# Thinking and Writing Persuasively

# Thinking and Writing Persuasively

## A BASIC GUIDE

**Candace Glass Montoya**
**Joan Mariner Roxberg**

The University of Oregon

**ALLYN AND BACON**
*Boston   London   Toronto   Sydney   Tokyo   Singapore*

*Vice President, Humanities:* Joseph Opiela
*Editorial Assistant:* Brenda Conaway
*Production Administrator:* Susan Brown
*Editorial Production Service:* P. M. Gordon Associates, Inc.
*Text Designer:* P. M. Gordon Associates, Inc.
*Cover Coordinator:* Suzanne Harbison
*Composition Buyer:* Linda Cox
*Manufacturing Buyer:* Louise Richardson

Copyright © 1995 by Allyn and Bacon
A Simon & Schuster Company
Needham Heights, Mass. 02194

**Library of Congress Cataloging-in-Publication Data**

Montoya, Candace Glass.
    Thinking and writing persuasively : a basic guide / Candace Glass
Montoya, Joan Mariner Roxberg.
      p.  cm.
    Includes index.
    ISBN 0–02–382431–X : $18.00
    1.  English language—Rhetoric.  2.  Persuasion (Rhetoric)
I.  Roxberg, Joan Mariner.  II.  Title.
PE1431.M66  1995
808′.042—dc20

                                      94–34638
                                        CIP

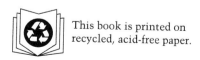

This book is printed on
recycled, acid-free paper.

Printed in the United States of America

10 9 8 7 6 5 4 3 2 1   99 98 97 96 95

Credits begin on page xx, which constitutes a continuation of this copyright page.

To my husband, Martin D. Montoya,
whose loving support has taught me
to value my own talents.

     —*Candace Glass Montoya*


To my mother, Ethel L. Smith,
upon whose intellectual legacy this book
is built and my husband, Dale W. Roxberg,
who provided the construction room.

     —*Joan Mariner Roxberg*

# Contents

*Preface*   xv
*Acknowledgments*   xix

## Part I / INVENTION                                                1

### *Chapter 1*   **Beginning a Discussion**                          1

How Ideas Are Formed   2
Why Write?   5
Using Information Sources   6
  *Exercises: Information Sources*   6
Writing and Revising   8
  *Computer Word Processing*   9
Revision Activities   10
  *Marie's First Draft*   10
  *Marie's Second Draft*   12
Chapter Review   15

### *Chapter 2*   **Reading and Writing for Ideas**                  16

Critical Reading   16
  *Forming an Interest*   18
  *Questioning Sources*   19

*What to Do If the Readings Are Hard to Understand*   19
*How to Read for Essay Ideas*   20
*A Reader's Journal*   21
*Writing Reaction Papers*   21
Why Use Argument?   26
Argument Structure   30
   *Exercises: Audience Responses*   31
   *Exercises: Dissecting a Question at Issue*   32
Arguing from Experience   34
   *How Experience Fits with the Readings*   35
   *Evaluate Your Experience*   36
   *First Person and Third Person*   37
Revision Activities   39
   *Darla's First Draft*   39
   *Darla's Second Draft*   45
Chapter Review   48

**Chapter 3   How Audience Shapes an Argument**      49

Common Ground   50
Diversity and Common Ground   50
   *Gender and Age*   51
   *Ethnic Background*   52
   *Religion*   53
   *Economic Status*   54
   *Political Opinion*   55
   *Regional Background*   56
   *A Classic Example of Common Ground:*
     *The Gettysburg Address*   57
The Challenge of English   58
   *English Variations*   59
   *Slang*   61
   *Correctness*   61
Common Ground and Argument   62
Revision Activities   63
   *Eric's First Draft*   63
   *Craig's First Draft*   68
Chapter Review   70

**Chapter 4   Exploring a Position**      71

Writing as Invention   71
Invention Methods   72

*Freewriting  72*
*Brainstorming and Clustering  73*
*Using Generative Sentences  73*
Building an Argument  74
*Addressing the Opposition  74*
*Purpose for Informing the Audience  75*
*Thoughtful Audience  76*
The Essay-Writing Cycle  76
*Read  77*
*Discuss  78*
*Take a Position  78*
*Use an Invention Method  78*
*Write a First Draft  78*
*[Peer Review]  79*
Revision Activities  79
*Kevin's First Draft  79*
*Kevin's Second Draft  84*
*Kevin's Final Draft  89*
Chapter Review  93

**Chapter 5   Peer Reviewing**                     94

You Know More Than You Think You Do  94
Individual Peer Reviewing  95
*Responding to the Argument  95*
*Reviewing Guideline Questions  96*
*Responding to Grammar and Mechanics  100*
Small-Group Peer Reviewing  101
*Avoiding Problems While Group Reviewing  102*
*Group Reviewing Activity  103*
Special Challenges with Peer Reviewing  104
*Spelling and Past Tense  104*
*English as a Second Language  105*
*English as a Second Language and Article Use  105*
*Standard English Verb Tense  106*
*Verbs and Time  106*
*Agreement Between Subject and Verb  108*
*Agreement Between Subject and Pronoun  109*
*Pronoun Reference  110*
Listening to Questions and Comments  111
Notes for the Next Draft  112
Chapter Review  112

# Part II / CONSTRUCTING A PERSUASIVE ESSAY                          **113**

*Chapter 6*  **Developing a Thesis**                                        114

Organizing a Thesis Statement   113
   *How Thesis Statements Work for the Writer*   *115*
   *Developing a Thesis Statement*   *116*
   *Testing a Thesis Statement*   *117*
   *Outlining with a Thesis Statement*   *119*
   *Sample Article for Practice*   *120*
Revision Activities: Natalie's First Draft   123
Things to Consider About Sentences   125
   *Thesis and Sentence Formation*   *125*
   *Sentence Structure*   *126*
   *Sentence Form and the Main Idea*   *127*
   *Subordination of Ideas*   *128*
   *Modifiers*   *130*
   *Prepositional Phrases*   *131*
   *Active and Passive Voice*   *134*
Revision Activities: Natalie's Second Draft   135
Paragraph Structure   137
   *Sentence Forms and Paragraph Structure*   *138*
   *Evaluating Paragraphs*   *141*
   *Sentences and Transitions*   *142*
Chapter Review   143

*Chapter 7*  **Shaping an Argument**                                        144

Starting from Familiar Ground   144
   *Induction*   *145*
   *Deduction*   *145*
   *Logic*   *147*
   *Elements of Persuasion*   *147*
Problem Areas in Arguments   149
   *Emotional Appeals*   *149*
   *Generalization*   *150*
   *Appeal to Popularity* (Ad Populum)   *150*
   *Doubtful Cause* (Post Hoc, Ergo Propter Hoc)   *151*
   *Slippery Slope*   *151*
   *Either/Or Dilemma*   *152*
   *Personal Attack* (Ad Hominem)   *152*

*Straw Man* 153
*Appeal to Tradition* 153
*Authority* 154
*Two Wrongs Make a Right* 154
Conclusions About Logical Fallacies 155
*Practice in Identifying Logical Fallacies* 156
Chapter Review 161

**Chapter 8 Revising a Draft** 162

Troubleshooting 162
Reviewing Your Writing 163
*Focus and Organization* 164
*Essay Structure* 165
*Testing a Thesis* 166
*Summary of Reviewing Guideline Questions* 167
Common Flaws in Argumentation 168
*Losing Common Ground* 168
*Failing to Address Opposing Arguments* 168
*Weak Question at Issue* 168
*Forgetting to Give the Audience Key Information* 169
*Conclusion* 169
Evaluate Writing Strengths 169
Be Aware of Writing Weaknesses 170
Punctuation 170
*Relax!* 170
*End Punctuation* 172
Chapter Review 174

**Chapter 9 Revising with a Computer** 175

Word Processing 175
Computer Terminology 177
Spell Checkers 181
*Homophones* 181
*Right Spelling, Wrong Word* 183
*Proper Nouns* 184
*Specialized Language* 184
*Auxiliary Dictionaries* 184
Grammar Checkers 184
*Standard English and Language Drift* 185
A Word of Caution 186
Chapter Review 187

***Chapter 10*** **Proofing**                                                                 **188**

   Proofing Strategies   188
       *Scanning Backward   189*
       *Reading Aloud   189*
   Apostrophe for Possessives and Contractions   190
       *Possessive Pronouns   191*
   Finishing Touches   191
       *Capitalization   191*
       *British English   192*
       *Gender-Neutral Language   192*
   Revision Activities: Connie's First Draft   193
   Common Comma Errors   196
       *Interrupting Material   197*
       *Compound Sentences   198*
       *Subordination   199*
   Commas in Detail   201
       *Lists   201*
       *Added Information   202*
       *Interjection   202*
       *Punctuation for Meaning   203*
       *Compound Subjects and Predicates   203*
   Revision Activities   204
       *Proofing Connie's Sentences   204*
       *Proofing Connie's Essay   205*
   Chapter Review   208

## Part III / FURTHER READINGS                          **209**

***Chapter 11*** **Readings for Discussion**                                209

   Wendell Berry, *The Ecological Crisis as a Crisis*
       *of Character   209*
   Vine Deloria, Jr., *This Country Was a Lot Better Off When*
       *the Indians Were Running It   219*
   John Langston Gwaltney, *Charlie Sabatier   228*
   Martin Luther King, Jr., *Letter from Birmingham Jail   245*
   Jonathan Kozol, *The Equality of Innocence:*
       *Washington, D.C.   259*
   Geoffrey Nunberg, *English and Good English   270*
   Robert C. Pooley, *The Definition and Determination of*
       *"Correct" English   274*

Elayne Rapping, *Local News: Reality as Soap Opera*   283
Studs Terkel, *C. P. Ellis*   302
Naomi Wolf, *The Beauty Myth*   312

*Appendix*   **Using Reference Material**                                          323

Brief Discussion of Format   324
    *1.1   Using Quotations in Your Essay*   324
    *1.2   Using References*   326
    *1.3   Citation Form*   327
    *1.4   Titles: Underline or Quotation Marks?*   328
Books   329
    *2.1   One Author*   329
    *2.2   Two or Three Authors*   330
    *2.3   One Editor of an Anthology*   330
    *2.4   Multiple Editors of an Anthology*   331
    *2.5   Encyclopedias or Dictionaries*   332
    *2.6   Pamphlets*   333
    *2.7   Government Publications*   334
Other Printed Material   334
    *3.1   Magazines*   334
    *3.2   Journals*   335
    *3.3   Newspapers*   335
Nonprint Sources   336
    *4.1   Television and Radio Programs*   336
    *4.2   Films or Videotapes*   337
    *4.3   Compact Discs, Audiotapes, or Records*   337
    *4.4   Lectures*   338
    *4.5   Interviews*   338

*Index*   339

# *Preface*

Writing in a manner that convinces other people that your ideas have merit is an increasingly important skill in the workforce. The nurse who records patient information, the lawyer who writes a brief, and the secretary who suggests a change in office procedure all want their information to be accepted as reasonable. To this end, their writing must be clear and to the point. They cannot afford to be misunderstood. This text is called *Thinking and Writing Persuasively: A Basic Guide* because, to some extent, all writing is persuasive. All writers have the goal of convincing an audience to pay attention to their information, or there would be no purpose in the act of writing. Even a private journal or diary strives to communicate events and feelings as the writer experienced them, trying to persuade an audience, even if it is only the writer, that those perceptions have merit. As you proceed through the activities outlined in this text, you will learn to write for academic success and for continued success after you leave school, because much of the writing in those settings involves persuasion.

One of the most important parts of persuasion is discussing controversial topics with others without antagonism. When people discuss a controversial issue, they often begin with supporting extreme positions and then attempt to persuade those listening to agree with those positions. This book emphasizes the method to identify a place of agreement, or common ground, and then, using an element of that agreement, to persuade an audience to consider your position. Finding this area of common ground is where real change, or persuasion, can begin. As you learn strategies of persuasive writing, you will also learn to think about writing in many different ways.

Writing is not a single activity. It is many activities occurring at once. Most textbooks have separate units on grammar, logic, audience, structure, and revision, as if each involves an isolated factor of writing and can be dealt with separately. In fact, before you write more than a word or two, you have to have some understanding of all these elements and more. This book is organized so that each chapter discusses topics in an order that responds to your needs as well as to the constraints of the classroom schedule, but you will find no chapters devoted to only one aspect of writing. Your instructor may wish to cover some of the material in a different order than we have arranged it; that is entirely a matter of personal preference. Given the understanding that virtually everything discussed in this book is related to the first paragraph you write, the order in which you cover the material is flexible.

As teachers, we acknowledge what you already know. You already reason, organize knowledge, and make decisions about what is important to you. You demonstrate these abilities when you vote, spend money, choose classes, and select your vocation. All of these thinking skills are used in persuasive writing as well. This text will help you put what you already know to work, and it will also help you to identify the components of good writing so that you can increase your control over the writing process.

By the time you finish this book, you will have been exposed to many methods for improving and focusing your writing. You will begin to write before you have read the entire book, probably within the first few chapters. The first drafts will serve as the foundation of more polished efforts that will follow as you gain confidence in reviewing and evaluating your writing. You will have many opportunities to revise. You might want to keep a file of all your work.

The Readings for Discussion in Chapter 11 will give you an opportunity to read material on a variety of topics and then to compare your responses to that material in discussions with your classmates. Those discussions will help you understand various viewpoints, contrast ideas, and respond to the topic under discussion. When you take a position in the discussion and develop an essay supporting that position, the comments of your classmates will give you an expanded understanding of the audience you are addressing.

This book does the work of a grammar handbook, a rhetoric, and a reader. It provides the grammar information you will need to write clear, error-free essays, and the appendix explains how to cite material you use to support your position. There are chapters on the writing process and readings to help you gather ideas for topics. You will find information to address every step of the writing process as you proceed through the chapters.

Both of us have spent many years teaching composition. We have taught adults and teenagers who did not read or write. We have worked with at-risk teens. We have taught at a variety of universities and community colleges. Over the years our students have also taught us many things about how to help people grow as effective writers. Some of our students have had a difficult time overcoming the poverty and neglect in their previous schools. Some have had to walk days and nights to escape the killing fields of their native lands. Others have struggled to become proficient in English as their second language. They have brought a wealth of knowledge and experience into our classrooms with them, and each student has made contributions to this book by being willing to learn.

Writing classes have often been the gatekeeper of education: the one class that decided who stayed in school and who did not. Our interest in our students prompted us to invite all students into the world of higher education by making convincing, error-free writing ability a reachable goal. Instead of being gatekeepers, we want the courses based on this book to function as passageways to increased confidence in your knowledge of persuasive writing methods and your ability to produce such writing.

So, welcome to *Thinking and Writing Persuasively: A Basic Guide.* By the time you have finished this text, you will have learned how to think of ways to convince an audience that your ideas have merit and how to develop strategies in organizing those ideas on paper. This book will also serve as a reference every time you organize a written assignment in the future. Information such as the questions for reviewing an essay, a quick guide to comma rules, a list of frequently misused homophones, and a brief guide to Modern Language Association (MLA) referencing format will continue to be helpful. Most of all, we hope you find the process of improving your writing to be interesting and rewarding, because you will see applications every time you write.

# Acknowledgments

We would like to express our gratitude to the following people: Holly Boone and Pat Braus, for deeply appreciated support; Center for the Study of Women in Society, for a grant to Candace Glass Montoya to support her writing; Mary Cote and Susan Fagan, for editing assistance; Beverly Donaghey, for editing, encouragement, and unflagging confidence in the worth of the task; John T. Gage, for his encouragement and the guidance provided by his pedagogical philosophy; and Kaseja Odanata, for word processing when deadlines loomed.

The following sources have generously extended their permission to reprint from copyrighted material:

Wendell Berry. "The Ecological Crisis as a Crisis of Character." *The Unsettling of America*. Sierra Club Books, 1977

Robert M. Bryce. "Oil Company Waste Pits: Big Killer of Migrating Birds." *San Francisco Chronicle*, March 19, 1990

Benjamin Chavis. "Race, Justice, and the Environment." *Nature Conservancy*. Sept./Oct. 1992

Vine Deloria, Jr. "This Country Was a Lot Better Off When the Indians Were Running It." *New York Times Magazine*, March 3, 1970

John Langston Gwaltney. "Charlie Sabatier." *Dissenters: Voices from Contemporary America*. Random House, 1986

Martin Luther King, Jr. "Letter from Birmingham Jail." *Why We Can't Wait*. HarperCollins, 1964

Jonathan Kozol. "The Equality of Innocence: Washington D.C." *Savage Inequalities*. Random House, 1991

Geoffery Nunberg. "English and Good English." *American Heritage Dictionary*, 2nd college ed. Houghton Mifflin, 1991

Robert C. Pooley. "The Definition and Determination of 'Correct' English." *Teaching and English Usage.* National Council of Teachers of English, 1946

Matthew Rabel. "The Call." Student paper, 1992

Elayne Rapping. "Local News: Reality as Soap Opera." *The Looking Glass World of Nonfiction TV.* South End Press, 1987

Studs Terkel. "C. P. Ellis." *American Dreams: Lost and Found.* Random House, 1980

Naomi Wolf. "The Beauty Myth." *The Beauty Myth.* William Morrow, 1991

Photo credits are as follows: p. 11, © Elliott Erwitt/Magnum Photos, New York; p. 40, ©1985 Kenneth Murray/Photo Researchers, New York, All rights reserved; p. 67, © 1984 Earl Dotter/Impact Visuals, New York; p. 69, © Leonard Freed/Magnum Photos, New York; p. 85, © 1994 Rick Gerharter/Impact Visuals, New York; p. 124, © Leonard Lee Rue III from National Audubon Society/Photo Researchers, New York; p. 194, © 1988 David H. Wells/The Image Works, Woodstock, NY.

*Thinking and Writing Persuasively*

# Chapter *1*

# Beginning a Discussion

How Ideas Are Formed

Why Write?

Using Information Sources

Writing and Revising

Revision Activities: Marie's Drafts

Chapter Review

It is the first day of school, and students take their seats. They look to the front expectantly to see what their teacher looks like and in the process, try to decide if this will be a good class or not.

All the students have opinions about the content of the class and expectations about how much they will enjoy it. In many ways those expectations will become reality, because people tend to look for examples that fit their previous experience.

In much the same way, you opened this textbook to begin reading. Most people want new things to be positive, and you may look for interesting and informative reading here. Composition textbooks do not have a reputation for being stimulating reading, however, and it is possible that you anticipate this one being much like all the others. To be perfectly honest, it is impossible to write a textbook that is as gripping as a novel or a short story. The purpose of textbooks is instruction, and the purpose of fiction is entertainment and forms of insight. While instruction may be interesting, it will seldom grip one's attention in quite the same way that a fine work of fiction will.

There are ways to make textbooks easier and more interesting, however, and if you use some of these methods, your time with this one may prove even more useful:

1.  As you read, watch for strategies you can apply to your writing.
2.  Underline, highlight, or make a few notes about the parts that explain new ideas that seem particularly useful to you.
3.  Read the chapter once quickly and then read carefully the areas that are discussing material that is new to you.
4.  When something is not clear to you or you have questions, trust yourself and ask your instructor. If you do not understand, it is likely that others are not understanding either. You will help everyone if you ask in class and get things clear, but if that makes you uncomfortable, you may ask your instructor privately.

This text is organized to assist you in focusing your ideas, recognizing the needs of your audience, and writing an essay that is clear, interesting, and convincing to those who read it. All students have some experience with that process, but that experience varies widely. Even if you understand some element being covered in one of the chapters, review it so that you will be prepared to assist others as you read and respond to their essays during peer reviewing exercises.

With those preliminary comments, you are now ready to begin examining the process of composing clear, informative essays.

## HOW IDEAS ARE FORMED

Writing begins with thinking. That seems obvious, but it is worth a few minutes of your time to consider how this process works for you and for others. Thinking is not something someone taught you how to do in the same way you were taught to read and write. From the time you were an infant, you have been taking in impressions of the world around you and sorting those impressions into some categories. That sorting process is called "thinking." As you learn new information, you compare it to what you already know and assign knowledge to what seems to be the most reasonable category. You do this so often that it is no longer a deliberate, conscious process but is almost completely automatic.

By the time you reach adulthood, you have an enormous volume of information, and you have established a variety of categories based on your experiences. For example, if the newspaper reported that your community had just won the bid for a new factory, there would be a wide variety of reactions. If you interviewed a group of people, these are some of the responses you might get:

**From a recent graduate:**

That's great! We need the jobs around here.

**From a 45-year-old with a high school education:**

It makes me mad, too. I'll bet every job will require a college degree.

**From a person interested in environmental issues:**

I'll bet our city officials waived all the environmental restrictions to get the approval.

**From a small-business owner who needs business:**

This will provide the economic boost that we've been needing.

**From a person concerned about taxes:**

How are we going to pay for the roads all those new people will require?

**From a farmer:**

They are building that factory on prime farmland. Someday we are all going to starve because there are buildings on all the good growing land.

**From an employed person who is very busy with personal concerns:**

Oh? Who cares?

**From a person irritated with restrictions on commerce:**

We are lucky they picked our town. In many places the environmentalists put up so many restrictions that the economy doesn't have a chance to grow.

Each of these responses is built on a variety of previously learned ideas that prepared each person for dealing with new information. All think the way that they do for what seem to them to be good reasons. It is sometimes hard to understand disagreement. People have had different experiences, and what they have learned from those experiences is slightly different. Sometimes those different ideas agree, and sometimes they contradict. Either way, the reasons *why* people hold the opinions they hold are as important as *what* they think, because the *why* explains how they came to the conclusion they did. It is not that what they think is not important, but the reasons *why* are the evidence they use for their belief.

The first big step in structuring effective communication of any sort is attempting to understand how people accept the ideas they believe to be true. If all people thought the same things, this would not be necessary, but they do not. If you do not understand some of the reasons used by those whose ideas are different from your own, you will have a difficult time communicating with them. Since communication with people who think differently is an essential professional skill, the first step in this communication is understanding how these differing ideas come into being.

---

### Application

What controversial issue can you think of that is presently being discussed in your community?

What are the various opinions on that issue?

Why might people have formed those different opinions?

---

People sometimes ignore those who hold opposing opinions. It is easier to think those who disagree are ignorant or misinformed than it is to try to figure out why they don't agree. In both educational and professional environments, however, it is expected that each person will try to understand sources of disagreement and, if possible, find ways to work around them. Professionals are placed in working situations with a variety of people, and because so much depends on clear, reasonable communication, it is important to overcome differences and see other points of view in order to find areas of compromise or concession. It is an important ability in many areas, from education to diplomacy.

The essays you write must show that you have tried to understand how your audience thinks, or you risk failing to communicate well. Communication and cooperation are central to your goal. If you cannot explain your ideas to others, including your professors and your peers, you will not succeed. You need to be able to enlist the cooperation of others if you are to direct their attention to ideas that you feel are important. You cannot get people to listen to you if you do not understand their reasons for thinking the way they do. People with whom we want to communicate are not always present when we want to communicate with them. While it may seem to make things more difficult to write out information, sometimes it is actually for the best. Communicating through writing can serve to improve communication when it is done well.

## WHY WRITE?

Writing is different from other forms of communication in several ways.

1. Writing is permanent because it has shape on a page.
2. Writing is revisable.
3. Writing is transportable.

Once you have said a word, you cannot unsay it, but you can revise a letter before you put it in the mail. Have you ever made a telephone call in anger and wished you could take the words back? Imagine how different the situation would have been if you had written a letter instead. By the time you finished writing out the same things you said on the telephone, you would have had time to think about whether you really meant them. In many such cases, the letter can be revised to express, in much calmer tones, what first caused the problem and to suggest possible solutions for it.

It is the time and thought it takes to write out ideas clearly and concisely that makes writing different from talking. When you speak to someone, you can answer any questions and clarify any points of misunderstanding. You can also respond to areas where your listeners may not agree with the position you have taken. When you write things out, you must try to anticipate these responses. In some cases, the wording of a communication may have legal consequences, so putting things in a letter may be less subject to confusion or misquoting.

---

### Application

Can you think of times where writing would be a better choice than a telephone call or personal conversation?

---

Writing can be used for more than communicating with other people. Writing can help you to understand more about yourself too. Sometimes when you look at your ideas as you are writing, you decide that they do not really express what you think. Because writing is permanent, you can return to exactly the same ideas later and decide if what you wrote expresses your thoughts. If not, you can decide what part to keep and what part you want to change. You can even go back to things you wrote years ago and see what was important to you then and how your perspective has changed or remained the same.

You can carefully think out something in advance and still forget how to say it when the time comes to tell someone about it. If, however, you write your thoughts down, they will still be as carefully thought out when the time comes to express them. No matter how many times you practice a speech, you cannot be as confident that it will remain in the same form as you can be with one that you write out.

Since written material stays in the same form over time, writing is increasingly important in modern communications. There was a time when it seemed as though writing would become less important as video images were used to transmit more and more information, but the exact opposite is happening. Fax machines and computers with modems not only have made writing more common but have made the ability to produce clear, understandable writing a professional requirement.

---

### Application

Name some examples of writing that are produced in the workplace. Why is it so important that these examples produce clear communication?

---

## USING INFORMATION SOURCES

The process of writing well is one that comes easily to some and presents challenges to others for reasons that are not always easy to identify. Good writers need an understanding of what makes their writing work well so they can increase their control of that process. Uncertain writers must gain effective strategies to write clearly and persuasively. Acquiring this ability makes a big difference in how confidently people continue with their education and careers. The first step is taking a close look at the various ways people process the information they receive.

### Exercises: Information Sources

The following exercises will allow you to examine your methods of receiving information. If you have a chance to share your answers with others, you may be surprised to find out how much they vary.

### Describe Yourself

A. Write a paragraph or two describing yourself.

B. In a brief paragraph, evaluate the writing classes you have had before and indicate what you consider your strengths and weaknesses as a writer.

C. List your everyday sources of information about the world around you. Answer the following questions about these sources.

   1. Which are the most likely to be factual?

   2. How do I know which sources are the most dependable? (List separate reasons if necessary.)

   3. What convinces me the fastest and why is it the most convincing?

D. List five opinions you have, and then answer the following questions about them:

   1. Why do I have these opinions?

   2. Do I have evidence that would convince people who hadn't made up their mind on the issue?

   3. What reasons do those who disagree with the opinions have for their disagreement? (Make separate lists as necessary.)

### Identifying Reasons

Read the five following questions. Pick two that you have opinions about and write down those opinions.

1. Should letter grades be eliminated and all classes be changed to Pass/No Pass?

2. Should colleges and universities require basic classes in writing and mathematics?

3. Should the music industry be ruled by the same rating system that the movie industry has accepted (R, PG, PG 13, etc.)?

4. Should poor women be sterilized if they have more than four children and receive public assistance? Should poor men be sterilized under the same circumstances?

5. What should be most important, environmental concerns or jobs?

### How Opinions Are Formed

For each of the questions you selected from above, write the answers to the following questions about how you formed those opinions.

1. What reasons do I use to support my opinions on this subject?

2. Where did I get the information that made me decide this way?

3. Whom do I know in agreement with me?

4.  What parts of the argument are most important to me?
5.  Can I identify a system or set of ideas that helps me sort new information? (Political identification, religion, regional identification, cultural identity, and a specific cause of intense interest are some of the idea clusters that assist people in categorizing ideas.)

# WRITING AND REVISING

Revision is a key strategy for a writer at any stage of ability. This book had to go through many rounds of revision before it was ready to be printed, and the same is true of almost everything you read. Many people who think they are poor writers have solid writing ability, but they have never been taught how to revise their work effectively. As a result, they quit before the work is complete, and the resulting product is unsatisfying to both the writers and their audiences.

It may seem odd to be reading about revision before you write your first essay. However, if you have a clear understanding of revision and how it works to improve everything you write, it will make the process of organizing your first essay much less stressful. Imagine you are having a conversation with someone, and you did not make one of your points clear. That person will ask you some questions, you will answer them, and the communication will be improved. When you write your ideas, you are not always present so your audience can ask you about the points that need clarification. It takes practice to learn how to anticipate the responses of your audience. The peer reviewing activities after your first draft will give you the chance to listen to your audience and see where you need to change your essay in order to answer reasonable questions and doubts. As you go through this process, you will gain a greater sense of audience and how to best communicate with the audience you have chosen.

The process of organizing an essay and then adjusting it to recognize the varying responses of an audience is where revision becomes essential. Virtually all writers go through a process of clarifying their ideas as they put them into sentences on paper. When they read those sentences aloud, they often see where they have left things out, included unneeded information, or could improve the clarity of communication by rearranging paragraphs. The willingness to do this often makes the difference between good communication and poor communication.

This book includes revision exercises using example essays that reflect the drafting or revision processes used by many students. Since each revision activity has a specific goal in mind, you will notice that these "students" display strengths and weaknesses in a variety of patterns. The important thing to keep in mind is that these essays are included to develop your abilities in recognizing structural problems in essays you or your peers are writing. Once you can recognize these problems, you will also develop methods for strengthening and improving your work while it is in the early stages.

The students in these revision activities have been given an assignment to do an essay on the topic of the environment. They were told to assess personal experiences that might be useful in developing an essay on that topic. In some cases, you will be able to follow the students' efforts through multiple drafts. The reason that there are multiple drafts is that essays virtually always improve with revision. You will write several drafts of each essay and change each draft in response to comments made by groups or individuals who read your work. Professional writers revise their work in exactly the same fashion until they feel their writing is in the best possible form. As a college student, you are in training to be a professional.

The hardest work in writing an essay is the first attempt to get the idea on paper. This is less difficult if you think of it as your first draft and as something you will have opportunities to change as you listen to what others say about it. Once you understand how to make the revision process work for you, you will feel more confident as you begin to organize your ideas. As you work with the sample essays in this book, each other's essays, and your own work, you will learn how to revise effectively. If you have not been in the habit of doing more than one draft of your work, you will be surprised at what a difference revising will make in the quality of your writing.

## Computer Word Processing

If you are not familiar with word processing, go to your school's computer lab and have someone help you learn how to write with a computer. It will also be useful for you to skip ahead to Chapter 9 and read the material on revising with a computer. After very little practice, word processing is easier, faster, and more accurate than typing because most mistakes are quicker and easier to correct. Working with a computer also gives you access to support systems, such as spell-checkers, which are wonderful for uncertain spellers. This technology can free you from some of the work of proofing. You are free to revise and change your paper until it reads the way you want it to without the drudgery of retyping. Once you type a paper into a computer and save it on a disk, making changes on that paper will take less than a quarter of the time it would take to retype the same paper.

# REVISION ACTIVITIES

### Marie's First Draft

Marie has a topic for her environment paper that seems important to her, but many others might disagree. Why has she focused on this topic? What does she need to think about if she is going to convince her audience? What would you like to have Marie tell you more about?

## Marie's Essay (Draft 1)

When I arrived here at the beginning of my freshman year, I saw many things I had never seen before. I grew up in a rural area, on an Indian reservation. One of the things that amazed me the most was dogs on leashes. On the reservation, dogs just walk around where ever they want to. On the farms in the area and even in the little town on the edge of the reservation where the high school is, it is the same.

I think the dogs look miserable. Maybe I feel this way because I am a little miserable so far from home. The girls in my dorm have told me not to go out by myself at night because it is dangerous for girls to be out alone after dark. I have also been told not to go to the park because that is where all the drug dealing is done. I have even been told not to get too close to the river because it is polluted. This is very new to me.

As a child I would just open the door in the morning and run as far as I could see. I would run until I was too tired to run anymore. Sometimes I would be out exploring with other kids, sometimes just with my dog. Now I have to be careful all the time. That is one reason that I feel sympathy for the dogs I see being dragged down the street underneath my dorm window.

Some of these dogs seem to live more like toys than actual animals. I have seen a dog grooming shop near the dorms. Dogs are in there getting hair cuts and being washed. They do not look happy to me. I wish I could take them with me back to the reservation.

If I could I would just turn them loose on the reservation, to live on their own, except for food. I know that this would not really work, though. These dogs have probably spent so much time in the city that they could not survive if they were able to roam free. They might be scared of other animals. Coyotes or foxes might eat them.

I do not think it is fair to treat dogs the way a lot of the dogs I see here are treated. They need room to walk around. They are not teddy bears. People treat them as though they were babies, but they are not. It is not

fair to the animals. They need the company of other animals just the way we need the friendship of other people.

I know that many people are afraid of the crime in the city and they keep dogs for protection. I can understand being afraid. I have been afraid many times walking the streets alone.

I do not think that watch dogs are the answer, though. If an assailant is armed, he is more powerful than you or the dog. An alarm would also make noise if someone entered the house.

I was walking to the store last week and a woman was walking a small dog. It tried to bark at me but only a rasping choking sound came out. I stopped and stared because I had never heard a dog make such a noise. The woman said, "I had its bark removed because it was bothering the neighbors." I could not believe my ears. How could anyone do such a thing? The noise it made was terrible. It was like the sound a dog would make in a bad dream.

People who live in cities who want animals for companionship can always have cats. Cats also deserve to go outside, I think, but they can take care of themselves. It is easy to have more than one so they will not be so lonely. However, I still do not like the idea of having their claws removed to keep them from scratching the furniture. If the furniture is so valuable then don't have pets at all.

Having dogs in the city may not seem like an important subject compared to air or water pollution, but I think that it is. It shows that people have lost touch with the natural world. They treat animals like they are human and they are not.

Native Americans believe that everyone is part of nature. Nature is not our servant. We all have the right to live our own life. Even dogs and cats.

---

### Reviewing Marie's First Draft

Marie has done a good job of presenting a controversy that she has drawn from her personal experience. She explains how she came to her conclusions and chooses the examples well. Her problem with this draft is that many pet owners will think her argument is unreasonable. She has not earned her conclusion because she has neglected to address many valid arguments for keeping dogs in the city.

In small groups discuss Marie's strengths and weaknesses:

1. What is Marie's purpose for writing? Does she state it clearly?
2. Does Marie have any valid ideas?
3. Does Marie succeed in making you sympathize with the animals she writes about?
4. Do Marie's memories of her home make the paper stronger?
5. Does Marie's anger seem justified?
6. Is it possible for Marie to be more flexible and still keep her anger?
7. Is it desirable for her to keep her anger?

To guide Marie's revision, answer the following questions:

1. What are some valid arguments for keeping dogs in the city?
2. How can Marie address these arguments in her essay?
3. What would you suggest Marie do to revise?
4. Are there other examples Marie might use to support her position?
5. Should Marie modify her position to a less extreme one?

### *Marie's Second Draft*

Marie read the responses given in the reviewing process carefully. The people who read her first draft felt her position that dogs should not be kept in the city was too broad to support, so she modified her argument. She may not like the kind of life she sees city dogs leading, but she has decided she cannot support her emotional response with enough compelling reasons to make the position reasonable to a thoughtful audience.

# *Marie's Essay (Draft 2)*

Coming to college was my first experience with living in an urban area. I grew up on an Indian reservation. I went to high school outside the reservation in a small ranching community, but it was still very rural. Ranching is the main business, on and off the reservation.

I was very shocked by many things I discovered in the city. Maybe I feel this way because I am a little miserable so far from home. The girls in my dorm have told me not to go out by myself at night because it is dangerous for girls to be out alone after dark. I have also been told not to go to the park because that is where all the drug-dealing is done. I have even been told not to get too close to the river because it is polluted. This is very new to me.

One of the things that I had never seen before is dogs on leashes. On the reservation, dogs just walk around wherever they want to. On the ranches in the area and even in the little town on the edge of the reservation where the high school is, it is the same.

To me, the dogs who are being led down the street on the leashes seem unhappy. Perhaps I am just seeing my own unhappiness at being confined reflected in them. As a child, I would just open the door in the morning and run as far as I could see. I would run until I was too tired to run anymore. Sometimes I would be out exploring with other kids, sometimes just with my dog. Now I have to be careful all the time. That is one reason that I feel sympathy for the dogs I see being dragged down the street underneath my dorm window.

Some of these dogs seem to live more like toys than like actual animals. I have seen a dog-grooming shop near the dorms. Dogs are in there getting haircuts and being washed. They do not look happy to me. I wish I could take them with me back to the reservation.

If I could, I would just turn them loose on the reservation, to live on their own, except for food.

I know that this would not really work, though. These dogs have probably spent so much time in the city that they could not survive if they were able to roam free. They might be scared of other animals. Coyotes or foxes might eat them. For this reason, I believe that, in fact, some animals do belong in the city.

I still do not think it is fair to treat dogs the way a lot of the dogs I see here are treated. Dogs need room to walk around. They are not teddy bears. People cannot treat them as though they were babies if they expect the dogs to be healthy and happy. It is not fair to the animals. They need the company of other animals, just the way we need the friendship of other people.

One of the things that would help is to have parks or beaches set aside for dogs to be able to be off the leashes and run free. I know this is done in San Diego, California, and other cities. My roommate is from San Diego, and she told me about beaches where dog owners take their dogs to allow them to run.

I know that many people are afraid of the crime in the city, and they keep dogs for protection. I can understand being afraid. I have been afraid many times walking the streets alone.

I do not think that watchdogs are always the answer, though. If an assailant is armed, he is more powerful than you or the dog. An alarm would also make noise if someone entered the house.

Not far from my dorm is a business where cars are repaired. Two dogs live there and guard the lot at night. During the day, I see the workers playing with the dogs, throwing sticks for them. Once I talked to the owner as he was feeding the dogs just before he left for the day. He said that he takes the dogs to the park whenever he has time. He said they are good dogs as long as no one enters the lot at night. I felt that he liked the dogs, and that they do not have such bad lives even though they live at a car repair shop in a city.

I was walking to the store last week and a woman was walking a small dog. It tried to bark at me but only a rasping choking sound came out. I stopped and stared because I had never heard a dog make such a noise. The woman said, "I had its bark removed because it was bothering the neighbors." I could not believe my ears. How could anyone do such a thing? The noise it made was terrible. It was like the sound a dog would make in a bad dream. This did not seem right to me. If the neighbors will not accept your dog, the dog should be given to someone who can take care of it.

People who live in cities in apartments where noise is a very serious subject and who want animals for companionship can always have cats. Cats also deserve to go outside, I think, but they can take care of themselves. It is easy to have more than one so they will not be so lonely. However, I still do not like the idea of having their claws removed to keep them from scratching the furniture. If the furniture is so valuable, then perhaps it would be best to have an animal that lives in a cage, such as a bird.

Compromises have to be made between people's desire for the companionship of animals and the living circumstances that the animals will be subjected to. I called the humane society, and they told me that they will not give a dog that weighs more than fifteen pounds to a family that does not have a yard. Perhaps pet shops should be required to also demand photos of the house the dog would be going to. Not everyone will always be able to have a dog. More attention should be paid to alternative pets. News programs could be encouraged to show different kinds of pets available for adoption from the pound, not just dogs, as they do now.

Having dogs in the city may not seem like an important subject compared to air or water pollution, but I think that it is. It shows that people have lost touch with the natural world. They treat animals like they are human, and they are not. It is another sign that humans do not think that they will ever have to change their ideas and plans to live in the world as one of many species.

Native Americans believe that everyone is part of nature. Nature is not our servant. We all have the right to live our own lives—even dogs and cats. People have to get used to the idea that we all have to live together and learn to get along with each other.

---

### Reviewing Marie's Second Draft

Discuss Marie's revision, referring to the first draft if necessary to note changes.

1.  What changes has Marie made?
2.  How has Marie improved her paper?
3.  Which is the stronger draft? Why?
4.  What remains to be done to improve Marie's second draft?
5.  Marie mentions her Native American heritage and its relationship with nature. Should she expand on this or do most readers recognize the relationship she is referring to?

# *C*hapter *Review*

1.  Why do some people ignore those who hold opposing opinions?
2.  Why did Marie modify her position in her essay?
3.  How can you help others by asking questions when something isn't clear to you?
4.  What makes writing different from other forms of communication?
5.  What is the hardest part of writing an essay?

# Chapter 2

# Reading and Writing for Ideas

Critical Reading
Why Use Argument?
Argument Structure
Arguing from Experience
Revision Activities: Darla's Drafts
Chapter Review

## CRITICAL READING

A benefit of the readings you do at the college level is the ability you develop in reading thoughtfully. This is sometimes called "critical reading."

**Critical reading**   Reading to make a careful evaluation of the accuracy and clarity of the material.

Critical reading requires more thinking on your part than an assignment that only requires you to remember what you read. You must think about what you read enough to make some of the ideas fit into your life and interests. You have to make some connection between yourself and the writer of the essay. For example, there might not seem to be any connection at all between you and an assignment to read the Gettysburg Address. However, you have opinions about war, remembering the dead, patriotism, or what makes a hero. Abraham Lincoln brings up some aspects of all those ideas in his famous speech.

Critical reading and clear writing are related activities. When you are able to identify the elements of effective persuasion in material you read, you are much more likely to produce those elements in your writing. People who have problems with their reading are often the same people who have difficulty with writing. The solution to both difficulties is practice. There is nothing magical about either reading or writing well.

Critical reading has broad applications. As you develop your abilities to read critically, you will find yourself better able to make clear assessments of things you read. From newspaper articles and editorials to political campaign materials, you will find yourself using many of the same analytical tools in your professional life. Even an office memo can be seen as an argument that requires some critical reading and thinking. Read an administrative assistant's reaction to an efficiency study that suggested workers should do only one task all day. What is the writer's argument? Would you be impressed if you were his boss?

---

### Application

MEMO

TO:        Sharon Rodriguez

FROM:      George Campbell

SUBJECT:   Efficiency Study

Putting the same workers on the same tasks for the entire day is not the best course of action to make the office more efficient. Instead, workers should have varied tasks. This will increase alertness and reduce the frequency of repetitive task injuries, such as carpal tunnel syndrome. While working at the same task all day might seem to reduce the distractions of moving from one activity to another, a varied workday reduces errors by reducing the boredom of repetitive tasks. I think a single-task workday is for machines, not for people.

---

If you were this person's boss, you would have to make some serious decisions based on your reading of this memo. You will be using the same critical reading skills as you read the essays in this book to develop ideas for your essays. You will think about the evidence the writer presented to see if it is convincing. You will also learn how to check for argumentative strategies that are misleading or invalid when you read Chapter 7, Shaping an Argument. When you find places where the points are either not clear or not convincing, you will also learn to trust your own judgment. Your opinions about the material you read matter. However, in order for those opinions to be accepted by others, you must be able to state clear reasons for how you came to form them. The reviewing activities you participate in are organized to help you in evaluating and responding to written material in an organized, convincing way.

### Forming an Interest

Essays are included in this book for you to read as you prepare to discuss topics selected by your instructor. Having a group read the same material in preparation for a discussion helps accomplish two important things:

1. Participants have more in common to start.
2. The group will have the sort of information that educated people use when they discuss ideas brought up in the readings.

The environment is the topic for the sample essays in this text. You may be asked to write about similar topics. In order to write an argumentative essay, you need a *question at issue* to address and an audience.

---

**Question at issue**   An area of disagreement or difference of opinion.

---

The readings in this text are chosen to provide you with questions at issue, but it is impossible to have topics that are automatically interesting to every student. If you cannot find ways to get interested in an assigned topic, the essay writing task will be more difficult and less likely to produce an effective essay. It is important that you find some part of the assigned topic that is interesting to you.

When you read that the environment was going to be the topic for the sample essays, you may have thought you had no interest in the environment so the essays would be boring. You might think,

The environment has nothing to do with me. I am not interested in camping, trees, nature walks, or anything to do with the environment.

Those things are part of the environment, of course, but only a part. Everything around you, no matter where you live, is part of your environment. You may not care about trees, but you may care if there are pesticides in the fruit you eat, if there are parks in your neighborhood, or if your city has a good transit system. All of those things are part of your environment.

---

### Application

How might environmental issues affect your professional life?

---

The first thing to do when you are asked to read about or discuss a topic is to find some way to connect that topic to your life. Even if you have not given it much thought before, try to figure out where this topic affects you. Once you find some part of the topic that affects your life, then you can start asking questions about how it affects the lives of others, too. During discussions, you will hear people say things about this issue with which you disagree. If you are willing to listen to the reasons they give for their positions, then you are well on your way to developing a focus on the topic.

### *Questioning Sources*

When you read essays, the writers of those essays have taken positions on questions at issue. In every question at issue, there are two or more opinions or positions and each has reasons that support it. The questions at issue that you write about will in most cases have a variety of positions ranging from moderate to extreme, and your task in writing an essay will be to support the one you believe in. One way to figuring out how to do this effectively is to take a close look at the position taken by the readings. Don't accept what the writers have to say just because the essay is included in the book. Ask some questions to see if the writers support the ideas that they present.

### *What to Do If the Readings Are Hard to Understand*

Reading does not come easily to everyone, and some will probably find the assigned readings difficult at first. Learning to understand material that is difficult is an inescapable part of getting an education, and no one will succeed by quitting when it gets hard. The readings have been chosen because they address a variety of ideas of concern to educated people. If you have trouble identifying what those ideas might be on the first reading, you should read the assignment a second time. Remember, the goal of the readings is to find ideas interesting enough to talk about in a discussion and expand on for an essay topic.

Here are a few questions that you should have in mind as you begin the readings. They will assist you in finding ideas to think about bringing up for discussion.

**Reading Questions**

1. What have you heard or read about this topic before? Where?
2. What is the question at issue in this essay? Is there more than one?
3. Have you made up your mind about this issue before now? Why or why not?
4. Does the writer have one or many points to make with this essay?
5. Can you think of reasons for or against ideas in the essay that the writer left out, or information that might change the conclusion of the essay?

With these questions in mind, you can begin to make the most of the readings. It is not possible to remember everything you read with enough detail to be useful to you later. There are strategies you can use to record what you read for later use in discussions and in generating essay ideas.

## How to Read for Essay Ideas

In most cases, reading material is assigned for the reader to gather information; a history reading assignment is a good example of this sort of reading. In English literature, you are assigned to read material and expected to understand the plot, characters, and theme of the work. You can develop a method for those reading assignments. Some students have trouble getting the ideas that teachers want them to get from assigned material, and, as a result, feel tense whenever they are assigned to read something. Some students have trouble remembering what they have read after they put the book down, and many students feel unqualified to disagree with material they are assigned to read.

The goal of these readings is to get you thinking about a question at issue or point of controversy, not to see how many pieces of information you can remember. Many reading assignments involve finding the "main" or "controlling" idea in the material. While the material you read may have a main idea, you do not necessarily have to figure out what it is to make use of the reading. Whatever you especially notice about the material is what is the most important to you, and you need to trust your responses. It does not matter if an idea you get from the reading is not the main idea of the essay. Your reading goal is to discover ideas brought up by the author that you feel are interesting and worth discussing with your classmates.

## A Reader's Journal

Many students find a *reader's journal* very useful for keeping a record of what they read and the ideas they gathered. In a reader's journal, you record the title of the work, the author, and the page of the book where you read the material. Then you record some of your responses and the conclusion the author came to in the essay. These journal entries don't have to be long; a paragraph or two will usually be enough unless the topic is one that you have thought about previously. If you bring the journal to class, you can add ideas that the class discussion of the reading adds to your thinking. When you get ready to write an essay on the assigned topic, the reader's journal will provide you with a record of the ideas you found in your first reading and what the class discussion added to those ideas.

## Writing Reaction Papers

An alternative to keeping a reader's journal is to write *reaction papers* to each assigned reading. A reaction paper is a series of responses you had to the readings, both the ideas you think are well presented and those with which you disagree. A reaction paper is not a summary of the reading. Most people can write a summary without understanding much of what they are summarizing. A reaction paper insists you think about what the writer has to say and then record your response to that position. The essays in this book have been selected because each has an argumentative focus of some sort. To write a reaction paper, you must identify the focus of the essay and determine if the writer supported that position well. You cannot respond to the writer's ideas if you do not understand the position. As with the reader's journal, it is useful to take the reaction paper to discussions and compare your reactions with those of others. That comparison will assist you in understanding the diversity that exists in your audience and finding ways to support whatever position you want to take.

To practice the skills involved in writing reaction papers, begin by reading the following essay and determining what questions at issue the author brings up.

## Race, Justice and the Environment

*Reverend Benjamin F. Chavis, Jr.*

For too long it has been assumed that people of color are not interested in conservation and the environment. The reality is, however, that environmental quality is viewed as a life-and-death issue in African American, Latin American, Native American and Asian American communities.

A 1987 study by the United Church of Christ's Commission for Racial Justice, "Toxic Waste and Race in the United States," revealed that people of color are disproportionately exposed to toxic and hazardous waste facilities throughout the nation. During the last five years it has become clear that people of color communities also are disproportionately exposed to lead poisoning, pesticide contamination and a host of other forms of air, land and water pollution. As a consequence, there is a sharp rise in the incidence of infant mortality, cancer, respiratory disease and other public health problems in these communities.

We believe the disproportionate exposure of people of color to environmental hazards is not an historical coincidence. It has often been the result of the way in which environmental policies were set by local, state and federal institutions and agencies.

The good news is that there is a growing multiracial environmental justice movement mobilizing people of all colors to join together at the grassroots level not only to demand justice but also to envision the transformation of society in the interest of ecological integrity. There should be increasing opportunities for constructive critical dialogue between conservationists and environmental justice activists.

The First National People of Color Environmental Leadership Summit last year adopted a set of 17 principles of environmental justice. Principle Three states: "Environmental justice mandates the right to ethical, balanced and responsible uses of land and renewable resources in the interest of a sustainable planet for humans and other living things." This perspective recognizes the interdependence of all species and the sacredness of all creation.

Some of the established national environmental groups have been slow to comprehend the vast reservoir of energy and interests in people of color communities on the vital issues of environmental protection and sustainable development. It is important for members of organizations such as The Nature Conservancy to view the desire to preserve the diversity of plants, animals and natural communities also as a need to understand and support the efforts of those who seek to ensure the diversity of human communities. The protection of human and natural communities from environmental degradation should not be viewed as being mutually exclusive.

The movement to combat environmental injustice involves organizing and mobilizing people at the community level and building regional and national environmental justice networks. There also needs to be more research performed—in particular, analyzing the correlation between environmental degradation and public health.

In addition, there must be greater coordination between federal and state agencies on environmental protection in the future. The public should be afforded significantly more access to environmental information held by these agencies. Technical assistance grants and projects should be encouraged as a means of increasing public awareness of the technical complexities of these issues.

A society that willingly tolerates environmental degradation is a society that will tolerate human degradation. The call for environmental justice affirms a vision and a mission to bring together peoples of diverse cultures, histories and struggles into a unified movement to ensure the health of the natural world for present and future generations. The demand for justice is not at odds with the desire to conserve; in fact, the desire to conserve natural resources necessitates the demand for environmental justice.

---

## Reading Questions

1. What have you heard or read about this topic before? Where?
2. What is the question at issue in this essay? Is there more than one?
3. Have you made up your mind about this issue before now? Why or why not?
4. Does the writer have one or many points to make with this essay? How many can you identify?
5. Can you think of reasons for or against ideas in the essay that the writer left out or information that might change the conclusion of the essay?

Here is the same essay with reading notes and a reaction paper written for it.

# Race, Justice and the Environment

*Reverend Benjamin F. Chavis, Jr.*

*I'm not sure this is true. Those are not know are not interested in environmental issues.*

For too long it has been assumed that people of color are not interested in conservation and the environment. The reality is, however, that environmental quality is viewed as a life-and-death issue in African American, Latin American, Native American and Asian American communities.

A 1987 study by the United Church of Christ's Commission for Racial Justice, "Toxic Waste and Race in the United States," revealed that people of color are disproportionately exposed to toxic and hazardous waste facilities throughout the nation. During the last five years it has become clear that people of color communities also are disproportionately exposed to lead poisoning, pesticide contamination and a host of other forms of air, land and water pollution. As a consequence, there is a sharp rise in the incidence of infant mortality, cancer, respiratory disease and other public health problems in these communities.

*Aren't there government regulations to control this?*

We believe the disproportionate exposure of people of color to environmental hazards is not an historical coincidence. It has often been the result of the way in which environmental policies were set by local, state and federal institutions and agencies.

The good news is that there is a growing multiracial environmental justice movement mobilizing people of all colors to join together at the grassroots level not only to demand justice but also to envision the transformation of society in the interest of ecological integrity. There should be increasing opportunities for constructive critical dialogue between conservationists and environmental justice activists.

*Where did this summit happen? Where could I get a copy of those 17 principles?*

The First National People of Color Environmental Leadership Summit last year [1991] adopted a set of 17 principles of environmental justice. Principle Three states: "Environmental justice mandates the right to ethical, balanced and responsible uses of land and renewable resources in the interest of a sustainable planet for humans and other living things." This perspective recognizes the interdependence of all species and the sacredness of all creation.

Some of the established national environmental groups have been slow to comprehend the vast reservoir of energy and interest in people of color communities on the vital issues of environmental protection and sustainable development. It is important for members of organizations such as The Nature Conservancy to view the desire to preserve the diversity of plants, animals and natural communities also as a need to understand and support the efforts of those who seek to ensure the diversity of human communities. The protection of human and natural communities from environmental degradation should not be viewed as being mutually exclusive.

The movement to combat environmental injustice involves organizing and mobilizing people at the community level and building regional and national environmental justice networks. There also needs to be more research performed—in particular, analyzing the correlation between environmental degradation and public health.

In addition, there must be greater coordination between federal and state agencies on environmental protection in the future. The public should be afforded significantly more access to environmental information held by these agencies. Technical assistance grants and projects should be encouraged as a means of increasing public awareness of the technical complexities of these issues.

*Does he support this statement? Is it true?*

A society that willingly tolerates environmental degradation is a society that will tolerate human degradation. The call for environmental justice affirms a vision and a mission to bring together peoples of diverse cultures, histories and struggles into a unified movement to ensure the health of the natural world for present and future generations. The demand for justice is not at odds with the desire to conserve; in fact, the desire to conserve natural resources necessitates the demand for environmental justice.

## Reaction

I enjoyed reading the essay by Reverend Chavis. I never thought about environmental pollution being a worse problem for people of color than for white people. I think that the environmental movement loses a lot of public support because it is perceived as a movement of upper middle-class, white, tree huggers. I saw a TV program once about the environmental problems of the lower Mississippi. This was an area of mostly African-American people, and chemical plants have polluted the atmosphere. There is a lot of cancer there. Also I have seen films about the problems of field workers who are exposed to pesticides. I think most people do not associate these problems with the save-the-whales environmental movement.

I wonder if there are any new laws that address this problem. I have been reading about apartment owners being forced to repaint buildings that have lead-based paint in them, but I do not know if health people are enforcing these laws.

# WHY USE ARGUMENT?

Sometime around 428 BC in Greece, a man named Plato was part of a community of thinkers that developed a new way of organizing information. This way of thinking was developed to find the truth about many aspects of both the physical world and abstract ideas such as love. Until then, in that culture there had been no method of sorting information in a way that allowed people to decide for themselves whether others had reasonable ideas. This method of inquiry relied on discussions (called "dialogues") by groups of people who were more interested in finding out what was true than they were in convincing others that their own opinion was correct.

All the writing in this text will be in this form of argument. The following is a definition of this academic kind of argument.

---

**Argument**   An exchange of ideas, and the reasons for those ideas, that allows every participant to examine the positions in a controversy.

---

The arguments you will be using in your essays have a relationship to the dialogues conducted by Socrates, Plato, and Aristotle. They wanted to search out the truth of matters that were important to the thinkers of their day. You will be searching out the best ways of convincing others that something you believe about an important issue is a reasonable position to take. You will be discovering new ideas for yourself just as the early philosophers used dialogues to discover truths that no one had ever thought about before.

When you are trying to convince someone that you are reasonable in a position you have taken, you must keep your audience in mind. That focus on audience will be an asset to you in all your writing. When you stop to think about it, much communication has some element of argument in it, and this is especially true of academic situations. If you are assigned to write an essay exam on the three most important characters in *Romeo and Juliet*, you must present evidence that your choices are valid. That process is an argument.

The same command of argument is used in professional situations. If you are writing a proposal for an innovative change in your work area, that proposal must present the reasons why you consider the change to be an advantage over the present system. If your argument is clear and well organized, your superiors will be persuaded to give it serious consideration.

When forming an argument, you will focus on convincing someone holding an opposing view because that will force you to keep the clearest line of reasoning possible as you develop your essay. As you write, you will be thinking about reasons people might use to disagree with you and how you will support the position you have taken. This process replaces having people present to tell you what they think.

A common definition of *argument* is almost the same as *fight*. A newspaper might report:

> The victim was having an argument with an acquaintance outside the supermarket when the alleged assailant drew a gun and wounded the victim in the abdomen.

Arguments of this kind do not rely on reasonable ideas or a search for truth. They rely on emotion, yelling, and, in extreme cases, force. In this definition of argument, you simply try to shout louder than those who disagree with you. Almost everyone knows that this kind of argument is not a good way to find out new ideas because it is hard to listen reasonably.

The following excerpts from the Platonic dialogue *Phaedrus* give a good example of how dialogue was used to inquire about ideas that were correct and those that were not. Phaedrus and Socrates are discussing the elements of speaking and writing and come to conclusions that still comprise much of what is considered to be good communication.

At this point, Phaedrus and Socrates begin to discuss whether the speaker needs to be speaking the truth to be effective. Phaedrus thinks the speaker need only be *seen* as good or noble to be persuasive. Phaedrus is responding to the ideas of the Sophists, a group of teachers who opposed Socrates, who felt that the highest art of rhetoric was to be compelling and persuasive, not to seek the truth. Socrates disagrees.

SOCRATES  Well, the subject we proposed for inquiry just now was the nature of good and bad speaking and writing; so we are to inquire into that.

PHAEDRUS  Plainly.

SOCRATES  Then does not a good and successful discourse pre-suppose a knowledge in the mind of the speaker of the truth about his subject?

PHAEDRUS   As to that, dear Socrates, what I have heard is that the intending orator is under no necessity of understanding what is truly just, but only what is likely to be thought as just by the body of men who are to give judgment; nor need he know what is truly good or noble, but what will be thought so, since it is on the latter, not the former, that persuasion depends.

. . .

SOCRATES   Well, here is my suggestion for discussion.

PHAEDRUS   Yes?

SOCRATES   Suppose I tried to persuade you to acquire a horse to use in battle against the enemy, and suppose that neither of us knew what a horse was, but I knew this much about you, that Phaedrus believes a horse to be that tame animal which possesses the largest ears.

PHAEDRUS   A ridiculous thing to suppose, Socrates.

SOCRATES   Wait a moment. Suppose I continued to urge upon you in all seriousness, with a studied encomium [praise] of a donkey, that it was what I called it, a horse, that it was highly important for you to possess the creature, both at home and in the field, that it was just the animal to ride on into battle, and that it was handy, into the bargain, for carrying your equipment and so forth.

PHAEDRUS   To go to that length would be utterly ridiculous.

SOCRATES   Well, isn't it better to be a ridiculous friend than a clever enemy?

PHAEDRUS   I suppose it is.

SOCRATES   Then when a master of oratory, who is ignorant of good and evil, employs his power of persuasion on a community as ignorant as himself, not by extolling a miserable donkey as being really a horse, but by extolling evil as being really good, and when by studying the beliefs of the masses he persuades them to do evil instead of good, what kind of crop do you think his oratory is likely to reap from the seed thus sown?

PHAEDRUS   A pretty poor one.

. . .

SOCRATES   Must not the art of rhetoric [speech], taken as a whole, be a kind of influencing of the mind by means of words, not only in courts of law and other public gatherings, but in private places also? And must it not be the same art that is concerned with great issues and small, its right employment commanding no more respect when dealing with important matters than with unimportant?

Socrates convinces Phaedrus that, in order to have any positive influence, the speaker must stick with the truth. Then they turn to the elements of an effective discourse or discussion. These elements apply to an effective piece of writing as well as to spoken communications.

> SOCRATES   Well, there is one point at least which I think you will admit, namely that any discourse ought to be constructed like a living creature, with its own body, as it were; it must not lack either head or feet; it must have a middle and extremities so composed as to suit each other and the whole work.

The closing comments set a pattern for written work that we still keep in mind today, even if we do not insist on a formal structure every time. An essay needs some form of introduction. The exposition explains the purpose of the work, and the evidence is the proofs or examples the writer offers to convince the audience of the reasonableness of the position. The refutation is the portion where the writer addresses the arguments of those who may disagree with the positions taken by the essay. This Socratic dialogue presents a foundation that still guides writers all these years later.

This form of discussion or dialogue, called *dialectic,* upset many people. Plato's teacher, Socrates, was forced to commit suicide by people who were angry because Socrates questioned beliefs they wanted everyone to accept. A student of Plato's, Aristotle, continued to develop this new way of thinking, and we still use many of the patterns of thinking that they began almost 2,500 years ago.

Socrates, Plato, and Aristotle relied on information that was accepted as reasonable by everyone. An idea could not be discounted until reasonable arguments were put forth that proved that the idea was unsound. Scientists in Western cultures have accepted this pattern of presenting proof or evidence to support an idea since Plato and his students started it.

Aristotle used the system of proofs and evidence to make new discoveries about nature and science, changing the way people saw education. Suddenly, students could discover things their teachers did not know. Previously, students had concentrated on remembering what their teachers had told them. Many older people did not like these new ideas, which questioned traditional ways of thinking about religion and the world. Some early scientists were even put to death for insisting old ideas were wrong.

Much of the writing you do will center on this form of argument. It is a method of learning to write clearly, because by organizing arguments on topics of interest to you and the others, you will learn to see the difference between an argument that fails to convince others of its reasonableness and one that convinces. When this kind of argument is done well, an order will emerge that makes both the disagreement and possible solutions for it clear. This form of argument is interesting because it makes you look for the strongest reasons to support your ideas. It can be frustrating if you can't find good enough reasons for an idea you really want to support, and sometimes you find surprising truths when you listen to what other people have to say about your topic. Before you can really listen, however, you have to think through your own opinions, because you cannot accurately evaluate their ideas if you have not carefully evaluated your own.

In this kind of argument, it is not a goal to convince your audience that your position is the correct one and all who disagree with it are wrong. In situations where formal arguments are conducted, there may be a wide range of reasonable positions to take. There may or may not be one single right or reasonable position. The important part of an argument is the way you support your position.

## ARGUMENT STRUCTURE

As you already know, an important element of an argument is the question at issue.

**Question at issue**   An area of disagreement or difference of opinion.

You cannot have an argument of any sort without some difference of opinion. As you begin to identify ideas that might be possibilities for an essay, however, the first ideas you come up with may be the ones you can most easily support and defend. Often those ideas will lack a clear question at issue. This happens because arguments of this sort have so many good reasons to support them that they seem appealing to defend. For example, you might think the following would be good topics for an essay:

Children would do better in school if their parents would give them more support.

Our society should stop discriminating against those who are perceived as different.

Women should not be sexually harassed at work.

These topics are not good for argumentative essays, though, because they do not have a question at issue or point of controversy. Who will say that parental support will hinder a child's education, people should discriminate, or women should be sexually harassed? When you have an essay topic that seems really easy to support, you need to check to see if you can identify people who disagree with the stance you are taking. If you cannot, you have a weak question at issue.

Some ideas do not make good arguments because they aren't important to enough people. You might think rainy days are better than sunny days, but you could not write an argumentative essay on that subject. Most people would not care enough about what kind of day you preferred to stay interested in the topic. As you begin the process of questioning ideas to see if they will work for an argumentative essay, the first questions you must ask are:

1.  Is this idea important enough to me that I will work to convince others?
2.  What are those who would disagree with me saying about this idea?
3.  What are their reasons for disagreeing?

If there are clear answers to these questions, then you know that people have been thinking and talking about your idea. This means that it is important enough to write about in an essay. If you cannot think of people who disagree or reasons they might use for disagreement, your problem is a weak question at issue.

## Exercises: Audience Responses

The following exercises will help you understand some of the key points we have covered. Divide into groups of three to five people, have each person give some answer to the questions, and take turns recording the answers. It is not necessary that the group come to agreement on a single answer. A good way to discover the range of assumptions is to listen to the various answers to the following questions.

### A. Comparing Sources of Information

Compare the sources for your information that you listed in item C of the Describe Yourself exercise in Chapter 1 (page 7).

1.  What sources do you have in common?
2.  What are the ones that differ?

3. Take a few minutes to discuss both the ones you agree on and the ones you differ on. Can you find any pattern in either the areas of agreement or the areas of disagreement?
4. In one or two sentences, write down a summary of your findings. Are your summaries all about the same? Why or why not?

## B. Identifying Differences of Perspective
1. What is a liberal?
2. What is a conservative?

In which category would you place the following people?

1. A member of a labor union.
2. A teacher who feels capitalism is a system with many weaknesses.
3. Someone who owns a business.
4. A person who votes against gun control.
5. A person who votes for gun control.
6. A teacher who feels socialism is a system with many weaknesses.
7. An unemployed person.
8. Someone who does not vote.
9. A teacher who feels both capitalism and socialism have weaknesses.

## *Exercises: Dissecting a Question at Issue*

From item D of the Describe Yourself exercise in Chapter 1 (page 7), read one of the opinions you hold that you don't think everyone agrees with. As a group, select an issue that you are interested in and about which there are differences of opinion.

1. Decide what aspects of this issue you all agree on. This may seem difficult at first, but keep breaking the issue down until you have some aspects of the controversy that you all agree about.
2. Make a list of the issues that make this topic controversial.

Once you have written down these lists, talk to each other about why you do not think alike on this issue.

1. What made each of you come to the conclusion that you did? If you are not sure why you have the opinion you do, then where did you get this opinion? Is it shared by your parents or your friends?

2.  If you listed reasons why you were right in your opinion, what would they be?
3.  What reasons do those who disagree with you give? Were they the same reasons you wrote down when you did this exercise in Chapter 1?

Now that you have thoroughly discussed this issue:

1.  What part of this controversy do you think you could most easily persuade your opposition to change their mind about?
2.  What reasons would you use?
3.  How would you avoid getting side-tracked into aspects of this issue where agreement would be difficult?

**Sample discussion.**   For comparison, the following lists summarize a discussion about a fairly controversial question at issue: Should student athletes be paid for the time they give to colleges and universities?

A.  Aspects of this issue most can agree on.
  1.  There should be student athletes at colleges and universities.
  2.  Being an athlete takes a significant amount of time.
  3.  It is difficult to maintain a high G.P.A. while playing a sport.
  4.  There are problems with the way student athletics is currently handled.
  5.  Athletes are rewarded for playing in a variety of ways.
  6.  Some athletes bring more money into the school than others.
B.  A list of the issues that make this topic controversial.
  1.  Paying athletes would remove their amateur status.
  2.  It would be impossible to pay each athlete fairly because not all generate the same money for schools.
  3.  Paying them would make sports a job instead of part of getting an education.
  4.  It would be expensive for the school.
  5.  It could increase the sexism in athletics.
  6.  The cheerleaders, band, and team managers would have to be paid, too.
C.  A list of arguments in support of this issue.
  1.  Athletes could concentrate on their sport better because finances wouldn't be a problem.
  2.  Pay could be set nationally so all schools would have an equal chance for good athletes.

3. Athletes would practice harder knowing the hours were earning them money.

4. It would reduce temptation to offer athletes hidden incentives or payments.

5. Athletes would not have to get jobs for spending-money in addition to the pressure of combining sports and academics.

6. Athletes would be more likely to finish their education rather than pursuing sports professionally before graduation.

D. A list of arguments in opposition to this issue.

1. Athletes already receive many preferences such as preregistration. This would widen the gap between them and other students.

2. An athletic scholarship is payment enough.

3. All students make sacrifices for their education; athletes should, too.

4. The small salary a college could pay will not compete with professional salary.

5. If athletes want to go professional, they should go. College is for education, not for professional sports demonstrations.

6. Sports are already too big and too expensive. They detract from the academic atmosphere.

# ARGUING FROM EXPERIENCE

Before you look for experts to support your position, make sure you are not overlooking the areas where your personal experiences have made you an expert on your topic.

---

**Expert**    A person who is known and respected by others in the same field.

---

People have a wide range of backgrounds and attitudes. This knowledge has to guide you when you choose the reasons you will use to convince them that you have taken a defensible position. Each person has had a different set of experiences and, when carefully explained, those experiences can assist others in understanding the conclusions that were reached based on those experiences. Too often, people ignore ways their life experience has made them experts on some topic or situation. Darla, the author of the sample essay at the end of this chapter, grew up in an area where there was strip mining. Because she has experienced the effects of this activity first-hand, she is an expert on the impact that that had on the people in the area.

As you progress in writing argumentative essays, you will find your own experiences, when used properly, can be very effective argument. Remember the point made in Chapter 1: *The reasons* why *you think the things you think are much more important than* what *you think, because the* why *explains how you came to the conclusion you did.* That *why* is most often connected to some experience that you have had. Other people cannot make an assessment of whether you can support what you are saying if you do not tell them why you have come to that conclusion. You have built a wide variety of understandings based on your experiences. Those conclusions are reasonable ones to you or you would not have kept them. If they are reasonable to you, it is very likely that they will be reasonable to your audience if you take the time to explain them carefully. It is also possible that others might look at the reasons why you came to your conclusion and see those reasons differently from the way that you did. As you listen to those different views of your reasons, you may come to alter your position to some degree.

You may think that your audience will not be interested in your experiences, but they will be if you let them know why your experience can either teach them something or serve as an example of a situation that affects their lives. The ability to learn from the experiences of others is one of the significant things that makes humans different from most other animals. Your audience can learn from you if you give them a chance, just as you can learn from them. When you think of an example you could draw from personal experience, however, there are things you need to ask before you use that example in your argument.

## *How Experience Fits with the Readings*

In the process of getting interested in the topic, you should have thought some about how the material you read connected with your life. Whatever way you found to relate to the assigned issue, now is the time to use that relationship to start focusing your ideas. You do not have to put personal experiences in every essay you write, but you must have clearly in mind what personal connection you have with the topic, or you will not be able to keep a consistent focus.

At other times, there will be a personal experience in your life, or in the life of someone you know, that will make the position you have taken clear to your audience. You know why you have your opinion on the topic; don't make the mistake of assuming your audience knows why, too. A well-presented description of that experience can assist your audience in understanding your position much more quickly than a long rationalization, and the description has the advantage of communicating your emotional connection to the experience. If you have chosen that experience carefully, that emotional understanding can assist the persuasive power of your essay.

Even if you make very strong statements about how much you believe in your position, you still have to offer your audience the necessary information to accept your word as reasonable argument. The more strongly you believe in a position, the more carefully you have to support it with information that has common ground with your audience. An emotional appeal alone is not reasonable argument. Emotional appeals often unintentionally cause you to lose common ground by triggering a defensive reaction in your audience because they do not share your strong emotions on the position. This is especially true if they do not know why you feel so strongly or if your reasons are not widely shared.

---

### Application

What experiences have you had that might be useful in an essay on the topic of education?

What position might you take when you tell your audience about your experiences?

---

Once you have made an assessment of how closely your personal experience fits with the essay you intend to write, you can start developing the strategies to support your essay.

 ## Evaluate Your Experience

1. *Will significant numbers of people have had similar experiences?* When you know that many others have had similar experiences, then you can build on them as support for your position. You must make it clear that you do not expect everyone to have had this experience, just enough people to make your argument reasonable.

If you are fairly sure that very few of your readers will have had a similar experience, then you must decide whether that experience will support your position. It still may work if you can be reasonably sure you know how the majority of your audience would react to a similar situation.

2. *Am I giving enough information to help my readers understand why I came to my conclusion?* Sometimes your responses to a situation are strong enough that you assume that others will know exactly why you reacted that way. Remember that your audience might not know why unless you tell them, and it is also true that, even if they think they know why, you will have a clearer argument if you explain carefully.

3. *Am I allowing for those who might respond to this situation differently than I did?* If you feel sure there are people who would react to the same situation differently, then you must give additional reasons for your response. If you do not, you have implied that your reaction is the only reasonable one, and that implication will cause you to lose common ground with those who respond differently. They will no longer feel your position is a reasonable one because they understand their reaction better than they understand yours.

4. *Have I been careful not to overgeneralize the experience?* A good example of overgeneralization is the person who has had a bad experience with someone who looked like a transient and came to the conclusion that all transients are criminals. While the bad experience might make the reader sympathize with the person who wrote about it, the experience does not justify making such a sweeping generalized judgment about all people who appear to be transients.

5. *Have I been careful to take into consideration all possible factors that influenced my response to the experience?* Highly emotional experiences can be used very effectively. All of us have had powerful events in our lives that changed the way we saw certain things, and telling about such an event can cause your audience to share your view. Remember the caution about overgeneralizing, however. Sometimes emotional experiences can cause people to lose sight of outside factors that affected their reactions. You cannot use emotional experiences effectively if you have not given some thought to why they caused you to come to the conclusion you did.

## First Person and Third Person

Students are sometimes told not to use "I" (the first person) when writing formal essays. Instructors who say this have reasons for doing so. They do not want to see papers that reflect only the students' own lives and experiences. Instead, they want students to go out and learn some things about the lives and experiences of others. This is a response to the fear that students will not learn anything unless they are encouraged to find out what others think.

Never using "I" does not work well for an argumentative essay, however. For an argumentative essay to work, the reader must first know what the writer thinks. It is possible to give an opinion without using "I." You could write "In this writer's opinion . . . " instead of "I think . . . ," but that is not the best method. It is not necessary to give credit for every statement. You can as easily write "The factory will cause long-range problems in the water quality of this town that will offset any employment benefits it might bring" as you can write "I think the factory will cause long-range problems in the water quality of this town that will offset any employment benefits it might bring."

You have learned that opinions must be backed up with facts and reasoning if they are to be acceptable to thoughtful people, regardless of whether you use the pronoun "I." When you write an argument, you choose the question at issue yourself. No one but you is responsible for the thoughts, ideas, and opinions contained in your essay. You are not able to share that responsibility with all Americans, all citizens of your state, all members of your political party, or the members of any other group. When you use the first-person plural "we" instead of the first-person singular "I," you are trying to accurately represent the feelings of a group, and this can rarely be done. It is not possible to evade responsibility for your own opinions. They are yours, and it is best to acknowledge them strongly. Once they are down on paper, you will get the credit or the blame in the long run in any case.

Of course, no paper would be as pleasant to read if every sentence begins with, or focuses on, the same word. This lack of variety frequently indicates that the reasoning in the essay is not good. Sentences that provide background for the opinions stated in the essay would not be likely to begin with "I," and an essay that goes from one unsupported idea to another would be wrong with or without the use of the word "I."

The second person is the person being addressed by the writer or speaker: *you.* It is not a good idea to write an argumentative essay in the second person, because writers can only give their own opinions or quote the opinions of others.  They cannot tell readers what their opinions should be.  If an essay tells the readers "You should not eat meat," it insults the audience by not letting them make their own decisions. A better approach, instead, is "I think eating meat is ethically questionable because the meat industry causes terrible suffering before it kills the animals." Or "Meat is only one of many ways to provide the essential proteins needed by the human body."

The third person is the person being spoken or written about: *he* or *she* or *they.* It is possible to use the opinions of a third person to develop an argument. That is what writers are doing when citing an expert for support and when offering acceptable information without giving a specific source. If a writer uses the opinions of other people exclusively, however, she will have difficulty because the essay will be about what others think, rather than the writer's thinking and conclusions.

---

**First person**   The person or people doing the speaking or writing (I, we).

**Second person**   The person or people being addressed by the speaker or writer (you).

**Third person**   The person or people being talked about by the speaker or writer (he, she, they).

---

## REVISION ACTIVITIES

### Darla's First Draft

Since Darla is from the Appalachian mountain region, she feels very strongly about the effects of strip mining on the landscape she knows best, and she wants her audience to be convinced by what she has to say. In order to make her argument as strong as possible, she has gathered as many experts as she can find to prove the importance of her subject.

As you read Darla's first draft, keep these questions in mind:

1.  What is her position on the question at issue?
2.  Does the information she gathered make you feel upset about strip mining?
3.  What kind of information seems to be missing from her essay?
4.  What kind of information does she seem to want most?

## *Darla's Essay (Draft 1)*

This essay concerns the effects of strip mining for bituminous coal on the ecology of eastern Kentucky. The Webster's New World Dictionary defines strip mining as "a method of mining, as for coal, by exposing a mineral deposit near the earth's surface." According to an article in Mother Jones, the September–October 1991 issue, by Tom Nugent and Donald R. Soeken, there are six thousand abandoned strip mines in the Appalachian area. This area consists of West Virginia, eastern Kentucky

and Tennessee, and western Virginia and North Carolina. (U.S. Department of the Interior)

The organization Save Our Cumberland Mountains discovered during a 1981 lawsuit against Republic Coal Company and Skiles Coal Company, two of the largest companies operating in the Appalachian mountain area (refer to earlier definition), over discharges into the Obed federally designated Wild and Scenic River, that, since the passage of the Surface Mining Reclamation Act, the federal government is owed 500 million (half a billion) dollars by mining companies. The states of Kentucky and West Virginia have not collected this money.

The Federal Office of Surface Mining Reclamation and Enforcement, under former director Vince Laubach, declares that only 100 million is owed, but admits that their accounting procedures for the years 1978 to 1990 are sloppy. (Nugent and Soeken, 57) We can therefore conclude, that the figure of 500 million given by Save Our Cumberland Mountains during the Obed Wild and Scenic River suit cannot be disproven.

The question now arises. Why have Kentucky and West Virginia not collected this money? The Appalachian area (see above) is unique in that the mineral rights to rural property are often not owned by the people who own the surface rights to the acreage, and who may live on the property and use it for agriculture and grazing. In fact, the majority of the mineral rights in this area are owned by businesses that are located outside that area. They are not locally owned, and may be large energy conglomerates with interests in oil, coal, nuclear power, and other forms of energy.

The definition given at the beginning of the essay for strip mining is not a complete definition of the activity. It also does not describe the effect that such mining activity can have on the area surrounding the mine. In order to fully understand the effect such activity has on the environment surrounding the site of the mining, it is necessary to consult those who, in fact, live there.

To do this, it will be necessary to get information from local organizations, such as Save Our Cumberland Mountains, as the representatives of official industry-regulating groups do not preserve the opinions of those local residents who live in the area and do not own mineral rights.

The report of the Committee on Disposal of Excess Spoil from Coal Mining of the Board on Mineral and Energy Resources of the United States Commission on Natural Resources does not include any conversations with the people most affected by the mining. The report encourages specific spoil (defined by the Board on Energy and Mineral Resources as: overburden that is not returned to the mine workings after mining is completed) handling procedures for the steep terrain of the central Appalachians. This is an improvement on previous procedures because it takes into account hydrological problems of runoff into mountain streams, but it still does not include the experience and desires of the landowners of eastern Kentucky and other related areas.

In this report, all data on cost of complying with the Surface Mining and Reclamation Act of 1977, mentioned earlier in this paper, is supplied by the National Coal Association and the American Mining Congress. Both of these organizations are lobbying groups that defend the interests of the coal companies who, in the past, have such a poor record of complying with the Surface Mining and Reclamation Act. This is mentioned at the beginning of this paper.

No alternative view of the costs of complying with the act are given in the report. Environmental organizations are not offered the opportunity to present other statistics on cost. The committee includes two representatives of the coal companies. Only one representative of an environmental point of view is on the committee, and he is an expert on air pollution from the John Muir Institute, not someone from a local group concerned with specific conditions in the coal fields.

I consulted another publication of the U.S. Natural Resource Council, Surface Mining: Soil, Coal and Society. This book was written by the Committee on Soil as a Resource in Relation to Surface Mining for Coal. The members of the committee are almost identical to those on the other committee. They represent the coal industry or they are professors at universities in the coal-producing states. I read reports by many committees, and the same people are consulted by all of them. I was surprised to find this practice was so common.

Surface Mining: Soil, Coal and Society was, in some ways, different from some of the other government publications on strip mining that I consulted for this report. It mentioned such subjects as social cost of surface (or strip) mining. "The quality of life may be degraded in the view of the local people. . . ."(6) The book, another publication of the Commission on Natural Resources, never considers the possibility that the stress of strip mining is too overwhelming for some communities to absorb, however.

The conclusions of this book focus on the need for additional reclamation. It considers the social costs in suggesting that some communities should not be mined near the center of town. This is the only conclusion directly aimed at the feeling of the people most affected. It also mentions the cultures of the Native American people directly affected by this mining technique in the western states, especially Arizona and New Mexico. I am sure that the effects on this community of people are very serious, but the government does not seem to realize that other communities are very close and have very strong ties, even though those ties are not protected by treaties and laws.

In the sections on reclamation and agriculture, the book debates whether to remake the Appalachians into new, less mountainous contours. During the discussion of this issue, it is mentioned that the soil in this area is thin and relatively unproductive for agriculture. (68) The virtues of living in the mountains that are no longer natural but consist of a series of terraces produced by hauling the mining waste (spoil) up from the pit in accordance with the 1977 Surface Mining Reclamation Law is discussed.

This discussion overlooks the fact that this land belongs to someone, at least on the surface. That individual, or family, does not have to wish what the commission's studies say they would wish. Even the commission's report, Surface Mining: Soil, Coal and Society, says,

> Social changes have psychological effects on individuals. The disruption of accepted cultural norms and the break-down of conventional systems of social relations and communication affect children and the aged especially strongly. Out-migration to escape the disorienting conditions is a common response. Relatively small communities affected by large facilities usually experience an increase in emotional disorders.

This seems to me a very serious side effect of any business activity. The commission seems to feel this is a cost of doing business that can somehow be passed along to the consumer with the cost of filling in open pits.

They also say that surface (strip) mining is superior to deep mining because "The deep mining of coal is a relatively hazardous occupation."

This is undoubtedly true, but it was the occupation of many people in the Appalachian region. Strip mining does not replace those jobs with other, less hazardous occupations. The former miners remain unemployed, and the younger generation joins the out-migration mentioned above.

A thorough search of the facilities at our library did not turn up a great deal on strip mining and its effect on the communities in which it is practiced. Of the articles and books I found, none actually questioned the need for continued strip mining. The people of the Appalachian coal fields have been asked to make sacrifices for the energy needs of the rest of the United States. Nothing can remake the destroyed land. No plan can even be put into place that is not based on the needs and wants of the people who were already living in the landscape before the strip mines came to the mountains.

---

When Darla did preliminary notes about her topic, she wrote this down:

> My house often shakes from the explosions in the coal pit. I hope the explosions aren't destroying the foundations of the house because my parents worked so hard to get it. My father has some lung problems, and things have not been easy for my family lately. My father was a miner, but he is retired, and my mother is a teacher's aide in an elementary class room, which does not pay that well. I hope we do not have to have the house repairs, which eat into the money my parents put aside for my education before my father retired. If they do, I do not know what I will do.

Darla sees things differently than the experts because her experience is different. She has lived with the impact of strip mining, whereas they have only studied it. Darla did not think the audience would listen to her experiences, so she tried to find experts who recorded the reactions of the people who lived with the sights, sounds, and emotions surrounding open pit mining. She couldn't find those references in the books she read, however.

What Darla has failed to recognize is that her experience has made *her* an expert on what it is like to live around strip-mining activity. She has insights into this aspect of the problem that the government publications have not recorded. If she had included her personal experience with mining, her audience would have understood why this topic was so important to her. Once the audience knew what Darla experienced, it would have been a reasonable conclusion that others near the mines were experiencing a similarly distressful effect on their lives.

Darla's essay ends very abruptly. The reason that she does not have a smooth conclusion is the same reason that the transitions between her paragraphs are very jumpy. Darla feels unable to include the personal experience that is her reason for choosing this topic, so she does not clearly articulate her position. She wants to convince her audience that strip mining has such a terrible effect on the nearby population that it should be discontinued, but, without her expert insight, she is not able to gather enough support for that conclusion.

## Application

It is possible to guess from what Darla has written that she knows more about this topic than she has told her audience. Individually or in small groups, make suggestions to Darla that will guide her in shaping this rough draft into a solid argumentative essay.

**Library use.**  Darla had problems finishing her essay because she tried to use the references in the library to replace her own ideas and thinking. The library can be useful when you want to see what others are saying about your position. When you try to write an essay using library sources alone, however, it becomes very difficult to maintain a clear contact with your audience. Each reference you read has a specific audience that is not the one you are writing for. Each audience has differences in vocabulary, background, and focus. If you were to try to write an essay for your psychology class using information you got from a discussion, you would first have to let the readers in the psychology class know what started the discussion, what material had been read, and why the discussion was being held. If you did not do that, the readers would not really understand why the people in the discussion had said the things that they said.

The same is true of using library references. You can gather pieces of information, but, if you gather too many pieces, they become disconnected from any central position, since each piece came from a discussion your audience does not know about. If you try to fill in all the background for every reference, soon your essay will be all background.

When you develop your ideas, try to find a topic that you have an interest in without doing any library research. If you have an interest, you also have some supports for the ideas already organized in your mind. If you think it would be useful to find quotations or statistics from a magazine, newspaper, or book to back up what you already know, then use the library. Just remember, there is not enough information in the library to replace your own thinking in support of your argument.

**Transitions.**   When you move from one idea to another, you need to let your audience know that you are making the change and that the new information has some relationship to the previous subject under discussion. These signals of change are called "transitions." You make them automatically when you talk, but sometimes people forget transitions when they write.

If you are talking with friends about the poor driving habits of a mutual acquaintance named Dave, and you think of a funny driving incident, you will introduce your story something like this: "Dave's driving reminds me of the time when . . ." You have provided your audience with a transition between what was previously under discussion to the story you want to tell. It is unlikely you would just begin by telling your story because you understand that your listeners would want to know why you were telling it to them. If you just began your story without a transition, your friends might feel that you had been rude and interrupted their conversation.

Transitions in writing accomplish the very same function of moving a conversation smoothly from one idea to another. Even though your audience is not present, you need to be at least as polite to them as you would be if you asked them to listen to you in person. Darla got so involved in recording the information she found at the library that she forgot her transitions. Many of the paragraphs in her essay do not seem to be connected to a central idea. Now that you have a little more information about what Darla is trying to accomplish, it will be easier to suggest ways she can put in some of those transitions.

**Paragraph order.**   Paragraphs are designed to visually signal a transition from one idea to another. They indicate that one part of the discussion is finished and another is about to begin. The combination of the written transition and the visual one of the indented first line or extra space makes your ideas flow smoothly from one point to another. Darla has started new paragraphs when she is still working on the same topic and not started new paragraphs when she shifts to a new idea.

## Darla's Second Draft

Darla used many of the computer's abilities when she revised her first draft. She moved some of her paragraphs around and reorganized her information so that her audience could see why she was so interested in this particular topic.

## *Darla's Essay (Draft 2)*

I would not be going to college if it were not for coal. My father was a miner. That is how the men in my town have supported their families for as long as the town has been there. Since there has been a union, mining has paid fairly well. There is another side to mining, though. My father is sick from his years in the mines. Our house shakes from the explosions in the open pit mine.

I do not know if I will ever be able to return to the area where I grew up. Many young people leave and don't return. They go to cities to work; they go to college and go on to take jobs elsewhere; they go into the military. The reason they do not stay is that there are no jobs. The jobs in the mines are disappearing because deep mining is giving way to strip mining. Strip mining is "A method of mining, as for coal, by exposing a mineral deposit near the earth's surface" according to the Webster's New World Dictionary.

Surface Mining: Soil, Coal and Society, a publication of the U.S. Natural Resource Council, says that surface (strip) mining is superior to deep mining because "the deep mining of coal is a relatively hazardous occupation." This is true, but strip mining is heavily automated and produces few jobs of any kind. Agriculture might be an alternative, but that ignores the state the surface of the land is left in after the minerals are gone.

Many people in the Appalachian region do not own the rights to the minerals that lie beneath the land they own. These rights were often taken from their ancestors unscrupulously when the value of the coal fields was first apparent. These people may have no control over mining on the land they use for farming or grazing and where they have their homes.

The Surface Mining and Reclamation Act of 1977 is supposed to guarantee the people of the Appalachians that the land will be restored to its original value. That act is the reason I doubt that I will ever be able to return to my home and earn a living.

According to Tom Nugent and Donald R. Soeken, writing in the September–October 1991 issue of Mother Jones, there are six thousand abandoned strip mines in the Appalachian area. These mines are the ones the Surface Mining and Reclamation Act is supposed to restore. The money for the reclamation should have been collected from the coal companies by the states that contain the mines and given to the federal government to finance the restoration.

In a 1981 lawsuit against the Republic Coal Company and the Skiles Coal Company for discharging waste into the Obed federally designated Wild and Scenic River, the environmental organization Save Our Cumberland Mountains discovered that, since the passage of the Surface Mining and Reclamation Act, the federal government is owed 500 million dollars by mining companies. The states of Kentucky and West Virginia have not collected this money.

The Federal Office of Surface Mining Reclamation Enforcement, under former director Vince Laubach, declared that only 100 million is owed, but admitted that their accounting procedures for the years 1978 to 1990 were sloppy. (Nugent and Soeken, 57) We can therefore conclude that the figure of 500 million given by Save Our Cumberland Mountains cannot be disproven.

The question that needs to be answered is: Why haven't West Virginia and Kentucky collected the money? The mineral rights in the Appalachian area that were signed away are not usually owned within the communities that live in the area. Instead they belong to businesses outside the area. These are often large energy conglomerates with interest in oil, coal, and nuclear power.

I consulted several federally financed studies before writing this paper. I was amazed to find that the reports, which came from different boards of the U.S. Commission on Natural Resources, were basically written by the same people. These people are professors from the state universities of coal-producing states, or they are representatives of the energy industry. Only one representative of an environmental organization was on any of the committees, and he was an expert on air pollution from the West Coast. No one from the area where the mining is being done was represented on any of the committees.

All the financial statistics used by the committees were provided by the National Coal Association and the American Mining Congress, lobbying organizations for the energy industry. No alternative statistics, such as those collected by Save Our Cumberland Mountains, were ever used.

One of these studies, quoted earlier, <u>Surface Mining: Soil, Coal and Society</u>, does address the issue of the feelings of the residents of strip-mining areas. This is called the social cost of surface mining. "The quality of life may be degraded in the eyes of local people . . ."(6) The book, another publication of the Commission on Natural Resources, never considers the possibility that the stress of strip mining is too overwhelming for some communities to absorb, however.

The conclusions of this book focus on the need for additional reclamation. It considers the social costs in suggesting that some communities should not be mined near the center of town. This is the only conclusion directly aimed at the feeling of the people most affected. It also mentions the cultures of the Native American people directly affected by this mining technique in the western states, especially Arizona and New Mexico. I am sure that the effects on this community of people are very serious, but the government does not seem to realize that other communities are very close and have very strong ties even though those ties are not protected by treaties and laws.

Nothing that has been tried so far can remake the destroyed land. The people of the Appalachian coal fields have been asked to make sacrifices for the energy needs of the rest of the United States. No plan has even been considered that is based on the needs and wants of the people who were already living in the landscape before the strip mines came to the mountains. This is why I do not expect to ever live in my home again. My father is ill, and my mother works as a teacher's aid in an elementary school classroom. It does not pay well. They are depending on me and my sisters and brothers to earn enough to take care of ourselves and help them. We cannot do that without leaving because the jobs are gone and the land is gutted.

---

### Reviewing Darla's Essay

1. List examples of ways in which Darla has succeeded in combining her first and second drafts.
2. List examples of places where she should have rewritten more.
3. Discuss whether Darla successfully integrated the paragraph she wrote about her personal experiences in her second draft.

# *Chapter Review*

1. What parts of discourse did Socrates name?
2. What are some applications for critical reading?
3. What is a question at issue?
4. What is the first step you can take to generate interest in a topic?
5. Why do you think Darla left her personal experience out of her first draft?

---

# Chapter 3

# *How Audience Shapes an Argument*

Common Ground
Diversity and Common Ground
The Challenge of English
Common Ground and Argument
Revision Activities
    Eric's First Draft
    Craig's First Draft
Chapter Review

A simple fact that often gets lost in the process of writing is that writing is an act of communication. Just as you do not ordinarily talk when there is no listener, it does not make sense to write when you have nothing to say to yourself or to others. Writing is different from talking, even though the same words may be used, because you cannot see your audience when you write. In some cases, such as writing a letter of application for a job, you may not even know who the audience will be. Often you know, or think you know, something about your audience, and that can help you tailor your writing to communicate with them. Still, you must think about them as you write because they are not physically present.

## COMMON GROUND

This invisible audience can cause trouble for a writer. Many writers assume an audience just like themselves because that is the easiest kind of audience to keep in mind. In a work setting, however, there are many ways your audience may differ from you, and, if you do not consider these differences, you will fail to persuade them that your argument is reasonable.

It is not always easy to tell when people are different from ourselves. When you first enter a room and look around at the people there, you may think their appearance tells you what you do and do not have in common with them. You will be right in some ways and wrong in others. The people in the room are varied in ways that are immediately identifiable: by race, gender, and age. However, those surface appearances may be deceptive, and there are many other significant differences that you are not able to see. To write to communicate, you have to have *common ground* or *warrant*.

---

**Common ground**   Reasonable justification for your ideas that your audience, especially those who disagree with you, will share with you. This concept is often called the *warrant* for a position.

---

## DIVERSITY AND COMMON GROUND

Common ground, or warrant, is an essential part of a solid argumentative essay. If those who read your argument cannot agree with or understand the points you make to support your main idea, the essay will not be persuasive. The reader will lose interest because you have already lost your point. Maintaining common ground can be difficult for a variety of reasons, but the key reason lies in the diversity of your audience. If you do not consider the possible differences between your assumptions and theirs, you will lose common ground and your audience's interest as well.

An assumption is something that you take for granted. Because you take an opinion for granted, you can make the mistake of thinking that others think just the way that you do about it. Common ground is a view of life that is shared to a degree that allows communication on a given topic. There are many not easily identifiable ways that diversity complicates common ground. To maintain common ground, you need to consider some of the ways your audience is different and, if those differences are not considered, how they will cause problems when forming an argument.

### Gender and Age   Don't gen. by this —

One of the first ways most people sort their peers will be by gender and age. They will compare their standing according to how many roughly match their position in those two categories. If they are in the minority in either category, it often reduces their comfort in that group. This reaction is based on the assumption that those who share their age and sex must be similar in other ways as well, and those who do not share those qualities will not be like them in ways that are significant.

In a general way, this is a safe assumption based on experience. Most societies have patterns of expectations for people based on gender and age that give these groups some similarities. The reason these factors fit in a discussion of common ground is that when the general perception of these similarities broadens into a stereotype including *all* women in their late teens, or *all* people over thirty, they will certainly cause the writer of that stereotype to lose credibility. It is certainly true that each of us has some similarities with others of our age and sex, but each of us also has individual characteristics that cause us to differ. No one likes to be put into a category that doesn't fit. A sentence such as

> All the old people voted against the tax levy because they hate paying for schools.

ignores the many senior citizens who support education and the taxes to pay for it. Absolute generalizations like *all*, *never*, and *every* will get a writer in trouble most of the time, especially when applied to other human beings.

Age is of particular concern to those nontraditional students who have had the courage to return to formal education after two or more years away from school. These students may feel out of place and hesitate to contribute. Once they have been in school for a while, however, most are pleasantly surprised to find their age an asset rather than a liability. Life experience allows the processing of material in a larger context than is possible for younger and less-experienced students. This context provides a wider range of choices in the method used to complete assignments and often provides an extra level of motivation as well. It is true that nontraditional students will often find differences in focus, attitude, and priority between themselves and students of traditional age, but those differences can form the basis for some stimulating and insightful conversations for both groups. Age reduces common ground only if a writer makes stereotypical generalizations about people based on their age that would present the same problems as generalizations about all of a gender group will.

## Ethnic Background

Ethnic distinctions have a great impact on common ground and are not always observable. There are many ways that people whose appearances are similar could be widely different in culture and language. African-Americans include the descendants of those forcibly imported as slaves, as well as many people who immigrated voluntarily from Africa, Latin America, or the West Indies. Some Asian-Americans are from families that have been Americans for three or more generations, while others are first-generation Americans still immersed in the language and culture of their parents. How much do a Cuban-American from Miami and a Mexican-American from Las Cruces, New Mexico have in common? They might not have the appearance some expect of a Latino. They could very possibly not speak the same home language, not share cultural traditions, and perhaps not even know a great deal about the differing problems each faces. Native Americans have a great deal in common as they deal with the dominant culture, but they also have the traditions, cultures, and languages of their own tribal groups. For example, the Sioux and the Navajo have very different patterns of living within their own cultures. You might assume that a person who spoke Standard English was American with certain values and attitudes, but that person could be Canadian or an immigrant still connected with another culture.

A person might take a position in a current question at issue with a statement similar to this:

People who cannot speak English should go back to where they came from.

This statement ignores the reality that there are people who are third- and fourth-generation Americans who do not speak English as their first language, not to mention that many of us are descended from people who "could not speak English." Several tribes of Native Americans, ethnic groups in large cities, and isolated rural groups of people each may have children growing up who seldom, if ever, hear English spoken. These people are born American citizens, and the above statement violates common ground by ignoring that fact.

It is not possible to anticipate all the reactions others might have to the things you take for granted in your culture, but you can acknowledge that you are arguing from your cultural position by not making assumptions about the ethnicity of those in your audience. If you are careful not to make sweeping generalizations about those from ethnic backgrounds different from your own, you will avoid losing common ground with this aspect of diversity.

## Religion   *Can't use bible (Not everyone believes. Hard to back it up)*

Few things are as controversial as assuming that others share your religious beliefs. It can quickly alienate those with whom you wish to communicate if you write or say something that, however accidentally, offends their religious values. In any large and complex society, many different religions exist side by side. To communicate in such a society, it is important to remember that people do not enjoy feeling that their beliefs count for nothing and are being ignored or that they are being asked to accept a belief against their will.

There are a variety of ways to violate this aspect of diversity and lose common ground. An example would be an argument that used as its main starting point an assertion such as:

> According to Scripture, capital punishment is wrong because the Bible commands us not to kill.

This has potential for losing common ground in several ways.

1. You assume that those in the audience accept the concept of divinely inspired writings as you do.
2. You assume the scripture you have quoted is the definitive reference on the subject.
3. You assume that all in your audience use the same scriptures you are citing, when it may include people of Buddhist, Moslem, Jewish, Catholic, Protestant, and Eastern Orthodox faiths, among others.
4. You assume those reading your essay put the same weight and emphasis on the scripture you have quoted.

As you think about it, you can see that these assumptions are not valid. You cannot expect an entire audience to see such important issues the way that you do.

An additional difficulty of an argument based on a religious principle is the position of the instructor who must evaluate such an argument. In essence, you are asking your instructor to evaluate whether your faith is strong enough to make this a compelling argument. It is not possible for instructors to evaluate your faith fairly, and it is not ethical for instructors to use their own religious views as an evaluation tool, either. There is no reasonable way to evaluate such an argument in a way that will be fair to everyone.

Given all these problems, avoid arguments that use religion as a basic premise except in the broadest and most general terms. For example, it would not violate common ground to write that the majority of the world's religions have some version of what is commonly called the "golden rule": A person should act toward others in the same way that that person would wish to be treated. After that general statement, the writer might then quote one of the rule's versions.

## Economic Status

Many schools have scholarship programs to allow those who could not otherwise afford to go to a college or university to get an education. Other students come from families who had to go into debt in order for the student to go to college. For some students, money is not a problem. They have family funds to use for their education without anyone in their family having to sacrifice. It is easy to assume that others have the same attitudes about money, poverty, and social standing that you do, but, if you make these assumptions, you will lose common ground.

Many people think they know what rich people or poor people look like. Some have a mental image of the person on public assistance. These mental images are commonly unrecognized stereotypes and can cause you to offend the readers of your essays if you do not recognize them in time to revise these preconceived attitudes. Avoid generalizations such as:

People on welfare really don't want to work.
White males are discriminated against.
All lawyers care about is the size of their paychecks.
All rich people are racist.

They will cause you to appear uninformed or uneducated and will distract your audience from reasonable consideration of your position.

### Political Opinion

Politics are very important to some families. They discuss political issues around the dinner table and during the evening news. Others do not feel politics have much to do with their daily routine of going to work and earning a living. If people agreed about political issues, we would not have to hold elections, so it is safe to assume that there are those who disagree with your political opinions, whatever they might be. If you consider the number of people who do not vote at all, it is not safe to think others are even interested in what your political opinions are. Since political views are always a matter of controversy, you must consider them a key part of your argument if you are going to include them in your essay in any form. If defending a certain political stance is a side issue to your main point, then think about eliminating the political references as a way of simplifying your argument.

It is sometimes difficult to recognize certain opinions as having their origin in a political philosophy. This is where you can use the comments made by peer reviewers. If the reviewers disagree on, or ask for more information about, a statement that you considered to be on common ground, it is possible that there is a political bias in the statement. The best way to learn to recognize these biases is to listen to the opinions of others. You will quickly see the areas of disagreement that relate to politics, because the reviewers will ask you to give support for your statements.

---

**Application**

Read the following statements and determine what bias is reflected in them:

The government should give more support to the homeless.
It is important that government not restrict businesses too much.
Health care should be available free to everyone.
Public assistance is costing too much and should be cut.

---

Look at your positions, decide what your personal bias is, and learn to recognize it in your writing. It is perfectly acceptable to use your political views in taking a position as long as you do not assume that others share the same views.

Most people will not fit in one political category with all of their opinions. The same person may have some opinions that are liberal, others that are conservative, and still others that don't really fit in either place.

## Regional Background

In a large and varied country like the United States, the region where people live, or spent their childhoods, can influence how they view the world. People from rural areas may view the economy differently, for example, than those from cities. People from certain parts of the country are traditionally perceived to be more conservative, more ecologically oriented, or more traditionally religious. It will almost certainly be a violation of common ground, however, if you assume all people from a certain area have a specific opinion.

People from the South are prejudiced against minorities.

It is a stereotype to think that all people from the South are poorly educated or racially biased. Those who grew up in a southern state will resent any implication of this attitude, and the person who includes this bias in an essay will lose common ground with that part of the audience.

If this is true for the United States, it is even more true for those who grew up in a country outside the United States, and in almost every college class there will be some students from another country. It will be helpful for you to think about some of the assumptions you have absorbed from the area where you grew up and compare them to the others you hear expressed. That process will assist you in avoiding unintentional assumptions in your writing that reduce the amount of common ground you share with your audience.

---

## Application

All the following statements violate some aspect of common ground. Either individually or in small groups, identify who will object to each statement and why. After making that identification, see if there is a way to revise the statement to avoid the common-ground violation.

1. People from New York are pushy.
2. Eve was created after Adam, so women are inferior to men.
3. Most people in minority neighborhoods use drugs.
4. Eschew imperspicuous expatiation.
5. Most women just work to get out of the house.

6.   Immigrants should learn America's language.
7.   Most college students are on some form of public dole.
8.   Americans believe capitalism is best.

## A Classic Example of Common Ground:
## The Gettysburg Address

An excellent example of a speaker who had to address an audience under extremely difficult circumstances is Abraham Lincoln when he gave the Gettysburg Address. The Civil War was one of the hardest fought, bloodiest, and most bitter wars this country has faced. The battle at Gettysburg, where over 38,000 men died, was seen as useless slaughter by many, and some of the audience felt the North was losing the war. President Lincoln came to the site four months after the battle for a cemetery dedication. The president's goal was to rally a weary and disheartened nation to support the Union effort. Read carefully and see how he managed to keep common ground with those who had lost loved ones in this terrible battle.

# *The Gettysburg Address*

## *Abraham Lincoln*

Four score and seven years ago our fathers brought forth on this continent, a new nation, conceived in Liberty, and dedicated to the proposition that all men are created equal.

Now we are engaged in a great civil war, testing whether that nation, or any nation so conceived and so dedicated, can long endure. We are met on a great battlefield of that war. We have come to dedicate a portion of that field as a final resting-place for those who here gave their lives that that nation might live. It is altogether fitting and proper that we should do this.

But, in a larger sense, we cannot dedicate—we cannot consecrate—we cannot hallow—this ground. The brave men, living and dead, who struggled here have consecrated it, far above our poor power to add or detract. The world will little note, nor long remember, what we say here, but it can never forget what they did here. It is for us the living, rather, to be dedicated here to the unfinished work which they who fought here have thus far so nobly advanced. It is rather for us to be here dedicated to the great task remaining before us—that from these honored dead we take increased devotion to that cause for which they gave the last full measure of devotion; that we here highly resolve that these dead shall not have died in vain; that this nation, under God, shall have a new birth of freedom; and that government of the people, by the people, for the people, shall not perish from the earth.

---

### Reviewing Lincoln's Speech

1.  President Lincoln had an argument built into this seemingly simple speech. What is it?
2.  How did he maintain common ground with that argument?

## THE CHALLENGE OF ENGLISH

One aspect of writing that is often either ignored or not clearly explained is the way the use of language can either increase or reduce common ground with an audience. English is one of the most widely used languages in the world. Currently, over 75 percent of the mail in the world is written in English. The problem with common ground becomes apparent when you understand that there are so many dialects of English that two people who grew up speaking English will be unable to understand each other. Variations in accent and dialect can make wide differences in how the same language is spoken. A Cockney mechanic from London, a teacher from India, a South African storekeeper, and a Hawaiian police officer may all be native speakers of English, but differences in the way they speak can make it almost impossible for them to communicate with each other. The way people have solved this problem is to use Standard English in all formal writing situations, so that when talking or writing for a general audience they can be sure of being understood.

---

**Standard English**   The form of English recognized in grammar books and used in educational and professional situations.

---

Written language has a standard form, and, if you do not follow that standard, you risk being misunderstood. In France there is an official governmental department to set the rules for a standard French language. The United States does not have such an official language standard, but rules governing the use of English are binding for those who wish to be successful in many professions.

If you grew up in a home where Standard English was generally used, you shared the grammar of the teachers and the textbooks when you went to school. If another dialect was used in your home, or another language completely, school presented some special challenges for you. Writing was especially difficult because Standard English was not your English. Standard English is used in schools, but often students who did not grow up using it are told that their home language is "wrong" and they should use "good" English when they write. In actuality, all language that communicates effectively is "good" language, and what needs to be done is to make clear the distinction between Standard English and other English variations.

This is a controversial topic because people's sense of identity is often tied to their home dialect. For our society to be as rich and varied as it has been throughout our history, we have to preserve home languages. This is not always easy, however, since Standard English is reinforced through the media, in business situations, and in the classroom. Home languages and dialects are often spoken in communities where people are separated from the larger society and united with each other by that language. These communities may be isolated economically, also. To take part in the power of the larger society, Standard English is necessary. It is easy to recognize that, for the time being, Standard English is the language people need if they are to be economically successful.

These variations in the use of English can be compared then to dressing for a variety of occasions. A wedding, a sporting event, a day at school, and a job interview will require different forms of dress. You would not go to most weddings dressed for the sporting event. Language can be thought of in the same way. You will comfortably use your home language when you are in your own community, regardless of whether it fits within Standard English. In formal situations, Standard English will serve you best even if it isn't as comfortable as your home language, just as your wedding clothes are not likely to feel as comfortable as the clothes you wear to a baseball game.

## English Variations

Almost all languages have variations within them—*dialects* that develop among groups of people. Examples of dialects in America are the Pidgin English spoken by some people in Hawaii; the dialect spoken by some groups of African-Americans; and Calo, the Spanish/English dialect of the urban barrio of the southwestern United States. Each of these dialects is at least partly English, with words from other language groups or older language patterns mixed in. Dialects differ from slang in having their own grammar as well as their own vocabulary. A dialect can be difficult for an outsider to understand, even though both speakers are native users of English. Without the guidelines set up by Standard English, elements of these dialectical patterns would cause their users to lose common ground because they would not be clearly understood.

Most dialects are oral language, in that they are not generally written. When a writer tries to write a dialect, much is lost because writing cannot reproduce the variation in tone or accent that gives dialect its character. Look at the following example of Pidgin English as a Hawaiian student expressed it in written form. Before you look at the translation, try to express the passage in Standard English.

> Standard English is made by da impohtant culchah in America. People ah discourage to use Pidgin oah any adah tongue in oah society. Even doh I lak ma own language, I muss learn dah language of da Haole in ordah to survive. Pidgen is chop suey. Get all kind words dat come from all ovah. Pidgen rulez in Hawaii. Even doh da teachah stress da Haole english, we still wen speek Pidgen. (Jon Menor, student)

Unless you have spent a great deal of time in Hawaii, it was probably difficult for you to be sure you had all the ideas the writer was trying to convey. Here is the translation of the above paragraph into Standard English:

> The dominant culture in America developed Standard English. This culture discourages people from using their home tongue because they will not survive in a society that is based on communicating in a single language. Although I see Standard English as a language developed for a culture other than my own, I must learn it to survive in my current surroundings. Pidgin is a culturally mixed language. It includes words that come from many different cultures. Pidgin uses words that come from any culture that has a significant population in Hawaii. Although teachers in grade school stressed the importance of Standard English, many of them accepted minor forms of Pidgin English.

Dialects are often a highly emotional topic for those who use them as a home language and have been criticized for using that language pattern in formal settings. Even though Jon Menor is from Hawaii and knows Pidgin English well, some people criticized the way he reproduced that dialect in writing. They felt he was making fun of Pidgin English. This sensitivity over English use variations is created by people who look down on dialect use because they do not understand the richness added to language by these speech patterns. Menor was not making fun of Pidgin English; his goal was to argue for the acceptance of Standard English in formal settings. It is true, however, that dialects, by their very nature, are understood primarily by those who use them as their home language. When the goal of writing is clear communication outside of a dialect-speaking community, Standard English will be more effective, especially since there are no rules for dialects in written form. Trying to write a dialect can offend, even if you are very familiar with its speech patterns, because your intent will not be clear.

## Slang  *Ẹ dialect  Ẹ how they are different*

Another variation from standard language is *slang*. Slang isn't a separate language subgroup with its own grammar like a dialect but a collection of words or phrases. Slang is especially important to those who are outside the dominant power structure. This is why slang is so important to teenagers. It is something that belongs to them that no one else can own. Almost every group you will belong to has some slang associated with it. This variation in the language adds richness, color, and a sense of belonging and is very important to some people. Because slang is so connected to the interests of the user, however, it can quickly lose common ground if it is included in a formal writing situation. Even if you can be sure that the members of your audience will know the meaning of the slang word or phrase, you cannot be sure that they will share the same feeling that word generates in you.

It is the nature of slang that it changes very quickly. Words such as *golly, gee whiz,* and phrases such as *the cat's pajamas* identify the age of the user and cause many people to either laugh or become confused. What do *the cat's pajamas* refer to, anyway? Maybe it's the same thing as *the bee's knees,* right?

### Correctness

Some people have been corrected for grammar or spelling errors to the degree that whatever they were trying to communicate was put in the background. The concern over using Standard English has overshadowed all other aspects of their writing for these people. They worry about spelling, punctuation, and sentence structure more than they worry about whatever they are trying to express in their writing. This concern over correctness has exactly the opposite effect from the one they want. They will usually find themselves making more errors and having less satisfaction with their finished work. Once you focus on correctness before you focus on your purpose for writing, you are in the category of a person who walks without a destination. There is movement, it is true, but there is no reason for that movement.

People who worry about correctness before they focus on what they want to say have more frequent errors instead of fewer mistakes, because language is for communication, not an exercise in correctness. When the writer focuses on the message being conveyed to the audience, much of the grammar and mechanical structure will fall into place because that will be the clearest way to convey the message. Correctness is a concern in the revision phase of a written work. That is where you look over what you have written to see if you have done the best job of explaining your points. Grammar and mechanical errors such as spelling and punctuation will cause communication breakdowns and need to be corrected, but this process is not the beginning stage of the writing process.

Even with an understanding about the use of Standard English, correctness is not what you should be thinking about when you begin to organize ideas for an essay. You have already begun to learn about revision as you looked at the essays at the end of each chapter. In exactly the same way, you will learn to look for variations from Standard English as you proceed through this book. You cannot decide how to write something, however, before you know what it is you want to say. Remember, writing is an act of communication. Once you have identified a topic you are interested in telling someone about, using Standard English will help you be sure the largest number of people in your audience will understand you clearly. The revision activity that follows demonstrates the difficulty with common ground that arises when writers do not use Standard English.

## COMMON GROUND AND ARGUMENT

As you see, common ground is more complicated than you might think. It is also one of the more interesting aspects of the educational experience. Educated people are expected to understand diversity, and learning to do that can also help us to understand a good deal about our own culture and ethnicity. We take for granted those things that have no contrast. If there has always been running water piped into your house, you will assume all people have grown up with that luxury. When you become aware that there are people living in rural parts of America, and many other parts of the world, who do not have water piped into their homes, you begin to realize what a difference that makes in how they see the life that you have taken for granted.

The only way you can be sure of maintaining common ground in your essays is to be positive that you understand to the best of your ability the reasons others have for taking the positions they take on the question at issue that you wish to address. For this reason, you will discuss the issues that you will be writing on with others before you form your argument. You will be able to express your opinions and listen to what others have to say about the topic. If you do not understand why a person takes a position on a topic, you will have an opportunity to ask for more information. Because an argumentative essay is really a discussion shaped into a single form, the discussions are a very important preparation for writing an essay that keeps common ground with the audience.

## REVISION ACTIVITIES

### *Eric's First Draft*

Eric has grown up in an inner city, and he speaks a dialect of Standard English. While he has trouble picking up places where his writing does not follow Standard English, he has an interesting aspect of environment to discuss for his essay. Read over his first draft and note where his first four paragraphs have deviations from Standard English that could cause him to lose common ground with a general audience.

As a result of the comments by his reviewers, Eric took his floppy disk over to the computer lab and used one of their grammar checker programs to assist him in revising the essay's grammar to Standard English. The grammer checker did not help him identify all of his grammar errors, but, with careful revising, he was able to identify most of the remaining ones. When you have errors that you are not sure how to correct, ask your instructor how to get assistance. Writing labs are available in some schools, and peer reviewing is also helpful in many cases. The remaining paragraphs of Eric's essay demonstrate the result of his careful revising.

As you can see, there are still differences from Standard English in Eric's writing, but many fewer than there were before. While they will not identify all grammar errors, grammar checker programs can provide a helpful first step for people who have not yet trained their ears to adjust to Standard English in formal writing situations. No machine can be expected to respond to all the complexities of human expression, however, and you cannot expect a grammar checker to "fix" all of the errors of spelling, punctuation, and sentence construction that you may make. You need to develop your own strategies for revising your writing with mechanical accuracy, as well as consistency of idea structures. For more information on grammar checkers, see page 000.

## *Eric's Essay*

### *Grammar Checker Not Used*

When I was a little boy I join a Boy Scout troop at the housing project where my mother and my brother and I lived. My parents divorced and my mother thought it would be good for me to be around a man who would be sort of like a father to me. Mr. Atwood, the Scout Master, is the football coach at the high school I went to when I was older. He a strict man but fair.

At this same time that I join the Boy Scouts, my grandparents were living in our same neighborhood in an apartment house just for old people. Next to their building were some old houses that were vacant because they were so run down. People with no place else to go sleep in the old buildings. They build fires to keep warm. One morning very early we wake up hear sirens coming from everywhere. One of the old buildings had burn.

Since the wood in the buildings was old and dry and they chimneys were broken and dangerous, the fire burn quickly and spread to the other abandon buildings. Soon the whole block from my grandparent's building to the corner was level. It was a mess with junk all over everywhere. The firemen only worried about saving the building with the old people living in it.

This fire turned out to be my first real experience with ecology. Before that, I never thought about it. I lived in Philadelphia which is a big city. My father take me to the Pocono's camping. I liked it, but I didn't connect much that I saw there with my life in Philadelphia.

### *Grammar Checker Used*

Most of the members of the Boy Scout troop lived in the same project as I did. The building where my grandparents lived was on the other side of the empty lots where the old houses had been. Mr. Atwood lived a few blocks away in an apartment with his family. The troop was out playing soccer in the parking lot by our building one day when Mr. Atwood looked at the empty lots. Some smaller kids were in there playing in the junk when he said, "This is no good. It's dangerous and a waste."

The city put a fence around the lots right after the fire, but it was not a very strong fence. Dogs dug holes under it, and anyone could bend it and walk right in. My mom told us never to go there because it might be dangerous, but kids like places like that. There's a lot of interesting junk, and it is a good place to play war and other games.

Once he made up his mind, Mr. Atwood didn't waste any time. He held meetings with the senior citizens and got them on his side. Then he had a meeting with the parents of the Boy Scouts, where they talked about the lots. Soon people were going to the city council and all kinds of city offices.

It worked. There were some problems, but basically Mr. Atwood got what he wanted. He wanted gardens, community gardens. This is when I started disliking the project. I wanted a playground and so did the rest of the Scouts. We didn't have enough room to play without having to worry about traffic.

I never had a garden. Some people in the city hauled dirt up to the roof of their buildings to plant flowers and stuff, but not us. I thought it looked like a lot of trouble for not much return. Mr. Atwood wanted the old people and the people where we lived to be able to have garden patches. I thought it was dumb to do all that work for flowers and was ready to quit Boy Scouts, but my mom made me keep going.

The city brought in some machines and big dumpsters and cleaned out all the junk in the lots. Next, scientists came from the city health department and took some dirt to test. It had lead in it. The machines came back and scraped it off, and it was hauled away. More trucks came with new dirt from a construction project across town. It was dumped on the lots, and a bulldozer spread it level. Now there was a lot of dirt with an old fence propped around it. I was not impressed.

At our next meeting of the troop, we got the bad news. Mr. Atwood wanted us to help get the gardens going. We would still have a baseball team, and we would still have cookouts, but, he said, Boy Scouts were supposed to help their communities, and this was a way for us to help ours. He had already gotten permission from our parents, so we couldn't say we had too much homework.

I didn't mind the building part so much. We built a wooden fence around the whole area and smoothed out paths between the 15′ × 15′ plots. Some policemen and women and firemen and women who worked in our neighborhood came and helped on their days off. The people from the neighborhood worked afternoons and weekends. Even the old people worked. We built big bins to hold compost, and this is where the trouble started, as far as I was concerned.

Gardeners who took care of parks in Philadelphia came to my grandparents' building and gave some talks. My mom said this was to help the old people, who were from the country, get used to growing things in the city. The gardeners said compost was, "decayed organic matter used to amend soil." Mr. Atwood made us go to those talks, too. Everyone said they would save compost. From then on, every day my mother saved coffee grounds, orange peels, even the cat's hair, and put it in a plastic bag. Guess whose job it was to carry this bag to the compost bin and empty it. I thought it was disgusting, and my older brother laughed.

This was not the worst, though. The zoo and a stable started to donate manure and straw to add to the compost. I had to rake the bins level and water them down. I am a city kid, and this was all new to me. I did not like it at all, but the old people did. They'd say things like, "Great-looking compost!" I thought they were losing their minds because they were so old. My grandparents bragged about all the work I did with the compost, and sometimes my friends from school overheard them. I got teased a lot.

When school got out in the spring, I thought my troubles might be over, but they were not. In fact, they got worse. Now all the plots were being planted, and the scout troop had to help the old people plant their gardens.

Looking back, I am embarrassed to admit that I didn't like old people. I loved my own grandparents, of course, but they seemed younger than the rest of them. I thought most of the old people were either grouchy or kind of dumb. Mr. Atwood said, "These people hold the wisdom of our community." I tried hard to see it that way because I liked Mr. Atwood, and I wanted to do what he said was right. The fact was, though, it was hot and boring working in the garden plots, and I didn't see any wisdom in all those old people.

After a few weeks, I got a chance to go to Boy Scout Camp. I was excited, and I spent the week before I left getting ready. I packed and repacked my suitcase. Camp was great! I swam, hiked, played games, roasted marshmallows, and sang songs. There was only one thing wrong with camp: there was a garden there. We all had to do some work in it each day.

It was a huge garden, and some of the plants had been there a long time. They had a greenhouse too, so some plants were there the whole year. Even I had to admit that it was great-looking. We only had to do a little bit of work because there were so many of us, so I got so I didn't mind it so much. I couldn't imagine the garden in our neighborhood ever looking so good.

When I got back to Philadelphia, I was eager to tell my friends about camp. I didn't think about the garden at first. After a few days, I came home to find my grandmother doing a few things to help my mom who was at work. "Eric," she said, "don't you want to see the garden?"

I walked home with her and we looked at it. Everything was different. Even though I had not been gone that long, it was different. All the plants had come up. None of the vegetables were big enough to pick, but some of the flowers were blooming. Every plot had green rows growing.

For the first time, I could see why the garden was important. I could see that it might someday look like the garden at camp. After that, it was easier for me to work in the garden. I still hated being teased and I still got impatient with the old people because they were so slow, but I was beginning to change.

The minister at our church said he was proud of our scout troop. The policemen stopped by to see the garden as they drove on their patrols. The firemen had a plot to get vegetables for the meals they cooked at the fire station. They would drive their fire truck to the curb so if they got a call they could move out fast. If they had to go, we would take their rakes and things back to the station for them. Even the teenagers would walk by and look at the garden.

When enough of the vegetables were ready, our troop was invited to a dinner at the church. All the ladies cooked what had been grown. They gave Mr. Atwood an award. I felt great.

My grandparents grew tomatoes, corn, okra, and bell peppers. My grandmother and my mom canned some vegetables because the garden grew so much. The jars were stacked up on some extra shelves my grandfather built in our front closet. I liked to see them there.

The rest of the time I was a scout, I worked in the garden. Every year it was better because we put all that compost in the soil to make it better.

I didn't mind taking care of the compost as much because the food from the garden tasted so good. It wasn't like the vegetables from the grocery store.

The gardens are still in my neighborhood. This was where I learned the meaning of ecology. I learned that it means recycling to get better soil, and that it means eating good, fresh food. I also learned about <u>human ecology</u>.

A neighborhood is an ecosystem, too. A neighborhood has to have clean air, good water, and different kinds of life in it to survive. I learned that not only does land take care of the people, but that people can take care of the land, too. Ecology is not just giant trees and mountains. It is also the way neighborhoods work or do not work.

When I get out of school, I want to be a neighborhood organizer and start recreational programs and adult education programs and gardens, of course, lots of gardens.

---

### Reviewing Eric's First Draft

1.  Eric has many strengths as a writer. What are some of the strengths you would want to point out to him if you were reviewing his paper?
2.  What is Eric's main message for his audience? How could it be made clearer?
3.  How can differences from Standard English cause Eric to lose common ground?

### *Craig's First Draft*

Craig's first draft has more serious common ground problems than Eric's because no computer program is going to assist him in correcting them. Read over Craig's draft and see if you can think of ways you might assist him in revising.

## *Craig's Essay*

Our environment here in the college area is being destroyed by transients. These guys are always hanging around, panhandling, and giving the place a bad name. Not only that, they build fires down by the river, which is dangerous. In the winter, they camp out in abandoned buildings. Anything can happen under these circumstances. Lack of plumbing can cause disease. Again, open fires in this situation are very dangerous.

One big problem that transients cause is that they are scary to women students. Some of the panhandlers are very aggressive. Most of the men have criminal records, and some have committed rapes. Women are

frightened by them, and they are afraid to walk around alone, even during the day. The environment around the school should belong to the women students, too. Women should have access to the entire neighborhood and be free to walk without being accosted.

Most of the transients are alcoholics or drug users. I would feel different if they really couldn't find work, but these people are not looking for work. The minute they get some money from begging, they immediately go to the convenience store near campus and buy alcohol or they buy drugs down by the river. I have seen them drinking over by the bike path, and needles show up there too. The transients are rowdy and obnoxious.

Some of the transients are women, and many have children. I think this is really terrible. The way they live is an awful environment for children. Someone should take the kids away and put them in a safe place. Those women are probably alcoholics or drug addicts or both. The kids are always neglected and dirty-looking. I have seen them on the streets as late as 11 o'clock at night. I wish I could take those kids home to my mom. She would at least clean them up and give them a decent meal.

I don't even think transients should be allowed to have dogs. I always see them dragging some poor puppy down the street by a rope that is tied around the dog's neck. I know they need protection from the other transients, but what about the poor dog? Doesn't it deserve a decent home? The dogs are always skinny. I'm sure they haven't had rabies shots or any of the other shots dogs need. It isn't fair for those people to have dogs or kids that they can't take care of.

These are the reasons I think transients ruin the campus environment for everyone. They make everybody uncomfortable, and they are a danger to the women students. They should do their drinking and doping somewhere else, and the police should arrest them if they come around campus.

---

### Reviewing Craig's First Draft

1. Identify the areas in Craig's first draft that will most likely cause him to lose common ground.
2. What are the opposing arguments that Craig has failed to take into consideration?
3. What revisions might Craig use to increase common ground and improve the reasonableness of his argument?
4. Are there places where Craig seems to lack the necessary information to form balanced conclusions?

## *Chapter Review*

1. What kinds of English usage can cause a writer to lose common ground?
2. Give an example of a way age assumptions can cause a writer to lose common ground.
3. What audience problems did Craig have with his first draft?
4. What is the warrant for a position?
5. How is writing different from talking?

---

# Chapter *4*

# *Exploring a Position*

Writing as Invention
Invention Methods
Building an Argument
The Essay-Writing Cycle
Revision Activities: Kevin's Drafts
Chapter Review

## WRITING AS INVENTION

The purpose of preliminary writing activity is to make the whole process of organizing and writing an essay as easy and stress-free as possible. The worst part of a writing exercise is when the writer is looking at a blank page or computer screen. Once you get a few ideas written, then it will be easier to start the process of putting those ideas into the best form to persuade whomever reads your work that you have made your point. Students often report problems getting ideas on a given topic, and this can create anxiety that makes recognizing reasonable ideas difficult. Learning how to use an essay-writing cycle can significantly reduce this frightening stage of beginning an essay.

**Essay-Writing Cycle**

The essay-writing cycle describes the natural steps that writers go through as they write an essay. When you are developing ideas, reading and discussing are very related activities because they are both ways of gathering information. You read essays organized to communicate a position as clearly as possible. In a discussion, you are able to listen, question, and offer ideas of your own. Both reading and discussing are methods of preparation for taking a position. Once you have decided what position you wish to take, you can use an invention method such as brainstorming or freewriting to organize information to support that position. After you sketch in your first draft, have someone review it and let you know how well you are getting your ideas across to your audience. The most important thing to remember is that the beginning efforts are the foundation of your essay, not the essay itself. Beginning an essay is a little like jumping into cold water: the anticipating is worse than the reality, and it feels much better once you are in.

**Read** for ideas.

**Discuss** those ideas with others to gain perspective.

**Take a position** that interests you.

**Use an invention method** to get started on your essay.

**Write a first draft.**

**Peer review** to test how well an audience understands your position.

---

Writing can generate ideas on an assigned essay topic, and there are a variety of ways to use this strategy. In using this method of getting started on your essay, the key thing to remember is that no idea is a bad one. Write down each idea that comes into your mind. If you are one of those fortunate people who easily identifies a focused topic for essay assignments, perhaps you will not need these activities most of the time, but almost everyone can use some first-draft strategies for getting started. No one method will work for every writer, just as no one style of dress suits every person. You may either try several of the activities suggested or just pick one that you already know will work for you. If you have not previously done first-draft writing to generate ideas, it will be most helpful for you to try one or two methods and see which suits you best.

## INVENTION METHODS

### *Freewriting*

Freewriting can be a very productive way of getting started with the first draft. You simply start to write down all the things you can think of that apply to the topic you want to write about. If you aren't sure of the exact topic, then do a freewrite on possible topics. In a freewriting activity, you do not worry about organization, transitions, or connecting ideas. You just write things down as they jump into your mind. If you see that you are starting on a new topic, you can begin a new paragraph, but even that isn't necessary. Don't try to develop ideas or add too much detail at this point. Just stay with main ideas or indicate how you think you might develop the ideas more fully. Don't worry, either, if some of the things that pop into your head seem unrelated to the topic. The purpose of a freewrite is to put down as much as you can until you are fairly sure you have run out of ideas.

## Brainstorming and Clustering

This activity works well in a small group and can also be used effectively by a single person. It is similar to freewriting but more focused. Use single words or short phrases and try to record everything you know about an issue. You can indicate any personal experience you might have had with the topic as well. After you have made a list of details, then see if you can group the ideas into related clusters.

If you were given an assignment to write an essay on the topic of "Safely Disposing of Nuclear Weapons," a brief example of a brainstorm/cluster activity would look something like this:

Radiation    Dangerous    Causes Cancer    Bombs
Long half-life    Poison the ocean    Concrete bunkers
Storage dumps    Research on reducing radiation
    Not near my town
Deserts    Don't make any more nuclear weapons    Outer space

Once you have this list to look at, you can start deciding whether your ideas can be grouped into related clusters. *Radiation, Dangerous, Causes cancer,* and *Long half-life* could all be grouped under the heading *Why This Is Such a Big Problem.* Topics such as *Poison the ocean, Concrete bunkers, Storage dumps, Deserts,* and *Outer space* could be grouped under the heading *Possible Methods of Disposal.* The remaining topics can be considered as a possible starting point for a new brainstorming session if the two larger topics you have developed are not what you want to write your essay on.

## Using Generative Sentences

This writing activity is similar to a freewrite, except that you will begin with a specific topic in mind. If you have an idea that you think

will work for an essay, simply begin to write on that topic. Do not concern yourself with organization yet. Just put down as much as you can
think of that you might use to develop this idea into an essay. You may
use brief sentences, fragments, and one-word keys to get as many things
down as quickly as you can, or you may want to at least partially develop
each idea.

# BUILDING AN ARGUMENT

## Addressing the Opposition

Now is the time to carefully organize the reasons why those who
disagree with you should listen to what you have to say. Remember our
definition of argument.

---

**Argument**   An exchange of ideas, and the reasons for those ideas,
that allows every participant to examine the positions in a controversy.

---

If you are going to make your position reasonable to those who
disagree, you are going to have to have reasons that persuade them to
reconsider the position they have taken. Sometimes students mix up this
part of argumentative essays with the idea that "argument" means
"fight." When that happens, the student tries to dispose of the opposition
by saying they are stupid or ignorant without offering proof of those
statements.

It is easy to form an attachment to the ideas that are important to
you. Those ideas are yours, and it feels uncomfortable when people question them. It feels so bad at times that those who question your ideas
seem like jerks. They may be jerks. They may disagree with you for fool-
ish or poorly thought-out reasons. However, people are not likely to agree
with you more, or more easily, if you call them jerks. If you give the
impression that you are thinking, "If you were smart, you'd agree with
me," you are less likely to make your audience see your position as reasonable.

The more people disagree with you, the more you have to hold
back your emotional responses to make your argument seem logical
and hard to ignore. It may be that, instead of being jerks, your audience
sees a weakness in your argument. If those who disagree with you seem

right, you may have to change your position. It is not fair and it is not effective to defend yourself by attacking your opponent's lifestyle or character when you can't think of any other way to answer opposing positions.

Do not forget that your goal for an argumentative essay is to persuade your opposition (those who do not agree with you) that your position is reasonable. If you had to convince only those who agreed with you in the beginning, there wouldn't be a question at issue. You would not be willing to listen to someone who said *you* were stupid, and neither will those who feel they have good reasons for the position *they* have taken. You lose common ground by making disparaging remarks about those who have come to a different conclusion about the question at issue you are addressing. Insulting people does not make them more likely to agree with you. You do not achieve your goal of making your position seem reasonable to those others.

---

**Common ground**   Reasonable justification for your ideas that your audience, especially those who disagree with you, will share with you. This concept is often called the *warrant* for a position.

---

If you are going to convince those who disagree with you, you have to take a position you are sure is a reasonable one. Then you must present those reasons in an orderly manner that will show those who disagree how you reached your conclusion. To do this, you must have a clear idea what caused disagreement in the first place. If you do not understand your opposition, you cannot be persuasive, because you do not know where to find common ground. A good argumentative essay requires you not only to have clear reasons why you think the way you do but to have a clear understanding of why others disagree as well.

## *Purpose for Informing the Audience*

A related part of understanding your opposition is having some purpose for telling your audience about your position. When we talk to others, we have a reason for doing so. The purpose can be as urgent as warning someone of danger or as simple as greeting a casual acquaintance as they pass on the sidewalk, but all speech has a purpose. When you take a position on a question at issue, you need to have some reason for doing that. If you clearly identify what you want your audience to do or to change their minds about, your writing will be more effective.

### *Thoughtful Audience*

When you look for a purpose for telling your audience about your position, you need to assume that you are talking to an audience of reasonable people. Sometimes, especially in highly emotional topics, writers form a mental image of an audience that will make fun of their ideas or refuse to listen to them. Argumentative essays are not operating in an environment similar to one you might find on "Donahue" or "Oprah."

On these talk shows, the person who interrupts the quickest gets the last word. An argumentative essay on a college level does not have an audience such as those on talk shows, even though you might be discussing similar topics.

You need to have a mental image of an educated audience that is willing to listen to ideas different from their own. They are interested in your ideas and have ideas they want you to hear and appreciate as well. This audience is a thoughtful audience.

---

**Thoughtful audience**   A group of people who are willing to listen to you as long as you respect their ideas and support your statements reasonably.

---

Your tone will be very different when you have a mental image of an audience such as this, and you will use different strategies to support your position. The ability to keep a picture of the audience you are trying to convince is one that every successful writer must develop.

## THE ESSAY-WRITING CYCLE

The first chapters of this book have covered some of the first steps in forming an argumentative essay. You don't have to go through the entire book before you begin to write your own essays, however. You now have enough information to begin writing on a topic of interest to you. As you proceed through the following chapters, you will gain information that will assist you in strengthening your work as you revise, but it is not necessary for you to wait.

The cycle of activities listed below will assist you in producing clear, persuasive essays with a structure that has broad application in educational and professional life. The peer review components are put in brackets because it is possible that you will not have time for more than one or two. It is very useful to have a peer reviewing activity at least once during the process of developing an essay, however. It is also possible that your instructor will pick one or more of those times to read and respond to your work rather than have a peer reviewing activity.

The first six steps in the essay-writing cycle are discussed in this chapter. The rest of the essay-writing cycle is covered in the following chapters of this book. You will use the strategies discussed in these chapters as you revise your essays and develop abilities in making your argumentative positions reasonable and persuasive.

**The essay-writing cycle**

Read
Discuss
Take a position
Use an invention method
Write a first draft
[Peer review]
Identify a focus (thesis)
Check persuasive strategies (logic)
Write an essay
[Peer review]
Revise essay
Proofing

Many of these steps flow together naturally, but some may seem strange at first. Peer reviewing takes a little practice before it feels right. It is most effective to learn many of the peer reviewing steps in the context of the sample essays, because then you can practice without risk. When you are predicting essays while you read and discuss ways to do that more effectively, you are better able to understand and apply instruction for improving your writing.

## *Read*

It is helpful to read essays guided by related questions at issue before you begin to formulate a position for your essay. You will have some ideas and opinions previously established on many of the topics covered by the essays in this text, but reading the essays will assist you in identifying what others are saying about these ideas as well. Reading is the first step in acquiring a good sense of what your audience will be thinking about the topic you choose. It is also by analyzing the arguments organized by other writers that you will learn effective and ineffective strategies for organizing your own.

Keep in mind as you read the assigned material that it is just as important that the writers of those essays convince you of the reasonableness of their argument as it will be for you to convince others. If you read statements that are unsupported, that you believe to be inaccurate, or that you feel are missing essential information, you have every right to question the validity of those writers' positions. It is in that questioning process that you will discover questions at issue that will form your essay ideas.

### Discuss

A discussion will add to the ideas you gathered from the readings, because you will hear opinions expressed by others who have read the same material. These discussions allow the topic to move from the time and place of the author of the essays to the place where the discussion is held. When you listen to the responses others make to the readings, you are better able to anticipate the responses they may make to your position as well.

### Take a Position

Once you have read and discussed a topic, you will be able to identify some aspect of that issue that interests you enough to develop an essay. In the beginning, you need only consider if you have thought enough about the topic to have some information on it and if you are interested enough to develop it carefully. If it seems that the topic that first occurs to you will require extensive research, you may wish to modify your position to some degree, unless your interest is keen enough for you to spend an hour or so in the library finding the necessary support.

### Use an Invention Method

Different people use different methods of beginning to write. Some of those methods were discussed earlier in this chapter, and your instructor may cover more. Whatever method works best for you, the important thing is to begin. Once you have written a paragraph or two, it will be much easier to begin organizing what it is you wish to accomplish with your essay.

### Write a First Draft

Once your invention strategy has you started in a direction, take your essay as far as you can. Try to explain, offer reasons, and convince your audience that you have a reasonable position on the question at issue you have chosen to discuss. Since this is your first draft, you can assume that you will have an opportunity to revise before the work is considered finished.

### [Peer Review]

Your first draft is a good time to have someone else read what you have written and give you some ideas on how well you are communicating. A first-draft review may assist you in avoiding time-wasting detours with unrelated paragraphs or poorly supported ideas. From the first draft to the final one, each revision can only benefit from your listening to how others respond to what you are writing.

Once you have the information provided by a peer reviewing activity, you will be ready to examine your essay closely for its argument and its technical accuracy. It is much easier to work on a draft and correct it than it is to attempt writing a perfect essay the first time around. Most people learn more about writing well by revising than they did when the first draft was composed. With each revision, you will find yourself with increasing numbers of strategies for fine tuning your essay.

## REVISION ACTIVITIES

### Kevin's First Draft

Kevin's essay is a good place to practice reviewing without the risk of hurting anyone's feelings. As you read Kevin's essay, think of ways he might improve it if he wanted to revise again. Has he convinced you? Why or why not?

Since Kevin grew up in a large city, he is familiar with the common problem of polluted air. He believes that the polluted air that his grandfather breathed for years contributed to his grandfather's illness, and Kevin is probably right. However, there is a difference between being right and making a convincing argument in an essay. Read through Kevin's first draft and decide whether he has put in enough information to prove his point.

## Kevin's Essay (Draft 1)

All my life, it seems, I dreamed about going to college. Now I am here in Berkeley and I don't feel as good as I thought I would. My grandfather, who is back in LA. has had a heart attack. He is out of the hospital but he can't work anymore. He has had to retire and he is just sitting home, not making any money. Since my parents were divorced when I was just a baby my grandfather has been more of a father to me. I feel bad being in Berkeley, so far away from home. What if my mother and my grandmother need me?

My grandfather's heart attack was caused by the smog in LA. In LA. the environment is really bad. The air is very polluted. Smog means smoke + fog, but really it's just dirty air from all the cars and factories. My grandfather worked in Wilmington. Which is a separate town or a neighborhood of Los Angeles. I don't know which. He felt bad a lot so he was always coughing.

My English teacher asked me the other day if I was all right. I guess my worrying about things at home must show. I said I was OK. I was surprised that she noticed. I didn't think teachers at college cared about students personal lives.

I read some racist graffiti in the bathroom yesterday. I didn't expect to see anything like that here at Berkeley. I thought everything here would be completely different from LA. I remember how hard I worked to get out of high school, missing parties and dances to sell souvenirs at the Dodgers games. Studying all the time. Now I'm here and some things are the same. Racism, and air pollution that is going to get worse and worse, it always does.

Even though the smog hurt my lungs all summer long, I miss LA. I didn't think I would. I miss my family. When my grandfather first went in the hospital I called my mother and told her I would come home and go to U.C.L.A. . . . . She said no because LA. is dangerous with lots of gangs. I'm glad now that she did. I am scared to go back there. The smog will always be there and every time my lungs hurt I think about my poor grandfather and how the smog is killing him.

This is my paper on the environment. The environment in Los Angeles is very bad. The air is full of smog (smoke + fog) and that is what made my grandfather so sick that he can't work because he worked in a dirty factory and he drove on the crowded freeway every day.

---

### Reviewing Kevin's First Draft

Individually or in small groups, write down the answers to the following questions.

1. What do you think Kevin most wants his audience to take from this essay?

2. What are some of the points Kevin could use for a primary focus for this essay?

3. What do you think he intended to be the main question at issue? What was he assigned to write on?
4. Who will agree with him, and what reasons will they use?
5. Who will disagree, and what reasons will they use?
6. What evidence does he present for his ideas?

**Common knowledge.** There is some information that almost everyone knows. For example:

Moss grows on the north side of a tree.
Studying grammar can make you a better writer.
Air pollution can make you sick.

Information such as this is called *common knowledge.* Common knowledge can be tricky, though. People once thought that night air caused malaria because those who went out at night got sick. That is where the name of the disease comes from: *mal*, Latin for "bad," and *aria*, Latin for "air." When scientists studied malaria, however, they found out that mosquito bites caused the disease, not the night air. Common knowledge had been wrong. It had seemed logical, though, just as it seems logical that the smog caused Kevin's grandfather to have a heart attack.

However, a problem with common knowledge is that it can have very weak supporting evidence. Moss can grow on almost any side of a tree depending on where the tree is growing, and studying grammar does not improve writing for most people. Air pollution can make you sick, but you need to carefully support the ways it does so.

In his first draft, Kevin has relied on the common knowledge that air pollution is bad to support the idea that the pollution caused his grandfather's illness. Kevin wanted something he could argue with confidence, but he does not have enough clear information linking the smog and his grandfather's illness. He wound up instead trying to prove that air pollution is bad, but who would argue that we *should* have air pollution? Kevin himself may not know at this point what he really wants to say about Los Angeles and the effects of the pollution.

**Practice in organizing ideas.** Still, Kevin has a good start on what could be a solid essay on the environment. Just because you can see problems at this stage does not mean that he has to throw this draft out and start with a whole new idea. One purpose of a first draft is to identify ideas that you can expand for your essay, and it will usually happen that there will be weaknesses and irrelevant material at this stage. Kevin's first focus seems to be "Air pollution is the cause of my grandfather's illness." This is not likely to be a serious issue for you because you do not know Kevin's grandfather. Still, if Kevin can offer some support for the relationship between the pollution and his grandfather's heart attack, he could then easily suggest that air pollution is a significant health hazard for everyone and should be seriously reduced, whatever the cost or inconvenience. That extension of Kevin's idea is a very good topic and would make the basis of a solid essay.

Kevin has left out the reasons why he blames air pollution for the heart attack. Because the bad effect of air pollution is common knowledge, Kevin assumed you would make the jump from that knowledge to this particular illness, but you may not have. Since he assumed you would agree with him, he did not include much information that you would need if you had any question in your mind about whether he was right. Did his grandfather smoke, or did he spend much time around someone who did? Was the grandfather overweight? Did he eat a healthy diet, and did he get some regular exercise? Kevin needs to give you answers to many of those questions before you have enough information to know whether he can use his grandfather as evidence that air pollution causes heart attacks. Does Kevin know anyone with similar problems? Does he know of people whose doctors have blamed air pollution for similar illnesses? Can he think of sources such as newspaper articles he might use to support his idea? If he has trouble thinking of answers to those questions, this might tell him that his argument is weak.

Kevin mentioned that his grandfather worked in a smoky factory. This leads to the conclusion that his grandfather was probably a laborer of some sort. Kevin could build an argument around the idea that the working environment is worse for people like his grandfather than for professional people. He would have to ask himself if he has ideas and information enough to develop this into a full essay.

**First-step review questions.**   The questions that might help Kevin decide where to go from here on this essay are the same questions you used for the essays you read for discussion. They are also the questions that you will use when reviewing each other's first steps in forming an argument.

1.   What is the question at issue in this essay? Are there more than one?
2.   Can you think of reasons for or against ideas in the essay that the writer left out or information that might change the conclusion of the essay?
3.   What have you heard or read about this topic before? Where?

4. Have you made up your mind about this issue before now? Why or why not?

5. Does the writer have one or many points to make with this essay?

Here are additional review questions that are helpful at this stage of forming an essay.

1. What could be done to help identify the main point for the audience?

2. What information is missing that would support the position of this essay?

4. Might there be readily available information to support the essay idea?

5. Are there any paragraphs in this draft that could be eliminated?

Notice that you are not asking Kevin to worry about mechanical problems like sentence fragments at this point.

When reviewing a first draft, here are the important things to question.

1. What part of this draft is the most important to the writer?

2. Which ideas suit the assignment?

3. Which ideas are the strongest?

4. Are there ideas that could be a better focus than this beginning has developed?

5. What support is offered to back up the position taken on the question at issue? If more than one question at issue is addressed, should one be reduced or eliminated in order to tighten the focus of the essay?

You may also notice that Kevin has no spelling errors in this draft. He has a spell checker in his computer word processing program that relieves him from that worry. Spell check programs will not resolve all grammar errors of word formation, and they will not screen out many typographical errors. It is easy to type "is" instead of "in," for example, and spell checkers will not pick up that error (since "is" is a correctly spelled word). However, they do speed the proofing process by allowing the writer to focus on other kinds of grammar problems. It might interest you to know that educational research has shown that spell checkers improve the spelling of those who use them. Not only are you improving your finished writing by using such a program, you are increasing your ability to spell correctly as well.

Kevin has ideas on this paper that have nothing to do with the environment, which is his assigned topic:

1. After Kevin's parents divorced, his grandfather was more like a father for Kevin.
2. Kevin objects to the racist graffiti he sees.
3. Kevin was surprised at his teacher's concern.

Ideas such as this will often be included in a freewrite, and should be revised out to improve the focus of the essay.

### Kevin's Second Draft

Kevin has listened to the ideas of the reviewers about his first draft and now he has tried to write a serious essay on the topic. However, he is still having trouble that you can help him correct. Read this revision carefully and see whether Kevin has backed up his argument this time.

## Kevin's Essay (Draft 2)

It is this writer's opinion that the air pollution in Los Angeles is destroying the health of people living in the central part of the city, because my grandfather, who was employed in the city of Wilmington, suffered a heart attack, and he isn't that old, and he already quit smoking. The Los Angeles Times stated that air pollution in Los Angeles is the worst in the United States. There is a very high rate of asthma in the central part of the city. It adds to the problems at inner-city hospitals such as Martin Luther King and USC Medical Center.

The city of Los Angeles is very inappropriately located for extensive circulation of air. The metropolitan area stretches from the coast by the ocean to San Bernardino mountains on the east side. The wind usually comes from the west—from the ocean. The mountains trap the air and form a big basin that fills up with pollution from cars and factories every day. Sometimes the wind reverses and blows from the desert east of the mountains. This condition is labeled a "Santa Ana." Then the smog is blown out to sea and the San Bernardino mountains and the Santa Monica mountains, and the Hollywood hills are clearly visible. On days like this, you realize how polluted the air is most of the time.

It rains very little in Los Angeles. The average annual rainfall is only 11 inches a year. For a long time, there has been a drought, and not even that much has fallen. This makes the problem a lot worse. Where it rains

more, for example San Francisco, the rain clears out the air by causing the heavy molecules of pollution to fall to the wet ground. The pollution is then washed out to sea with the other effluent loosened by the precipitation.

The poorer communities in the central part of L.A. bear the unfair brunt of the air pollution. People with money live on hills where the air is not as bad. They live in estates in Beverly Hills or Bel Air, or they live in Malibu, where they can enjoy the tradewinds off nearby the ocean.

It makes me angry that poor people cannot live in safer places or have the good medical care the rich have. They drive down the freeway with their windows rolled up and their air conditioning on, talking on their car phones while everybody else is stuck in traffic breathing the toxic exhaust from the miles of vehicular traffic that clog the arterial highways in L.A.

L.A. had 350 days of moderate-to-high air pollution last year. Most of the other cities with records of very high air pollution are in the Los Angeles Basin; San Bernardino and Riverside are examples of this phenomenon. The most serious cause of this terrible problem is internal combustion engines, i.e., automobiles. There are 11 million cars for 14 million people, almost one car for every person. No one walks in L.A. This is also unfair. The poor people breathe most of the pollution, yet they are the ones who take the bus. The bourgeoisie do most of the driving.

The buses need to be made better. According to the <u>L.A. Times</u>, the public transportation system is antiquated and inefficient compared to most other major American cities. The cinematic portrayal <u>Who Framed</u> <u>Roger Rabbit?</u> was true. The petroleum companies, which are owned by America's richest families, agitated to get the freeways built to take people out in the country to live so they would have to drive back and forth for hours every day. This also contributed to racism because the suburbs excluded blacks, and that left them behind in the inner cities. All this driving made the air unbreathable.

Factories also contribute to pollution. Factories are an unavoidable facet of urban life. You have to have factories so material objects can be created so the economy will triumph and people can have employment. On the network news they talked about careers being sent overseas in order to assist corporations in employing less expensive employees and avoiding American environmental protection laws.

This practice has to be made illegal. No one has the right to take away another persons career. My neighbor from L.A., Mr. Vasquez, says the factories in Mexico are very unsafe and they produce a lot of toxic waste and polluted air.

Automobile transportation and industrial development are ruining the physical health of people in the Los Angeles Basin. These enterprises cause air pollution, which contributes to asthma, heart disease, cancer, and birth defects. It is worse for the poor. They get the least benefit and have the most medical conditions.

---

### Reviewing Kevin's Second Draft

Write down the answers to the following questions and then advise Kevin on changes he might make to strengthen his environment essay.

1.  What is the main argument of this essay?
2.  What paragraphs support this argument?
3.  What paragraphs seem to be on another topic?
4.  Where is Kevin getting his information?
5.  Is Kevin's grandfather still central to the essay's focus?
6.  Does Kevin have a clear question at issue yet?

**Citing sources of information.**   Once you have given Kevin some advice on his idea organization, then it would be useful for you to look at some of the other problems he has run into. Kevin clearly tried to gather some information from various sources for his topic of air pollution. He did not mention any sources except the *Los Angeles Times*, however, and he did not cite a specific reference in the *Times*. The following sentences sound very much as if Kevin has used all or part of sentences written in one of the sources found.

> Where it rains more, for example San Francisco, the rain clears out the air by causing the heavy molecules of pollution to fall to the wet ground. The pollution is then washed out to sea with the other efflu-ent loosened by the precipitation.

The language and vocabulary are not like what Kevin ordinarily uses. He needs to give clear references on what material he read and used for this essay. Otherwise, he has *plagiarized* the material, regardless of whether he intended to do that.

---

**Plagiarism**   To use ideas, words, and/or information provided by an identifiable source without acknowledging that source.

---

Plagiarism is a serious kind of cheating, even if you did not intend to do it, and it will often result in a person being denied credit for a writing class if it is proven. Many times, as in Kevin's case, students will unin-tentionally plagiarize because they do not understand how to properly cite their sources. The only course to take if you are going to look up information to support your argument is to become familiar with how to properly give credit to the person who supplied you with that informa-tion. The Modern Language Association (MLA) method of citing material recommends that citations be given in the text rather than in footnotes or endnotes. It is easier to put a brief reference in parentheses right where you use the information you found than it is to cite it any other way, so we suggest you use the MLA method. Please see the appendix of this text for examples of the MLA method.

**Editing for wordiness.**   Kevin needs to think about the language he used as he revises in preparation for his final draft. Such language often comforts students because it seems to sound academic, so they can try to appear more at home in college with unnecessary words. The best writing is always clear and straightforward, though. For example, when Kevin opened his essay with, *In this writer's opinion*, he was trying to sound formal. Since this entire essay is Kevin's opinion, he does not need to write that down. He would make a better beginning by writing a clear statement about the air pollution in Los Angeles that would bring his readers into the topic he intends to discuss. Phrases like the one he used and others, such as *I am going to write about* and *This essay is about*, are unnecessary fillers that distract rather than add.

Kevin also wrote: *Los Angeles is very inappropriately located for extensive circulation of air.* This is not the easiest or clearest way of expressing this idea. Choose words for meaning and not for size or important sound. A writer who wants to communicate clearly should not try to fill an essay with words intended to impress. They usually confuse. There are other examples demonstrating this type of wordiness in Kevin's essay. In groups of three or four, you might underline a few and suggest clearer alternatives.

Look at the words in bold print in the following two paragraphs written by Kevin. They will remove none of the meaning when they are gone.

> The city of Los Angeles is **very** inappropriately located for **extensive** circulation of air. The metropolitan area stretches from the coast **by the ocean** to San Bernardino mountains **on the east side.** The wind usually comes from the west—**from the ocean.** The mountains trap the air and form a big basin that fills **up** with pollution from cars and factories **every day.** Sometimes the wind reverses and blows from the desert east of the mountains. This condition is **labeled** a "Santa Ana." Then the smog is blown out to sea and the **San Bernardino** mountains **and the Santa Monica mountains** and the Hollywood Hills are clearly visible. On days like this you realize how polluted the air is most of the time.
>
> It rains very little in Los Angeles. The average annual rainfall is only 11 inches a year. For a long time, there has been a drought, and not even that much has fallen. This makes the problem a lot worse. Where it rains more, for example San Francisco, the rain clears out the air by causing the **heavy molecules of** pollution to fall to the **wet** ground. The pollution is then washed out to sea with the other effluent loosened by the precipitation.

**Dictionary and thesaurus.**    Still, sometimes a writer with a difficult idea to express needs to pick exactly the right words to explain that idea or the reader will not understand. Two sources that are very useful are a dictionary and a thesaurus. Just as a hammer and a saw are essential tools for a carpenter, these are essential tools for a writer. It is worth noting that both hammers and saws can cause injuries if they are used carelessly, and the same can be said of using a dictionary and a thesaurus. If writers look up words in either book, but the words do not correspond with the ideas they have in mind, the result can confuse or mislead a reader.

There are several kinds of dictionaries sold, and most are acceptable. However, it is important to have more than just the spelling dictionaries that list words alphabetically for people to look up the correct spelling. This book does not define the words, so you will not know if the word you are spelling correctly means what you think it means. For example, *bare* and *bear* mean different things. There are more words in the English language than you might think that can confuse you in this way, so be sure to have a dictionary that defines the word you are planning to use and gives examples of correct usage of each word and every part of speech possible for that word. For example, *To celebrate, a celebrant, a celebration,* and *a celebrated* event are all forms of the same word, but they mean different things depending on how they function in a sentence.

The thesaurus is very useful if you find yourself using the same word over and over or if you cannot think of the right word to say exactly what you want to express. It will give you a list of words that have similar meanings to the one you look up. If you do use a thesaurus, however, be sure you know the meaning of the word you use. A synonym is not ever an exact duplicate, and you could wind up saying something quite different from what you intend to say. An example of this is the reference to ecclesiastical titles for the word *Mother* in *Roget's Thesaurus.* If you did not understand that *ecclesiastical* means *religious,* you might think that *Monsignor* could be used in place of *Mother.* You can avoid this kind of mistake only by looking up the definition of every word you find with the thesaurus. A thesaurus can create as many problems as it can solve unless it is used very carefully.

### Kevin's Final Draft

In this draft, Kevin has made significant progress in meeting his audience halfway. He had taken the time to establish some links between the air pollution and his grandfather's heart attack. Even a final draft can be revised if necessary. What would you advise Kevin on this draft?

## Kevin's Essay (Final Draft)

Because of a heart attack that my grandfather suffered, I have been thinking about the air pollution in my hometown, Los Angeles. I think air pollution contributed to his heart problems. Air pollution contributes to heart disease because it makes breathing difficult, adding stress to the systems of many people with pre-existing heart conditions.

<u>Popular Science</u> of September, 1990, in an article on air pollution by Richard Marini, states that the air of Los Angeles is, "the most polluted in the United States." According to ABC News, January 5, 1992, the central area of Los Angeles also has the highest rate of respiratory illness in the United States. This is the area where my grandfather has lived since right after World War II.

He worked in an automobile assembly plant that entire time, and some of the pollution he has encountered is related to his job in the factory. However, many parts of the United States have heavy industry, and they do not have the embarrassing title of worst air in the United States. What makes Los Angeles unique are its location and its high concentration of automobiles.

The word commonly used to describe polluted air, especially air polluted by automobile exhaust, is smog. The word is made by combining two words: smoke and fog. This common nickname for polluted air was invented in Los Angeles because of the factors that combine there to make air pollution severe.

Los Angeles has a very bad location for air circulation. The metropolitan area stretches from the coast to the San Bernardino mountains to the east. The wind is generally off the ocean: from west to east. The mountains cut off the flow of air and form a large basin that fills up with the pollution from cars and factories. When the wind flows from the desert east of the mountains to the ocean, a condition called a "Santa Ana," the pollution is blown out to sea and the San Bernardino mountains, the Santa Monica mountains, and even the Hollywood hills, which are close to downtown, are clearly visible. This makes it obvious how much of the city is filled with pollution most of the time.

The same article in Popular Science said, "In 1988 Los Angeles had 232 days that exceeded federal air pollution limits." (71) That only considers very bad days. An article in the Los Angeles Times I read several years ago said Los Angeles had 350 days of moderate to severe pollution. The Environmental Protection Agency considers only very severe smog unhealthy.

The movie Who Framed Roger Rabbit? although it seemed silly was right about the first freeways in Los Angeles. The streetcar line was driven out of business, and the suburbs were built so people would have to drive to get to work. My grandfather, who was a young man when this was going on has told me about it. Automobiles cause most of the pollution in Los Angeles. There are 11 million cars for 14 million people in metropolitan L.A. This is the highest proportion of automobiles to people of any city in the world (Los Angeles Times). This is the source of the smog.

A high rate of heart disease is the effect of the smog. The two main hospitals serving the central part of Los Angeles are Martin Luther King and University of Southern California Medical Center. Both these hospitals are named in an article in the September 17, 1991, issue of the Los Angeles Times as hospitals with high rates of admission for asthma and other respiratory problems.

Many things besides air pollution can lead to respiratory difficulties. Smoking is an especially bad habit for breathing difficulties. Most of the admissions at these hospitals, however, are children. They do not yet smoke but they already have the health problems often seen in people who have been smoking for years.

Peter Jaret, in an article in Health magazine in March 1989 writes about Los Angeles, "Non-smokers in smog have that same lungs as smokers without smog." (49) This same article says of ozone, an common element of smog, "Ozone constricts vessels, making the heart and lungs work harder." Mr. Jaret writes of carbon monoxide, another common element of automobile emissions, that it "impairs the ability of red blood cells to carry oxygen."

These quotations are taken from the results of studies done by respected scientists. They prove that smog makes the heart work harder. This can lead to heart attack. Not just my grandfather in Los Angeles is affected by this. According to an editorial in Science magazine, May 5, 1989, 75 million Americans breathe sub-standard air for at least part of the year.

We must make cleaning up our air a national priority. If we do not, we are all in danger from the cumulative effects of labored breathing and reduced lung capacity.

___

## Reviewing Kevin's Final Draft

Use the following questions to look at the organization of Kevin's finished essay.

1. Discuss what you feel is the focus of his essay.
2. What is the message that Kevin wants his audience to receive?
3. Write a sentence that describes each paragraph.
4. Write a sentence that gives the conclusion.
5. Do Kevin's paragraphs give evidence to support his conclusion? Can you see any areas where Kevin could have added information? Are there places where he is still putting in material that does not support his argument?

Kevin has made substantial improvement in his final draft. When Kevin started on this essay, he was so involved in his feelings about his grandfather's illness that he forgot that his audience would not share all of those feelings. He did not really try to argue that air pollution contributed to the heart attack; he just said that he was sure that it did. Kevin is not an expert in the field, and he did not give us support from experts, so you could not decide if he was right or wrong. Since he did not organize a clear argument for himself, he included information that did not apply to his original position.

When Kevin got the comments on his first draft, he could have changed his topic to some aspect of air pollution that did not include his grandfather. He decided not to do that because it was his anger over what he believed air pollution had done to his grandfather that kept him interested in this topic. Instead of giving up, he went to the library for information that would support what he was fairly sure was true: air pollution contributes to heart attacks. Once he got the facts to back up his position, Kevin was able to *earn* or support his conclusion.

---

**Earned conclusion**   An argumentative position supported with clear, persuasive evidence that convinces a thoughtful audience that the position is reasonable.

---

By the time Kevin finished his essay, he had made his grandfather stand for all the millions of people who are breathing polluted air and either suffering health problems now or risking those problems in the future. We no longer have to know his grandfather personally to feel interest in the issue.

**Library use.**   Kevin went to the library to get more information about air pollution so he could support his position on his grandfather's illness. Every topic you pick will not require research, but Kevin felt strongly enough about his position that he wanted to keep it for his essay. When you have a position you feel strongly about, it is worth a trip to the library to support it for your audience. It took less than an hour and a half to find the articles on air pollution using the reference materials in the library. Kevin was excited to find the necessary information to support his argument, and you will feel that excitement, too, when you find support for yours. If you take the time to get acquainted with the resources in your library, it may take even less time than it took Kevin to find the necessary information. Most libraries offer tours that assist students in efficiently using the various library resources.

Too often, students will give up on a position they cannot immediately think of solid support for when they could easily find that support if they looked. Remember, you think the things that you do for good reasons. You may have heard something on the news or read something in the paper that helped you come to your conclusion. It is easy to forget just where you got the information that forms your opinions, but just because you cannot remember does not mean you are wrong. While library references cannot take the place of your own thinking, they can supply you with information to support your ideas. However, it is also true that the people who are close to you may have had an influence on your opinions without having the necessary support to convince a diverse audience. The only way you can be sure whether that clear support is available is to look and find out.

**Citing experts.** When you watch the news or read the newspaper, you often hear or read the phrase *Experts agree that* . . . Kevin looked for expert opinion for his paper, because he understood that his opinion was not informed enough to convince an audience.

Notice that an expert is known and respected, but not necessarily agreed with. Experts often disagree without losing the respect of their peers. There may be articles about air pollution that indicate heart disease is outside the effects of breathing smog, but, until the matter is proven beyond a doubt by research, Kevin supports his argument by the articles he cited.

Children acquire their view of the world from their parents because, to a child, the parent is the supreme expert. As you mature, your definition of *expert* broadens. Parents are still experts on some things, of course, but they are no longer *the* expert on all things. You have learned to ask questions about how people who say they are experts came to have the knowledge they say they have. Your audience has gained the same ability. Since the audience doesn't know you, you have to back up your position with support that you could trust if you had to take someone else's word for that position.

# *Chapter Review*

1. Why is Kevin's first draft unconvincing?
2. Why is it important to understand the reasons people disagree with your position?
3. What is common knowledge?
4. What are some methods to get started in writing an essay draft?
5. What is plagiarism?

# Chapter 5

# *Peer Reviewing*

You Know More Than You Think You do
Individual Peer Reviewing
Small-Group Peer Reviewing
Special Challenges with Peer Reviewing
Listening to Questions and Comments
Notes for the Next Draft
Chapter Review

## YOU KNOW MORE THAN YOU THINK YOU DO

Peer reviewing is writers assisting each other with their revisions by trading essays and making comments suggesting ways the essays are effective and ways they could be improved. This is useful to both reviewer and writer in a variety of ways. It is easier to see places of confusion or contradiction in someone else's writing. You know what you meant to say, so sometimes you might find it difficult to see where you could confuse your audience. It is not difficult to know where you get lost when you are reading, though. Each time you indicate to the writer of an essay that you cannot follow a point or that you do not have enough information to decide if an argument is valid, you also learn a little bit about how to make sure you do not have the same problems in your own writing.

The benefit to the writer lies in the opportunity to obtain your responses to the essay before completing the final draft. Even if the writer does not agree with your assessments, those comments must be considered when completing the essay. This process gives the writer another opportunity to evaluate the strength of the argument and to improve its validity.

When peer reviewing, you must give the writer comments based on your opinions and responses, and this is uncomfortable for some people. Some reviewers say: *I'm not a good enough writer myself to feel comfortable criticizing someone else's work.* This feeling is easily understood, but you do not have to be able to do a thing to understand when it is done well. Many people who are not musicians have a clear definition of what constitutes good music. Most of us know when we see good acting even if we have no acting ability at all. In the same way, you are able to tell when something you read is convincing and when it is not. You know when you feel confused by the way something is organized and when a writer gets off the topic. These are the feelings that can guide you to be an effective peer reviewer, but you must learn to trust yourself as a part of the writer's audience. While it is possible that not everyone will have the same responses you have, it is also unlikely that you are the only person in the writer's audience who will have your reactions. Your reactions will be useful to the writer if you give clear reasons for them and clear suggestions for resolving any problems. This chapter is designed to assist you with the process of identifying those reasons and making those suggestions.

## INDIVIDUAL PEER REVIEWING

### *Responding to the Argument*

Since you will probably not have a large amount of time to do the peer reviewing, you will have to focus on the areas that you feel will be of most help to the writer. Before you can decide what kind of comments will most assist the writer, you have to read the essay all the way through without trying to make any kind of response. This will allow you to get the fullest possible understanding of where the writer wanted the argument to conclude and what proofs were used to support that argument. If the following questions are used as a guideline, they will make your job easier.

## Reviewing Guideline Questions

Use the following list of questions to identify areas needing revision. Do not try to give detailed answers to all the questions, but use them as a guide for focusing attention on the structure of the essay. Read the discussion of each question before participating in the reviewing activity.

A.  *Does the introduction assist the audience in understanding why they should be interested in the essay?* When you start a conversation with people, you do not just start talking about something that is interesting to you. First, you give them enough information about why you are interested in the topic to allow them to get interested, also. The introduction of an argumentative essay serves to get the attention of the audience.

A few general statements about why the topic has become a question at issue, or a few of the positions on the question at issue, allows an audience to join the discussion mentally. However the writer begins, be sure there is a method to focus audience attention on the topic before the draft launches into the argument.

B.  *Does the conclusion have a clear connection to the thesis?*

---

**Thesis**   A position supported by reasoned argument.

---

A good thesis statement indicates what the essay will conclude. By the end of an effective argumentative essay, the writer will have earned the conclusion by giving evidence or proof to support the thesis. If the conclusion of the essay does not have a clear connection to the thesis, the argument has gotten off topic somewhere, and the writer needs to correct that problem. Chapter 6 has questions to test the effectiveness of a thesis.

C.  *Is the conclusion earned by the information in the body of the essay?* Determine that there is a clear connection between the thesis and the conclusion. Then check to make sure it is an *earned* conclusion based on support a reasonable audience would accept. Each paragraph in the essay should provide some new piece of evidence or proof that the thesis is valid.

D.  *Does each paragraph have ideas that relate to the previous one?* Sometimes it is easy to get caught up in writing and lose sight of the focus. Once a paragraph is written, it is difficult to think all that writing might not apply to the thesis. If you see that there is a paragraph in an essay that does not seem to tie to the thesis, think about why the ideas in the paragraph might fit the other ideas in the essay. Is there information left out that would make the connection clear? If it seems that the writer just got off-topic, now is the time to eliminate the paragraph. A paragraph that is off the topic can seriously distract an audience from the focus of an essay and, in the process, cause the argument to fail. It is better to eliminate whole paragraphs in the draft stage than it is to lose the audience with material that has no application to the issue under discussion.

I am sure you have known people who could not stay with a topic under discussion. It is irritating to have comments or stories that have no connection interjected into a conversation. Exactly the same good manners apply when writing an argumentative essay, and your audience will expect an essay to hold to the topic promised in the beginning.

E.  *Are the paragraphs in the best order possible?* Consider if it will make the essay stronger to move a paragraph to a different position to make the focus clearer or give a better progression of ideas. It may be that some point in the beginning turned out not to have very good support. It also happens that some idea toward the end of an essay turns out to be the strongest part of an argument and should be moved to an earlier point.

F.  *Is there enough support for each paragraph to seem reasonable to a thoughtful audience?* The support for each paragraph should be strong enough for that paragraph to seem reasonable to a thoughtful person. If the audience doesn't have enough information to agree with or clearly understand the position, now is the time to go back and add more information to support the argument.

G.  *Is there at least one paragraph that addresses the concerns of the opposition on this topic?* In any question at issue, there are people who will disagree with the position taken in an essay. The writer must respect the opposing opinions enough to address the reasons why they do not agree. The writer must explain carefully why the essay position is a reasonable one. It is not necessary that the opposition be proved wrong. It is necessary, however, that even those who disagree be able to see that the conclusion is reasonable. If the question at issue has strong opposition from more than one viewpoint, then there may have to be two or more paragraphs addressing those various views.

Keep in mind that it is a positive move to admit that the opposition has some valid points. A good question at issue will have reasonable arguments on a broad range of positions, and no one has to argue that they are all wrong. The goal is to present a specific position in such a way that reasonable people will see solid support for that position.

It may seem to some writers that the best way to deal with those who disagree with their position is to ignore that opposition. This will not work for a thoughtful audience, however. A clear question at issue also has a clear opposition. Writers must have reasons for believing their thesis is persuasive in spite of those opposing opinions, and they must give those reasons to their audience. Neglecting this important step will give the impression that the position is so weak that it cannot answer the arguments of the opposition.

H. *Does each paragraph stay with the topic it started with or do new topics turn up that require new paragraphs?* It helps to check to see if the writing has kept its focus within each paragraph. Sometimes writers get started in a paragraph and ideas occur to them that just don't fit. It also happens that writers start a paragraph and realize after two or three sentences that they do not have enough information to really support that topic. The result is often a series of sentences that do not connect with the idea that began the paragraph or do not advance the thesis.

Also, some paragraphs start with topics that are too big to cover in a single paragraph. When that happens, there are often places where parts of that topic can be divided into a new paragraph as a way of preventing confusion.

I. *Are there statements that offend or irritate you or might have that effect on others?* When you find yourself reacting in this way, that means the writer has lost common ground with you. Something in the statement may be too broad or general to keep a valid connection with the argument. Try to figure out just what bothers you about the statement, and give the writer the clearest explanation you can on how the statement might be revised to avoid the problem. If the statement brings up a problem that is outside the main focus of the thesis, the writer may wish to eliminate it completely.

J. *Are there any statements concerning questions at issue that have no supportive evidence or proof to back them up?* It is easy to spot these statements when you disagree with what they say. However, it is easy to just accept statements when you agree with them unless you remind yourself to look for the support. If a statement touches on a question at issue, it should have clear support for coming to that conclusion. If that support is lacking, the argument will not seem reasonable to a thoughtful audience.

K. *Is the audience treated with respect?* An argumentative essay must always address the audience in a respectful tone if the argument is to be seen as reasonable. Let the writer know if any comments seem to make fun of any part of the audience.

### Summary of Reviewing Guideline Questions

A. Does the introduction assist the audience in understanding why they should be interested in the essay?

B. Does the conclusion have a clear connection to the thesis?

C. Is the conclusion earned by the information in the body of the essay?

D. Does each paragraph have ideas that relate to the previous paragraph?

E. Are the paragraphs in the best order possible?

F. Is there enough support for each paragraph to seem reasonable to a thoughtful audience?

G. Is there at least one paragraph that addresses the concerns of the opposition on this topic?

H. Does each paragraph stay with the topic it started with or do new topics turn up that require new paragraphs?

I. Are there statements that offend or irritate you or might have that effect on others?

J. Are there any statements concerning questions at issue that have no supportive evidence or proof to back them up?

K. Is the audience treated with respect?

Once you have read through the essay, you might want to quickly read over the reviewing questions to see if there is any one that might be a special strength or weakness of this particular essay. Do not forget to look for strengths as well as areas that might need reworking. Knowing what was done well is as important as, if not more important than, knowing where an argument ran into trouble.

The reviewing guidelines are designed to be just that, guidelines. You are not expected to answer every question for the writer or even to answer every one for yourself if they do not seem to be of special concern for the essay you are reading. Every argumentative essay is a conversation between the reader and the writer. No questions that were written separate from that conversation can possibly address the specific elements of that conversation. That is why your comments as a peer reviewer are so important.

When you make comments about the argumentative structure of the essay, be as clear as you can about what you think the writer has done to cause your reaction. A comment such as *This is a great essay!* does not give the writer any idea of what caused you to have that reaction. Adding an additional comment or two giving specific examples of things that you felt were especially well done will resolve that difficulty. This is just as important when you feel something was done poorly. The writer cannot correct the problem if you do not give specific examples from the essay to be evaluated and revised.

If you have a response to an argument, but you have trouble identifying exactly why you feel as you do, tell the writer about it anyway. The writer may be able to think of a revision that will resolve the problem.

The quickest and clearest way to make comments about an essay is to write brief comments in the margin by sentences or paragraphs that you decide merit comment. When you reach the end of the essay, write a brief note to the writer assessing the argument as a whole. In each case, tie your comments closely to some specific part of the argument. This will keep the communication between you and the writer as clear as possible.

### Responding to Grammar and Mechanics

Your primary purpose as a peer editor is to help the writer to fine-tune the argument in the essay, but that does not mean you cannot mark grammar and mechanical errors when you notice them. Errors of this nature can really interfere with the clear communication of an argument, and they need to be corrected before the final draft. You may feel that you have some weaknesses in this area of your writing and therefore should not presume to criticize someone else's. Keep in mind, though, that you are trying to help the writer produce the best essay possible. If you do not inform people of errors, how are they supposed to correct them? Also, you may have mastered skills that others lack. Your responsibility as a peer editor is to let the writer know what you think and what you see in the essay you read. You do not have to be a perfect writer yourself to do this. The writer can double check to see if there is an error. It does not hurt to check twice. If nothing is wrong, no harm is done, and errors will be caught before the final draft.

Address possible mistakes by putting a check in the margin next to the sentence where you think there may be one. If you tell the writer what the error is or simply correct it, then the writer will not develop the necessary ability to recognize that error without assistance. A check in the margin will indicate that something may be incorrect in the sentence, and the writer will then review the sentence. If writers cannot find mistakes on their own, they can always ask, but the process of finding errors unassisted is where the learning takes place. Most people only make a few grammar or punctuation errors in the sentences they write, but they make the same ones over and over. Once a writer learns to recognize how to correct these few errors, then the problems with grammar and mechanics will be greatly reduced.

**Spelling.**　You do not have to be a good speller to notice that a word looks wrong or odd. If you are not sure if a word is spelled correctly, put a circle around it. That will let the writer know that it looks misspelled to you and prompt a double-check with the dictionary.

**Wrong word or poor word choice.**　These words can be circled, too, but you should add an indication that something other than the spelling of the word is bothering you. A mark of "WW" for wrong word will indicate your intent that the writer look to see if another word would better express the idea of the sentence.

**Unclear or awkward sentences.**　A question mark (?) or the abbreviation "awk." in the margin next to a sentence that has one of those two problems will indicate to the writer that you had trouble following the ideas in that area. If the problem is bigger than just one sentence, you will need to write out just what you feel is missing or what confuses you. Whenever possible, write these comments as a question so the writer can supply the missing information or clarify the issue by answering the question in the essay.

**Summary.**　The main thing to keep in mind as you review an essay is that you are assisting the writer by giving clear, focused comments on what you thought of the argument in the essay. You are part of the audience that the writer is trying to convince, and knowing how you reacted to the argument is useful information. It is not picking on the writer to note areas of confusion or sentences with errors. It is assisting that writer in the revision process so that the final draft can be as convincing and error-free as possible.

## SMALL-GROUP PEER REVIEWING

Another method of reviewing each other's essays is to work in small groups. Small-group reviewing allows you the experience of being present when an audience reads your essay. You can listen to what the audience has to say about the essay, and you have an opportunity to answer questions. This interaction allows you to see the strengths and weaknesses of your arguments in a manner that will assist you in clarifying your points or understanding why to take a new approach in some area.

The competitive view of education that students have learned from testing and grading in earlier classes makes peer reviewing a difficult process for many because it is a cooperative exercise where everyone is both a teacher and a learner. The goals of this activity are that you learn to give useful comments on the material you read and to listen to the comments given by others. When effectively done, group reviewing assists the participants in identifying essential components of a successful argumentative essay. Since everyone has skills others do not possess, all will have something to offer. Each person will also learn from others in the group.

You will learn to give writers responses to their essays so that they feel supported and encouraged rather than criticized and discouraged. To accomplish this, the members of the group have a responsibility to express in a positive, friendly way what they see as the strengths and weakness of the essays they read. The members of the group must take particular care to focus their comments on the writing and not the writer. Saying *I do not understand this sentence* is very different from saying *I do not understand this person.*

## Avoiding Problems While Group Reviewing

**Critical comments directed at the writer.**   One way to do this activity incorrectly is to put a writer down rather than focus on the writing. Direct all comments at helping writers discover ways to improve their writing. It always feels good to help someone, so the reviewing activity should be satisfying and useful to everyone. When you read something in an essay that doesn't seem to have much thought behind it or with which you strongly disagree, pause before you say anything. Remind yourself that the purpose of this activity is to assist the writer in improving the essay, not to express personal opinions concerning the position the writer has taken. It is appropriate to say that you do not feel writers have adequately supported a statement or that writers have ignored opposing opinions. It is not appropriate to say writers are stupid or that they have no right to the opinion expressed.

**Getting distracted onto other topics.**   Sometimes a topic will remind the group of a related idea, and they will get distracted into a discussion of that idea instead of the essay being edited. The easiest way to avoid this problem is to appoint one member to remind them if they get off-task. A group leader can ensure that the time will be used in the most productive way. Rotate this position to avoid making anyone feel like a police officer.

**Saying that everything is fine when it isn't.**   Sometimes students handle feelings of discomfort connected with analyzing someone's essay by saying the essay is well done when it is not clear or convincing. This reaction cheats writers of the assistance they need if they are to understand how to strengthen their writing. If you do not feel an essay is done well, say what you think even if you cannot find words to explain why you react that way. Others may be able to assist you by adding their reactions in a way that makes the problem clear for the writer.

It is unlikely that a group will have an essay to review that is so perfect that no one can suggest improvement. You appreciate help with your essays, and your partners expect help with theirs. It may seem quicker and more comfortable to gloss over places where the essay is not clear to you, but that choice slows down the writer's progress in revising the essay. You would not like to be left with errors of organization and grammar that someone else was unwilling to point out to you. Your partners most likely have the same feelings.

If you do not see areas that you feel need improvement, then you can help your partner by pointing out the areas you think are the strongest. This can help the writer decide if those areas should be expanded.

**What to do with a poorly written essay.**   Occasionally, a group will face an essay that appears to be of exceptionally poor quality. It is appropriate to comment something like: *It looks like (person's name) had trouble with this essay.* Avoid adding comments about how bad the essay seems to you, however. The writer could not help feeling personally attacked by such comments, and those feelings will interfere with that person learning how to improve the situation.

Even in a poorly written essay, there is often something to comment positively about. Focus on finding a strength. The initial idea, the introduction, particularly effective sentences, a piece of support for the argument could be areas of strength in an otherwise weak essay.

The next challenge when responding to a poorly written essay is to assist the writer in finding ways to improve. A writer picks a topic because something about it interested him or her. In essays that communicate poorly, the writer failed to effectively inform the audience what that area of interest was in such a way as to interest the audience. The group should attempt to figure out from the writing what the writer has left out or what could be included to improve the essay.

## *Group Reviewing Activity*

Groups should be no fewer than three people and no more than five people.

1.   *Bring two copies of* your *first draft, typed and double-spaced.* Each student will keep one copy of her/his own essay to make notes on as the others talk. The other essay will be given to the person on the left.

2.   *Select a volunteer to read an essay aloud while the writer notes any awkward sentences or areas needing improvement.* While the essay is being read, everyone should listen carefully and make a few notes about areas of strength and weakness in the essay. The writer should listen for places where the reader seems to have trouble following sentences or ideas. Since the writer will have a copy of the essay to mark on, notes can be made right where changes need to occur.

3.   *Each person will make some positive comment about the essay to the writer.* Perhaps there is an interesting experience included in the essay. It may be that the writer has some good comparisons or there are some clear supports for an idea. Virtually every essay has some area of strength, and the writer needs to know what was done well to build on that strength. The writer will make a brief note of the positive comments.

4.   *The group will discuss these revision questions as they apply to the essay while the writer listens and makes notes.* The writer may answer questions or offer more information when necessary, but that necessity usually indicates the need for clarification or additional information during revision.

5.   *When the group finishes the reviewing process, the writer can comment, ask questions about how to revise, or answer questions that came up during the discussion.* This is the time when the essay writer gets to explain things that seemed unclear to the group and get some help in making those things clearer. It is also a good time to ask questions of the group about why they responded to some parts of the essay the way they did. The writer needs to understand audience responses if the essay is to be effective, and someone may not have said enough in the discussion to make a point clear.

6.   *Once the cycle is complete for one essay, begin again with the next essay to the left.*

## SPECIAL CHALLENGES WITH PEER REVIEWING

### *Spelling and Past Tense*

A problem that arises when writing about a past time concerns the *-ed* ending added to many verbs to indicate past tense. *I talk*: present tense; *I talked*: past tense. This becomes a problem when the *-ed* is not strongly pronounced in speech and is, therefore, easily forgotten when the word is written. In some words it is almost impossible to hear the *-ed* when the word is spoken. The word *prejudice* is a good example. It is difficult to hear any difference between *prejudice* and *prejudiced* when the two are said aloud, even if the speaker says the word carefully.

Most of us use an internal voice to sound out words for spelling as we write them. If this voice does not pronounce the *-ed* ending, it will not be used, and, since the word is spelled correctly, a spell checker will not help this problem. If a writer uses *prejudice* instead of *prejudiced*, this problem is further complicated by the fact that *prejudice* is not a verb. It is a noun that means a thing, "prejudgment," instead of the verb meaning the *"act of* prejudgment." Both peer reviewers and writers must learn to be alert for such problems and correct them in the draft stages of an essay or the audience will be confused about whatever idea the writer is trying to develop.

## English as a Second Language

Many classes include students who are not native speakers of English. Some of these students may have learned English in other countries. Such students often make excellent peer reviewers for native speakers because they learned a more formal English when they studied it in the classroom. This makes them more informed on the grammar rules for Standard English than many who grew up speaking a less formal English. On the other hand, non-native speakers are rarely as comfortable with the informal exchange of conversation and writing as are native speakers. These differing areas of exposure to the language can allow each student to benefit from the strengths possessed by the other.

Another advantage is that testing an argument with a person from a different cultural background is an excellent way of determining if the argument is given adequate support. If the argument bridges the differences in cultural viewpoints, then it is a clear, well-constructed one. The writers of such arguments know they are doing a good job of communicating their ideas.

## English as a Second Language and Article Use

For some, especially those coming from the Chinese language group, the English uses of articles (*a, an,* and *the*) present special problems. The purpose of articles in English is to modify nouns by making them general or specific. *I saw the cat* is very different in meaning from *I saw a cat.* There are variations between British and American English in article use, also. In British English it is correct to say *I went to university.* American English uses the article *the*: *I went to the university.* Peer reviewers need to be aware of these areas of concern and be prepared to assist second-language users of English in the standard patterns.

## Standard English Verb Tense

There are many dialects in the United States that handle verb tenses differently from Standard English. When a person grows up using English in one way, it is difficult to remember to change those patterns in other settings. These dialects also make it difficult for people learning English as a second language. They learn one pattern in the classroom, and, often, they hear another pattern being spoken in the cafeteria as they eat their lunch. All people who struggle with Standard English tenses know the feeling of using a pattern that sounds fine to them only to have it marked as incorrect. English has borrowed heavily from other languages, so many verbs do not follow regular patterns. There are many tense-change patterns, and a non-native speaker of English can use a grammar checker program to check for these tense changes or have a grammar handbook as a reference.

The important thing to remember is that everyone who understands spoken English understands how these tense changes work. When you listen to the radio or watch television, you do not have to stop and think about whether the announcer is talking about the past, the present, or the future. These announcers are, with few exceptions, using Standard English, so you do understand the rules of Standard English grammar when you hear it. If native speakers of English keep in mind that they understand more than they give themselves credit for, it will make it easier to think of the Standard English pattern when they review an essay. It may help, however, to do a brief review of how tense changes function to inform an audience when the action of the sentence happens.

## Verbs and Time

Verb tenses signal the time in which events occur. Verbs tell what the actor in the sentence is doing or being, and the tense change in the verb indicates *when* that doing or being happened.

---

**Verb tense**    Forms of a verb that indicate whether the action of the sentence happened in the past, the present, or the future.

---

The past includes all the time that has gone on before this minute. The future includes all the time that will take place after this minute. Without clear tense indicators, all communication would quickly become confused. Suppose you wanted to tell someone a story and you could only use present tense.

> I see a play with a friend and it is very funny. All kinds of things they do not plan happen. A door is locked by mistake and the person who is suppose to be on stage cannot get in. Another man cannot come on stage because he run into a board and is knock unconscious. The person who is on stage is stuck with nothing to do. The audience is confuse. We learn all about the problems in the newspaper in the morning.

What could be an amusing story of theatrical mishaps is instead confusing. To communicate complex ideas, you must be able to use a mix of verb tenses to indicate time sequence for those ideas.

> I saw a play with a friend and it was very funny. All kinds of things they did not plan happened. A door was locked by mistake and the person who was supposed to be on stage could not get in. Another man did not come on stage because he ran into a board and was knocked unconscious. The person who was on stage was stuck with nothing to do. The audience was confused. We learned all about the problems in the newspaper this morning.

A variety of time-change indicators signal the reader which time the teller of the story is talking about.

Time is a simple thing for a child. There is very little past to worry about, and all but the next day or two are too far away to imagine. In a child's view, time is past (was), present (is), and future (will be). This might be called *simple time* because the child worries only about events that happen in specific moments in the past, present, or future. As a person grows up, however, time becomes much more complex. Most of the things you will want to write about will cover many finely tuned references to time. Consider this brief autobiographical statement:

> I went into the armed forces right after high school and stayed there until my children were born. Then I went to a community college where I studied bookkeeping for several semesters. Since returning to civilian life, I have wanted to get my CPA license. When I receive it, I would like to return to government service so I can build up my retirement there. Perhaps I will work for the IRS or as a civil servant assigned to the military.

Some of these sentences are in the *simple past* indicating something that took place entirely in the past, and some are in the *past perfect* indicating something that took a larger amount of past time. Native speakers use these time markers without having a vocabulary to describe them. They know which is appropriate for the meaning they are trying to communicate. People learning second languages need to have instruction on how the new language indicates the time shifts that were done automatically in the home language. The diagram of a more complex view of time might look something like this:

Would have been

| had been | have been | am being | will have been |
|----------|-----------|----------|----------------|
|          | was       | am       | will be        |

Depending on the intent of the idea being expressed, *would have been* can refer to past (*I would have been a good student if my parents had bought me a computer*), present (*I would have been here earlier but the traffic held me up*), or future (*He would have been an actor if music hadn't distracted him*). The long line represents verb tense phrases that show more complicated time references than simple past, present, or future. Each of the verb tenses on the long line refer to a period of time rather than a specific point in time. *I had been playing baseball* conveys a different time-frame than *I was playing baseball*. The simple past, present, and future are still there, but now there are signals to indicate events that covered longer periods of time in each category. It is not necessary to know the rules that govern this pattern to understand what is indicated when you read the sentence. All the dialects of English have these patterns, but the words used to indicate the pattern can be different in different dialects. Since Standard English is the pattern recognized by the greatest number of people, you must use it in writing for an academic or a professional audience.

## Agreement Between Subject and Verb

All parts of every sentence must connect in a reasonable way to the subject. It is the actor of the sentence, and the purpose of the sentence is to tell something about that actor. *There is a bird at the feeder. There are three birds at the feeder.* The way the verb shifts from *is* to *are* keeps the sentences clearly focused on the subject of the sentence in each case.

---

**Subject/verb agreement**   If there is only one actor, or subject, then the verb must be singular; if there are two or more subjects, then the verb must be plural.

---

Subject/verb agreement helps those who listen to you or read your writing to keep track of what the subject or subjects are doing.

To make all parts of the sentence agree with the subject, it is always necessary to know what noun or pronoun is the subject. Sometimes a noun phrase forms the subject, which can complicate the process of identifying it: **What you possess** *is often* **what possesses you.** This sounds complicated, but it is easy to ask what the sentence is about. The answer to that question will always be the subject. If you cannot clearly identify what the subject is, your readers might get confused and not understand what you are trying to tell them, so learning to identify the subject is essential. When you are not sure, read the sentence aloud. That will help you to hear the sentence focus.

### Agreement Between Subject and Pronoun

A different problem with agreement comes up with sentences such as this one: *Everyone has his head on the table.* In the past, it has been correct to refer to a person whose gender is not specified as *he.* This dates back to the time when women were not recognized as part of the public world. They were not allowed to hold jobs that involved public speaking, and they often could not read and write because only males were allowed an education.

That has changed greatly, and women are now part of the public world. Writers cannot afford to ignore the women in their audience by using the masculine pronouns *he* and *him* to refer to words like *everyone, person, student, each,* and *anybody.* The most practical way of avoiding this problem is to use plural subjects such as *students* and *people.* Then you will use *they* or *them* instead of singular pronouns, thereby avoiding having to worry about the awkwardness of writing *he/she* or *her/him.*

Many people try to avoid calling everyone *him* by writing *he or she* instead of just *he.* This is better than only addressing the male half of your audience but it can be repetitious and awkward. Compare the following two paragraphs and see how much more direct the second seems.

When a student goes into registration, he or she has to have his or her schedule already made out or he or she will find that a great deal of his or her time is being spent filling out forms that he or she could have just as easily filled out in the comfort of his or her home where he or she could at least be comfortable.

When students go into registration, they have to have their schedules already filled out or they will find that a great deal of their time is being spent filling out forms that they could have just as easily filled out in the comfort of their homes where they could at least be comfortable.

It is important to remember that when the subject is plural, the rest of the sentence must be plural as well.

---

**Subject/pronoun agreement**   When the subject is singular, the pronoun that refers to that subject must be singular, also. When the subject is plural, the pronoun must be plural.

---

You will avoid the problem of having a singular subject with a plural pronoun if you use plural subjects. *Everyone has their head on the table.* This avoids the problem of calling everyone *he*, but it does not have agreement between the subject and the pronoun. *Everyone* is a singular word, and *their* is a plural word. The two do not go together. *All the students have their heads on the table.* This takes care of both problems. The subject and the pronoun agree, and you do not have to worry about whether the students are male or female.

### Pronoun Reference

Another common problem with pronouns occurs when they are used in a manner that makes unclear to which noun the pronoun refers.

Don and I went to George's house, but *his* car was out of gas. (Whose car, Don's or George's?)

Society does not give enough attention to the environment. *They* seem to feel the air and water will stay clean with no effort. (What noun does *They* represent? Society is an *it*.)

*They* say that moss grows on the north side of trees. (What noun does *They* represent? Unless the previous sentence makes that clear, revise.)

When you read, check to make sure that the pronouns have a clear connection to the nouns they represent. If you aren't sure what the pronoun represents, suggest the writer revise the sentence.

## LISTENING TO QUESTIONS AND COMMENTS

There are not many times in our lives when we have to sit and listen while others discuss something we have done. Some may find it uncomfortable. Keep in mind that when you write, you will very seldom be present when your audience reads your work. They will have many of the same questions and comments that your peer reviewers have, however. This is an opportunity for you to hear how well your writing has communicated with your audience.

Be sure to take as many notes as you can. Even if a comment seems unfounded at the moment, it might make more sense when you begin to revise. Remember, the members of the group are students, too, and they may not express some of their comments in the clearest way possible at first. If you do not understand why someone makes a particular comment, you need to ask for more information.

Some people have a difficult time making comments in a way that focuses on the writing and not the writer. If you feel personally attacked by something someone has to say, try to figure out whether something you wrote could have caused the person to react that way. While the attacking comment is not appropriate, it may be that something you wrote has caused an unintended negative reaction in your audience. If you can learn to identify and avoid writing that causes antagonistic reactions, your audience will have a much easier time seeing your position as a reasonable one.

When someone criticizes in a way that seems unfair, a common response is to devalue that person. It is easy to write people off as being jerks whose opinion is valueless. As noted in an earlier chapter, the person may be a jerk, but in academic situations, that evaluation is not enough to make the opinion invalid. Even a jerk can be right. Your responsibility as the person defending the thesis you have chosen is to make sure you have made the most reasonable and clear defense that you can. The comments made in reviewing can assist you in discovering if you have been successful in that task and, if you have not, in finding ways to improve.

However, when it is your turn to ask questions, it is perfectly reasonable to ask the person who seemed to be attacking what you wrote to explain what triggered the negative response. Sometimes the person will add further comments that are much more helpful than the first ones. If at any time you do not understand why someone made a comment, be sure to make a note requesting more information.

## NOTES FOR THE NEXT DRAFT

Try to make note of as many of the comments as possible, regardless of whether they are negative or positive. Some of the comments may not really help much in your revision process. It will be difficult to instantly decide which is helpful, however, and it will be useful for you to have as complete a record as possible.

When you revise, keep the notes you have made during the group reviewing activity nearby. They will help you to fine-tune your argument. You may also wish to have your partners write down their impressions of your essay so you can refer to them as you are reworking. Writing something down takes more time and thought than just saying what you think, so they will probably put their most serious and clearly thought ideas down for you to refer to.

# *Chapter Review*

1. Why is it important to acknowledge the concerns of those holding opposing views?
2. Why is it a problem to say that everything is fine with an essay when it isn't?
3. How would you note a grammar or punctuation error in a sentence?
4. What is the goal of the reviewing process?
5. What makes competition a problem with peer reviewing?

Chapter **6**

# *Developing a Thesis*

Organizing a Thesis Statement
Revision Activities: Natalie's First Draft
Things to Consider About Sentences
Revision Activities: Natalie's Second Draft
Paragraph Structure
Chapter Review

## ORGANIZING A THESIS STATEMENT

Once you have written the first draft of your essay, then you need to check for a clear thesis statement.

**Thesis statement**   A statement of position in an area of controversy that forms the focus of a unified essay.

The definition given above can be put in many different ways, and the term *thesis statement* is used in almost every English class. It seems useful to break that term down so that you clearly understand what it is you are looking for.

**113**

As used by writers of essays the definition of a thesis is as follows.

---

**Thesis**   A position supported by reasoned argument.

---

Remember the definition of argument.

---

**Argument**   An exchange of ideas, and the reasons for those ideas, that allows every participant to examine the positions in a controversy.

---

As you can see, asking you to have a thesis statement is asking you to identify a position for your argument and put it into a sentence. The reason the word *statement* is added to the thesis is to make it clear that your thesis cannot be a question. A question is not a position in a controversy; it is a request for more information.

Imagine yourself walking into a room and finding a group of people discussing whether a new factory should be built near your community. You take a seat and listen for a few minutes, and then you say

> I think a factory would be good for this area because it would provide many people with jobs.

You have just taken a position. You could then try to convince the others that having the opportunity for so many jobs in the area would be an advantage that would outweigh any disadvantages they might be worried about. However, if you had asked someone

> How many people will the factory hire from around here?

you would have been conducting research before you felt ready to take a position. A question cannot serve the function of taking a position.

The arguments you write about will be similar to the situation described in the previous paragraph, but, instead of all the participants being present, some will present their positions in things they have written. It is impossible for you to sit down with everyone who has an opinion on a topic such as the environment. If you wish to form an educated opinion on any important issue, you must do some reading and find out what those familiar with it are saying. When you are informed on the controversy, you will then decide which positions are the most reasonable. When you come to a conclusion and form an opinion, you have formed a thesis concerning the question at issue.

## How Thesis Statements Work for the Writer

Once you have identified a clear thesis statement, you are well on your way to writing a clear, organized essay. Because there are several functions that an effective thesis statement performs for you, it is well worth your time to develop one carefully.

**Focus.** A thesis keeps you focused on a single topic. One problem writers often face is that their essays jump from one topic to another. Some essays end on a completely different topic than they began on. This not only confuses the reader, it fails to support the position the essay took in the beginning. If writers have a thesis statement to refer to as they write, they can tell quickly if they are getting off the topic.

**Earned conclusion.** If you have a thesis, you will have in mind the effect you wish to have on your audience. In the sample thesis about the factory coming to your town, by the end of your essay you would have given your audience enough information to support the position that the factory will affect unemployment positively, which will benefit the town in many ways. This supported position is an *earned conclusion* because you have earned the right to be heard by reasonable people.

---

**Earned conclusion** An argumentative position supported with clear, persuasive evidence that convinces a thoughtful audience that the position is reasonable.

---

A good thesis guides a writer, and the readers as well, toward an earned conclusion. The cycle of an essay guided by a clear thesis might look something like this:

*Introduction*   thesis statement = position taken or asserted.
*Body*   proofs or examples = evidence to support the position.
*Conclusion*   position supported (or earned) based on evidence given.

As you can see from the cycle above, if the thesis is flawed, the essay probably will be, too. Learning to develop an effective thesis statement will make your essay writing task much easier.

## Developing a Thesis Statement

Once you have a first draft, you need to start testing it to see if it has a good thesis statement. If your thesis is flawed, you will probably find problems with the draft as well. Just because a draft has problems does not mean you cannot use it, however. You need to back up a little and organize a solid thesis. Then the material that you can use from your first draft will be clear to you.

The method of organizing a solid thesis is not as difficult as it may sound. Using the argument concerning the factory outside town, you might start with a thesis that sounded something like this: *This new factory will employ three hundred people.* You believe that you can support this because you read it in the paper, but it is not a question at issue. This is a statement of fact, not a position in an argument. Facts can be proven without a doubt, so they do not form an area of disagreement or a difference of opinion.

The next thing you might try as a thesis is: *Do you want the high unemployment in this town to get higher?* You know unemployment is a problem, and you intend to argue that the factory will reduce that problem. You have phrased your thesis as a question, however, and since you do not really want anyone who reads that sentence to answer "Yes," the focus is unclear. No one wants high unemployment, but people do have differing opinions about how to solve the problem. Your question does not give any hint of how you intend to address this problem. The type of question you have used is a *rhetorical question.*

---

**Rhetorical question**   A question asked for effect, or to emphasize a point, where the answer is implied in the question itself.

---

A rhetorical question does not work as a thesis, because it assumes your audience will either answer it exactly as you would, or that no one has a clear answer. In both cases, the rhetorical question hinders a clear development of your position.

The sentence used when you joined the conversation of the people discussing the factory, *The factory would be good for this area because it would provide many people with jobs,* could be a solid thesis statement. It says clearly what forms the basis of your opinion. You have clear information to support your position, and it allows you to address the concerns of those who do not agree with you. You may wish to strengthen the idea that jobs are desirable by saying why the community needs new jobs. That would add another phrase to your thesis. *The factory would be good for this area because it would provide many people with jobs, which would reduce the unemployment.*

One possible area of vagueness, however, is the word *good.* What kind of *good* do you have in mind? If you see the jobs as providing an economic benefit, say that instead of *good.* Words like *good, bad, strong, weak, right,* and *wrong* can mean many things to your audience, and it will benefit you as a writer to say exactly what you intend to prove without using such vague terms. So, to finish the development of this thesis you would say: *The new factory would economically benefit this area by providing many new jobs, which would reduce the unemployment.*

## Testing a Thesis Statement

Since the thesis will provide the central focus that will guide your essay, you must be sure it is an effective one. Once you have a thesis statement written down, there are questions you can ask that will help you to know if your thesis will work to guide your essay's development.

1. *Is this topic something that is important to me?* This question is asked first because a bored writer is a boring writer. A bored writer is also often one who makes many grammar and mechanical errors simply because of indifference. If you don't care about this topic, why should your audience? It isn't necessary that you be wildly excited about every topic, but it is highly desirable that you be interested in letting others know why you have taken your position.

2. *Is this topic something my audience will want to know about?* If you feel that they are not interested but they should be, then you must begin the essay by telling them why you feel they should be interested.

3. *Do I have enough information to explain my position thoroughly? Am I willing to take the time to do that?* A quick sentence outline can answer part of this question. Write a brief sentence or phrase that indicates how you plan to develop your essay. If you have trouble outlining how you will explain and support your position, then you may need more information. If you do not have enough information readily at hand, do you care about this topic enough to look up the necessary information?

4. *Do I have the right amount of time and essay length to cover this topic thoroughly?* If your answer to this question is uncertain, it will help to narrow your topic. If you begin with a broad, general topic, it will result in broad, general, poorly supported statements as you try to explain your position. These broad statements will cause you to lose common ground with some of your audience because they will see the lack of support. You will need specific examples if you want people to accept your position as reasonable.

5. *What is it exactly that I want my audience to conclude from my essay?* Every essay needs a purpose. In an argumentative essay, that purpose is getting your opposition to look differently at the question at issue you have chosen. At the end of your essay, your conclusion should be a message to your audience concerning that difference.

6. *Are there knowledgeable people who agree with me? Disagree with me?* When people begin exploring an idea, they need to learn from those considered experts, if only to find out how much knowledge is available and why those experts think as they do. The experts may still be wrong. No new knowledge would be discovered if no one ever disagreed with thinkers who went before. When Louis Pasteur first suggested vaccines, most of the scientists of his day disagreed with him. Pasteur spent years in experimentation to back up his theories, and he was able to prove that he was right and they were wrong. The newer your ideas, the more carefully you have to support them to get your audience to understand your position and agree with your reasoning.

7. *What reasons do the people who do not agree with this position give to support their disagreement?* If you cannot think of an immediate, clear answer to this question, your thesis has one of two problems:

  a. *Poor or absent question at issue.* If you have a solid question at issue, the reasons given by those who oppose your position should be clear. This will be especially true of a topic that you have discussed in a group, because you will have had a chance to listen to what your opposition said on the issue.

  b. *Need for more research.* If you know that your topic is a question at issue but you cannot understand why anyone would disagree with your position, then you need to do more research before you write on this topic. Since part of your job in defending a position is giving reasons why others should see your position as reasonable, you cannot organize an effective essay without understanding why others support different positions.

8. *What proofs or evidence do I have to present to my opposition to persuade them of the reasonableness of my position?* This is when you

have to be most careful to tell your audience *why* you think the way that you do. When you believe something, it is easy to think that everyone else believes it, also. This is especially true when you have had an experience that strongly supports that belief. However, forgetting to include the reasons why your audience should accept your belief may cause you to lose common ground. If those in your audience have had experiences that brought them to different conclusions or they cannot understand why you believe as you do, they will not be able to accept your argument as a reasonable one.

## Outlining with a Thesis Statement

With a good thesis, you can do a brief outline of the paragraphs you intend to write to support your position. This does not have to be a complicated, formal outline, and it can help you in several ways. Using the same thesis, *The new factory would economically benefit this area by providing many new jobs, which would reduce the unemployment,* a sample outline might look something like this:

*Thesis*   The factory will benefit the area by reducing unemployment.
*Introducing paragraph*   Growing unemployment in town caused by mills closing.
*Paragraph*   Description of closed stores and rise in welfare claims. (Cite newspaper stories.)
*Paragraph*   Personal story of an uncle who has been laid off and how his family struggles.
*Paragraph*   Your account of looking for work without success.
*Paragraph*   Argue that everyone in town will suffer economically if people start leaving the area to look for work somewhere else.
*Paragraph*   Recognize the concerns of the opposition by acknowledging the need for controls to ensure environmental protection.
*Paragraph*   Use newspaper article to support the economic benefit of a large number of new jobs coming into the area.
*Concluding Paragraph*   Reduced unemployment caused by the new factory will benefit everyone in the town.

As you can see, this is not a complicated outline, but it would guide you through the essay-writing process. You might even decide that it would make your argument more effective if you started with your uncle's story and then followed it up with the more general newspaper article reference. Making an outline in advance allows you to assess your organization to see if your ideas are in the most effective order.

The first thing you will learn from an outline is whether you have enough information to write the essay without doing further research.

You will also be able to see if you have developed this idea enough to carefully explain why you took your position. You will usually know how long the essay has to be, and, if you run out of information within a paragraph or so, you need more information.

An outline can also help you to organize your essay ahead of time. Many people feel outlines are a waste of time, but even in in-class essay situations, an informal outline can prevent the problems that arise when a writer gets off-task in the middle of an essay. Some people may want to write a formal outline with details listed in subheads under each paragraph, and that is fine. However, it is not necessary to do a formal outline with roman numerals followed by Arabic numerals. A brief outline similar to the one written above is enough to prevent many essay-writing problems and will save you time and energy.

## Sample Article for Practice

The following newspaper article would be an excellent source of support for an essay on environmental damage caused by some industries. You will be using the information from the article to develop and test a few thesis statements, so read through it carefully.

# Oil Company Waste Pits—Big Killer of Migrating Birds

19 March 1990

*Robert M. Bryce*

### Big Spring, Texas

Cash Schriefer says he knew the bird he was fishing out of the oil waste pit in southern Oklahoma in late January was big. The U.S. Fish and Wildlife Service special agent said he thought it was a goose at first.

But when Schriefer finally pulled the oil-covered bird out of the abandoned waste pit, he was amazed at its size. A six-foot wingspan, massive talons and yellow beak told Schriefer immediately that the bird was a bald eagle.

Thousands of oil waste pits such as the one that killed the eagle dot the arid plains of Texas, Oklahoma and New Mexico.

Biologists say more than 600,000 migratory birds die annually in the open waste pits of the three-state region; twice as many birds die each year in pits than were killed by Alaska's Exxon Valdez oil spill.

"The birds think the oil pits are water, so they land on them," says Midge Erskine, a bird rehabilitator from Midland, Texas, who has treated birds rescued from the tar-like goo.

"Very few birds escape death once they touch the oil," says Rob Lee, a special agent with the Fish and Wildlife Service, stationed in Lubbock.

Sometimes a bird can escape from the pits, but they are going to die anyway because they have no way of cleaning their feathers. Anything more than minute amounts of oil is fatal."

### U.S. Crackdown

Authorities say most such birds die of hypothermia, because oil destroys their ability to retain body heat. Others die of poisoning while preening oil from their feathers.

The Fish and Wildlife Service began cracking down on companies that operate open waste pits after a yearlong voluntary compliance period that ended in October. During the compliance period, federal officials encouraged oil companies to cover pits with screens or nets to prevent birds from touching the oily water.

On October 1, agents began collecting dead birds from oil waste pits, and more than 15 companies in Oklahoma and 30 in Texas face federal prosecution under the Migratory Bird Treaty Act.

Passed by Congress in 1918, the act protects 842 migratory birds from unlawful killing. Companies found guilty under the law face fines up to $10,000 and six months in jail for each violation. But despite stiff fines and possible prosecution, many oil companies have not covered pits.

The probe puts many oil and gas producers in an unusual position: Even though their waste pits may be operating legally under state law, they may still face federal prosecution.

Open waste pits and open-topped storage tanks are common sights in oil-producing areas. Brine is a byproduct of oil production. Pits or tanks are used to store saltwater and occasionally for emergency storage of oil.

### State Commissions

Although federal officials have been lobbying for a rule change, the Oklahoma Corporation Commission and the Texas Railroad Commission—the state agencies responsible for regulating the oil industry—have not passed new rules requiring open pits and tanks to be covered.

Erskine and other conservationists blame the Railroad Commission for lax enforcement of a 1939 rule that prohibits the storage of oil in open earth pits. Using 130 inspectors, the commission found 834 violations of the open pit rule last year. Yet it issued only 10 fines.

"I suppose if we had 1,000 inspectors, we could fine a higher percentage of these oil pits," says John Sharp, a Texas Railroad Commission member. "Whenever someone reports them to us, the open pit rule is enforced."

But a lack of enforcement is evident. In Oklahoma, the pit that killed the bald eagle was reported to Oklahoma Corporation Commission inspectors last fall, but the inspector assigned to the case could not find the pit.

According to Schriefer, the company that owns the pit will be prosecuted under three federal laws: the Eagle Protection Act, the Endangered Species Act and the Migratory Bird Treaty Act. Fines up to $50,000 and jail sentences could face company executives.

### The Oil Lobby

Colorado and California have required open pits to be covered with screens for years. Last June, in response to requests by Fish and Wildlife Service officials, New Mexico passed a similar measure.

But the oil industry in Oklahoma and Texas has lobbied hard to prevent rule changes. Jim Allen, chairman of the Texas Mid-Continent Oil and Gas Producers Association's Regulatory Practices Committee, explains that his group opposes new rules requiring that the facilities be covered.

"We believe an emphasis on compliance and enforcement of existing rules appears to be the appropriate response as opposed to a new rule," Allen says.

To date, no oil companies have been prosecuted, but Fish and Wildlife Service officials say it is only a matter of time.

---

### Exercises in Developing and Testing a Thesis

1. Make a list of questions at issue in this article.
2. List positions that could be taken in an argumentative essay based on this article.
3. Pick two or three positions, and develop each of them into thesis statements.
4. Using the questions given for testing a thesis, test your thesis statements to see if they would work.
5. What more information, if any, would you need to write an essay on the position that many businesses are indifferent to environmental damage?

# REVISION ACTIVITIES: NATALIE'S FIRST DRAFT

When Kevin from Chapter 4 did his first draft, he had a clear topic in mind, which made it a generative sentence draft. Natalie isn't as clear about what she wants to say about the topic of the environment, but she knows it was a battle over the environment that changed her life. As you read her draft on the assigned topic of the environment, try to find areas that she might be able to expand into an argumentative essay.

 *Natalie's Essay (Draft 1)*

I couldn't believe my ears when my mother told me we were going to move to Seattle. The mill in my hometown, Elkton, Oregon, closed last year. Except for people who owned stores and things like that, everyone in Elkton worked at the mill. My father worked there. My mother never worked.

After the plywood mill closed a lot of people moved out of town, I thought we might have to move too. My father went to community college for job retraining. He studied airplane mechanics. I thought we might have to move to a larger town, Coos Bay or Eugene. A town with an airport. I never thought we would move all the way to Seattle.

Another shock was that my brother was not going with us. He finished his junior year at Elkton High School. Where he played football and basketball. He stayed with his coach and his wife so he could finish at Elkton High. It was very strange to think of leaving him behind. He was also going to keep Wolf, our German shepherd, with him. Our cat stayed with my grandparents. My mother said we couldn't take them because we might have to live in an apartment. I never lived in an apartment, I never lived without pets.

Before we left I went out by the river to think and say good-bye to the only place I ever lived. Where we lived there were lots of trees, it was never very sunny because of the trees. The back of our lot was the Umpqua River. My uncle, who was young and single and worked for the State Fish and Game would live in our house now. As I sat by the river thinking I looked up and an elk was looking across the river at me. Elk came close to the river sometimes but this one was big, a five or six point buck. It seemed almost as if he was going to say something to me, good-bye maybe.

I don't know why the mills closed. My father said it was because of the environmentalists, they want to preserve everything so rich people can go hiking. My science teacher at my high school in Seattle said the

temperate rainforests of the Northwest are an invaluable ecosystem and they have to be preserved. I don't know what to think.

Since I've been in Seattle, I've been to a Seahawks game and I've been to the top of the Space Needle. Now I'm going to college. Which I could probably never have done if I'd stayed in Elkton. But I still don't feel at home here. I still miss rural Oregon and the trees and the river.

---

### Reviewing Natalie's First Draft

1. Natalie needs some help with identifying the ideas in this first draft that will work best for her final environmental essay.
   a. What do you think are the strongest parts of this draft?
   b. What idea does Natalie want to be the focus for her audience?
   c. Do you see possibilities for a stronger argument hinted at by information she has put down?
2. Acting as reviewers, pick out places Natalie could expand on her ideas to clarify her essay. Write her a brief note in the margin of those paragraphs suggesting these ideas as a possibility for a clearer focus.
3. When you have finished your margin notes to Natalie, write a brief note at the end of her essay telling her what parts interested you and what you think she should do to make it better fit the assignment.
4. After you have finished the other notes, then comment about the sentence-structure errors in her essay. Mark five of these errors and indicate the sentence problem. You may not be marking grammar

errors when peer reviewing essays for each other, so Natalie's essay gives you a chance to practice seeing similar errors in your own rough drafts.

# THINGS TO CONSIDER ABOUT SENTENCES

### *Thesis and Sentence Formation*

If you were constructing a building made of bricks, a single brick would be similar to the place a single word holds in language. A row of bricks would be similar to a sentence. If one brick is the wrong length or shape, then the whole row will be off, which will affect the strength of the building. In a sentence, every word must fit its place in much the same way. A single word stands for an idea or thing. A sentence is a group of words combining ideas or things to form a single larger idea. Each of you understands this, and you demonstrate that understanding every time you talk to someone.

Speech is not learned in quite the same way that writing is, however. You *acquired* speech as little children from listening to the speech of those around you. Writing is a different learning process. You have to learn to write by the same process that you would use in learning to construct a building. If you were learning to be a bricklayer, you would have to learn how to place the bricks properly, one at a time. It is a similar process when you learn to write, but there is one big difference. Sometimes the way language is organized seems simple and obvious because you are already skilled at using spoken language. Other times, you may know what sounds right, but you do not know how to explain why that particular word pattern is correct. You already know a great deal about how your language works, but sometimes people have problems organizing clearly written ideas in spite of that knowledge. The solution to that problem is to organize what you already know about language, so you can use your knowledge about spoken language when you write. Natalie's draft demonstrates how connected the intent of the writer is to the way sentences are constructed.

One of the problems you encountered with Natalie's first draft was that there were sentence-structure errors. In a first draft, it is not important to worry about sentence structure, but it is still useful to consider this question: Why has she made these errors?

Sentence structures have to be chosen according to the overall goal of an essay. Natalie's thesis is not clear. Is it her life in Seattle compared to her life in rural Oregon? If so, does that fulfill the assignment to write an essay on the subject of the environment? Her experience of having to

move from rural Oregon because of a battle to save part of the environment could be an excellent thesis, but she did not really develop that
idea. No helpful improvements can be made on the sentence errors of
Natalie's essay until it is clear what she wants for her thesis. Then she
will know how to write to accomplish her goal.

Keep this in mind for your own writing. It is much more likely that
you will run into grammar errors if you try to write an essay with an
unclear or poorly thought out thesis. There is a strong relationship between a well-organized thesis and good grammar.

## Sentence Structure

A sentence is a group of words forming one clear idea. In every sentence, something has to happen or to be. Each sentence has to have an
*actor,* that is, the word or phrase that represents the *source of the action*
or the *being* in the sentence. This word is a *noun.*

---

**Noun**   The name of a person, place, or thing.
**Pronoun**   A substitute for a noun.

EXAMPLES   *Walla Walla, WA,* doesn't have a *zoo,* but *it* does have a
balloon *race.*

---

In the sentence *The picture hangs on the wall, hangs* is the verb
because it tells what the picture does. It hangs.

---

**Verb**   The word that tells what *acting or being* is going on in the
sentence.

EXAMPLES

*Being:* Love *is* the salsa on the rice of life.
*Acting:* Salsa *puts* spice into eating.

---

Some words can confuse by fitting into more than one part of speech.
These words are called homonyms. Look at the following sentences, and
you will be able to see why it is useful to understand how to identify the
parts of speech in order to avoid sentence errors.

Cats *spring* out of trees. (verb)
The house needs a *spring* cleaning. (adjective)

Flowers bloom in the *spring.* (noun)
The pond was fed by a *spring.* (noun)

---

**Application**

Discuss or write these words in as many different sentences as you can generate: *race, top, can.*

---

Most sentences must have these two things: (1) an actor (a subject that is being or doing something) and (2) action or being. Sometimes the actor or subject can be understood rather than written, as in commands. When parents look at their children and say "Do the dishes," they mean "*You* do the dishes." That is not all that is needed for a complete sentence, however. It must also be a complete idea. One whole thought must be in every sentence for it to be complete. It is possible to make technically complete sentences with just a subject and a verb: *Dogs run. Horses neigh. Babies cry.* As you can see, however, these simple sentences are more like baby talk than complete sentences. To convey adult-level communication, sentences need to be more complex.

### Sentence Form and the Main Idea

Sentence structure is the servant of what the writer wants to emphasize. For example:

I sat in the backyard.
The backyard was shady.
The shade was caused by many tall trees.
The backyard was bordered by a river.
It is the Umpqua River.
Elk graze along the Umpqua.
An elk was looking across the river.
It was a large male.
Its antlers had five or six points.
It seemed to be saying good-bye.

Most of these sentences are ordinary information. The three most important facts are that there were (1) tall trees, (2) a river, and (3) an elk. The other information can be subordinated or put in the background as a way to emphasize the main points. Natalie makes errors in sentence structure because she has not decided which of the pieces of information that she is giving her readers is the most important. Without a thesis to guide her choices, she cannot guide her readers by the way she constructs her sentences.

The last sentence—"It seemed to be saying good-bye"—is different from the others because it is not ordinary information. It is something unique. When an idea is presented in a simple sentence, it seems stronger and more emphasized than if it is in a complex sentence with modifiers. You know that when you talk, so you save simple sentences for important or key ideas. Natalie would have helped her reader focus on the elk as a messenger if she had eliminated all modifiers as in: "His look said good-bye."

## Subordination of Ideas

Not all ideas are equally important, and the choices you make in forming your sentences tell your audience which ideas you want them to pay the most attention to. One of the ways to help your audience to do this is to subordinate ideas within a sentence. One idea is singled out as the most important, and the others are put in phrases that are not complete sentences. These phrases, called *dependent clauses* because they depend on a sentence to be a whole idea, contain information that the audience needs to know, but is not essential to the main idea.

In the sentence *Because a shark ate Father, we left the beach early,* the purpose is to tell the audience that the writer left early. The sentence also tells *why* the writer left. The reason has no meaning on its own: *Because a shark ate Father.* A subordinate clause needs to be connected to a sentence in order to have meaning.

---

**Independent clause**   The main clause in a complex sentence.  An independent clause could be a complete sentence if written alone.

**Dependent (or subordinate) clause**   An idea that depends on an independent clause to be a complete idea.

EXAMPLE   Because a shark ate Father (dependent clause), we left the beach early (independent clause).

---

The sample sentence also demonstrates the way meaning can become confused if the writer puts important information in a dependent clause. If a shark ate your father, it is unlikely you would consider that event less important than that having to leave the beach early. The sentence *Because a shark ate Father, we left the beach early* sounds as if the writer was not as affected by the loss of a parent as much as the early departure from the beach.

Some people write in simple sentences because they feel safer. There are no tricky commas, conjunctions, or dependent clauses to worry about. The result of this is that the reader has trouble knowing which points are important and which are just background information. The writing seems choppy and fragmented even though all the sentences are technically correct. You will more likely find yourself doing this and writing other faulty sentences if you don't know how your ideas relate to each other, because you have the problem of not being sure what ideas are guiding your sentence decisions.

Natalie had trouble with choppy writing because she wrote in short simple sentences that contained primarily a simple subject, a verb, and an object. The verb and its object are the *predicate* of a sentence.

---

**Subject**    The thing doing the *being* in a sentence. It is the part that the sentence is *about.*

EXAMPLE    *The picture* hangs on the wall.

**Predicate**    The verb that tells what the subject is or does combined with all the verb's modifiers.

EXAMPLE    Elk *graze along the Umpqua.*

---

She needed to subordinate some of her information about where she lived to guide her audience in recognizing what was most important. There are a variety of ways to arrange these pieces of information, depending on what point you want to make with the audience. If Natalie wanted to put the audience in the setting of her yard so she could describe seeing the elk, she could write it like this:

*Bordered by the Umpqua River and shaded by tall trees,* my backyard was a good spot to sit and think. *While sitting there shortly before we left,* I saw an elk grazing along the opposite bank. Elk often grazed over there, but this one was unusually large: its antlers had five or six points. It looked at me so long that it seemed to be saying good-bye.

By putting the background information in subordinate clauses, Natalie could guide her audience to focus on the important information of her feelings about leaving her home and seeing the elk. Normally, a sentence puts the important information first, so when a subordinate clause comes first, it is set off with a comma. If you read the sentences with the subordinate clauses aloud, you will hear the pause that indicates that a comma will have to be there when the sentence is written.

Any information that interrupts the normal flow of information (subject—verb—object) is set off with commas unless it is very brief or unless it is essential to the meaning of the sentence. A subordinate (or dependent) clause is set off with a comma when it begins the sentence. A speaker or reader will pause to focus attention on the information that the sentence is about: the subject and the predicate. Sentences would be very simple and boring if they only contained subjects, verbs, and objects, however. It takes additional information about each of these sentence parts to add color and interest. The additional information is frequently added by modifiers.

### Modifiers

*The famous, beautiful, indescribable picture of the Mona Lisa hangs on the wall of the Louvre in Paris.* This is still the same basic sentence: *The picture hangs on the wall.* The original subject is now surrounded by words that make its meaning more specific. Those additional words are called *modifiers,* because they modify the meaning of the words they refer to. These modifiers come in a variety of patterns that allow the speaker and writer to communicate information and ideas on very complex levels.

Modifiers cannot be the subject in a sentence because they cannot *be* things, they can only *talk about* things. What is the subject of this sentence? *There is a bird at the feeder.* The sentence is about birds. Therefore, that is the subject. An adverb such as *there* can never be the subject, because a sentence cannot be about *there.* If someone were to say *At the feeder is a bird there,* it would not make sense because the subject is not in the place where the patterns of English insist it needs to be.

---

**Extended, or complex, subject**    The noun or pronoun of the sentence together with all the words that modify its meaning.

EXAMPLE    *The vicious, snarling poodle* tried to break the chain.

---

The same idea applies to the verb. In *The picture hangs on the wall,* the verb is modified because we know where the picture hangs: *on the wall.* In the second sentence, we learn even more about where it hangs:

*on the wall of the Louvre in Paris.* This part of a sentence is a *complex predicate.*

### Prepositional Phrases

When prepositional phrases are used to modify the subject, writers may get confused. The subject word is not necessarily the only noun or pronoun in the sentence. Prepositions connect the subject word in time or space (position) with another noun or pronoun. *The dog with the floppy ears . . .* The preposition *with* shows the relationship between the words *dog* and *ears.*

In the phrase *The dog with the floppy ears, dog* is singular, and *ears* is plural. Writers can confuse the noun or pronoun that is the subject of the sentence with the noun or pronoun that is the object or the receiver of the connection made by the preposition. Words that are modified by a preposition or that receive the action of the verb are called "objects." Sentences are often written subject—verb—object, but other patterns are correct, depending on what idea the sentence is intended to convey. Questions often start with the verb: *Are you ready to go?* (verb—subject—object).

Some students are afraid of confusing prepositional phrases with the subject of the sentence, so they avoid using prepositional phrases. There are ways to avoid this confusion, however, and still write sentences that express all the complex ideas that you are able to express when you talk. All you have to do is ask what the sentence is about: What is the subject? When you know the answer to that question, then you can make sure that all parts of the sentence focus on the actor.

Modifiers can be single words: **The dog ran. The skinny** *dog ran* **free.** When you talk, you sometimes use more complicated modifiers, though. Often, you use a phrase or phrases along with one-word modifiers to modify the original word. **The skinny** *dog* **with the floppy ears** *ran* **free during the day.** These phrases are called prepositional phrases because they begin with a preposition, and they are a very common form of modifier.

---

**Preposition**   A word that shows a relationship in space or time.

---

These are some of the most commonly used prepositions:

| to | on | at | in | as | by |
|------|------|------|------|------|------|
| of | up | off | for | out | onto |
| into | like | over | next | past | near |

| | | | | | |
|---|---|---|---|---|---|
| upon | until | with | inside | beside | outside |
| toward | after | down | against | during | despite |
| through | about | without | before | opposite | among |
| considering | around | between | behind | unlike | regarding |
| underneath | beyond | respecting | above | across | |

---

**Prepositional phrase**    A word or group of words modified by a preposition.

---

The *position* part of **preposition** can help you remember what these words are and what their function is. Prepositional phrases can often show more information than a single-word modifier. *He went there. He went **to the airport.***

**Exercise on prepositional phrases.**    Look at the way the underlined prepositions function in the following little story. Each prepositional phrase is in bold to show how they add information to the sentence that would be difficult to include without writing many tiny, choppy sentences. In one case, however, the writer of this example has put in one sentence that has mistaken a prepositional phrase for a complete sentence. This is a common mistake, and one reason that it is useful to be able to recognize a preposition. Can you find the sentence fragment?

Judy went **to work at the construction site until sunset**. She was working **inside the structure** directly **underneath the roof above a tile floor** when she leaned **across the scaffold toward her toolbox.** After Judy fell **off the scaffold,** breaking her arm, she realized she had fallen **onto some plaster** spilled **on the floor.** She fell down again when she tried to stand up. She leaned **against the wall beside the scaffold throughout lunch. About an hour** later, workers **outside the building** heard her call. They came **into the room** and found her **by the scaffold.** She said, "I can't walk **without pain,** and my arm feels like it is broken." She sat **in the cab as the boss** drove the company truck **over the bridge past the main entrance of the hospital** and parked **near the emergency door. Inside the hospital,** Judy sat **in the lobby during the wait for a doctor. Despite her injuries,** others were sicker than Judy. The doctor came **with a nurse** and said Judy was **in good shape** considering how far she had fallen.

Now that you have had a chance to see prepositional phrases marked, see if you can mark them in the rest of Judy's story.

Despite her cast and twisted ankle, Judy hated sitting around the house. She read, and, between books, she saw reruns of every TV show made since she was in high school. Her friend Lupe called her before the boredom was too bad. She and Judy often went along the river and sat under the trees and talked concerning the future. Lupe talked about Judy's ability as a carpenter. Lupe wanted Judy to teach carpentry at the women's center opposite the hospital where Judy could sit upon a stool among the students next to the equipment. Judy was in her car and over the speed limit to get there. At first she felt behind the other teachers, but soon the students were respecting her advice, unlike some of the other jobs she had done. Judy felt good regarding her work. Everyone thought she had something between her ears. By falling below the scaffold, she had risen above her expectations and was happy.

If you are able to identify a prepositional phrase and how it functions in a sentence, you will not mistake it for a sentence by itself. It must be connected to the item it is designed to modify, a sentence with a complete idea, or it has no function.

Once you understand prepositional phrases, however, you must also learn to use them wisely. Technically, it is possible to have a correct sentence with many prepositional phrases linked, but this is not the clearest way to express your ideas. Judy's story has too many prepositional phrases because it was written to provide an example. Look at the same story when the number of prepositional phrases is reduced to add to the clarity.

Judy went **to work at the construction site**. She was working inside, directly **under the roof,** when she leaned **across** the scaffold. After Judy fell, breaking her arm, she realized she had fallen **onto some spilled plaster**. She fell down again when she tried to stand up. She leaned **against the wall during the lunch break**. **About** an hour later, workers **outside the building** heard her call. They came in and found her. She said, "I can't walk **without** pain, and my arm feels like it is broken." She sat **in the truck** as the boss drove **to the hospital**. Judy sat **in the hospital lobby** waiting **for a doctor**. **Despite her injuries**, others were sicker than Judy. The doctor said Judy was **in good shape** considering how far she had fallen.

Again, see if you can identify the prepositional phrases in the second paragraph.

Despite her cast and twisted ankle, Judy hated sitting around the house. She read and saw reruns of TV shows between books. Her friend Lupe called, relieving Judy's boredom. She and Judy often went along the river and talked about their future. Now Lupe talked about Judy's ability as a carpenter. Lupe wanted Judy to teach carpentry at the women's center. Judy was out the door, speeding to get there. At first she felt unprepared, but soon the students respected her advice unlike the attitude of those at some of her other jobs. Judy liked her work. Everyone thought she had valuable knowledge. By falling, she had risen to a new, rewarding career that made her happy.

## Active and Passive Voice

Many sentences have objects: *The catcher threw* **the ball.** The ball is not the actor of the sentence, but it receives the action. **The ball** *was thrown by the catcher* is a sentence written with the object first because it is the focus of the sentence. Sentences like these are in passive voice.

---

**Active voice**   The subject is the main focus of the sentence.

EXAMPLE   I drove your Ferrari into a tree.

**Passive voice**   The focus of the sentence is on the word receiving the action of the subject.

EXAMPLE   Your Ferrari has been wrecked.

---

A writer will use the passive voice when there is a reason why the object is more important than the actor in the sentence. Perhaps the next sentence will focus on the Ferrari's mechanical failure, or how the driver had nothing to do with the accident. In cases such as this, the driver, who was the actor of the sentence, is less important than the car, which is the passive receiver or object of the action. Even in the passive voice, however, the writer still has to know who the actor of the sentence is to keep the idea expressed by the sentence clear.

One reason why the passive voice can be confusing is that it keeps the actor from getting credit, or blame, for the action. This is how the passive voice is often misused. Imagine yourself walking into a kitchen where a child is standing next to a spilled glass of milk. The child may feel bad about the spill and say, "The milk got spilled" rather than "I spilled the milk."

Without knowing the definition, the child understands that the passive voice puts the emphasis on the receiver of the action (the milk) rather than on the actor (the child). The child also knows that using the passive voice can have a confusing effect, because the meaning of the sentence can be clouded when the intent is to avoid having the actor take responsibility for the action in the sentence.

*I spilled the milk.*   This is the active voice, and the event is clear.

*The milk got spilled.*   This is the passive voice, and it is not clear how the milk spilled. There is no actor in this sentence, only an object of the action.

What is understandable in a child is not always acceptable for an adult. When a scandal erupts in government, it is not acceptable for those in charge to say "Mistakes were made." As in the child's excuse, this sentence has no actor. It is an incorrect use of the passive voice. Only use the passive voice if there is a good reason to focus on the receiver of the action. If there is not such a good reason, then use the active voice, and say who spilled the milk or who made the mistakes.

## REVISION ACTIVITIES: NATALIE'S SECOND DRAFT

After her essay was reviewed, Natalie could see that she needed to focus more on the assigned topic of the environment. She learned that her experience gave her special information on people whose lives are disrupted as the laws protecting the environment are enacted. As she got a clear focus on what she wanted to say, many of the previous sentence problems disappeared.

### *Natalie's Essay (Draft 2)*

One of the most important issues in the area of ecology is rain forest destruction. Many people think of this in terms of the destruction of the Amazon Basin forests, but I would like to discuss the destruction of the temperate rainforests of the Pacific Northwest.

The ecosystem of the Pacific Northwest is unique. The huge conifers, Douglas firs, and redwoods, among others, that dominate the forests of the Northwest are found in very few places on earth. They are part of a very rich habitat for many animals large and small. They also make very valuable lumber.

Many communities have grown up around the harvesting and milling of this lumber. I was born and grew up in such a community, Elkton, Oregon. Elkton is a small, quiet town where I grew up leading a happy, safe, small-town childhood that many urban people might envy.

The end of this rural life was directly related to environmental controversy. The mill where my father worked closed due to scarcity of logs. Timber sales that might have kept the mill open were stopped by the Environmental Protection Agency in order to protect the habitat of the northern spotted owl.

There are other endangered species in the Northwest forests. My high school science teacher said that the entire ecosystem of the temperate rainforests is invaluable and has to be preserved. Already a drug called Taxol, which fights certain kinds of cancer, has been found in the bark and needles of the Pacific yew tree. No one knows what other valuable plants may be in the forests.

However, I feel that my life in Elkton and the lives of the other people who lived there and had to leave were also valuable. Except for those who owned stores or worked for the forest service, everyone in Elkton worked at the mill. The cost of living in Elkton was never very high, and many women did not work. My mother did not have a job when we lived there. She was always there when my brother and I got home from school.

My father received job retraining from the federal government. He went to community college in Eugene, Oregon, about 60 miles from Elkton. He was able to commute there, so our lives did not change that much, except we had less money. When he graduated, everything changed.

We moved to Seattle, Washington, so my father could work at an airplane manufacturing company. Seattle is a large city. My life in Seattle is very different from the life I led in Elkton. I have opportunities I would not have had in the small town I left, but I also left many important things behind. The most shocking thing for me was the breakup of my family.

When we had to leave, my brother was finishing his junior year at Elkton High. He was on the school football team and he did very well at football. He also got pretty good grades. My parents talked to his coach and to the principal and everyone felt there was a better chance for him to get a scholarship to go to college if he stayed behind. He lives with the coach and his family and my parents pay his expenses. Even our dog stayed behind with him.

My grandparents, my aunts and uncles, our family friends, everyone is scattered since the mill closed. In Seattle my mother has to work. When I come home I am alone. I wish I knew who to blame for the changes in my life.

My father says it is the fault of the environmentalists. For a long time I agreed with him, but I now think it is not that simple. My science teacher here in Seattle has helped me to see that the harvests of timber from the Northwest have to be curtailed. I do not know if that means that they have to be ended. I think that it is a shame that towns such as Elkton may end up being abandoned. A way has to be found to preserve these communities.

The day I left my home I went out into the backyard alone. Our backyard was very large and shaded by many trees. It backed up the Umpqua River. As I sat there thinking, I looked up to see an elk watching me from across the river. Elk often came to the river to drink, but this one was unusually large and pretty. He was big, a six-point buck. He stared at me for a long time. I think he was saying good-bye. The forest belongs to the elk and the owls, of course. I also think the people of Elkton, Oregon, and so many other communities belong there. I don't know what can be done to change the current economic slump in the timber-dependent Northwest, tourism or harvesting Taxol, but we want to live in the forest, too.

---

**Reviewing Natalie's Essay**

Alone or in small groups, look over Natalie's essay.

1. Has she made her thesis clear?
2. Is her argument balanced?
3. Has she adequately addressed her opposition?
4. How does her sentence structure show increased confidence?

Natalie's second draft is much more focused than her first. She has given her audience enough background information to assist them in understanding why she has chosen this topic for her essay, and she has now connected her ideas with the assignment on the environment. Now Natalie has focused her argument, and her sentences flow together smoothly. There are a variety of sentences reflecting the different points that Natalie wants to make and how important they are to the thesis.

## PARAGRAPH STRUCTURE

As you choose the subjects you want to write on, you will often have more than one reason for your choices. The subject you choose is probably one you have strong feelings about, and the reasons for those feelings will form your thesis, assuming those feelings are based on valid reasoning. Those feelings and the reasons you formed them are the motivation for you to want to communicate with your audience.

If the words we use to express an idea can be compared to the single bricks used in constructing a building, then paragraphs can be compared to the walls of brick that hold the structure together. A single wall protects the building from a single direction. The more walls that are added, the stronger and more complex the building becomes. You can build a wall of three rows of brick, just as you could make a paragraph three sentences long, but neither the wall nor the paragraph would be very complex. Most paragraphs require five to ten sentences to fully develop an idea.

Each paragraph in your essay needs to have a purpose in the development of your argumentative position. That is why the examination of your essay has often involved a paragraph outline that assisted you in reviewing where each idea fit in that development. When a paragraph seems to lose its focus or not accomplish exactly what you intended it to, then you can start asking some questions about the way the sentences in that paragraph work together. Perhaps a paragraph/wall in your argument has some weak spots. You would want a weak wall repaired before you moved into a building. It is a similar expectation that you repair weak paragraphs before handing in an essay for evaluation.

It is important that you have a goal in mind for each paragraph you write as you develop your essay. When you wrote your first draft, you just put ideas down as they came into your mind. When that draft was reviewed, you may have been told about areas that did not seem to fit with your thesis or places where some of your argument was not properly developed. In response to those reviews, you have revised to fine-tune and strengthen your essay. Now, in the final revision, you can analyze some of your argument in a way that it would not have been useful to do when you were first generating ideas to support your position.

### *Sentence Forms and Paragraph Structure*

Your sentence structure should serve to showcase your strongest idea, the one you feel is the most important. This should not be your only idea on the subject, however. You have already learned that besides knowing the reasons why you hold the ideas you do, it is important to understand why others hold the ideas they do. This understanding is the background for your own strongly felt position, and it needs to be included in your argument.

The sentence and paragraph structures you choose help to focus your readers' attention on the ideas that are most important to you. While you may not have stopped to think about this while you wrote your first draft, you have already made some effective choices as you shaped your argument in response to comments made by reviewers. However, now is a good time to do some conscious evaluation of the way sentences and paragraphs are formed to guide readers in the directions chosen by the writer.

When you review the paragraphs in your essay, you can evaluate whether you have organized each paragraph for the best possible development of your idea. If there is an especially effective part of your argument in the middle of your essay, you might consider moving it to the beginning or the end, where it will have maximum impact. Natalie did that with the story of the elk, and it was very effective.

Once you have reviewed the structure of your argument, then you can look at the sentences you have used. You have almost certainly changed some sentences as you adjusted areas that were not as effective as you wished them to be. It is difficult to look at each sentence just by itself, however, because sentences tie together to form a larger idea. That is why paragraphs are set apart by indenting the beginning line five spaces. That indent tells the reader that you are either shifting to a new aspect of your discussion or you are expanding the idea in the previous paragraph.

Whether a writer chooses to present ideas alone, coordinated equally with other ideas, or subordinated to other ideas is controlled by the importance those ideas have in the essay. Attention will be drawn to ideas that stand alone and ideas that have other ideas subordinated to them. The most important ideas should be expressed in this way. The choice of a simple sentence: *The elk said good-bye,* a coordinated sentence, *I moved to Seattle, and I attended the University of Washington,* or a subordinated sentence, *I left my dog in Elkton because he would not have been happy in a city,* is one you must make for the sake of the meaning you want to communicate and not just to add variety to your writing.

The variety has to come logically out of the points you are trying to make. The same is true of paragraphs. Some will be longer and more complicated than others, depending on how much information you have to convey on a specific subject, what you want to focus the readers' attention on first, and how much attention you think should be focused on a particular part of your argument. When you are talking to someone, you know how to organize your words so that the sentences best communicate what you want to say. You cannot see spoken language the way you see written language, however, so you need to give some extra attention to ensure the best possible sentence and paragraph form to convey your position to your audience.

In her first draft, Natalie talked about an elk looking at her from across the river. That same elk is in her second draft, but the paragraph structures are quite different.

**Natalie's first draft**

Before we left I went out by the river to think and say good-bye to the only place I ever lived. Where we lived there were lots of trees, it was never very sunny because of the trees. The back of our lot was the Umpqua River. My uncle, who was young and single and worked for the State Fish and Game would live in our house now. As I sat by the river thinking I looked up and an elk was looking across the river at me. Elk came close to the river sometimes but this one was big, a five or six point buck. It seemed almost as if he was going to say something to me, good-bye maybe.

**Natalie's second draft**

The day I left my home I went out into the backyard alone. Our backyard was very large and shaded by many trees. It backed up the Umpqua River. As I sat there thinking, I looked up to see an elk watching me from across the river. Elk often came to the river to drink, but this one was unusually large and pretty. He was big, a six-point buck. He stared at me for a long time. I think he was saying good-bye. The forest belongs to the elk and the owls, of course. I also think the people of Elkton, Oregon, and so many other communities belong there. I don't know what can be done to change the current economic slump in the timber-dependent Northwest, tourism or harvesting Taxol, but we want to live in the forest too.

The elk was a touching part of Natalie's first draft, and she has not lost that clear emotional appeal in the second. She has, however, taken that moment and built it into her conclusion in a way that strengthens her focus. It seemed like an unrelated part of her first essay, but it did have a connection to what she wanted to tell her audience. If you take a close look at the way the sentences are formed in the two paragraphs, you can see that when Natalie had a better idea of what she wanted to say, her sentences became more complex in a way that guided her audience to her main point. Her experience with the elk was in the middle of her first draft in roughly the chronological order of her story about leaving Elkton, Oregon, to move to Seattle, Washington. In the second draft, she saved the elk for the end and made it part of her conclusion. While she may not have thought it out in just this way, the elk is something almost everyone can respond to, and she understood that it would help her audience to understand some of what she felt about a complicated environmental issue.

An analysis of paragraph structure is a function of the review process, not a function of the beginning draft stage. Worrying about revision-stage evaluations can cause you to become almost paralyzed when you try to write. If you find places where you need to revise a paragraph, that does not mean you are a poor writer. That means you are following the pattern of all writers who are serious about having their writing in the best possible form before giving it to their audience. This revision process allows you to change and strengthen your writing so that you are more likely to convince them of the reasonableness of your argument. There is a time to relax and just put ideas down, and there is a time to focus on revision of those ideas to polish your work.

## *Evaluating Paragraphs*

There are ways to question the purpose of each paragraph that will speed the process of evaluating your essay. If you just read it over, it is possible that you will miss places where the revision of a sentence or two would make a positive difference. When you write your essay, the first drafts are intended to assist you in getting your ideas down in some organized fashion. Now that you have accomplished that, you can begin to do an analysis of what you have done to see if a few changes can improve it even further.

1.   *What do you want each paragraph to accomplish for your audience?* Each paragraph should have a reason for being where it is. You cannot always think about that when you first write your essay, but you can do it once you have gotten this far. If it doesn't seem clear to you why you included one of your paragraphs, go back to a brief sentence outline of your essay and see where the paragraphs fit together. If you know what you want each paragraph to tell your audience, it is much more likely that you will have earned your conclusion by the end of the essay.

2.   *How does this paragraph fit with the one that came before it and the one that follows it?* Paragraphs are the walls that hold your argument together. They must have a clear connection to each other, and there must be a clear connection between the ideas in them. If the ideas in your paragraphs do not seem to fit together, then you need to pay careful attention to providing transitions for your audience.

3.   *What role does this paragraph play in supporting the conclusion?* Each paragraph should provide information that supports the position you have taken in your argument. Even if the paragraph contains interesting information, if that information does not support your conclusion, you need to either make that connection or eliminate the paragraph. Just as Natalie connected the story of the elk with her essay's conclusion, it is often possible to use information that at first might not seem to fit.

You wrote each paragraph because something about the idea in it came to mind as you developed your argument. If you did not let your audience know what brought that particular idea to mind, now is the time to fill in that information.

4. *Which sentences have the key information, support, or persuasion in them?* Each paragraph has key ideas and key sentences. If it does not, you may have a paragraph that needs reorganizing. The main idea does not have to be the first or the last one, but there should be some adjustment of the sentences in the paragraph that helps the audience to know just why you are giving them the information in the paragraph. You do not have to know exactly which sentence is the topic sentence or be able to write down the main idea of the paragraph to know if you have a paragraph that has a single focus. If part of the paragraph seems to be on one topic and part on another, perhaps you should break it into two paragraphs. If they would be two very short paragraphs, consider if you need both of them. If you need to add more information, it would be better to eliminate one of the ideas.

5. *Are there any sentences that do not fit or that seem awkward?* If you have not already done so, read the essay aloud. Do the sentences flow together? Does each sentence sound clear and smooth? Is there some variety to the length and organization of your sentences or are they all about the same? Lack of variety in sentences can make otherwise good writing seem monotonous and boring.

6. *Is the language you have chosen suitable to the purpose of the paragraph?* Word choices are very important to establishing the tone of an argument. If your essay is light and humorous, some slang or less formal phrases would be appropriate. If you wish to convince your audience of the seriousness of your position, however, you must use Standard English.

Even mild profanity will weaken your position, because profanity is a form of emotional appeal rather than reasoning. Profanity might also cause you to lose common ground, because some people object to its use. As a rule, profanity does not belong in argumentative essays intended for a thoughtful audience.

## Sentences and Transitions

If you have problems with transitions in your writing, the problem is one of organization of ideas. When a reviewer writes on your paper "Needs better transition between paragraphs," that indicates that the paper jumps from one idea to the next without any logical connection.

Sticking in words such as *therefore, next, first,* and *however* will not solve the problem in every case. You need to see if there is a better order for the ideas you have in your essay that will make each paragraph connect with the one before and after it. If there does not seem to be an order that will accomplish that, then perhaps you need a new paragraph or two that will make the connections clear for your audience.

You cannot just change sentence forms to make the necessary connections either. Coordinating ideas that are not connected by meaning and subordinating unrelated ideas will not make up for the missing information needed to provide the transition. Natalie could not have made her point using the elk just by forming a coordinating sentence such as: *The elk belongs in the forest, and people have a right to live in the forest too.* Without the extra information she gave about the complex issue of endangered species and the economic implications of reduced harvesting of timber, the coordinated sentence would not seem reasonable.

Usually, the reasons behind the ideas in each paragraph are what is needed for successful transitions. With all the reasons clearly presented, it is easy for the reader to see why you go from one idea to another and why one idea proceeds logically from the one before it.

# Chapter Review

1. How does a thesis guide the sentences in an essay?
2. Why is it important to be able to recognize a preposition?
3. What function does a clear thesis statement perform?
4. What is choppy writing?
5. What is an earned conclusion?

# Chapter *7*

# *Shaping an Argument*

---

Starting from Familiar Ground
Problem Areas in Arguments
Conclusions About Logical Fallacies
Chapter Review

---

## STARTING FROM FAMILIAR GROUND

Many students feel uncertain about their own thinking processes. They have not been able to express themselves in writing very well in the past, and when it comes to defending an argumentative position that they are interested in, they would rather find material to support their position than try to use their own reasoning. This uncertainty forms a large barrier to these students when they begin to write essays.

If you are having a discussion with a group of people, you can ask them questions about why they have come to the conclusions they have. If their background or culture is different from yours, you can adjust your position to consider that. When you write for a thoughtful audience, you cannot sit down with them and make the same kind of assessment.

It is possible, however, to write a clear, convincing essay for this audience without knowing anything more about them. There are certain kinds of information that will be convincing to a thoughtful audience no matter how diverse they may be. Before you can test to see if you are

including this sort of information, you have to know a few things about how a thoughtful audience expects you to present your arguments.

## Induction

One of the ways each of us gathers new information is to put each new experience into a category of similar experiences. After a few related experiences, you learn to anticipate what will happen next and prepare for it. People who ride bicycles don't have to have a car turn into their path very often before they learn to watch carefully to see what nearby automobiles are going to do. A strong experience might make you prepare for a similar one. A small child who is bitten by a dog will possibly be afraid of all dogs, even though the parents take great care to see to it that all the dogs that get close to the child are friendly. Both people on their bicycles and the child who is afraid of dogs are using individual experiences to come to a conclusion about all experiences of the same kind. This kind of reasoning is called "induction."

---

 **Induction** The drawing of a general conclusion from a number of known facts.

---

While you might sympathize with the child and understand the reason for the fear of all dogs, you also know the child has allowed the bad experience of being bitten to force a hasty conclusion. You have been exposed to many dogs, and you know that some are friendly and some are not. By using induction, you have concluded that most dogs are friendly, but you take a few precautions with strange dogs until you are sure. In time, the child will most likely re-evaluate the experience of being bitten and come to the same conclusion.

You can use this understanding about how a series of facts or experiences leads to a conclusion when you write your essays. Known pieces of information lead to an argumentative conclusion by induction. If you carefully present information that supports your thesis position and there is no opposing information to prove your position inaccurate, then you will be able to prove or earn your conclusion.

## Deduction

This form of reasoning looks like the reverse of induction at first. In deduction you have a general piece of information you are sure of and start reasoning from the general to the specific piece of information you want to prove.

> **Deduction**    Reasoning from the known to the unknown or from the general to the particular.

This is an example of the deductive reasoning pattern called a *syllogism:*

> *Major premise:* My cat has white fur.
> *Minor premise:* There is white fur on my bedspread.
> *Conclusion:* My cat has been on my bed.

The conclusion is reasonable only as long as no other animals with white fur are able to get into the house. That is where the deductive premise often runs into trouble: other factors are not considered when the conclusion is drawn. If the thinking of the child that was bitten by the dog is outlined in a syllogism, it would look like this:

> *Major premise:* All dogs have big teeth.
> *Minor premise:* A dog with big teeth bit me.
> *Conclusion:* All dogs are dangerous.

The child did not consider the temperament of the dog, so the conclusion is faulty. When you use any form of a syllogism to support your thesis, you have to carefully take all aspects of the argument into your premise statements.

It is unlikely that you will be using formal syllogisms in the essays you write. Knowing about this form of argument can help you to test a conclusion you want to use for your essay, though. For example, Kevin's conclusion (in Chapter 4) could be tested using a syllogism to see if it seems reasonable. His conclusion was: *Air pollution contributes to heart attacks.* Written as a syllogism, his reasoning looks like this:

> *Major premise:* Air pollution contributes to respiratory problems.
> *Minor premise:* Respiratory problems increase stress on the heart.
> *Conclusion:* Air pollution contributes to heart attacks.

Kevin acquired enough information to support the reasonableness of his conclusion. In his final draft, he supported both his major premise and his minor premise before he asked his audience to accept the conclusion.

## Logic

Both induction and deduction are part of a system of reasoning called *logic*. When you hear someone say in response to a suggested course of action "That's logical," they might not know what induction or deduction is, but whether they know it or not, they are referring to these principles of reason that are formed in logical argument.

---

**Logic**   A way of reasoning or arguing; the way conclusions can be proved valid by using certain principles of evidence.

---

Notice that the definition says that logic is *a* way of reasoning, not *the* way of reasoning. Some groups of people use stories and songs to sort information and then use those stories to convince others. You might hear some people use proverbs as a way of responding to situations needing a solution.

---

**Proverb**   A short, common saying expressing a well-known truth or fact.

---

A mother is using a proverbial saying when she tells her child who is calling another child names, "Honey catches more flies than vinegar." She is, of course, not talking about flies at all. She is telling her child that being pleasant will have better results in life than being unpleasant. The proverbial saying provided a short way of expressing that idea without trying to reason with the child. These sayings are not reasoned argument, but they are usually sensible and accepted as sound thinking.

The reason that argumentative essays in a school setting use logical reasoning instead of proverbial sayings, songs, or stories to support conclusions is that, with a diverse audience, you cannot be sure everyone will be familiar with the same proverbs, stories, and songs that might help you to organize your ideas. The patterns of logic will, however, be clear to everyone no matter what their background.

## Elements of Persuasion

It is a common belief that logic is cold and unfeeling. Indeed, when logic alone is the basis of an attempt to persuade someone, it may fail because the audience feels the writer does not fully understand all the elements of the question at issue. Other components of reasonable persuasion are emotion and ethical considerations. All ideas that are questions at issue are important to people because they affect their emotions or their sense of right and wrong. If you ignore that emotional or ethical connection, you risk losing common ground because those in your audience may think that you are discounting their feelings or their values in the matter.

Feelings are often thought to be opposed to logic, but this is not necessarily the case. When you present an emotional example to support your position, you can often assist your audience in coming to a reasonable (logical) conclusion based on that emotional evidence. In much the same way, almost everyone has a sense of fairness in common, and if you present an example that supports that value, you can also use that example to lead your audience to a reasonable conclusion. These elements have the formal names of "logos" (logic), "ethos" (values), and "pathos" (emotion). Learning how to balance these elements of persuasion will make the process of convincing your audience much easier. Finding a balance of these elements in reasonable persuasion is part of the challenge of constructing an effective argument.

Here is an example of an effective and reasonable ethical and emotional appeal:

> In a country as prosperous as ours, it is not right to allow a system of medical care delivery in which the illness of a family member can cause the economic destruction of the family. An example of this is families with an Alzheimer's disease victim. Often they could care for that person at home if families could get help with at-home care. Instead, people often have to be destitute before they can get help and even then it is often necessary to institutionalize the sick family member before financial help is available. An electrician, approaching retirement, and his wife had this experience with Alzheimer's disease. They were considered too prosperous to receive help because they owned their home and had a retirement income. She was forced into an institution. Her illness undid years of frugality and saving. We need a system of health care that does not punish those who try to take care of themselves and their families.

The relationship of logic, emotional appeal, and ethics is, of course, a much bigger and more complicated field of study than we have presented here. This is a composition text, though, so the information you have now should be enough for you to start organizing reasonable support for your positions as long as you develop an understanding of how to avoid some common problem areas.

# PROBLEM AREAS IN ARGUMENTS

Sometimes people find it difficult to understand the rules of logical argument. There are many instances when the media violate the rules of logic; they often use errors in reasoning called *logical fallacies*.

---

 **Logical fallacies**   Positions taken in argumentative situations that are not reasonable when considered logically.

---

You hear logical fallacies so often that it seems that it must be all right to use the same strategies in your argumentative essays. You must remember that your audience is a thoughtful one and will expect you to avoid these logical errors. Before you can avoid these errors, however, you must have a clear picture of just what they are.

## *Emotional Appeals*

Some element of emotional appeal is usually involved in argument. It is often tempting to use emotional appeals when you strongly believe in a position you have taken, and it adds to that temptation that emotional appeals are such a common occurrence in advertising. When you are exposed to something so regularly, it is easy to believe that the same strategies will work to support your thesis no matter what the facts are.

If you were called and offered a vacation to Europe, absolutely free, you would most likely ask what the person was trying to sell. If you got an envelope in the mail asking you to send money for a pathetic-looking child shown in an enclosed picture, you might ask how much of that money would be spent on that child or similar children.

In both of these cases, you ask logical questions when you are presented with an appeal to your emotions. You may wish you could go to Europe, and you may feel upset that so many children are neglected, but you do not let these emotions overrule your logical responses.

To be effective with a thoughtful audience, emotional appeals must be founded on evidence. Just as you have learned to ask reasonable questions when someone makes an appeal to your emotions, an audience will not accept an emotional appeal that has no support. A thoughtful audience has learned that it is often true that the stronger the emotional appeal, the weaker the logical support is likely to be. Instead of accepting the appeal, your audience may look even more carefully to see what support you give them for accepting it.

## 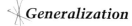Generalization

One of the most serious mistakes that a writer can possibly make in forming an argument is the error called *All Italians love opera*. This sentence can never be true as long as only one Italian dislikes, is neutral about, or is only mildly interested in opera. It might *seem* to be true. Aren't some of the world's great opera houses in Italy? Haven't there been many famous Italian opera stars? Weren't many of the most famous operas written in Italian? All of these things are true; knowing that, it might seem that all Italians must love opera. They do not, though. *Many* Italians may love opera, but that does not make the original statement true or even close to being true.

The statement *All Italians love opera* is a harmless example of overgeneralization. Many overgeneralizations are much more destructive. If all the people in a group were asked to close their eyes and raise their hands if they have ever judged an entire group of people by the actions of a few members of that group, almost every honest person would have a hand up. Racism, sexism, religious prejudice, and many other destructive patterns of thinking are often rooted in overgeneralization.

## Appeal to Popularity (Ad Populum)

One method advertisers often use is saying that many other people have purchased the same product, that all good Americans have such a product, or that pretty women or handsome men will like you better if you have one. These messages are not always spoken, of course. Pictures often carry the message, but, however it is conveyed, it is an appeal that has nothing to do with the quality of the product itself. No one wants to be different from others, unpatriotic, or unattractive. If you stop to think about it, you know that the things you buy do not solve any of those problems, but advertisers do not want you to stop and think about it.

A thoughtful audience will know that if you tell them something must be all right because "everyone" does it, you are asking them to believe that large numbers of people cannot be wrong. A large number of people supported Hitler, and they were profoundly wrong. A very large number of people can vote for a particular candidate without proving that that candidate is a great leader. The only thing proved by a large number of voters is that the candidate was better liked than the opposing candidates.

### Doubtful Cause (Post Hoc, Ergo Propter Hoc)

Imagine you went to a political rally and heard the speaker say,

"Since my opponent, Mayor Jones, has been in office, crime in our city has gone up by ten percent."

Whom would you be inclined to vote for? What exactly has been said about Mayor Jones? The speaker has not offered any evidence that the mayor is responsible for the rise in the crime rate. It is very possible that Mayor Jones has done everything possible to combat crime and that the crime rate might have gone up twice as much with another mayor. In a *doubtful cause* argument, facts are put together in this way in an attempt to get an audience to accept something that has little or no supportive evidence. It might seem to be a good shortcut to link ideas in this way if you are sure that you can prove the connection, but you must prove that connection. If you do not, you are trying to manipulate your audience with a logical fallacy just as Mayor Jones's opponent did.

### Slippery Slope

A *slippery slope* logical problem is related to doubtful cause. If the speaker in the doubtful cause argument decided the audience was believing that the 10 percent rise in the crime rate was Mayor Jones's fault, then the doubtful argument might continue something like this:

"If you vote for Mayor Jones, crime will continue to rise, the police will be helpless, and none of us will be safe in our beds at night."

This is the slippery slope argument: one doubtful cause argument leading to another doubtful cause argument until some terrible, doubtful conclusion is reached. Usually the conclusion predicted is unpleasant enough that any reasonable person would want to avoid it, and the presenter of the slippery slope is counting on just that reaction to keep the audience from looking too closely for evidence that the argument is accurate or valid. The politician who presented the doubtful cause and slippery slope arguments against Mayor Jones was also presenting an emotional appeal. Almost everyone is upset about crime, and if the audience could be swayed into believing that Mayor Jones could not reduce crime, the opponent could possibly win the election.

## Either/Or Dilemma

Have you ever seen or been involved in a quarrel where you heard something like this:

"I don't want you to go out with your friends tonight. I want you to go to the show with me!"

"But I told them I would spend the evening with them. We haven't seen each other for a long time."

"If you go out with your friends tonight, then you don't love me!"

"That has nothing to do with it!"

This is an example of an *either/or dilemma*, trying to force an audience into a choice that they do not have to make. Writers sometimes tell their readers that they must agree with the writer's thesis or accept the ideas of the opponents. This is not true. Not all decisions have to be either/or, and there may be a wide range of opinions. The readers might have their own opinions, or they may not accept any of the ideas presented so far.

If you are going to present your readers with a dilemma, make sure that it is a real situation where one problem is going to have a specific result. Be very careful about using either/or dilemmas because in most situations there are more than two options.

## Personal Attack (Ad Hominem)

It may happen that you find you are unable to defend a thesis you want to write or speak about. Your opponent may be able to counter all your arguments. No matter how much your emotions get involved, it cannot make your argument more reasonable to say negative things about your opponent, even if those negative things happen to be true.

Take, for example, a person who has been dating the same person exclusively for quite a while. This person has to study and so says "no" to a chance to go to a film with the regular date. Later, the student takes a break from studying and goes out for a walk. While passing the theater, the student notices the regular date entering the theater with another person! They seem to be very friendly. The next day, this conversation occurs:

*Student:* "Were you out on a date with someone else last night?"

*Regular date:* "You were spying on me!"

The regular date has not answered the student's question but resorted to a personal attack instead. You cannot, in logical argument, use such strategies to defend your position. A personal attack may allow the regular date to avoid answering the student's question by starting a new argument, but a thoughtful audience will not allow itself to be distracted from the thesis in this fashion.

### Straw Man

When considering problems such as the environment, it is sometimes tempting to wish that a simple answer could be found that would take care of all parts of the problem at the same time. This is just not possible, however. Complex problems almost never have simple solutions, and it will take many kinds of changes in human behavior to solve all the problems occurring in the Earth's environment.

Many centuries ago, people had a ceremony where they symbolically took the evils of the community, gave them to an animal, and then drove the animal out into the wilderness to rid the community of the evils. This animal was known as a *scapegoat*. Other groups of people built a person of straw, had the same kind of ceremony transferring whatever trouble they wanted to be rid of, then burned the straw image.

The logical error of focusing on a person or group of people to blame for some complex problem instead of looking at the actual situation is called using a scapegoat or *straw man*. Many terrible things have happened because of this search for simple answers to complicated problems. The best example is Hitler blaming the Jewish people for the problems Germany faced after World War I. Hitler is dead, but this kind of thinking is still very common. When forming argumentative essays, you must take care not to oversimplify either the problem or the solution to your question at issue or you will be using the straw man logical fallacy. A thoughtful audience will be looking carefully to see what support you give for your position, and straw man fallacies do not have such support.

### Appeal to Tradition

Everything changes over time. Still, it is natural to expect things to continue as you have known them during your lifetime. Almost every family has traditional ways of conducting holiday dinners, for example, and those traditions become an expected part of the holiday. Certain foods, fancy dishware, or a pattern of sitting at the table add to the sense of this being a special occasion. However, these traditions, important as they may be, are not the same as logical reasons for doing things in certain ways.

Dr. Martin Luther King, Jr., led a movement that changed the traditional ways that African-Americans were treated in this country when many people said it was just too big a change to be accomplished in one lifetime. Earlier reformers such as Florence Nightingale and Louis Pasteur met resistance when they tried to change the world of medicine because their methods were not according to the traditional ways of treating illnesses. In each of these cases, once people got used to the new ways, they could see that the traditions needed to change.

That something has been done a certain way for a long time only shows that there is a pattern in the behavior of people in that specific area. It does not prove that the behavior is reasonable or efficient.

## Authority

When you were little, you had to obey the adults in your life to be safe. Sometimes it was hard to understand adult reasoning:

> "I want to play ball in the street."
> "No, you might get hit by a car."
> "I'll be careful."
> "No! You cannot play in the street. It's too dangerous."

As you grew older, you began to understand why adults forbid certain behaviors for children. You no longer accept authority without question, but you try to figure out why certain things are dangerous or wrong.

It is the same with your readers. They will accept an authority that can provide evidence to support the reasons behind the rules or the claims. Sometimes, however, people try to present themselves as authorities when they do not have enough evidence to support that claim. If you use some authority to support your thesis, be sure to let your audience know why they should accept that person's information as true. An authority is almost the same as an expert. Authorities and experts have to be known and recognized before they can provide good support for your thesis. If you feel your audience lacks knowledge of the authority you want to use, give them the information that they need in order to believe that the authority can supply accurate information.

## Two Wrongs Make a Right

When someone does something to you that you see as wrong or unfair, the first impulse is usually to "get even" for the offense. It is a very human reaction that springs from the emotions connected to being treated unfairly. The newspapers often report the extreme reactions of frustrated drivers who ram their cars into other cars, assault people, or even shoot others when they feel crowded by another driver. Most of us see these behaviors as extreme and unreasonable, but we also understand the emotions that caused them.

This logical problem is called *two wrongs make a right*. You know that it is not appropriate to physically attack someone who cuts your car off on the freeway, but you might not think it is inappropriate to lie to a person who has lied to you. The pattern of response is exactly the same. In both cases, someone did something wrong and another person reacted with the same wrong behavior, or another just as wrong. The result of this kind of thinking is that there are two problems instead of just one. Engaging in irrational or inappropriate behavior in response to an injury does not either prevent a repetition of the injury or correct it.

## CONCLUSIONS ABOUT LOGICAL FALLACIES

The reason you found so many of the examples of logical fallacies to be familiar is that you see and hear them everyday. They are used so often because they work. Logical fallacies have been proven over and over to be an effective way of persuading people to change their behavior in a variety of ways. The emotional part of logical fallacies often causes people to accept them even when they might suspect the logic is not sound. People sometimes choose to accept unsound, persuasive arguments, just as dieters often choose to believe weight loss advertisements because they *want* to believe there is an easy way to lose weight.

Sometimes people will refuse to recognize a logical fallacy even when it is exposed. Most people dislike being wrong, and the dislike is even stronger when they must admit being wrong about something they wanted to believe. This often happens when people are not sure whose word they can trust on an issue. Uncertainty will often cause people to look for someone who seems to offer a solution, because to be unsure is an uncomfortable feeling.

Logical argument can reduce uncertainty, but the person who looks for logical support for argument must be willing to keep an open mind until there is enough evidence for a reasonable conclusion. Keeping an open mind in emotionally charged questions at issue is often difficult, and it requires that the person be really interested in finding out which position has the best support. In other words, you must be willing to set aside your emotions on an issue until you have some real evidence to support those emotions.

Most people would find it difficult or impossible to be completely logical all the time. If you do not like liver, all the reasonable arguments in the world about how good it is for you will not make you like it any better. However, the role of education is to help people to reach a better understanding of themselves and the world around them. Better understandings require facts. In educational settings, people learn to use logic as a means of communication, because logic allows you to be sure that the findings of an expert are trustworthy. You can then use their conclusions to discover new findings of your own.

Because new knowledge cannot be discovered using logical fallacies, it is important that students learn to recognize and avoid them. It will become clear as you work with logical argument that it works best in the long run. Fallacies always expose themselves over time. Eventually, even the most determined dieter will learn by experience that the only way to keep weight off is to permanently reduce the number of calories eaten, to exercise regularly to burn more calories, or a combination of both. All the attractive advertising in the world will not change that reality.

### Practice in Identifying Logical Fallacies

The following political speech contains a variety of logical fallacies. Identify the sentences and name the fallacy. Remember that some statements may contain more than one fallacy.

Mayor Jones is the wrong candidate for governor. Since Mayor Jones has been in office, there has been a forest fire and an earthquake. Before she was mayor, there had never been an earthquake in this entire state. Is this the kind of person you want for your governor? After the earthquake, when there was looting in the ruins, Mayor Jones called the state police to help restore order. No other mayor ever needed the state police to restore order in their city after an earthquake. Is this the kind of person you want for your governor? Also, Mayor Jones colors her hair. How can you trust a person who would do such a thing to be honest with the voters? This is an example of how manipulative women are. Do you want a manipulative woman for your next governor? If you elect a woman governor, she will fill the state house with women, gays and lesbians, and other riffraff. The next thing you know, wild, emotional people will take over the state government, and decent people will be driven out.

It is true that I, Governor Smith, have been governor during the most scandal-plagued administration in the history of the state, but that proves I should be reelected! I am the only candidate who understands scandal. Mayor Jones knows nothing about scandal! Since I have been found diverting funds from the state coffers, I should be reelected because I should be held responsible for cleaning up the mess. Also, I should be put back in office because I know how to be governor. How could Mayor Jones know how to do that? She has never been a governor in her life. Remember, all my problems in office were caused by the press. If those vultures hadn't printed all that depressing news about me robbing the state treasury, everyone would like me.

The following essay has a clear argumentative position: The administrators at the Warren G. Harding School censored Matthew Rabel and his friends because they disagreed with their opinions. In the essay, Rabel responds in a variety of ways to the administrators' attempts to control students' activities. The censorship changed the school environment for him and for others in ways not anticipated by school officials. As you read, try to put yourself in this student's place. Would your responses be similar, or do you agree with the administrators? Do you believe Rabel supports his position?

## The Call for Change

### Matthew Rabel

For the second two years of my high school career, I changed to a small private school of about one hundred and eighty people called the Warren G. Harding School. In some aspects, this was a dreadful idea, but I ended up being more aware of my own opinions and more apt to voice them because of it. It was in my junior year that an underground paper, not necessarily a newspaper, began to circulate. It was entitled "The Call," symbolizing the call for information, the call for organization, and most of all, the call for change. This biweekly chronicle brought up issues of censorship, challenged many rules in our fair school, and offered ideas of how the student body could deal with those problems. The people of "The Call" got more than they bargained for when the administration began to censor the scripts that spoke out against school policies. At the same time, the administration was getting more than they expected since their attempt at squashing "The Call" gave the writers new issues to talk about and a more highly fueled need to do so. Many examples of censorship unfolded in these two years. In the end, a good number of students had been, or were being, banned from presenting some of their most powerful pieces of art and script. The kids involved knew and recognized the censorship, and we became more deviant because of it.

"The Call" was the work that gave students the most hope for change, but it was not the only work on campus that brought about a confrontation. With the coming of the first few issues of "The Call," any student that showed a friendship with the writers was watched to make sure every action was acceptable. The Readerboard is a glass display case to which only one student had the key. That student, however, was one of those watched students. He was accused of being sexist when a *Weekly World* headline made its way onto the board. The title read, "Women Are Taking over the Planet." When confronted with this accusation, this student responded by laughing and asking, "Who takes the *Weekly World* seriously, anyway?" Obviously, his response questioned the validity of their complaint, but he was still forced to remove the headline.

Other "Call" staff members and "accomplices" were confronted by the administration for their smoking habits. In the student handbook it stated that no students could smoke on campus or on any adjacent property since it would give any passer-by a bad image of the student body. With this rule in mind and the fact that the school had an open campus, two of this "problem group" made their way up a short hill away from the school, but the administration's objections to their smoking persisted. At this point, the administration was not only censoring school behavior but also attempting to restrict what kids did on their own time. The accusing, protesting, and censoring continued throughout the remaining months of the "problem" group's high school career, and through those months, they were more vocal than ever.

This group came to be known as the "core group." The school authorities viewed these students as the center of all the smoking, drinking, and skipping problems that plague any high school. The term "core group" didn't emerge, however, until the end of my junior year when I found myself to be part of it. All of a sudden my writings and art works were found to be too objectionable to be posted in the front hall where student work was displayed upon completion. Three days after its posting, I received a memo from the fourth-grade teacher claiming that my final silk-screen project was giving one of her students nightmares. The piece was not meant to be all that horrifying, especially not to a fourth-grader, but for some unknown reason, a child couldn't rest without the disappearance of my poster.

The work was simple yet powerful. It was made to show some truths of nuclear power and depicted a human face that gradually changed into a skull. I can't imagine how a child as old as a fourth-grader hadn't encountered these images before, especially since my first major project at this school had been of a skeleton standing upright, holding its bleeding heart from falling out of its ribs. Both my teacher and I agreed that the "horrifying" poster was my best piece all term, and when I was forced to remove it, I was filled with a strangely exhilarating desire for vengeance and need to do more work of the same sort. The memo asking me to remove it, by the way, now resides in my dusty, emerald-green scrapbook and marks one of the first milestones of my journeys at the Harding School.

Since I was part of the '91–'92 "core group," I was constantly watched. Some of my projects were banned before they were finished, even when they were not intended to be either objectionable or backstabbing. To my advantage, however, I had the support of many teachers, such as my silk-screen teacher, who encouraged me to persist.

Most of my creative work revolved around dark ideas and concepts, and the administration found this to be good enough reason to ban them. One of the few pieces that actually stayed on the presentation wall was about the same idea as my silk-screen project, a nuclear blast. In this one, however, I added variables to confuse those who were just out to ban me. This work consisted of a series of paintings showing a forest-covered hillside. By the second frame, a glowing orb began to emerge from behind the hill. By the end, the glow had disappeared and all that remained was a bald hillside. This in itself had the administration fooled, but to be safe, I added humor into this work. Since I was a known coffee drinker, I labeled each frame with a delectable type of coffee (Kona, Vienna, French Roast, etc.) except the last one, which had to be the worst kind of coffee around: Folgers. I had made my point that nuclear power is a great thing, especially when it is used strategically, but the final product is quite possibly the worst situation to live in, hence, the addition of Folgers in the final frame. I had also left the administration in the dust since they seemed to think that my work was just about a sunrise, and since coffee and sunrises go hand-in-hand, it just strengthened their idea. I'm still confused, however, about why they thought the sun rises and sets on the same horizon.

Though I had fooled the school, I didn't feel good about my work. It's like when kids lie to their parents so they can go to a party they aren't supposed to be at. The final product never equals the effort it took to get there. Just as the party always seems boring, so did my project. Even though it did give me a good laugh, I felt too confined, as if I wasn't being allowed to express myself. After this experience, I went back to my old style. My old style was fought in the same old ways. The more work I produced, the more I was censored. A few of my future paintings in that same class were taken off the art room walls before they even had the chance to dry. I was enjoying myself again. My work made me happy and occasionally I would get to witness some reactions to it. Unfortunately, I didn't get anything for the scrapbook that term.

During the next term, I was not in any art classes so writing had to suffice. Since my creations in these classes wouldn't be presented anywhere, I had a no-holds-barred kind of attitude. In both my essay class and my poetry class, I wrote on the darker side. Some short stories made certain administrators, to say the least, look like fools and others were of odd deaths and suicides. Of course, some of my poems were directed to my girlfriend, Marie, because I do have a heart, and to her, it gives its undivided attention. When these strange words of love made it into my papers, the teachers said I was making a great turn in my ways. Needless to say, it wasn't a turn, maybe a slight veer. To the majority of my assignments, I got notes saying that my work was well written, but if I needed to talk to anyone, they were there for me. It wasn't until the end of the term that I gained support for my writing style.

My poetry teacher actually came to me about one particular poem that was included in my journal. Strangely enough, he picked my favorite, which, consequently, was the most objectionable. I then decided to further that piece by adding in one of my favorite art forms, photography, and by the end of the third trimester, I had created my best piece ever. The poem explained the life of a man who is too structured, too controlled by an outside variable. In his case, it was his job. It starts by telling the monotonous way he greets each day, from having grainy coffee out of a stained, chipped mug to the way he holds his generic cigarette between two of his most yellowed fingers as he sits in an empty white room. The photographs that accompanied each line of the poem were some of the dreariest and most obscure works I had ever produced, centered around a series of self-torturous and/or unappealing activities. At the end of the poem, the man begins another day, but before he steps down from the porch, he tightens his noose rather than his tie.

After the completion of this project, I left, having finished my final year of high school. I went back and apologized to the few people I felt I may have truly offended. I think I gained some worthwhile knowledge from what the classes were attempting to teach me, but I think "The Call" was the key to my deviance since it clued me into the problems that plague the Harding School. I still have a lot of offensive ideas, but throughout my senior year, I learned to redirect those feelings. I put them into my band where we sang of corruption, our overall resistance to authority, and generally badmouthed the particular folks we found to be censoring us. Needless to say, we had a lot to sing about, especially when we were banned from practicing at school.

### Reviewing Matthew Rabel's Essay

1. Is making undesired behaviors against the rules an effective way to eliminate those behaviors?
2. How does Rabel define deviance?
3. Would you want Rabel in your class if you were a teacher? Why?
4. What message did the school administrators send about creativity?
5. Briefly suggest how the school should have handled the "core group."
6. Was Rabel's "coffee" project more effort than it was worth?
7. Does Rabel support his argument reasonably?
8. What are some ways Rabel might revise his argument to improve it?

# *Chapter Review*

1. Give an example of deductive reasoning.
2. What is a proverbial saying?
3. What are the elements of effective persuasion?
4. Why didn't Rabel feel supported by the staff at his school?
5. Give an example of an overgeneralization.

# Chapter **8**

# *Revising a Draft*

Troubleshooting
Reviewing Your Writing
Common Flaws in Argumentation
Evaluate Writing Strengths
Be Aware of Writing Weaknesses
Punctuation
Chapter Review

## TROUBLESHOOTING

Many people do not take serious care with the revision of a draft. Because of this lack of attention, their finished essays wind up without the effectiveness they could have had. There are some things you can check for at this stage of your writing that will increase your communication with your audience and decrease the possibility of failing to convince your audience of your reasonableness. The more practice you get with writing, the better you will become at it. A large part of writing well is connected to this process of learning to revise your own work.

## REVIEWING YOUR WRITING

Revising a draft is similar to organizing a piece of writing for publication or the final review you will give the materials you use in a job application process. In each case you want the written material to be in the best form possible. While an essay may not have quite the same impact as those two examples, the ability to present a well-organized, error-free body of work is a valuable one with many uses.

Almost all professions involve some written work, ranging from memos to extensive written proposals. You will find yourself writing in a variety of settings after you finish your education. If you have confidence in your ability to write with conciseness and accuracy, this aspect of your profession will be a comfortable one. Those who lack confidence in their ability to write, however, often avoid writing situations. This can severely limit personal and professional growth, and now is the best time for you to avoid having this problem.

It is unfortunate that many people feel anxious about their writing when it can be improved with practice. As you have experienced, first drafts need revision to achieve the best possible effect. The anxiety about writing is seldom that people do not know what they want to communicate. The problem lies in understanding how to revise their drafts with the audience and purpose in mind. The reviewing activities you have participated in so far have increased your abilities in reviewing and revising your own writing. The exercises would be pointless if you learned to revise only when you had others review your work. While you might arrange for someone to review your writing for your other classes, you are going to have to do it yourself in many cases.

Even if you could always have someone review your work, you still have to know what it is you want the material to accomplish and how to effectively revise with that goal in mind. If you do not have that knowledge, you will not be able to assess whether a comment about your writing is valid. The final responsibility is yours. It is not reasonable to tell a professor or a prospective employer that the problems in the written material you handed to them are the fault of the person who inadequately or incorrectly reviewed your writing.

Grammatical and mechanical errors made by writers follow a pattern that reflects the particular rules of language those writers have yet to learn. Perhaps you have seen some of your own grammatical or mechanical errors disappear as you learned how to correctly form sentence patterns. Spell checkers help many people improve their spelling as they see the correct spelling displayed on the same screen near their incorrect spelling.

The same sort of learning pattern applies to the ways people form their arguments in their writing. Just as you have learned which grammatical and mechanical errors you commonly make, you can use the reviewing feedback from your peers and instructor to learn where your writing most often fails to communicate effectively. Each of you supports your arguments differently, and the way you organize your ideas may have some connection to the kinds of errors you most often make in your writing. As you organize your ideas, you will follow a pattern that has a relationship to previous ideas you have organized. The advantage of reviewing exercises is that you learn to identify the ways that the essays written by other people need revising to best convince the audience. Responding to other writers gives you some tools to do the same assessment of your own writing.

Besides the insights you gain from reading what others have written, you also have the comments made by others about your own writing. As the term goes on, you will have several essays that others have read and reviewed, and it is possible that you will see a pattern in the comments that they have given you. While each essay must be revised on its own merits, each revision will teach you things about your individual way of writing.

### *Focus and Organization*

One of the biggest mistakes beginning writers make is to hurry the process of revising. It is very common for students to do a quick scan for mechanical problems such as spelling errors or comma faults before printing the final draft. When people find writing difficult, the relief of getting a draft finished may be strong enough to cause them to forget what their first purpose for writing was. You want to be able to express your ideas with the confidence that others will clearly understand those ideas and how you came to your conclusions. If you do not do a careful revision of your first draft, you risk losing that confident feeling about how well you have supported your argument. The more skilled writers become, the more careful they are about revising their work before giving it to an audience. Unlike talking, you will not be there to answer questions when your audience reads your essay, so you must take care to see that you have made yourself as clear as possible. An effective revision can make the difference between a flawed and unconvincing argument and a clear, reasonable, and persuasive one.

Once you have a draft completed, then you begin the process of checking to adjust areas that do not express your ideas and the support for them clearly. This process is as much a part of writing an essay as organizing a solid thesis statement or avoiding logical fallacies.

### *Essay Structure*

As you review your work, you will do best if you have a systematic approach. Then you will not overlook some key area that needs attention. Some of the steps suggested in the paragraphs that follow will go very quickly as you gain practice with the review process. You will be aware of these aspects of a well-structured argument even as you develop your essays, and the review before the final draft will be a double-check. Still, even professional writers understand the need for review and revision before submitting their writing to an audience. Here are a few methods to use in revising your own work, and, while they are a good idea at any time in the revision process, they are especially effective in the first-draft stage.

1. If you are word processing, print out a copy of your draft.
2. Let the writing sit at least one night before you start to revise. That will allow you to see problem areas that you would not have seen right after you wrote the material.
3. Read the essay aloud to yourself. This sounds too easy to some students, so they skip this step. That is a mistake. You will hear many awkward sentences, mechanical errors, and faulty reasoning areas when you read the essay aloud that you will not catch by reading silently.

Then continue revising your draft by:

1. Writing out your thesis statement.
2. Writing a brief sentence describing the content of each paragraph in the essay.
3. Stating your conclusion in a brief sentence.

When you have finished this, you will have a sentence outline of your essay that will allow you to examine some of its structure in detail. It is often difficult for writers to be objective about their own writing, and this outline will help you avoid that problem by reducing the essay to a skeleton form.

You may want to compare this outline with the planning outline you did when you organized ideas to support your thesis statement. This outline may be quite different. Whether or not it has changed, you can learn a few things about your personal composition style by comparing the two. If they are similar, then you felt comfortable with following the original outline as you wrote out the rough draft.

If the two outlines differ widely, then you changed or added ideas as you wrote. This is very common and is only a problem if the added material does not support the thesis statement. Some people discover new ideas in the process of writing, and sometimes the new ideas are even stronger and more persuasive than the first ones.

## Testing a Thesis Statement

If you have not tested your thesis statement using the guidelines from Chapter 6, it is not too late to do it now. If you decide at this point that the thesis is unclear, you will have to rework it and then make adjustments to your essay, but it is much better to do this than risk failing to support your conclusion. Now is the time to make sure that your argument is clear and convincing. Check back if you need to review exactly what each question is asking.

1.  Is this topic something that is important to me?
2.  Is this topic something my audience will want to know about or is interested in?
3.  Do I have enough information to explain my position thoroughly? Am I willing to take the time to do that?
4.  Do I have the right amount of time and essay length to cover this topic thoroughly?
5.  What is it exactly that I want my audience to conclude from my essay?
6.  Are there knowledgeable people who agree with me? Disagree with me?
7.  What reasons do the people who do not agree with this position give to support their disagreement?
8.  What proofs or evidence do I have to present to my opposition to persuade them of the reasonableness of my position?

When you have finished with the questions concerning the thesis, then you can review your draft with the same questions you have been using for peer reviews. Now that you have gained experience with reviewing writing produced by others, you can use those abilities in reviewing your own writing.

## Summary of Reviewing Guideline Questions

Answering the following questions will help you to take an objective look at your own writing and correct some problems before your essay goes to an audience.

- Does the introduction assist the audience in understanding why they should be interested in the essay topic?
- Does the conclusion have a clear connection to the thesis?
- Is the conclusion earned by the information in the body of the essay?
- Does each paragraph have ideas that relate to the previous paragraph?
- Are the paragraphs in the best order possible?
- Is there enough support for each paragraph to seem reasonable to a thoughtful audience?
- Is there at least one paragraph that addresses the concerns of the opposition on this topic?
- Does each paragraph stay with the topic it started with or do new topics turn up that require new paragraphs?
- Are there statements that offend or irritate you or might have that effect on others?
- Are there any statements concerning questions at issue that have no supportive evidence or proof to back them up?
- Is the audience treated with respect?

Once you have answered these questions, you can go back into the computer and change the areas that are not clear or convincing. If you are not word processing your essay, it still is worth the effort to clear up problem areas rather than risk confusing your audience with a flawed essay.

As you acquire more practice, you will increasingly keep the revision questions in mind as you write. Writing improves with practice. The more you do it, the more comfortable you become. Each time you revise something you have written and correct a problem area, you are less likely to have the same problem in the next writing assignment. The first essay or two you revise may take some time, but you will need less revision time as you become increasingly familiar with the strategies that are involved in producing a well-organized, argumentative essay.

# COMMON FLAWS IN ARGUMENTATION

### Losing Common Ground

Some arguments run into trouble when writers get so involved in presenting what they consider to be the correct view of a question at issue that they forget to maintain common ground with their audience. Any statement that takes a position on a question at issue must be supported with reasons for a thoughtful audience to accept the statement as valid. Otherwise, the writer risks losing common ground with those who may disagree with the position.

### Failing to Address Opposing Arguments

Another common problem that develops in arguments is that the writer forgets to address the valid points made by the opposition. There are reasons for every position taken on a solid question at issue. Sometimes writers think the best way to deal with the opposition is to present the strongest arguments they can and ignore the people who disagree with them. This strategy will fail with a thoughtful audience. What are your reasons for not accepting the positions taken by the opposition? Remember, your goal is to convince your audience that your position is a reasonable one. You do not have to convince them that opposing positions are wrong and that yours is the only correct one.

A good question at issue has reasonable arguments for a variety of positions. If it were clear from the beginning that one position had the strongest reasons for support, the question at issue would be a weak one. The strongest way to address the opposition in an argumentative essay is to identify the strongest points of the opposition and concede that the points are valid. Then it will be possible to shift audience attention to the aspects of the argument that will best support the position you have taken.

### Weak Question at Issue

If all the reasons given for the position taken by the opposing side to your argument are invalid, then the question at issue is not a strong one. It would be common knowledge for that audience that the opposition did not have a valid position. There are people who insist on believing the world is flat in spite of evidence presented by photographs taken in space.

An argument defending the position that the Earth is a sphere would seem to be an easy one to win, but it has a weak question at issue, therefore, the essay would not hold the interest of a thoughtful audience.

### *Forgetting to Give the Audience Key Information*

Just because you know key things that support your position does not mean your audience will assume you have that information. You must carefully check to see if a reasonable audience will have questions about information that you have left out of your essay.

### *Conclusion*

It does not take long to check the various parts of your argument to make sure that it has a clear focus. Often, the addition of a sentence or two of additional information can make a big difference in how reasonable an entire paragraph will look, and this review of your argument's development can assist you in catching such areas before you do your final revision.

## EVALUATE WRITING STRENGTHS

Each writer has areas of strength. You have some aspects of your writing that appeal to an audience with particular effectiveness, and it is to your advantage to know exactly what those strengths are. As the reviewers responded to your essays, they have commented on things they feel you did especially well. It might not seem that these comments have much in common at first, but, if you think about it, you will find things that work together.

For example, perhaps one essay had a positive comment about the way you tied in some of your personal experience to support your thesis, and in the next essay a reviewer praised a story you told about the way a high school classmate handled some aspect of your argument. These two pieces of feedback put together indicate that you have a strength in describing a situation in a way that engages audience attention. In addition, you can isolate aspects of those situations to describe in support of your thesis. This is a positive asset that you can draw on when you organize your ideas for writing. Even essay questions in other classes can often be effectively addressed with these abilities. Since you know you have a strength in descriptions, look for ways to use that strength as you respond to essay questions.

# BE AWARE OF WRITING WEAKNESSES

By this time, you will most likely be aware of the patterns in your writing that most often cause you problems. That awareness is a great strength as you review your own writing in preparation for the final draft. Just scanning an essay to see if any mistakes jump to your attention is not a very effective strategy for reviewing. You made your mistakes because they were in areas where you were not sure of the correct pattern. This is true in both the argumentative structure and the mechanical/grammatical structures. It is unlikely that errors that you made will be obvious to you unless you take some care to check for the specific areas where you know you have weaknesses as a writer.

The reviews that the people who responded to your essay gave you will assist you in learning where you need to pay extra attention when you begin the revision for your final draft. Whether or not the specific suggestions they have offered are ones you wish to use, you should seriously consider that they saw a problem with the area they commented on. As time goes on, you will have several essays that have been reviewed by peers and evaluated by your instructor. Be sure to pay attention to repeated problems you encountered in those essays and check to see that you have not repeated the problem in the one you are currently revising.

# PUNCTUATION

## *Relax!*

The next few pages are going to discuss some of the most-used patterns of sentences that require punctuation, and they will show you how to recognize those patterns. (Other types of punctuation, such as commas and semicolons, are discussed in Chapter 10.) The way you read these pages can make a big difference in how useful they are for you. If you try to memorize everything in the discussions or focus very hard so you can recognize these sentence patterns in your own writing, you may find you are able to remember very little of what you have read when you finish.

Many people have experienced frustration in trying to produce mechanically correct writing. Sometimes frustration can produce a level of stress that makes it impossible to focus on what you are trying to say. This stress makes it almost impossible to write *without* making errors because the rules will change depending on what the sentences are to communicate.

The best way to use this material is to read it over so you understand it. Then, when you begin to revise your essays, refer to the sections that you recognize as problem areas.

---

**Note**

Most people have fewer than five problems with punctuation, and repeated errors involving those five rules make their writing appear to have serious mechanical or grammatical problems.

---

Each person writes in a pattern that is unique. The sentences you form are different in tiny ways from the sentences produced by any other person. If you have a problem with some form of punctuation, that means that you use a certain type of sentence as a comfortable way of expressing the ideas you have, and you never learned the punctuation rules for that type of sentence. It is less a matter of learning the rules than it is a matter of learning to recognize the rule that applies to your sentence. When you say the sentences, you never say them incorrectly. That means you understand the rule of voice change that the punctuation is designed to indicate.

It sounds odd to some people, but the best way to write clear, correct sentences is to think only about what you are trying to tell your audience when you first write the sentences. You cannot decide what punctuation to use or which grammar rules apply to your sentences until you have a clear picture of what you want to tell your audience. Once you have your ideas organized on paper, then is the time to go back and revise so that the grammar rules you use make your ideas as clear as possible to your audience. Revision is the time for a writer to fine-tune sentences so that they come as close as possible to expressing exactly what the writer has to say. Writing is communication, not an exercise in correctness. All grammar rules, including punctuation, are formed to make sure that written communication is as close as it can be to saying the same sentences aloud to your audience. As an example, read the following paragraph.

Today is a beautiful day I think I will go the park I will take my dog and I will throw the Frisbee for her she loves to chase the Frisbee she would chase the Frisbee all afternoon if I let her she has a lot more energy than I do my arm is tired after about half an hour of throwing the Frisbee but Sophie my little dog is just getting started when I am running out of steam.

This is an example of the importance of punctuation. If you try to read the above passage aloud, you will find first that you are running short of breath before you finish. Then you might wonder why the writer is telling you this information. What ideas are the key ones? Depending on how these ideas are punctuated and what words are used to connect or modify some of them, these sentences could have a focus on the lovely day, the dog, or the exercise. Without using the guidelines that grammar provides, the reader of these sentences cannot decide what the writer thought was important when they were written.

Talking came before writing in history just as it does in the lives of people, and punctuation is an attempt to reproduce on the page the voice changes that occur in speech. When you read all the rules that go with various punctuation marks, it can seem like an impossible job to remember them all. You already use the voice changes that punctuation marks represent on paper when you speak, and you already know the majority of the rules. All you have to do is learn to listen to the sentences that you write, and you will often know how to punctuate them correctly.

As you read the following pages, just relax and follow along as the sentence patterns are discussed. Each section is designed to let you put into words some of the things you already know about English patterns of punctuating sentences. When you are finished, remember the parts of the discussion that cover areas where you have had problems in the past. Refer to those discussions when you begin to revise your writing. Soon you will find many of those problem areas are no longer problems.

## *End Punctuation*

Sentences, since they contain separate ideas, are separated from each other on the page as they would be by pauses in speech. This is called *end punctuation.* End punctuation is easy because there are only three types: a period (.), a question mark (?), and an exclamation mark (!). Each type of end punctuation is followed by two spaces when you type or word process to indicate a longer pause than is given to other punctuation marks. There are only three kinds of end punctuation, because in English there are only three ways to end a sentence.

You will find out.
Will you find out?
You will find out!

If you are familiar with speaking English, you will not confuse the meaning of these three sentences. Each sentence would end with a different kind of voice change to indicate the meaning of the idea, and the punctuation indicates that voice change when the sentence is written down.

If we did not have a general agreement on how written language had to look, we would not be sure we understood clearly what written material was trying to communicate to us. When you write, you are working on your ideas and your grammar at the same time. The grammar is just the agreed-upon pattern of putting ideas on paper, instead of the pauses and voice changes that you would use if you were expressing the same ideas in a speech. You may not know the grammar rule, but you do know how to say the sentence correctly.

Read the following sentences aloud:

1.  Look at that car.
2.  Look out!
3.  Take a look at that outfit.
4.  Will you look for it yourself!
5.  Will you look for my pen?

Because you know the rules of spoken language, your voice changes with each sentence. In most end-punctuation errors, there is an element of losing the rhythm of the spoken word.

**Period.**   A period ends most sentences. It marks the end of one idea and the beginning of another. The period is the written indicator of the pause we take between sentences to catch our breath.

**Question mark.**   Question marks indicate the rise in speech tone when questions are asked. Anytime a sentence begins with a verb—*Are you ready? Can you go today? Would he baby-sit tonight?*—you need to check to see if you need a question mark.  Some commands can begin with a verb also—*Close that door*—but you will hear the difference clearly if you read the sentence aloud.

Even questions that have no clear answer end in question marks. Sometimes writers ask questions to make their audience think about an issue: *Why is our environment so polluted?* This kind of question is called a *rhetorical question.*

---

**Rhetorical question.**   A question asked for effect, or to emphasize a point, where the answer is implied in the question itself.

---

It is easy to overuse rhetorical questions, especially in argument. It is usually stronger to make statements rather than ask questions: *Why is our environment so polluted? Our environment is so polluted because . . .* As you can see, the statement requires the writer to add more information, that is why it seems easier to write the question. A thoughtful audience will want to hear that additional information, however, and rhetorical questions will not assist the writer in evading the responsibility of providing it.

**Exclamation mark.**  An exclamation mark is the indicator of a shout. No sentence that a writer would say quietly or calmly should end in an exclamation mark. Tabloid newspapers, such as those you see near grocery-store checkout stands, are full of exclamation marks. They are trying to make everything they write seem important, though it really isn't. Too many exclamation marks give readers the impression that the writer is trying to convince them through creating a false sense of urgency, and a thoughtful audience will resent the deception.

# *C*hapter Review

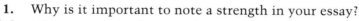

1.  Why is it important to note a strength in your essay?
2.  Why is scanning for mistakes an ineffective strategy?
3.  Why does lack of confidence about your writing have potential for becoming a professional handicap?
4.  What are the common flaws in argument?
5.  Why should you read your paper aloud?

# Chapter *9*

# *Revising with a Computer*

Word Processing
Computer Terminology
Spell Checkers
Grammar Checkers
A Word of Caution
Chapter Review

## WORD PROCESSING

Few products of technology have had as great an impact as the personal computer, or PC, has had on writing. *Word processing* is the term used for writing with a computer. Some students have used word processing since elementary school, while others feel intimidated by computers and continue to use a typewriter or write by hand because it is familiar. Computers have not been available to many students because they were too expensive for home use, and many schools have not been able to provide them in adequate numbers. Some students have had very little experience with computers, so we'll give a brief description here of word processing and how it differs from typing.

The differences between typing and word processing are not clear when you read a page of material, but they are distinctly separate experiences from the viewpoint of the writer. Typing requires practice and manual dexterity to be both fast and accurate. Typing a three-page essay can be the work of two or more hours for an unskilled typist. Because typing is so time-consuming, typed material is often not revised, even when the writer can see flaws. It takes not only discipline to rework typed material but also sufficient time to get it done. Many students find both time and energy lacking when papers are due.

Word processing removes the burden of hours over a keyboard for even weak typists. You can type in the words as fast as you can find the letters on the keyboard without the anxiety of having to retype if you make a mistake. It is possible to go back and make changes whenever spelling, typing, grammar, or other errors are discovered. With word processing, you can insert words or phrases in order to clarify a point in the middle of a sentence or a paragraph anywhere in the essay. Getting your original draft on paper can be much quicker and easier, which gives you more time to work on revision. It is easy to move sentences and paragraphs around to improve the organization of ideas so the first typing of an essay forms the foundation for all revisions of that work. When material is saved on a disk, it can be changed at any time the writer desires.

When people are introduced to using a computer after struggling with a typewriter, the relief and ease of producing neat, accurate written material often significantly reduces the stress of writing. That is why students were urged to become familiar with the computer labs on their campuses early in this book. Not all students can afford to have their own computers, but colleges and universities have made great efforts to make sure that computers are available to every student. They have done this because word processing provides a significant advantage for writers over typing.

Computer labs provide assistance to students for understanding how to operate the computers and word processing programs used in that particular lab. Many facilities have more than one kind of computer, so if you have had some exposure to a certain model, you can probably continue to use that machine. While there may be a fee involved for using the lab, the investment is a sound one for students without another access to a computer. Students with financial restrictions should check with the financial aid and student services departments on their campus. There are often computers with time set aside for student use in departments around campuses. It is also common to have roommates or dorm mates who have computers and are willing to share them with responsible friends.

## COMPUTER TERMINOLOGY

As with all forms of technology, computer users have terms that are so common that those familiar with them tend to assume that everyone knows what they mean. If you have worked with a computer, then this section may not tell you anything new. If you are just getting introduced to computers, this book will not replace the manuals designed to assist you with the specific machine or software you will be using. The terms that follow are in general use and might apply to any brand of computer or word processing software. They are presented to give students a vocabulary of terms to use in suggesting revision strategies. These are *not* all the terms needed to understand computer function and operation, so the computer users reading this list will find many omissions.

**Disk or floppy disk.** Disks are the portable portions of computer memory. Think of a disk as a very small portable filing cabinet. Disks can hold many "files," or pieces of writing, and usually can be "read" on another computer of the same type.

The outside of a disk is covered in a case of heavier material, but inside is a thin sheet of plastic, coated with electronically charged pieces of metal. The computer reads the patterns of the metal arrangements and translates them into information that is then displayed on the monitor screen. This plastic film can be damaged by excessive heat or a magnetic field. Never store disks on a car dashboard, for example, or you risk losing all the information you have stored there when the sun heats them up. They should always be kept at the same temperature that keeps a person in shirtsleeves comfortable. Never put disks on top of a television set or on the computer monitor. The magnetic field there may erase them.

**Saving text.** Saving material is one of the big advantages of using a computer to word process. Once a piece of text is saved, it can quickly and easily be changed in a variety of ways without retyping the whole thing. Learning how to save your work on your own disk should be one of the first things you do as you become familiar with the computer system you are using. It is important to save material on both the regular or working disk and on a backup disk. That way, no accident can cause you to lose the work you have written into the machine.

You could type an entire essay into a computer, revise it, and print it out without saving any of the material on a disk, but to do so reduces the computer to a very complicated typewriter and wastes many of the advantages of word processing. Some computers have memory storage on *hard drives* built into them, where text can be saved without using a disk. This is very convenient, and, if you are using the same computer every time, it is tempting to save on the hard drive instead of saving your work on a disk. Resist the temptation, and *back up* your text on a disk. *Backing up* means having a second source for your computer work if something happens to the material on the hard drive. Even professional computer-users occasionally make mistakes, and hours or days of work can be erased in less than a second. If you have your work saved on a disk, all you will lose in the case of an accident is the material done since you last saved on the disk, not all the work of a term.

Disks can be bought in almost any store that sells calculators and typewriters, and they are not too expensive. As soon as you begin to work with a computer, you should get at least two disks of your own so you can save the work you do. You will need to know the type of computer you will be working on so you can get the right kind of disk. If you are not sure, ask the computer lab assistant or the store clerk which disk you need for the computer you are using. When you buy a disk, it has to be prepared by the computer and the word processing program you are using to store information. Each program uses slightly different instructions, and the disk cannot follow those instructions unless especially prepared to do so. This preparation is called *formatting* or *initializing* the disk.

Another type of saving text is important, also. As you type material into the computer, there is a *save* function that will load your work into the computer memory. Until you *save*, the material you type is only displayed on the screen. If there is a power failure or if your program develops a problem, the work you have done can vanish in an instant. It is easy to get involved in typing and forget to save your material, but you will not work around computers very long before you hear some sad stories from people who have lost hours of work that way. Develop the habit of hitting the *Save* key combinations every time you pause for thought, and you will never regret it.

**Programs.**   Programs are the instructions that tell a computer what to do. There are word processing programs to assist a writer, drafting programs that will draw blueprints, mathematical programs that will write equations, a wide variety of game programs, and so on. Some programs are inexpensive, and others cost hundreds of dollars because they are so complex.

You may have people offer to make you a copy of their program so you can use it when they are not there. Getting copies of programs from friends and acquaintances is not a good idea because you very seldom get the documentation with the programs. The documentation is the written instructions for running the program and detailed explanations of how to solve problems you might encounter with it. Without the documentation, the program will almost certainly be a source of frustration and seldom accomplish all of what it was designed to do for the user.

In most cases, making copies of programs is a violation of copyright laws, and there have been some extensive lawsuits over these violations. The people that write computer programs work a long time to get them perfect. These people deserve to be paid for their work, and the law enforces that right. It is better to buy an inexpensive program than to violate these laws and risk facing the penalties for that illegal activity.

**Viruses.** You may have read about computer viruses in the newspaper. It seems silly to talk about a machine having a virus, but these destructive programs are not funny. There are people who are very skilled with computers and find it amusing to write computer programs that will cause damage when put into someone else's machine. These "virus" programs are hidden within another program, so it is almost impossible to know when you put one in your machine until the "virus" begins to work. Some of these "viruses" are fairly harmless, but many will cause damage to other programs in any machine they "infect," so it is very wise to take precautions against these vandal programs. Just as you need to be careful in other aspects of your life to avoid dangerous infections, you should not take chances with computer viruses, either.

Any time you borrow and use programs used by friends or acquaintances, you risk picking up a virus that could wipe out some of the memory on your computer or even damage files in the "hard drive" (the permanent storage part of the computer). If you use a modem to access bulletin boards or electronic mail, you might consider getting a virus protection program and updating it regularly. These protective programs are designed to identify and erase many viruses before they can do any damage.

The best way to avoid computer viruses is to only use programs in your machine that you have purchased and opened the seal on yourself. The computer lab at your school will have virus protection programs in use to protect the equipment. You can be reasonably confident that your work will be safe if you use the programs provided there.

**Memory.**   This refers to the amount of information a computer can store. Questions asked about how much memory a computer has are most often referring to how much information can be used at one time. Some computers have only enough memory to work with a limited amount of text when the word processing program is activated. Others have more memory and can handle large amounts of material besides the program at one time.

**Monitor.**   This is the display area that looks like a television screen where material is read by the computer operator. You will need some instructions to understand the commands you read on the monitor screen, because each computer program has a different set of commands. They are usually fairly easy to understand once you have been over them a time or two. Most commands are used frequently while writing, so you will learn them quickly.

Some monitor screens can be damaged by being left on with the same picture displayed for too long. Ask if the unit you are using has, or needs, a screen protector program, or "screen saver." This program will change if the display does not shift after a preset amount of time. It would be upsetting to be called away by the telephone and come back to a damaged monitor.

**Hardware.**   The physical parts of the computer such as the keyboard, the printer, and the monitor are called the "hardware."

**Hard copy.**   If you are asked to hard copy something, you are being asked to print it out. While paper might not be hard, it is more physical than the print on the screen.

**Software.**   The programs that tell the computer what to do are called *software.* These are sometimes called *applications* instead of programs.

**Word processing typewriters.**   Word processing typewriters also make writing easier. They allow the writer to easily change typing errors without rewriting the entire paper or using messy correction devices, but the screen is so small that it takes away the advantage of seeing whole paragraphs of text at once. That disadvantage reduces the full range of revision advantages offered by the computer. Still, they are much less expensive than a computer and are a big improvement over the traditional typewriter. Even with the improvements offered by word processing typewriters, however, it is worth making the necessary effort to find access to a computer and, if needed, instructions for using it.

## SPELL CHECKERS

Computer-generated aids such as spell checkers have raised the standard of accuracy expected by instructors at colleges and universities even if they do not require work to be written with a computer. It is not an intentional expectation, but, increasingly, spelling errors are considered to be a matter of carelessness rather than an involuntary error. Because spelling accuracy is so easy with a computer, it will take much of the anxiety out of writing for people who have difficulty with spelling. Spell checkers also pick up typographical errors and highlight them as spelling errors, so those mistakes can be eliminated, too. The computer is a purely logical machine, however, and there are a variety of errors that a spell checker will not be able to correct.

### *Homophones*

One common problem with computer spell checkers is that most of them cannot help you with *homophones*. Some of the programs have a check for some homophones, but there are so many of them in English that most of them have to be checked another way.

A few of the most commonly misused homophones are listed below, but there are many more of them. The important thing to remember is that most people have problems with at least one homophone, and, if you have trouble with more than one of them, you are not alone. It is an easy problem to resolve. Once you discover that you mix up one of these words, write yourself brief sentences using each correctly, similar to the examples given below. If you write the examples on self-stick notes, you can place them in your dictionary, in the front of another reference book you commonly use, or on the wall near where you regularly write. Then, as you write your essay, you can check to see that you have used the correct word.

A way to proof for homophones that takes advantage of the computer's abilities is to use the *Find* or *Search* command that is present in word processing programs. This command will find every example of the requested word. Once the word is highlighted, you can check to see if you have used it correctly. If, for example, you know you have trouble with mixing up *there* and *their*, you can have the computer find every place you use those words, and you can correct the ones you mixed up.

The extra benefit of correcting the errors using the *Find* or *Search* command is that you will make fewer and fewer of these mistakes as time goes on. The repetition of correcting the misuse in your own sentences teaches you how to use the words correctly, just as correcting spelling errors will improve your spelling.

If you have trouble with mixing up any of the homophones listed here, you can highlight the examples or write them out as described above. The main thing to remember is that misusing them and not correcting that error is going to be distracting for your audience. It can make the audience conclude that, since you did not take the time to correct these simple errors, you are not likely to have checked all aspects of your argument, either.

**there:** Meet me over *there.*
**their:** *Their* parties are great.
**they're:** *They're* (they are) throwing another party next weekend.

**theirs:** *Theirs* are the best parties in town.
**there's:** *There's* (there is) no place else to be on Saturday night.

**to:** Throw the ball *to* Terrell.
**too:** He's *too* good to miss the shot.
**two:** He's hit the basket on the last *two* tries.

**its:** The cat licks *its* paw.
**it's:** *It's* (it is) contented.

**your:** *Your* opinion counts.
**you're:** *You're* (you are) in training to be a professional.

**who's:** *Who's* (who is) paying the bill?
**whose:** *Whose* wallet is fattest?

**bare:** I stepped on a thorn with my *bare* foot.
**bear:** The grizzly *bear* looked huge.
**bear:** I cannot *bear* Brussels sprouts.

**no:** There are *no* apples left.
**know:** I *know* my roommate ate them.

**knew:** I *knew* her before she became famous.
**new:** My *new* shoes hurt my feet.

**hole:** The bill really put a *hole* in my budget.
**whole:** The *whole* class did well on the test.

**threw:** He *threw* the ball.
**through:** It went *through* the net.

**here:** *Here* is your pet snake.
**hear:** When you *hear* it hiss, feed it.

**brake:** *Brake* your car before going into a curve.
**break:** Don't *break* the window!

**by:** I went *by* your house on the way home.
**buy:** I want to *buy* a new coat.

The following words are not exact homophones, but their sound is so close that they are often confused:

**weather:** The *weather* is going to be beautiful.
**whether:** I was going to go *whether* it rained or not.

**are:** *Are* you going to the store?
**our:** *Our* cupboards are getting low on food.

**effect:** The *effect* of her entrance was stunning.
**affect:** She *affected* him strangely.

**accept:** I do not *accept* lame excuses.
**except:** I count absences *except* for illness or emergencies.

**than:** Apples have fewer calories *than* pizza.
**then:** She ate and *then* he washed the dishes.

There are many more examples of homophones than these. These are just the ones that are most commonly confused. If you find one that you have trouble with, jot it down on this page so you can refer to it when you proof your essay.

## Right Spelling, Wrong Word

Spell checkers will not highlight a word that is spelled correctly even if it does not make any sense in the sentence. For example, a typographical error can easily make *exiting* out of *exciting*, or *love* out of *live*, and it will not be caught by the computer. The only way to check for this kind of error is to read your work carefully. It helps slow down the reading process and increases the probability that you will pick up the error if you read aloud.

### Proper Nouns

Proper nouns do not follow the spelling patterns of other words, and most computer dictionaries do not list them. You will have to use an encyclopedic dictionary or an encyclopedia to look up the spelling of proper nouns such as the spelling of cities, countries, and the names of famous people. The spell checker will probably highlight your name as misspelled also, unless your name has a word definition. White, Brown, and Smith are examples of names that will not be highlighted by a spell checker. They are in the dictionary with definitions that have nothing to do with their function as names. When you are using proper names in your writing, be sure to double-check the spelling before you print your final draft.

### Specialized Language

Spell checker dictionaries have words that are in general use, but specialized language or technical terms will be highlighted whether or not they are spelled correctly. If the word is not in the program's dictionary, it will be highlighted. There are additional dictionaries for some fields that include this specialized language, and if you are certain of your major, you might consider purchasing a specialized dictionary supplement for your computer. An alternative to buying these programs is to see if your computer lab has them available. Many of the computers available for students have a library of programs that students may check out and use.

### Auxiliary Dictionaries

An easy way to speed checking your spelling is to add frequently used proper nouns and specialized terms to the dictionary's auxiliary dictionary. Spell checkers can add terms to their list and then check them with all the others. Bilingual people can add words in another language as long as the alphabet is the same as English, and the specialized vocabulary used for a particular class can be added to the auxiliary dictionary of your spell checker as well.

## GRAMMAR CHECKERS

Grammar checkers are computer programs that have been designed to highlight words and sentences that may contain common grammatical errors. They will check writing for some departures from Standard English and ask if there should be changes made in the highlighted text. These programs were designed for Standard English users so, while these programs can be useful and educational for either a non-Standard English user or for someone who speaks English as a second language, they are not, by themselves, useful tools for revising and correcting essays. They often do no explain what error the computer is asking you to check for, so they may be more confusing than helpful.

Grammar checkers take a long time to run even on a three- or four-page essay, and many errors will not be highlighted by these program. Problems with subject/verb agreement, errors in punctuation, and words that are spelled correctly but have the wrong meaning for their sentence placement will not be highlighted. Remember that grammar checkers suggest, but they do not tell you what is correct. They note things that *may* be wrong or *may* be improved with changes, but you must decide what best expresses your ideas. The grammar checker may also highlight a sentence that is correct and best communicates the idea you had in mind. You cannot expect a computer program to be a substitute for your own thinking as you organize ideas.

One helpful thing about these computer programs is that they can teach you as they highlight possible errors in your writing. When you recognize an error in a highlighted sentence, you will be less likely to make that error in the future. If your native language is not English or if you are a non-Standard dialect speaker of English, using a grammar checker as a first step of your revising process may be useful for you. Just remember that it is the *first* step and not a substitute for careful proofing. For a clearer idea of what grammar checker programs can and cannot do, look at the errors that are left after both Eric's essay in Chapter 3 and Connie's essay in Chapter 10 are grammar checked.

## Standard English and Language Drift

As with spell checker programs, grammar checkers are mechanical devices that cannot think. They have been programmed to pick up certain departures from Standard English and highlight them. Once the program is written, it cannot adapt to changes that happen in language from that time forward.

All language changes over time. If you have ever looked at anything written in Middle English or Old English, you understand how much our language has changed over the centuries. People sometimes find Shakespeare difficult to read because of the changes in English since he wrote in the sixteenth and seventeenth centuries.

Language changes every year. New words come into common use, and sentence forms that were once common become outdated or practices that were considered errors become acceptable. For example, read these brief paragraphs:

The Cat tried to answer, but became confused. Therefore the Fox said immediately:

"My friend is too modest, and that is why she doesn't speak. I will answer for her. I must tell you that an hour ago we met an old wolf on the road, almost fainting from want of food, who asked alms of us. Not having so much as a fish-bone to give him, what did my friend, who has really the heart of a Caesar, do? She bit off one of her fore paws and threw it to that poor beast that he might appease his hunger."

These paragraphs are taken from a 1916 edition of the fairy tale *Pinocchio, The Tale of a Puppet* by C. Collodi. Can you hear how awkward and formal the sentences sound compared to the language we use today? It seems odd to think that such formal-sounding language was considered appropriate for a children's book a little over seventy-five years ago. If you are interested to see how much language has changed, type the above paragraphs into the computer you use and see what the modern spell checker and grammar checker do with them.

Another thing that can be seen from these paragraphs is that the word choices would not be appropriate for a modern child even if the sentences are technically correct. Some of the words do not seem appropriate for an adult audience, because they are not commonly used today. What does it mean to "ask alms," for example? In addition, would you want to read a story to a small child that included an example of a cat biting off its paw to feed a wolf? Many people today would question this content for a child.

## A WORD OF CAUTION

A computer program cannot help you with the meaning of sentences. It can only tell you if the sentences are technically accurate. While that is often useful to know, it is not the most important part of language. Language is used to communicate, and accuracy alone does not indicate whether the passage has communicated appropriately for your chosen audience.

If you did not test the paragraphs from *Pinocchio* with your spell checker and grammar checker, it will interest you to know that those programs will find very little to change. They are technically correct, but they fail to address a modern audience in many ways. The responses spell checkers and grammar checkers have to these paragraphs demonstrate that you cannot depend on computers to make sure you are communicating well with your chosen audience.

# *Chapter Review*

1. What is a computer virus?
2. What types of words will spell checkers often not highlight?
   a.
   b.
   c.
3. In what ways can a grammar checker be useful?
4. Why is word processing better than typing?
5. What will you do if you are asked to hard copy an essay?
6. What is a homophone?

# Chapter *10*

# *Proofing*

Proofing Strategies

Apostrophe for Possessives and Contractions

Finishing Touches

Revision Activities: Connie's First Draft

Common Comma Errors

Commas in Detail

Revision Activities: Proofing Connie's Sentences and Essay

Chapter Review

## PROOFING STRATEGIES

Almost every task has little finishing touches that make the difference between a job that is done and one that is done well. A holiday meal requires extra attention to trimmings and garnishes to make it special. Painting a house is not complete until the trim is done. The same is true of writing an essay. There are finishing touches that make a difference in how well an essay accomplishes its purpose, and indicate how seriously the writer was interested in presenting the argument convincingly. Small errors scattered throughout the essay may not interfere seriously with audience comprehension, but they indicate a carelessness and lack of attention to detail on the writer's part that can easily be interpreted as indifference to the reading audience and their opinion of the writer's ideas.

By the time an essay is finished, you have worked hard to convince the audience that the essay position is a reasonable one, and that it should be taken seriously. When you do not proofread for problems such as typographical errors, simple comma faults, absent or misplaced capital letters, and similar minor problems, it appears you did not take seriously the obligation to put the argument in the best possible form for the audience. It is unfortunate to see an essay that is otherwise well argued but has clusters of surface errors.

Proofreading is a very different form of reading than just checking your essays for logic and organization. It is easy to overlook minor errors while simply reading the essay. There are several kinds of errors that the computer cannot help you with, such as the wrong word that is spelled correctly. One writer had a problem with typing the word *love* instead of *live. Loving in the country* and *living in the country* have two very different meanings, and the computer will not pick up that typographical error. This kind of mistake needs to be picked up with proofing, or the result is distracting for the audience and possibly embarrassing for the writer.

## Scanning Backward

One quick way to proof for errors is to read from the last sentence of the essay to the first. You will not be reading the sentences for meaning that way, but you will be able to concentrate on each word, patterns of capitalization, and apostrophe use. By now, you are aware of the kinds of surface errors you make frequently. Look for the word patterns where that grammar or punctuation pattern is involved and make sure you made the correct choice. This is also a good time to check for sentence end punctuation and make sure it has not been accidentally left off.

## Reading Aloud

Some pieces of advice sound so simple that it is hard to believe that they are worth listening to, and the instruction to read all work aloud as part of the finishing process can seem like just such simple advice. It works, however. Many grammar errors can be heard when a paper is read aloud. Commas can be placed, for example, by listening for the pause that indicates where they belong in a sentence.

This entire text was read aloud several times while it was in the revision process. Many errors that would not have been caught by the authors were corrected before the editor saw them because we took the time to read the material aloud. Try it. After you do it once or twice, no one will have to tell you to do it again. You will automatically do it to every piece of writing you care about from then on.

## APOSTROPHE FOR POSSESSIVES AND CONTRACTIONS

One error that will not be helped by reading aloud concerns the possessive apostrophe. The possessive apostrophe is used to show belonging, and its use is exclusive to the English language. In Spanish a speaker would say *That book is the book of John.* An English speaker will say *That is John's book.* This English shortcut allows the indication of possession or belonging without restructuring the sentence. The reason this shortcut presents problems is that the apostrophe cannot be heard when said aloud, so the possessive cannot be distinguished from a plural. The possessive apostrophe cannot be avoided, though, even if it is easy to forget when you are writing. The sentence *This is the book of my sister* would be an awkward and unnatural use of English. A writer must develop some strategies for learning when to insert the apostrophe.

1. The neighbors got together to solve the problem of speeding drivers on their street.
2. The neighbors' plan involved taking down license numbers and turning them into the police.

In sentence 1, the group of *neighbors* was discussing their problem. In sentence 2, *neighbors'* is a possessive that modifies *plan.* While the words sound exactly the same, the function is different.

The word *aunt* is usually the noun that names your relationship to the sister or sister-in-law of one of your parents. It could, however, be used to describe another word. For example, *my aunt's house* uses the word *aunt* to describe the house.

The possessive apostrophe turns a noun into a modifier.

---

**Noun**   The name of a person, place, thing, or idea.
**Modifier**   A word that gives information about another word.

---

Since the plural of many words is formed by adding an *s* or an *es* to the end of the word and showing possession usually involves adding *'s* to the end of words, it is easy to confuse them, especially if the possession is not immediately easy to see.

*boss's desk:* one boss and one desk belonging to that boss

*bosses' desks:* plural bosses and their desks

*bosses and desks in a room:* plural of both *boss* and *desk* but no possessive

Not all uses of possessives are as clear-cut as *my aunt's house. Yesterday's news* and *tomorrow's weather* are also possessives, but they are not simple, physical possession. You may have to think about words such as these for a moment before the possessive connection is clear.

### Possessive Pronouns

Pronouns have several forms. Some can be used as subjects, some as objects, and some as possessives. Since possession is already built in to some pronouns *(my, your, yours, his, her, hers, its, our, ours, their, theirs, whose),* they never need possessive apostrophes.

Some possessive pronouns can be confused with certain contractions. Contractions are words that eliminate one or more letters and use an apostrophe in place of the missing letter. An example is the word *o'clock.* It is a contraction of the words *of the clock.* One commonly used type of contraction combines a verb with the word *not* and eliminates the *o* in not. Examples are *do not (don't)* and *is not (isn't).* The apostrophe always appears at the spot where the letter is missing.

The confusion of possessive pronouns and contractions comes from contractions such as *they're, who's,* and *it's. They're* is the contraction for *they are.* It sounds exactly like *their,* a possessive pronoun meaning *belonging to them. Who's* is the contraction of the words *who is.* It has the same sound as the possessive pronoun *whose,* meaning *belonging to whom. Its,* the possessive pronoun meaning *belonging to it,* and the contraction *it's* meaning *it is,* seem to be the most confusing. The following sentences show them used correctly: *See the cat! It's eating its dinner.* Check the list of homophones in Chapter 9 if you are not sure which form of one of these words you need.

## FINISHING TOUCHES

### Capitalization

Capitalization is another part of a sentence that cannot be heard when it is read aloud. It is more common to overcapitalize than to undercapitalize. Some words are so important it seems that they should always have a capital letter, but they don't always require one. There are rules governing what should and should not be capitalized. In his essay about gardening in Chapter 3, Eric capitalizes Scout Troop. This is an error. *Boy Scouts* is capitalized, and that is correct because *Boy Scouts* is the name of one specific organization and no other. *Scout troop* is a more general term that can refer to any number of troops, even if in Eric's mind it only refers to *his* scout troop. You may have to stop and think twice to remember what is and is not a specific organization.

## British English

Many foreign students and immigrants to the United States come from countries of the British Commonwealth or countries who use British English. This creates an extra proofing problem for nonnative speakers who may not even be aware that the rules they learned are not standard in *American* English. For example, the *u* has been removed from the spelling of many American words: *color, neighbor,* and *parlor* are a few examples of such words. Words that end in *re* in British spelling may end in *er* in the United States. Words such as *center* and *theater* are examples of this pattern. The British *plough* is *plow* in the United States. These differences make it especially important for those who learned English under the British system to use a spell checker on their writing until they become familiar with the differences in American spellings.

## Gender-Neutral Language

Earlier in the book there was a discussion about coordinating the parts of the sentence, and it was pointed out that using plural subjects helps to avoid writing *he/she* over and over down the page. You also read why *he* is no longer acceptable as a reference to a word such as *student,* which may refer to either a male or a female.

There are other instances when a writer can include both men and women readers very easily. This is a controversial subject to some. Many jokes are made about "personhole" covers and other awkward changes made to language to avoid the exclusion of women in terms that previously made it sound as if only males were involved. Many of these changes are easier and more comfortable than the jokes indicate, however.

The word *mankind,* for example, is often used to describe the human race. It is often easy to switch to *humanity.* It is not awkward or wordy. Instead of the sentence *Man has always used tools* it is easy to say *People have always used tools.* The second sentence is not uncomfortable, and it is also more accurate than the first. In Chapter 2, Eric had trouble with his description of the police who came to see the garden and the fire fighters who grow vegetables there. He wrote:

The policemen stopped by to see the garden as they drove on their patrols. The firemen had a plot to get vegetables for the meals they cooked at the fire station.

Eric knew it was appropriate to acknowledge the women who work as police officers and fire fighters, because in an earlier sentence he wrote:

Some policemen and women and firemen and women who worked in our neighborhood came and helped on their days off.

He wasn't sure how to do it as a regular pattern however, so he slipped back into the familiar, *policemen/firemen*. It is just as easy to say *"The police stopped . . ."* as *"The police officers stopped . . ."* The same is true of *fire fighters, letter carriers,* and *paper carriers.* All of these designations are as easy to say as the former *firemen, policemen, mailmen,* and *paperboy* designations, and the new ones do not cause the writer to lose common ground with an audience who wishes to have all people recognized for the contributions they make. It also shows that the writer recognizes that many of these designations are the correct, official names for these positions.

## REVISION ACTIVITIES: CONNIE'S FIRST DRAFT

Connie has quite a few mechanical problems with her essay. As you read over her argument, you will see that she has a good topic for her environment paper, but the punctuation and spelling errors interfere with the clear expression of those ideas.

Some of Connie's spelling problems could have been corrected by a spell checker, but others may not have been. If you have Connie's problem with using the correct form of *there, their,* or *they're,* you might look at the spell checker section on homophones in Chapter 9 again.

For the first reading of her essay, focus on the ideas and see if she has included the basics of what she needs for her final draft.

### *Connie's Essay (Draft 1)*

After I graduated from high school I got married. 18 months ago my little boy was born. Now he stays with my mother in law while I go to class. I want to go into the program in early childhood education so I can open a child care center for the children of the field workers in the area.

Since the birth of my baby I have changed my feelings about ecology alot. I was never very interested in it before. I read the <u>San Antonio Star</u>

about the ozone layer but it never seemed important to me. Now that I have the baby though I am concerned about the future and the kind of world he will have to live in.

When I get out of school I drive home and I walk to my inlaws house which is right around the corner from our trailer to get my baby Joey. I bring him home and put him in a sandbox his father made for him. It is in the yard right outside the kitchen window. I go in and make snacks for us and come back out and play with him.

When you read this you may think, what a nice life. What could be wrong their. It is nice and I love the time I spend outside playing with Joey. We have alot of shade in our yard and it is cool even on hot days. I love to see the baby exploring his world and learning things for the first time.

The Rio Grande valley is in an agricultural area. That is about the only thing going on around here. That is not what bothers me though. The farmers spread chemicals to kill weeds and bugs on there fields from airplanes. The fields come right up to the edge of our yard. Even though the planes are very careful not to fly over our trailer I still worry that something will blow near us and hurt the baby. The smell gets really strong sometimes.

I don't know much about the chemicals that are used in the fields around here. They must be poison though. They kill the bugs dont they. They also spray for weeds. It worries me too because I don't know exactly what is in it. Anyway I take the baby inside while they are spraying even if it is hot. I dont want to take any chances.

My husband works as a mechanic for the crop dusting planes. He says I shouldn't worry so much the chemicals wont hurt the baby. He says that the farmers have to use the planes to spread the chemicals. If they hired people to do it by hand he says, they would go broke.

When I was in high school I worked at the child care center at Out Lady of Guadalupe after school. Lots of the children there lived in the migrant housing and played in the fields. They were always sick.

My husband says that I cannot prove that they were sick because of the chemicals. He thinks they were not being fed right by there parents. I know the chemicals caused there parents to have health problems because doctors told them they were hurt by going into the fields to soon or handling the chemicals wrong.

You may think that this does not prove my point. If they handled them correctly they would not have gotten sick. But what I want to know is; if they are safe why do they have to wait 24 hours before going back into the fields?

I worry about all the children who are near the spreying, not just by baby. I saw a program on tv about the San Joaquin valley in California which is a place like the Rio Grande valley. Alot of the kids in some of the little towns there had cancer. Many more than there usually is in towns that size.

I dont know if the chemicals they use there are like the chemicals they use here. Maybe they are worse but now that I have Joey I am worried about all the children who breathe the air near the chemical spreying.

When I am out of school and have my day care I am going to want the kids to play outside. What will I do if they get sick. I do not want to have the kids here if they are going to get sick, also the parents may get angry at me and take there kids away if they get sick while i am taking care of them.

I know their is not anything one person can do to influence the way things have been done for a long time. Also I know that the farmers have to make a living. There farms keep most of the people around here working. Without them there would not be anything for the people here. Everyone in the valley makes there living from the farms one way or another including my husband Joe.

Usually when people think of pollution they think of a big city where there are lots of cars and lots of factories. It is nothing like that here. It seems impossible that there would be any pollution here not like Houston with all the oil refineries. My uncle lives there and I visited him there with my family when I was younger, it is a terrible place with tons of traffic and trash beside the roads.

The spreying is bad though. By now everyone, even way out in the country here knows there is a whole in the ozone layer to large to ignore.

Maybe that is caused partly by the spraying to. Chemicals are bound to float away in the air.

If everyone in the valley got together including the farmers and the other people and talked about the spreying maybe something could be done to make this a better place to raise helthy kids.

I know this is not likely to happen because their are rich people here and their are poor people here and they dont have much in common or know each other.

Alot of people in the valley go to church though and if people met at their churches they could talk to each other and find out how many people here are sick and if they were in the fields at the wrong time or what is the matter.

That would be a beginning and that way everyone would know what all the chemicals are. The science teachers from the schools could help and nurses could come and explain how to do the best to take care of the kids so they wont get sick.

These are my ideas to help the children of the Rio Grande valley, especially the children who are in or near the fields to keep them completely safe from the chemicals that are spreyed on the fields from the crop dusting planes. Maybe other farm areas could do this to and all the children would be safe.

---

**Reviewing Connie's Essay**

1.  Organize a clear thesis statement for Connie using the information she has given in her first draft.
2.  Using that thesis statement, do a planning sentence outline of the paragraphs she could use to support her position.
3.  Indicate what other information, if any, Connie will need to write a persuasive essay on her topic that will seem reasonable to a thoughtful audience.

# COMMON COMMA ERRORS

People don't make only one kind of grammar error when they write because these writing problems are connected to the way people learn to write. Often, grammar is separated into little chunks and taught part by part as if it were a mathematical process. This kind of teaching ignores the fact that all elements of grammar are connected to each other and to what the writer intends to say. The result of teaching grammar separately from these connections is that students come to think of writing as an activity that requires remembering an impossibly long list of rules at the same time they are trying to communicate a message to someone.

Connie's writing is not an unusual response to this conflict between the rules of grammar and a message the writer wants to communicate. She gave up worrying about the grammar rules and just wrote down what she wanted to say. When writers react this way, the result is the kind of flawed essay that Connie produced for her first draft. Now that she has her ideas down, she can go back and revise so that the grammar problems do not interfere with an argument that is clearly important to her.

Many of Connie's punctuation errors could have been corrected if she had read her essay aloud. She got so focused on writing her ideas down that she lost the feeling of how she would say it. Words only form part of the meaning of any sentence. The rest of the meaning comes in the pauses and voice changes that we use when we say the words, and the rules of written grammar tell the reader how the writer intended the sentence to sound. When you read a draft aloud, read a little slower than if you were reading some finished work to a friend. A slower pace will allow many problems to show up more clearly because the rhythm changes in your voice will be more obvious.

Connie seems to have a large number of comma errors, but the majority of her errors fall into three main groups of comma faults.

1.  Interrupting material.
2.  Compound sentences that link two related ideas.
3.  Subordination, or putting less important ideas in a dependent clause.

This is true of most of the errors other people make, too. Once they figure out the small number of patterns where they commonly overlook the punctuation that indicates the way they want the sentence to sound, the problems with commas are dramatically reduced.

Since Connie's sentences have a pattern of comma errors that many people make, let's look at those errors so you can avoid them in your writing.

### *Interrupting Material*

One of the words that Connie uses frequently is *though.* The use of words such as *though, although,* and *however* is the pattern to ensure a smooth flow of thought from one idea to another. These transition words interrupt the main flow of the sentence, but they also tie the present idea to either the one before or the one that comes next. These words provide a smooth, finished quality to the ideas as the readers follow through the essay.

To understand why Connie put these words in her sentences, you must go back to the essay. It does not seem necessary to have these interjections, or added words, when you read the sentence by itself, but they serve a clear function when you read the sentence where Connie put it in her essay.

Because these words interrupt the smooth flow of the sentence, they are set off with commas. If they begin a sentence, the comma will come after the word, if in the middle of a sentence, commas will be on both sides, and, if at the end of a sentence, the comma will be before the word.

> *However,* a waist is a terrible thing to mind.
> A waist, *however,* is a terrible thing to mind.
> A waist is a terrible thing to mind, *however.*

### Compound Sentences

Some ideas are so closely related that it makes them clearer to hook them together even if they are equally important. Connie knew this, and she included this pattern in her writing. She forgot, however, to include the comma that indicates the pause used in speech for this kind of sentence. When sentences are hooked together with conjunctions such as *and* or *but,* those words must be preceded by a comma to indicate the pause used in speech.

---

**Conjunction**   A word that connects other words, phrases, or sentences.

---

If there are two sentences that have ideas that are very closely related, rather than being separate sentences, they can be connected. There are several ways of connecting closely related ideas and each one is suited for a different kind of idea communication. The first two ways of connecting sentences are with the semicolon (;) and with a conjunction.

Both of these ways of connecting sentences work for ideas that are equally important. The semicolon is used as a substitute for a period and makes one sentence out of what could be two sentences. A writer will use a semicolon to stress to the reader that the two ideas are closely related in meaning. Semicolons work only in the place of a conjunction to connect two complete sentences.

> My cat clawed my nylons; I was really angry.

Here is a list of things you cannot do with a semicolon:

1.  You cannot use a semicolon to connect phrases unless both are sentences (subject + predicate = complete thought).
2.  You cannot use a semicolon to set off a word or phrase for drama. You need a full colon for that:

    *It is easy to see what is destroying our environment: waste!*

3.  You cannot use a semicolon to introduce a list. To do that you need a full colon. There is an example of that above this list.

Conjunctions are more flexible than semicolons. Ideas that are equally important are connected by order or by contrast with conjunctions. These are also called *coordinating conjunctions.*

I will go to the store, *and* I will go to the movies, too.
I will go to the store, *but* I will go to the movies, too.
I will go to the store, *or* I will go to the movies.

Notice that each of the conjunctions has a comma before it. That comma is the pause that a reader will give at the end of a sentence, but the pause is not as long as it would be if the sentence was by itself. Since the sentence is connected to another sentence, the pause is shorter. This lets the listener or reader know that the two sentences tie together to make a related idea.

Each of the sentences above changes in meaning depending on the conjunction used. If they were connected with a semicolon, those changes would be left out, and the reader would not understand as much about what connected the two ideas. That is why coordinating conjunctions are used much more frequently than semicolons to link sentences.

The following common coordinating conjunctions connect roughly equivalent ideas or sentences: *and, but, or, nor, for, so, yet.*

## Subordination

Another sentence pattern occurs when the main idea is interrupted with extra information that explains something about that main idea. In the sentences where Connie often fails to put in a comma, the extra information comes before, instead of after, the main idea. Connie chose to give her readers this extra information first because it seemed to her that it made the idea more balanced and complete. Speakers make these choices every time they form a sentence, but when they write the sentence, they must keep an eye on the way the punctuation indicates the pattern. This pattern, which was discussed after Natalie's first draft, in Chapter 6, is called *subordination.* A dependent clause is a phrase that begins with a modifier so that it does not form a complete idea all by itself. The phrases in this paragraph that are in **bold** print are subordinate clauses.

---

**Dependent (or subordinate) clause**    An idea that depends on an independent clause to be a complete idea.
**Subordinate** simply means less important.

---

When you read a sentence aloud, your pauses will indicate where the commas go. Listen to these two sentences:

1.  I still worry that something will blow near us and hurt the baby even though the planes are very careful not to fly over our trailer.
2.  Even though the planes are very careful not to fly over our trailer I still worry that something will blow near us and hurt the baby.

Even though both sentences contain exactly the same information, the arrangement of the information has a slightly different impact on the reader. Which sentence has the missing comma? Why is the comma needed?

Other patterns of adding extra information also use commas to indicate the pause you make when you say the sentence. Connie had one of these sentences almost correct (the words in **bold** print contain errors that will be examined later in this chapter):

By now everyone, even way out in the country here knows there is a **whole** in the ozone layer **to** large to ignore.

She included the first comma after *everyone,* but she forgot the second one after *here.* There is a pause both before and after information that is added in the middle of a sentence like this, so the phrase must have a comma both before and after it.

By now everyone, even way out in the country here, knows there is a *whole* in the ozone layer *to* large to ignore.

You can check for the pattern that indicates subordinate clauses by looking for the beginning word that causes the rest of that phrase to become dependent upon another sentence. This is a very similar activity to learning to identify prepositional phrases that are often subordinate clauses. Here is a list of common words that may indicate a subordinate clause:

| after | although | as | as if | because | before |
|-------|----------|-----|--------|---------|--------|
| even | even | though | how | if | in |
| rather than | since | so that | than | though | unless |
| until | when | where | whether | while | |
| in order that | | | | | |

When Connie learns to identify the comma patterns in interrupting material, compound sentences, and subordinate clauses, she will have eliminated the majority of her comma problems. It seemed as if it were a large problem for her, but she only needs to recognize three sentence types and remember the rules for punctuating them correctly. That is probably the case for you as well. If you have any problems with commas at all, correcting those problems will only require you to learn to recognize those sentence patterns where the comma is required. Keep this in mind while you read over the next discussions of commas.

## COMMAS IN DETAIL

When you talk, you pause for effect at places other than at the end of a sentence. That is why there is punctuation within a sentence as well. Commas, like end punctuation, can often be heard if you read the work you have written out loud *carefully* and *slowly*. You will hear many of the places where you pause within a sentence, and commas belong in those places. People such as Connie often get confused about how to use commas because they do not "listen" to what they are saying to their audience. With a little practice, you will learn to hear the pauses in your sentences that indicate the need for a comma when the sentence is written. It is important to do this because your readers expect to find the rhythms of spoken language indicated with your punctuation (even if they don't realize they expect it).

In the paragraphs that follow, we will discuss some of the uses of commas and how they function in sentences. Remember, you are not trying to memorize all of this. Just follow along and make note of the places where you know you often omit needed commas or add unneeded ones. Then you can refer to those areas when you review your writing to remind yourself of the correct patterns.

### Lists

A very common use of commas is to set off items in a list. If you read the sentence carefully, you will hear the commas when you say the sentence aloud.

I bought apples, tomatoes, and chicken at the store.

The commas keep the listener and the reader from running the items on the list together and getting confused. Some lists are more complicated, but the principle is the same.

I bought spiced apples in a jar, Roma tomatoes for the spaghetti, and a chicken for the casserole when I went to the store.

You can see that the more complex the sentence, the more important it is to include the commas in the right place or you will confuse your audience. They will not be able to be sure where one item on the list ends and the next begins.

## Added Information

When a piece of information is given twice, there is the same need for a pause. This usually occurs when something is said once and then restated in different words.

Mrs. Wong, the art teacher, has a show in a gallery downtown.

Since *Mrs. Wong* and *the art teacher* are the same person, the information is given much like a list to avoid confusion. Remember that in this case the information is set off by commas, not followed by a comma. There is a comma on both sides of the phrase *the art teacher*, to clearly set it aside as an additional piece of information about Mrs. Wong. If a phrase of the same kind were to appear at the end of a sentence, then the comma would come before the phrase.

There is a show in a gallery downtown by Mrs. Wong, the art teacher.

The comma serves to set off words that repeat information about something already identified in the sentence.

## Interjection

When a piece of information is added for effect or for clarity, it is often set off with commas. Some words are added for emotional impact.

Oh dear, I left my book bag in the library.

It is also easy to hear this comma when you say the sentence aloud. It is set off from the real information of the sentence to allow the reader to see in print what can be heard in the spoken sentence.

The same pattern is followed when writing a direct address. A *direct address* is when you use someone's name just as you would if you were talking to that person.

Louise, did you do the wash yet?

If you were speaking to Louise, you would pause after saying her name to give her a chance to respond. The comma records that pause when you write the sentence.

## Punctuation for Meaning

The intended meaning will determine when the comma will come between some modifiers.

He wore a faded, blue hat.
She wore a faded blue hat.

In the first sentence, the hat he wore was both faded and blue. In the second sentence the color of the hat was faded blue. The comma tells the reader which meaning is intended by the sentence.

In these sentences, the placement of the comma indicates whether the speaker is talking about a color (faded blue) or describing the condition and the color of the hat (faded and blue). Both sentences are correct, but they mean different things.

## Compound Subjects and Predicates

Conjunctions that are often mistakenly assigned a comma connect compound subjects and predicates. The way to tell if you have a compound sentence, a compound subject, or a compound predicate is to listen for the pause.

Sarah *and* I will go to the store *and* buy dog food *and* broccoli.

There are three conjunctions in the previous sentence, but none of them is preceded by a comma because they are connecting subjects and predicates. It is not a compound sentence because it does not contain two closely related ideas in complete sentences. It only tells about one thing, the trip to the store. *Buy dog food and broccoli* is not a complete thought, and the sentence could not be divided into two equal halves.

Items in a series or a list will be separated by commas, and there will be a conjunction at the end to tie them all together, but the material after the comma and conjunction will not be a complete sentence.

Sarah will go to the store *and* buy dog food, broccoli, *and* tomato soup.

Several conjunctions can be in the same sentence, but the pauses as you read the sentence will indicate where to place the commas.

Sarah *and* I will go to the store, *and* we will buy dog food, broccoli, *and* tomato soup.

If you read this sentence slowly, you would probably know which conjunction needed a pause and which did not. Even if it seems difficult to "hear" the commas at first, it will get easier with practice. If you "listen" to what you already know, you know where to place the comma when using conjunctions.

# REVISION ACTIVITIES

### *Proofing Connie's Sentences*

To check your knowledge of comma use, look at the following list of Connie's sentences, find the sentence patterns we have discussed, and punctuate the sentences correctly. These are not all the sentences that Connie wrote that contained errors. Connie, like many writers, does not have just one kind of problem with her writing, and trying to correct all problems at once is confusing for both the writer and the editor. It is better to focus on one problem at a time even if you can see others. Do notice, however, how many of Connie's sentences can be corrected by applying the comma rules for three different kinds of sentences. (This list of sentences also contains some spelling or grammar errors, indicated by **bold** print. We will deal with these kinds of errors in the next section.)

1. After I graduated from high school I got married.
2. Now that I have the baby though I am concerned about the future and the kind of a world he will have to live in.
3. When I get out of school I drive home and I walk to my **inlaws** house which is right around the corner from our house to get my baby Joey.
4. We have **alot** of shade in our yard and it is cool even on hot days.
5. That is not what bothers me though.
6. If they hired people to do it by hand he says, they would go broke.

7. If they handled them correctly they would not have gotten sick.

8. **Alot** of people in the valley go to church though and if people met at their churches they could talk to each other and find out how many people here are sick and if they were in the fields at the wrong time or what is the matter.

9. That would be a beginning and that way everyone would know what all the chemicals are.

10. The science teachers from the schools could help and nurses could come and explain how to do the best to take care of the kids so they **wont** get sick.

11. These are my ideas to help the children of the Rio Grande **valley**, especially the children who are in or near the fields to keep them completely safe from the chemicals that are **spreyed** on the fields from the crop dusting planes.

12. Maybe other farm areas could do this **to** and all the children would be safe.

Even though some of Connie's comma faults are corrected, others are still present, and she still has quite a few mechanical problems in what could be an excellent argument on the topic of crop dusting. The mechanical problems are going to seriously distract her audience, and she needs to learn to correct them before she gets to her final draft.

Many students who return to school after some time away bring life experiences that are excellent resources to draw upon, and Connie has collected some solid support for her position. Her examples are clear and reasonable. If she allows the mechanical problems to dominate her assessment of her writing, she will become discouraged. It's important for her to recognize that the correction of these problems is not the monumental task it might seem at first. She does not have a great number of mistakes, just repeated examples of each.

### *Proofing Connie's Essay*

The comments made by the reviewers made Connie decide it was worth the effort to go to the computer lab and word process her essay. Then she used the programs there to spell check and grammar check her essay. But there were still proofing problems in Connie's essay even after she had run the programs.

When Connie went to the lab to use the grammar checker, she discovered that it is much more complicated than the spell checker, because the grammar checker has to do many more functions than the spell checker. Sentence structure, word choice, and punctuation are examples of areas where writers may want help from the grammar checker.

Grammar checkers do not correct errors. They point out places where there might be mistakes. The writer has to decide if the sentences actually have errors in them.

Also, some errors are not caught by the grammar checker. No writer can depend on grammar checkers to take over the responsibility for writing correctly. The grammar checker can help, but it cannot do as much to correct grammar as spell checkers can spelling. Grammar is too complex and too connected to the meaning intended by the writer for a machine to know what to change. Many aspects of grammar are part of the writing process and can only be changed by the writer.

Look at the **bold** print portions of Connie's essay and see if you can identify the nature of the problems that the grammar checker left for the proofing process.

## *Connie's Essay (Draft 2)*

After I graduated from high school, I got married. Eighteen months ago my little boy was born. Now he stays with my **mother in law** while I go to class. **I want to go into the program in early childhood education so I can open a child care center for the children of the field workers in the area.**

Since the birth of my baby I have changed my feelings about ecology a lot. I was never very interested in it before. I read the <u>San Antonio Star</u> about the ozone layer but it never seemed important to me. Now that I have the baby, though, I am concerned about the future and the kind of world he will have to live in.

When I get out of school, I drive home, and I walk to my in-laws' house that is right around the corner from our trailer to get my baby, Joey. I bring him home and put him in a sandbox his father made for him. It is in the yard right outside the kitchen window. I go in and make snacks for us and come back out and play with him.

When you read this you may think 'What a nice life. **What could be wrong there. It is nice and I love the time I spend outside playing with Joey.'** We have a lot of shade in our yard, and it is cool even on hot days. I love to see the baby exploring his world and learning things for the first time.

The **Rio Grande valley** is in an agricultural area. That is about the only thing going on around here. That is not what bothers me, though. The farmers spread chemicals to kill weeds and bugs on their fields from airplanes. The fields come right up to the edge of our yard. **Even though the planes are very careful not to fly over our trailer I still worry that**

**something will blow near us and hurt the baby**. The smell gets really strong sometimes.

I don't know much about the chemicals that are used in the fields around here. **They must be poison though. They kill the bugs don't they.** They also spray for weeds. It worries me, too, because I don't know exactly what is in it. Anyway I take the baby inside while they are spraying even if it is hot. I don't want to take any chances.

My husband works as a mechanic for the crop-dusting planes. **He says I shouldn't worry so much the chemicals wont hurt the baby**. He says that the farmers have to use the planes to spread the chemicals. If they hired people to do it by hand, he says, they would go broke.

**When I was in high school I worked after school at the child care center at Our Lady of Guadeloupe.** Many of the children there lived in the migrant housing and played in the fields. They were always sick.

My husband says that I cannot prove that they were sick because of the chemicals. He thinks they were not being fed right by their parents. I know the chemicals caused **there** parents to have health problems because doctors told them they were hurt by going into the fields **to** soon or handling the chemicals wrong.

You may think that this does not prove my point. If they handled them correctly, they would not have gotten sick. **What I want to know is; if they are safe why do they have to wait 24 hours before going back into the fields?**

I worry about all the children who are near the spraying, not just **by** baby. I saw a program on TV about the **San Joaquin valley** in California that is a place like the **Rio Grande valley.** Many of the kids in some of the little towns there had cancer. Many more than there usually is in towns that size.

I don't know if the chemicals they use there are like the chemicals they use here. **Maybe they are worse but now that I have Joey I am worried about all the children who breathe the air near the chemical spraying.**

**When I am out of school and have my day care I am going to want the kids to play outside.** What will I do if they get sick? **I do not want to have the kids here if they are going to get sick, also the parents may get angry at me and take their kids away if they get sick while I am taking care of them.**

I know there is not anything one person can do to influence the way things have been done for a long time. **Also** I know that the farmers have to make a living. Their farms keep most of the people around here working. Without them, there would not be anything for the people here. **Everyone in the valley makes there living from the farms one way or another including my husband Joe**.

Usually when people think of pollution they think of a big city where there are many cars and factories. It is nothing like that here. It seems impossible that there would be any pollution here not like Houston with all the oil refineries. My uncle lives there and I visited him there with my family when I was younger, it is a terrible place with tons of traffic and trash beside the roads.

The spraying is bad **though**. By now everyone, even way out in the country here knows there is a <u>whole</u> in the ozone layer too large to ignore. Maybe that is caused partly by the spraying **to**. Chemicals are bound to float away in the air.

If everyone in the <u>v</u>alley got together including the farmers and the other people and talked about the spraying maybe something could be done to make this a better place to raise healthy kids.

I know this is not likely to happen because there are rich people here and there are poor people here and they don't have much in common or know each other.

Most of the people in the valley go to church, though, and if people met at their churches, they could talk to each other. They could find out how many people here are sick, if they were in the fields at the wrong time, or what is the matter.

That would be a beginning, and that way everyone would know what all the chemicals are. The science teachers from the schools could help, and nurses could come and explain how to do the best to take care of the kids so they won't get sick.

These are my ideas to help the children of the Rio Grande valley, especially the children who are in or near the fields to keep them completely safe from the chemicals that are sprayed from the crop dusting planes. Maybe other farm areas could do this **to**, and all the children would be safe.

---

## *C*hapter Review

1. How does an apostrophe change a noun?
2. How is proofreading different than reading for meaning?
3. Why is it important for writers not to become discouraged over mechanical errors such as the ones Connie made?
4. What is gender-neutral language?
5. What contractions are often confused with possessives?

Chapter **11**

# Readings for Discussion

"The Ecological Crisis as a Crisis of Character" by Wendell
    Berry

"This Country Was a Lot Better Off When the Indians Were
    Running It" by Vine Deloria, Jr.

"Charlie Sabatier" by John Langston Gwaltney

"Letter from Birmingham Jail" by Martin Luther King, Jr.

"The Equality of Innocence: Washington, D.C." by
    Jonathan Kozol

"English and Good English" by Geoffrey Nunberg

"The Definition and Determination of 'Correct' English" by
    Robert Pooley

"Local News: Reality as Soap Opera" by Elayne Rapping

"C. P. Ellis" by Studs Terkel

"The Beauty Myth" by Naomi Wolf

## The Ecological Crisis as a Crisis of Character

*Wendell Berry*

Wendell Berry is a teacher, an essayist, and a farmer who does not
admire many facets of modern life. He quarrels with many aspects of

consumer culture and technology. Berry worries about the decline of respect for agriculture and deplores our dependence on "expert" advice.

In July of 1975 it was revealed by William Rood in the *Los Angeles Times* that some of our largest and most respected conservation organizations owned stock in the very corporations and industries that have been notorious for their destructiveness and for their indifference to the concerns of conservationists. The Sierra Club, for example, had owned stocks and bonds in Exxon, General Motors, Tenneco, steel companies "having the worst pollution records in the industry," Public Service Company of Colorado, "strip-mining firms with 53 leases covering nearly 180,000 acres and pulp-mill operators cited by environmentalists for their poor water pollution controls."

These investments proved deeply embarrassing once they were made public, but the Club's officers responded as quickly as possible by making appropriate changes in its investment policy. And so if it were only a question of policy, these investments could easily be forgotten, dismissed as aberrations of the sort that inevitably turn up now and again in the workings of organizations. The difficulty is that, although the investments were absurd, they were *not* aberrant; they were perfectly representative of the modern character. These conservation groups were behaving with a very ordinary consistency; they were only doing as organizations what many of their members were, and are, doing as individuals. They were making convenience of enterprises that they knew to be morally, and even practically, indefensible.

We are dealing, then, with an absurdity that is not a quirk or an accident, but is fundamental to our character as a people. The split between what we think and what we do is profound. It is not just possible, it is altogether to be expected, that our society would produce conservationists who invest in strip-mining companies, just as it must inevitably produce asthmatic executives whose industries pollute the air and vice-presidents of pesticide corporations whose children are dying of cancer. And these people will tell you that this is the way the "real world" works. They will pride themselves on their sacrifices for "our standard of living." They will call themselves "practical men" and "hardheaded realists." And they will have their justifications in abundance from intellectuals, college professors, clergymen, politicians. The viciousness of a mentality that can look complacently upon disease as "part of the cost" would be obvious to any child. But this is the "realism" of millions of modern adults.

There is no use pretending that the contradiction between what we think or say and what we do is a limited phenomenon. There is no group of the extra-intelligent or extra-concerned or extra-virtuous that is exempt. I cannot think of any American whom I know or have heard of, who is not contributing in some way to destruction. The reason is simple: to live undestructively in an economy that is overwhelmingly destructive would require of any one of us, or of any small group of us, a great deal more work than we have yet been able to do. How could we divorce ourselves completely and yet responsibly from the technologies and powers that are destroying our planet? The answer is not yet thinkable, and it will not be thinkable for some time—even though there are now groups and families and persons everywhere in the country who have begun the labor of thinking it.

And so we are by no means divided, or readily divisible, into environmental saints and sinners. But there *are* legitimate distinctions that need to be made. These are distinctions of degree and of consciousness. Some people are less destructive than others, and some are more conscious of their destructiveness than others. For some, their involvement in pollution, soil depletion, strip-mining, deforestation, industrial and commercial waste is simply a "practical" compromise, a necessary "reality," the price of modern comfort and convenience. For others, this list of involvements is an agenda for thought and work that will produce remedies.

People who thus set their lives against destruction have necessarily confronted in themselves the absurdity that they have recognized in their society. They have first observed the tendency of modern organizations to perform in opposition to their stated purposes. They have seen governments that exploit and oppress the people they are sworn to serve and protect, medical procedures that produce ill health, schools that preserve ignorance, methods of transportation that, as Ivan Illich says, have "created more distances than they . . . bridge." And they have seen that these public absurdities are, and can be, no more than the aggregate result of private absurdities; the corruption of community has its source in the corruption of character. This realization has become the typical moral crisis of our time. Once our personal connection to what is wrong becomes clear, then we have to choose: we can go on as before, recognizing our dishonesty and living with it the best we can, or we can begin the effort to change the way we think and live.

The disease of the modern character is specialization. Looked at from the standpoint of the social *system*, the aim of specialization may seem desirable enough. The aim is to see that the responsibilities of government, law, medicine, engineering, agriculture, education, etc., are given into the hands of the most skilled, best prepared people. The difficulties do not appear until we look at specialization from the opposite standpoint—that of individual persons. We then begin to see the grotesquery—

indeed, the impossibility—of an idea of community wholeness that divorces itself from any idea of personal wholeness.

The first, and best known, hazard of the specialist system is that it produces specialists—people who are elaborately and expensively trained *to do one thing.* We get into absurdity very quickly here. There are, for instance, educators who have nothing to teach, communicators who have nothing to say, medical doctors skilled at expensive cures for diseases that they have no skill, and no interest, in preventing. More common, and more damaging, are the inventors, manufacturers, and salesmen of devices who have no concern for the possible effects of those devices. Specialization is thus seen to be a way of institutionalizing, justifying, and paying highly for a calamitous disintegration and scattering-out of the various functions of character: workmanship, care, conscience, responsibility.

Even worse, a system of specialization requires the abdication to specialists of various competences and responsibilities that were once personal and universal. Thus, the average—one is tempted to say, the ideal—American citizen now consigns the problem of food production to agriculturists and "agribusiness men," the problems of health to doctors and sanitation experts, the problems of education to school teachers and educators, the problems of conservation to conservationists, and so on. This supposedly fortunate citizen is therefore left with only two concerns: making money and entertaining himself. He earns money, typically, as a specialist, working an eight-hour day at a job for the quality or consequences of which somebody else—or, perhaps more typically, nobody else—will be responsible. And not surprisingly, since he can do so little else for himself, he is even unable to entertain himself, for there exists an enormous industry of exorbitantly expensive specialists whose purpose is to entertain him.

The beneficiary of this regime of specialists ought to be the happiest of mortals—or so we are expected to believe. *All* of his vital concerns are in the hands of certified experts. He is a certified expert himself and as such he earns more money in a year than all his great-grandparents put together. Between stints at his job he has nothing to do but mow his lawn with a sit-down lawn mower, or watch other certified experts on television. At suppertime he may eat a tray of ready-prepared food, which he and his wife (also a certified expert) procure at the cost only of money, transportation, and the pushing of a button. For a few minutes between supper and sleep he may catch a glimpse of his children, who since breakfast have been in the care of education experts, basketball or marching-band experts, or perhaps legal experts.

The fact is, however, that this is probably the most unhappy average citizen in the history of the world. He has not the power to provide himself with anything but money, and his money is inflating like a balloon and drifting away, subject to historical circumstances and the power of other people. From morning to night he does not touch anything that he has produced himself, in which he can take pride. For all his leisure and recreation, he feels bad, he looks bad, he is overweight, his health is poor. His air, water, and food are all known to contain poisons. There is a fair chance that he will die of suffocation. He suspects that his love life is not as fulfilling as other people's. He wishes that he had been born sooner, or later. He does not know why his children are the way they are. He does not understand what they say. He does not care much and does not know why he does not care. He does not know what his wife wants or what he wants. Certain advertisements and pictures in magazines make him suspect that he is basically unattractive. He feels that all his possessions are under threat of pillage. He does not know what he would do if he lost his job, if the economy failed, if the utility companies failed, if the police went on strike, if the truckers went on strike, if his wife left him, if his children ran away, if he should be found to be incurably ill. And for these anxieties, of course, he consults certified experts, who in turn consult certified experts about *their* anxieties.

It is rarely considered that this average citizen is anxious because he *ought* to be—because he still has some gumption that he has not yet given up in deference to the experts. He ought to be anxious, because he is helpless. That he is dependent upon so many specialists, the beneficiary of so much expert help, can only mean that he is a captive, a potential victim. If he lives by the competence of so many other people, then he lives also by their indulgence; his own will and his own reasons to live are made subordinate to the mere tolerance of everybody else. He has *one* chance to live what he conceives to be his life: his own small specialty within a delicate, tense, everywhere-strained system of specialties.

From a public point of view, the specialist system is a failure because, though everything is done by an expert, very little is done well. Our typical industrial or professional product is both ingenious and shoddy. The specialist system fails from a personal point of view because a person who can do only one thing can do virtually nothing for himself. In living in the world by his own will and skill, the stupidest peasant or tribesman is more competent than the most intelligent worker or technician or intellectual in a society of specialists.

What happens under the rule of specialization is that, though society becomes more and more intricate, it has less and less structure. It becomes more and more organized, but less and less orderly. The community disintegrates because it loses the necessary understandings, forms, and enactments of the relations among materials and processes, principles and actions, ideals and realities, past and present, present and future, men and women, body and spirit, city and country, civilization and wilderness, growth and decay, life and death—just as the individual character loses the sense of a responsible involvement in these relations. No longer does human life rise from the earth like a pyramid, broadly and considerately founded upon its sources. Now it scatters itself out in a reckless horizontal sprawl, like a disorderly city whose suburbs and pavements destroy the fields.

The concept of country, homeland, dwelling place becomes simplified as "the environment"—that is, what surrounds us. Once we see our place, our part of the world, as *surrounding* us, we have already made a profound division between it and ourselves. We have given up the understanding—dropped it out of our language and so out of our thought—that we and our country create one another, depend on one another, are literally part of one another; that our land passes in and out of our bodies just as our bodies pass in and out of our land; that as we and our land are part of one another, so all who are living as neighbors here, human and plant and animal, are part of one another, and so cannot possibly flourish alone; that, therefore, our culture must be our response to our place, our culture and our place are images of each other and inseparable from each other, and so neither can be better than the other.

Because by definition they lack any such sense of mutuality or wholeness, our specializations subsist on conflict with one another. The rule is never to cooperate, but rather to follow one's own interest as far as possible. Checks and balances are all applied externally, by opposition, never by self-restraint. Labor, management, the military, the government, etc., never forbear until their excesses arouse enough opposition to *force* them to do so. The good of the whole of Creation, the world and all its creatures together, is never a consideration because it is never thought of; our culture now simply lacks the means for thinking of it.

It is for this reason that none of our basic problems is ever solved. Indeed, it is for this reason that our basic problems are getting worse. The specialists are profiting too well from the assumptions, evidently, to be concerned about cures—just as the myth of imminent cure (by some "breakthrough" of science or technology) is so lucrative and all-justifying as to foreclose any possibility of an interest in prevention. The problems thus become the stock in trade of specialists. The so-called professions survive by endlessly "processing" and talking about problems that they have neither the will nor the competence to solve. The doctor who is interested in disease but not in health is clearly in the same category with the conservationist who invests in the destruction of what he otherwise intends to preserve. They both have the comfort of "job security," but at the cost of ultimate futility.

One of the most troubling characteristics of the specialist mentality is its use of money as a kind of proxy, its willingness to transmute the powers and functions of life into money. "Time is money" is one of its axioms and the source of many evils—among them the waste of both time and money. Akin to the idea that time is money is the concept, less spoken but as commonly assumed, that we may be adequately represented by money. The giving of money has thus become our characteristic virtue.

But to give is not to do. The money is given *in lieu* of action, thought, care, time. And it is no remedy for the fragmentation of character and consciousness that is the consequence of specialization. At the simplest, most practical level, it would be difficult for most of us to give enough in donations to good causes to compensate for, much less remedy, the damage done by the money that is taken from us and used destructively by various agencies of the government and by the corporations that hold us in captive dependence on their products. More important, even if we could give enough to overbalance the official and corporate misuse of our money, we would still not solve the problem: the willingness to be represented by money involves a submission to the modern divisions of character and community. The remedy safeguards the disease.

This has become, to some extent at least, an argument against institutional solutions. Such solutions necessarily fail to solve the problems to which they are addressed because, by definition, they cannot consider the real causes. The only real, practical, hope-giving way to remedy the fragmentation that is the disease of the modern spirit is a small and humble way—a way that a government or agency or organization or institution will never think of, though a *person* may think of it—one must begin in one's own life the private solutions that can only *in turn* become public solutions.

If, for instance, one is aware of the abuses and extortions to which one is subjected as a modern consumer, then one may join an organization of consumers to lobby for consumer-protection legislation. But in joining a consumer organization, one defines oneself as a consumer merely, and a mere consumer is by definition a dependent, at the mercy of the manufacturer and the salesman. If the organization secures the desired legislation, then the consumer becomes the dependent not only of the manufacturer and salesman, but of the agency that enforces the

*(handwritten margin note: unless individuals change, society won't change)*

law, and is at its mercy as well. The law enacted may be a good one, and the enforcers all honest and effective; even so, the consumer will understand that one result of his effort has been to increase the number of people of whom he must beware.

The consumer may proceed to organization and even to legislation by considering only his "rights." And most of the recent talk about consumer protection has had to do with the consumer's rights. Very little indeed has been said about the consumer's responsibilities. It may be that whereas one's rights may be advocated and even "served" by an organization, one's responsibilities cannot. It may be that when one hands one's responsibilities to an organization, one becomes by that divestiture irresponsible. It may be that responsibility is intransigently a personal matter—that a responsibility can be fulfilled or failed, but cannot be got rid of.

If a consumer begins to think and act in consideration of his responsibilities, then he vastly increases his capacities as a person. And he begins to be effective in a different way—a way that is smaller perhaps, and certainly less dramatic, but sounder, and able sooner or later to assume the force of example.

A responsible consumer would be a critical consumer, would refuse to purchase the less good. And he would be a moderate consumer; he would know his needs and would not purchase what he did not need; he would sort among his needs and study to reduce them. These things, of course, have been often said, though in our time they have not been said very loudly and have not been much heeded. In our time the rule among consumers has been to spend money recklessly. People whose governing habit is the relinquishment of power, competence, and responsibility, and whose characteristic suffering is the anxiety of futility, make excellent spenders. They are the ideal consumers. By inducing in them little panics of boredom, powerlessness, sexual failure, mortality, paranoia, they can be made to buy (or vote for) virtually anything that is "attractively packaged." The advertising industry is founded upon this principle.

What has not been often said, because it did not need to be said until fairly recent times, is that the responsible consumer must also be in some way a producer. Out of his own resources and skills, he must be equal to some of his own needs. The household that prepares its own meals in its own kitchen with some intelligent regard for nutritional value, and thus depends on the grocer only for selected raw materials, exercises an influence on the food industry that reaches from the store all the way back to the seedsman. The household that produces some or all of its own food will have a proportionately greater influence. The household that can provide some of its own pleasures will not be helplessly dependent on the entertainment industry, will influence it by not being helplessly dependent on it, and will not support it thoughtlessly out of boredom.

The responsible consumer thus escapes the limits of his own dissatisfaction. He can choose, and exert the influence of his choosing, because he has given himself choices. He is not confined to the negativity of his complaint. He influences the market by his freedom. This is no specialized act, but an act that is substantial and complex, both practically and morally. By making himself responsibly free, a person changes both his life and his surroundings.

It is possible, then, to perceive a critical difference between responsible consumers and consumers who are merely organized. The responsible consumer slips out of the consumer category altogether. He is a responsible consumer incidentally, almost inadvertently; he is a responsible consumer because he lives a responsible life.

The same distinction is to be perceived between organized conservationists and responsible conservationists. (A responsible consumer is, of course, a responsible conservationist.) The conservationists who are merely organized function as specialists who have lost sight of basic connections. Conservation organizations hold stock in exploitive industries because they have no clear perception of, and therefore fail to be responsible for, the connections between what they say and what they do, what they desire and how they live.

The Sierra Club, for instance, defines itself by a slogan which it prints on the flaps of its envelopes. Its aim, according to the slogan, is " . . . to explore, enjoy, and protect the nation's scenic resources . . . " To some extent, the Club's current concerns and attitudes belie this slogan. But there is also a sense in which the slogan defines the limits of organized conservation—some that have been self-imposed, others that are implicit in the nature of organization.

The key word in the slogan is "scenic." As used here, the word is a fossil. It is left over from a time when our comforts and luxuries were accepted simply as the rewards of progress to an ingenious, forward-looking people, when no threat was perceived in urbanization and industrialization, and when conservation was therefore an activity oriented toward vacations. It was "good to get out of the city" for a few weeks or weekends a year, and there was understandable concern that there should remain pleasant places to go. Some of the more adventurous vacationers were even aware of places of unique beauty that would be defaced if they were not set aside and protected. These people were effective in their way and within their limits, and they started the era of wilderness conservation. The results will give us abundant reasons for gratitude as long as we have sense enough to preserve them. But wilderness conservation did little to prepare us either to understand or to oppose the general mayhem of the all-outdoors that the industrial revolution has finally imposed upon us.

Wilderness conservation, we can now see, is specialized conservation. Its specialization is memorialized, in the Sierra Club's slogan, in the word "scenic." A scene is a place "as seen by a viewer." It is a "view." The appreciator of a place perceived as scenic is merely its observer, by implication both different and distant or detached from it. The connoisseur of the scenic has thus placed strict limitations both upon the sort of place he is interested in and upon his relation to it.

But even if the slogan were made to read " . . . to explore, enjoy, and protect the nation's resources . . . ," the most critical concern would still be left out. For while conservationists are exploring, enjoying, and protecting the nation's resources, they are also *using* them. They are drawing their lives from the nation's resources, scenic and unscenic. If the resolve to explore, enjoy, and protect does not create a moral energy that will define and enforce responsible use, then organized conservation will prove ultimately futile. And this, again, will be a failure of character.

Although responsible use may be defined, advocated, and to some extent required by organizations, it cannot be implemented or enacted by them. It cannot be effectively enforced by them. The use of the world is finally a personal matter, and the world can be preserved in health only by the forbearance and care of a multitude of persons. That is, the possibility of the world's health will have to be defined in the characters of persons as clearly and as urgently as the possibility of personal "success" is now so defined. Organizations may promote this sort of forbearance and care, but they cannot provide it.

---

## Review Questions

1.   Why is specialization a problem?
2.   Does expert care always help people?
3.   What was the problem with the Sierra Club investments?
4.   How should organizations such as the Sierra Club invest? Shouldn't they get the best return for their money?
5.   Is it possible to consume as much as you want and still be a conservationist? Give reasons for your answer.

# This Country Was a Lot Better Off Whe the Indians Were Running It

*Vine Deloria, Jr.*

This essay was written during the takeover of Alcatraz by Native Americans in late 1969, but, in his stories of growing up near the Pine Ridge Reservation in South Dakota, Deloria winds up presenting a picture of larger interest.

On November 9, 1969, a contingent of American Indians, led by Adam Nordwall, a Chippewa from Minnesota, and Richard Oakes, a Mohawk from New York, landed on Alcatraz Island in San Francisco Bay and claimed the thirteen-acre rock "by right of discovery." The island had been abandoned six and a half years ago, and although there had been various suggestions concerning its disposal, nothing had been done to make use of the land. Since there are Federal treaties giving some tribes the right to abandoned Federal property within a tribe's original territory, the Indians of the Bay area felt that they could lay claim to the island.

For nearly a year the United Bay Area Council of American Indians, a confederation of urban Indian organizations, had been talking about submitting a bid for the island to use it as a West Coast Indian cultural center and vocational training headquarters. Then, on November 1, the San Francisco American Indian Center burned down. The center had served an estimated thirty thousand Indians in the immediate area and was the focus of activities of the urban Indian community. It became a matter of urgency after that, and as Adam Nordwall said, "It was GO." Another landing on November 20, by nearly one hundred Indians in a swift midnight raid, secured the island.

The new inhabitants have made "the Rock" a focal point symbolic of Indian people. Under extreme difficulty they have worked to begin repairing sanitary facilities and buildings. The population has been largely transient: many people have stopped by, looked the situation over for a few days, then gone home, unwilling to put in the tedious work necessary to make the island support a viable community.

The Alcatraz news stories are somewhat shocking to non-Indians. It is difficult for most Americans to comprehend that there still exists a living community of nearly one million Indians in this country. For many people, Indians have become a species of movie actor periodically dispatched to the Happy Hunting Grounds by John Wayne on the "Late, Late Show." Yet there are some 315 Indian tribal groups in twenty-six states still functioning as quasi-sovereign nations under treaty status; they range from the mammoth Navaho tribe of some 132,000 with sixteen million acres of land to tiny Mission Creek of California with 15 people and a tiny parcel of property. There are over half a million Indians in the cities alone, with the largest concentrations in San Francisco, Los Angeles, Minneapolis, and Chicago.

The take-over of Alcatraz is to many Indian people a demonstration of pride in being Indian and a dignified, yet humorous protest against current conditions existing on the reservations and in the cities. It is this special pride and dignity, the determination to judge life according to one's own values and the unconquerable conviction that the tribes will not die, that has always characterized Indian people as I have known them.

I was born in Martin, a border town on the Pine Ridge Indian Reservation in South Dakota, in the midst of the depression. My father was an Indian missionary who served eighteen chapels on the eastern half of the reservation. In 1934, when I was one, the Indian Reorganization Act was passed, allowing Indian tribes full rights of self-government for the first time since the late 1860s. Ever since those days, when the Sioux had agreed to forsake the life of the hunter for that of the farmer, they had been systematically deprived of any voice in decisions affecting their lives and property. Tribal ceremonies and religious practices were forbidden. The reservation was fully controlled by men in Washington, most of whom had never visited a reservation and felt no urge to do so.

The first years on the reservations were extremely hard for the Sioux. Kept confined behind fences, they were almost wholly dependent upon Government rations for their food supply. Many died of hunger and malnutrition. Game was scarce, and few were allowed to have weapons for fear of another Indian war. In some years there was practically no food available. Other years rations were withheld until the men agreed to farm the tiny pieces of land each family had been given. In desperation many families were forced to eat stray dogs and cats to keep alive.

By World War I, however, many of the Sioux families had developed prosperous ranches. Then the Government stepped in, sold the Indians' cattle for wartime needs, and after the war leased the grazing land to whites, creating wealthy white ranchers and destitute Indian landlords.

With the passage of the Indian Reorganization Act, native ceremonies and practices were given full recognition by Federal authorities. My earliest memories are of trips along dusty roads to Kyle, a small settlement in the heart of the reservation, to attend the dances. Ancient men, veterans of battles even then considered footnotes to the settlement of the West, brought their costumes out of hiding and walked about the grounds gathering the honors they had earned half a century before. They danced as if the intervening fifty years had been a lost weekend from which they had fully recovered. I remember best Dewey Beard, then in his late eighties and a survivor of the Little Bighorn. Even at that late date Dewey was hesitant to speak of the battle for fear of reprisal. There was no doubt, as one watched the people's expressions, that the Sioux had survived their greatest ordeal and were ready to face whatever the future might bring.

In those days the reservation was isolated and unsettled. Dirt roads held the few mail routes together. One could easily get lost in the wild back country as roads turned into cowpaths without so much as a backward glance. Remote settlements such as Buzzard Basin and Cuny Table were nearly inaccessible. In the spring every bridge on the reservation would be washed out with the first rain and would remain out until late summer. But few people cared. Most of the reservation people, traveling by team and wagon, merely forded the creeks and continued their journey, almost contemptuous of the need for bridges.

The most memorable event of my early childhood was visiting Wounded Knee where two hundred Sioux, including women and children, were slaughtered in 1890 by troopers of the Seventh Cavalry in what is believed to have been a delayed act of vengeance for Custer's defeat. The people were simply lined up and shot down much as was allegedly done, according to newspaper reports, at Songmy(also known as My Lai Four, a village in south Vietnam where hundreds of civilians were reportedly shot by American infantrymen in March, 1968). The wounded were left to die in a three-day Dakota blizzard, and when the soldiers returned to the scene after the storm, some were still alive and were saved. The massacre was vividly etched in the minds of many of the older reservation people, but it was difficult to find anyone who wanted to talk about it.

Many times, over the years, my father would point out survivors of the massacre, and people on the reservation always went out of their way to help them. For a long time there was a bill in Congress to pay indemnities to the survivors, but the War Department always insisted that it had been a "battle" to stamp out the Ghost Dance religion among the Sioux. This does not, however, explain bayoneted Indian women and children found miles from the incident.

Strangely enough, the depression was good for Indian reservations, particularly for the people at Pine Ridge. Since their lands had been leased to non-Indians by the Bureau of Indian Affairs, they had only a small rent check and the contempt of those who leased their lands to show for their ownership. But the Federal programs devised to solve the national economic crisis were also made available to Indian people, and there was work available for the first time in the history of the reservations.

The Civilian Conservation Corps (CCC: A Federal agency which hired unemployed young men for public conservation work in the 1930s) set up a camp on the reservation, and many Indians were hired under the program. In the canyons north of Allen, South Dakota, a beautiful buffalo pasture was built by the CCC, and the whole area was transformed into a recreation wonderland. Indians would come from miles around to see the buffalo and leave with a strange look in their eyes. Many times I stood silently watching while old men talked to the buffalo about the old days. They would conclude by singing a song before respectfully departing, their eyes filled with tears and their minds occupied with the memories of other times and places. It was difficult to determine who was the captive—the buffalo fenced in or the Indian fenced out.

While the rest of America suffered from the temporary deprivation of its luxuries, Indian people had a period of prosperity, as it were. Paychecks were regular. Small cattle herds were started; cars were purchased; new clothes and necessities became available. To a people who had struggled along on fifty dollars cash income per year, the CCC was the greatest program ever to come along. The Sioux had climbed from absolute deprivation to mere poverty, and this was the best time the reservation had ever had.

World War II ended this temporary prosperity. The CCC camps were closed, reservation programs were cut to the bone, and social services became virtually non-existent; victory gardens (homeowner's personal gardens cultivated during World War II to increase food production) were suddenly the style, and people began to be aware that a great war was being waged overseas.

The war dispersed the reservation people as nothing ever had. Every day, it seemed, we would be bidding farewell to families as they headed west to work in the defense plants on the Coast.

A great number of Sioux people went west and many of the Sioux on Alcatraz today are their children and relatives. There may now be as many Sioux in California as there are on the reservations in South Dakota because of the great wartime migration.

Those who stayed on the reservation had the war brought directly to their doorstep when they were notified that their sons had to go across seas and fight. Busloads of Sioux boys left the reservation for parts unknown. In many cases even the trip to nearby Martin was a new experience for them, let alone training in Texas, California, or Colorado. There were always going away ceremonies conducted by the older people who admonished the boys to uphold the old tribal tradition and not to fear death. It was not death they feared but living with an unknown people in a distant place.

I was always disappointed with the Government's way of handling Indian servicemen. Indians were simply lost in the shuffle of three million men in uniform. Many boys came home on furlough and feared to return. They were not cowards in any sense of the word, but the loneliness and boredom of stateside duty was crushing their spirits. They spent months without seeing another Indian. If the Government had recruited all-Indian outfits, it would have easily solved this problem and also had the best fighting units in the world at its disposal. I often wonder what an all-Sioux or Apache company, painted and singing its songs, would have done to the morale of élite German panzer units.

After the war Indian veterans straggled back to the reservations and tried to pick up their lives. It was very difficult for them to resume a life of poverty after having seen the affluent outside world. Some spent a few days with the old folks and then left again for the big cities. Over the years they have emerged as leaders of the urban Indian movement. Many of their children are the nationalists of today who are adamant about keeping the reservations they have visited only on vacations. Other veterans stayed on the reservations and entered tribal politics.

The reservations radically changed after the war. During the depression there were about five telephones in Martin. If there was a call for you, the man at the hardware store had to come down to your house and get you to answer it. A couple of years after the war a complete dial system was installed that extended to most of the smaller communities on the reservation. Families that had been hundreds of miles from any form of communication were now only minutes away from a telephone.

Roads were built connecting the major communities of the Pine Ridge country. No longer did it take hours to go from one place to another. With these kinds of roads everyone had to have a car. The team and wagon vanished, except for those families who lived at various "camps" in inaccessible canyons pretty much as their ancestors had. (Today, even they have adopted the automobile for traveling long distances in search of work.)

I left the reservation in 1951, when my family moved to Iowa. I went back only once for an extended stay, in the summer of 1955, while on a furlough, and after that I visited only occasionally during summer vacations. In the meantime I attended college, served a hitch in the Marines, and went to the seminary. After I graduated from the seminary, I took a job with the United Scholarship Service, a private organization devoted to the college and secondary-school education of American Indian and Mexican students. I had spent my last two years of high school in an Eastern preparatory school and so was probably the only Indian my age who knew what an independent Eastern school was like. As the program developed, we soon had some thirty students placed in Eastern schools.

I insisted that all the students who entered the program be able to qualify for scholarships as students and not simply as Indians. I was pretty sure we could beat the white man at his own educational game, which seemed to me the only way to gain his respect. I was soon to find that this was a dangerous attitude to have. The very people who were supporting the program—non-Indians in the national church establishments—accused me of trying to form a colonialist "élite" by insisting that only kids with strong test scores and academic patterns be sent east to school. They wanted to continue the ancient pattern of soft-hearted paternalism toward Indians. I didn't feel we should cry our way into the schools, that sympathy would destroy the students we were trying to help.

In 1964, while attending the annual convention of the National Congress of American Indians, I was elected its executive director. I learned more about life in the NCAI in three years than I had in the previous thirty. Every conceivable problem that could occur in an Indian society was suddenly thrust at me from 315 different directions. I discovered that I was one of the people who were supposed to solve the problems. The only trouble was that Indian people locally and on the national level were being played off one against the other by clever whites who had either ego or income at stake. While there were many feasible solutions, few could be tried without whites with vested interests working night and day to destroy the unity we were seeking on a national basis.

In the mid-nineteen-sixties, the whole generation that had grown up after World War II and had left the reservations during the fifties to get an education was returning to Indian life as "educated Indians." But we soon knew better. Tribal societies had existed for centuries without going outside themselves for education and information. Yet many of us thought that we would be able to improve the traditional tribal methods. We were wrong.

For three years we ran around the conference circuit attending numerous meetings called to "solve" the Indian problems. We listened to and spoke with anthropologists, historians, sociologists, psychologists, economists, educators, and missionaries. We worked with many Government agencies and with every conceivable doctrine, idea, and program ever created. At the end of this happy round of consultations the reservation people were still plodding along on their own time schedule, doing the things they considered important. They continued to solve their problems their way in spite of the advice given them by "Indian experts."

By 1967 there was a radical change in thinking on the part of many of us. Conferences were proving unproductive. Where non-Indians had been pushed out to make room for Indian people, they had wormed their way back into power and again controlled the major programs serving Indians. The poverty programs, reservation and university technical assistance groups were dominated by whites who had pushed Indian administrators aside.

Reservation people, meanwhile, were making steady progress in spite of the numerous setbacks suffered by the national Indian community. So, in a large part, younger Indian leaders who had been playing the national conference field began working at the local level to build community movements from the ground up. By consolidating local organizations into power groups, they felt that they would be in a better position to influence national thinking.

Robert Hunter, director of the Nevada Intertribal Council, had already begun to build a strong state organization of tribes and communities. In South Dakota, Gerald One Feather, Frank LaPointe, and Ray Briggs formed the American Indian Leadership Conference, which quickly welded the educated young Sioux in that state into a strong regional organization, active in nearly every phase of Sioux life. Gerald is now running for the prestigious post of chairman of the Ogalala Sioux, the largest Sioux tribe, numbering some fifteen thousand members. Ernie Stevens, an Oneida from Wisconsin, and Lee Cook, a Chippewa from Minnesota, developed a strong program for economic and community development in Arizona. Just recently Ernie has moved into the post of director of the California Intertribal Council, a statewide organization representing some one hundred thirty thousand California Indians in cities and on the scattered reservations of that state.

By the fall of 1967 it was apparent the national Indian scene was collapsing in favor of strong regional organizations, although the major national organizations such as the National Congress of American Indians and the National Indian Youth Council continued to grow. There was yet another factor emerging on the Indian scene: the old-timers of the depression days had educated a group of younger Indians in the old ways, and these people are now becoming a major force in Indian life. Led by Thomas Banyaca of the Hopi, Mad Bear Anderson of the Tuscarora, Clifton Hill of the Creek, and Rolling Thunder of the Shoshoni, the traditional Indians were forcing the whole Indian community to rethink its understanding of Indian life.

The message of the traditionalists is simple. They demand a return to basic Indian philosophy, establishment of ancient methods of government by open council instead of elected officials, a revival of Indian religions, and replacement of white laws with Indian customs; in short, a complete return to the old people. In an age dominated by tribalizing communications media, their message makes a great deal of sense.

But in some areas their thinking is opposed to that of the National Congress of American Indians, which represents officially elected tribal governments organized under the Indian Reorganization Act as Federal corporations. The contemporary problem is therefore one of defining the meaning of "tribe." Is it a traditionally organized band of Indians following customs with medicine men and chiefs dominating the politics of the tribe, or is it a modern corporate structure attempting to compromise at least in part with modern white culture?

The problem has been complicated by private foundations' and Government agencies' funding of Indian programs. In general this process, although it has brought a great amount of money into Indian country, has been one of cooptation (pre-empting or seizing for oneself before others are able to do so). Government agencies must justify their appropriation requests every year and can only take chances on spectacular programs that will serve as showcases of progress. They are not willing to invest the capital funds necessary to build viable self-supporting communities on the reservations, because these programs do not have an immediate publicity potential. Thus the Government agencies are forever committed to conducting conferences to discover that one "key" to Indian life that will give them the edge over their rival agencies in the annual appropriations derby.

Churches and foundations have merely purchased an Indian leader or program that conforms with their ideas of what Indian people should be doing. The large foundations have bought up the well-dressed, handsome "new image" Indian who is comfortable in the big cities but virtually helpless at an Indian meeting. Churches have given money to Indians who have been willing to copy black militant activist tactics, and the more violent and insulting the Indian can be, the more churches seem to love it. They are wallowing in self-guilt and piety over the lot of the poor, yet funding demagogues of their own choosing to speak for the poor.

I did not run for re-election as executive director of the NCAI in the fall of 1967, but entered law school at the University of Colorado instead. It was apparent to me that the Indian revolution was well under way and that someone had better get a legal education so that we could have our own legal program for defense of Indian treaty rights. Thanks to a Ford Foundation program, nearly fifty Indians are now in law school, assuring the Indian community of legal talent in the years ahead. Within four years I foresee another radical shift in Indian leadership patterns as the growing local movements are affected by the new Indian lawyers.

There is an increasing scent of victory in the air in Indian country these days. The mood is comparable to the old days of the depression when the men began to dance once again. As the Indian movement gathers momentum and individual Indians cast their lot with the tribe, it will become apparent that not only will Indians survive the electronic world of Marshall McLuhan (author of books which explored the effects upon society of worldwide electronic communication), they will thrive in it. At the present time everyone is watching how mainstream America will handle the issues of pollution, poverty, crime and racism, when it does not fundamentally understand the issues. Knowing the importance of tribal survival, Indian people are speaking more and more of sovereignty, of the great political technique of the open council, and of the need for gaining the community's consensus on all programs before putting them into effect.

One can watch this same issue emerge in white society as the "Woodstock Nation," the "Blackstone Nation" (a Chicago street gang which renounced violence in 1967), and the block organizations are developed. This is a full tribalizing process involving a nontribal people, and it is apparent that some people are frightened by it. But it is the kind of social phenomenon upon which Indians feast.

In 1965 I had a long conversation with an old Papago. I was trying to get the tribe to pay its dues to the National Congress of American Indians, and I had asked him to speak to the tribal council for me. He said that he would but that the Papago didn't really need the NCAI. They were like, he told me, the old mountain in the distance. The Spanish had come and dominated them for three hundred years and then left. The Mexicans had come and ruled them for a century, but they also left. "The Americans," he said, "have been here only about eighty years. They, too, will vanish, but the Papago and the mountain will always be here."

This attitude and understanding of life is what American society is searching for.

I wish the Government would give Alcatraz to the Indians now occupying it. They want to create five centers on the Island. One center would be for a North American studies program; another would be a spiritual and medical center where Indian religions and medicines would be used and studied. A third center would concentrate on ecological studies based on an Indian view of nature—that man should live *with* the land and not simply *on* it. A job-training center and a museum would also be founded on the island. Certain of these programs would obviously require Federal assistance.

Some people may object to this approach, yet Health, Education and Welfare gave out ten million dollars last year to non-Indians to study

Indians. Not one single dollar went to an Indian scholar or researcher to present the point of view of Indian people. And the studies done by non-Indians added nothing to what was already known about Indians.

Indian people have managed to maintain a viable and cohesive social order in spite of everything the non-Indian society has thrown at them in an effort to break the tribal structure. At the same time, non-Indian society has created a monstrosity of a culture where people starve while the granaries are filled and the sun can never break through the smog.

By making Alcatraz an experimental Indian center operated and planned by Indian people, we would be given a chance to see what we could do toward developing answers to modern social problems. Ancient tribalism can be incorporated with modern technology in an urban setting. Perhaps we would not succeed in the effort, but the Government is spending billions every year and still the situation is rapidly growing worse. It just seems to a lot of Indians that this continent was a lot better off when we were running it.

---

**Review Questions**

1.  What did the Indians want to do with Alcatraz? Was it a reasonable suggestion?
2.  What was the condition of the people Vine Deloria, Jr., grew up with?
3.  Did these people have a sense of possessing their own country?
4.  What purpose would there be for having a Native American cultural center?
5.  Does Deloria have a valid argument for allowing them to establish one?

# *Charlie Sabatier*

### *John Langston Gwaltney*

The speaker in the following essay gives some of his impressions of what it means to be handicapped, to be an American, and to be a veteran. This interview first appeared in Gwaltney's *The Dissenters*. Gwaltney is a professor of anthropology at Syracuse University who has studied people who, for various reasons, do not fit in the mainstream of American experience. His first major book, *Drylongso*, was a series of interviews on what it means to be African-American. Gwaltney understands the problems encountered by those who are physically challenged because he himself is blind.

*Combat duty in Southeast Asia left Charlie Sabatier with a need for a wheelchair, but it is difficult for me to think of him as confined. The truth is, his mind is infinitely freer now than it was for most of his pre-Vietnam life. In that pre-Vietnam, South Texas existence, Charlie and I would probably not have had very much to do with one another. But in July of 1982 we met and talked in his suburban Boston home and he turned out to be civil, hospitable, direct, and a formidable raconteur. The talking and listening were facilitated by the array of thick sandwiches and cold beer he provided. Late in the afternoon of our day of talking and listening Charlie's wife, Peggy, phoned. He maneuvered his wheelchair out of the house they are remodeling, down the drive, and into his car and drove off to pick her up.*

*The May 1982 issue of the American Coalition of Citizens with Disabilities newsletter had carried a story about Charlie's successful battle with Delta Airlines over one of their policies regarding disabled persons. The story read, in part:*

> *On March 17, 1982, in East Boston, Charles Sabatier fought with Delta Airlines over evacuation. Sabatier was arrested when he refused to comply with a Delta Airlines safety policy which stipulates that a disabled person must sit on a blanket while in transit so that he/she can be evacuated in case of emergency. . . . When Sabatier refused to sit on the blanket (which was folded), the flight was delayed, and Sabatier was eventually arrested for disorderly conduct.*
>
> *The court in which he was charged was located in an inaccessible courthouse. Sabatier refused to be carried up the courthouse steps and was therefore arraigned on the steps. The location of the trial was then moved to an accessible courthouse. Charges against Sabatier were dismissed in court when the parties reached a pretrial settlement. Delta agreed to change its policy so that use of a blanket to evacuate persons will be optional and paid Sabatier $2,500.00 for legal fee expenses, $1.00 of which would be for punitive damages at Sabatier's request. Sabatier agreed not to sue Delta over the incident.*

This blanket thing had happened to me at least a dozen times before, and in the last three years I've flown at least three dozen times. I mean, I've been *everywhere.* I've been to Seattle and Los Angeles and San Francisco and New Orleans and Chicago and any place you can name that's on the map, practically, any major city, I've been there in the last three years. I've been subjected to that probably ninety percent of the times I flew Delta or Eastern. I would protest. I would get on just like this time. I would get on out of the wheelchair and into this aisle chair that Delta, by the way, likes to call the "invalid" chair—I've even written them letters about that. You know, about how language means things. Like you don't call black people niggers and you don't call women broads and chick and honey and you don't call disabled people cripples and invalids. You know, I told 'em what an invalid meant. That that's somebody in a bed, totally helpless. I said, "I'm not totally helpless and stop calling me names." And I'd write them nice bureaucratic-type letters. Yeah, they write back all the time, bureaucratic-type things. They got a standard-type letter, I'm telling ya. They hire somebody, you know, whose only qualification is—can you write a bureaucratic meaningless letter? You know, at least a one-pager. That guy's probably paid twenty-five thousand dollars a year to answer people like me. And I never got anywhere by it, but that didn't stop me from writing them. I had to write to get it out of my system, I think. One of the things I contended was that the whole damn policy was arbitrary and capricious because it happened to me a dozen times before and I always talked my way off the blanket! I'd get in there and argue with 'em and talk about my rights and all this self-worth, dignity, humiliation, and stigma and they'd go "Jesus Christ! Get him out of here. Forget about it." You know, "Just go sit down." They'd go, "Hey, we gotta take off, man!" So they'd say "Listen, forget it." And so that's what would happen. They would just forget about their dumb policy. And so I expected the same thing to happen this time. I mean, they're gonna subject me to this and I'll argue and get away with it. And this time I ran into a captain. The stewardess actually said forget it, and I went down—that's how I got into the seat. 'Cause this all happened at the door of the plane by the captain's cabin when I transferred from my chair to the aisle chair that gets me down the narrow aisle. And we argued and someone behind said, "Forget it." And so we went down. I got in the chair, got in the seat, had my seat belt on, they moved the chair out of the aisle and she comes down and says, "I'm sorry, the captain insists that you sit on the blanket." I said, "Look, you tell the captain what I told you. That I'm not about to sit on this blanket." And we went through this whole thing and I argued with every Delta person in probably the whole terminal over the course of about forty-five minutes and naturally, you know, this plane's going to Miami and everybody's saying, "Let's get going!" Yeah, I mean, it's not like it's wintertime and you're going to Minneapolis. They wanted to get going. Everybody's kinda wondering. I think the people on the plane, who saw me coming on, see, in this chair, they figured, this guy is sick or something and they were pretty nice. Well, finally the stewardess got irritated about this delay and she walks down the aisle and she used to like stoop down to talk to me but this time she comes down and just stands there and says, "Look, if you don't sit on the blanket, we're gonna have to de-board the plane and cancel the flight." Out loud, see? So everybody said, "Wait a minute, this guy's not sick. This delay's just 'cause he won't sit on a blanket." So some guy yells out, like about five rows behind me, "You mean to tell me that this delay is because this guy won't sit on a blanket?" And she says "Yes!" And he says, "Look, man, if I sit on a blanket, will you sit on a blanket?" And I said, "No. But if everybody sits on a blanket, I'll sit on a blanket." And he says, "Well, why do you have to sit on a blanket?" And she says, "It's for his safety." He says, "It's for your own good, do it." I said, "Look, seat belts are for people's safety. *Everybody* gets one. If blankets are for my safety, I want everybody to get one, Okay? If it's so good for my safety, it's so good for everybody else's. But if I'm the only one that has to do it, it's like puttin' a bag over an ugly man's head, you know? I mean, that's a stigma. So the guy says, "Okay, then we'll all sit on blankets." Everybody says, "Yeah!" So half these people started chanting, "We want blankets! We want blankets! We want blankets!" I kinda enjoyed it, 'cause I was getting some support finally. I was getting a kick out of it, but at the same time I was a little bit nervous. It was funny except for the fact that the State Police officer was comin' down the aisle at the same time they were chanting on the plane. So he says, "Either you sit on this blanket or I'm gonna have to arrest you." I said, "What charge? Where's the blanket charge?" He says, "Disorderly conduct." And that got me mad. Disorderly conduct? *These* are the people chanting "We want blankets," it's their conduct. I said, "If anybody's being disorderly, it's them. And it's this airline that's treating me like dirt who should be arrested." I said, "Besides, you don't work for the airline. You work for the State of Massachusetts, just like me. You shouldn't be arresting people that are violating some policy they have. This is not a Federal Aviation Administration regulation. And even if it was, it should be the feds making the arrest here, not you. You're out of your jurisdiction." Well, he didn't get ahold of all that and goes, "Oh well, I don't care. Look, these people are gonna have to get off, you're interrupting and costing them a lot of money. I'm going to arrest you. I'll worry about that later." I says, "You bet you will, 'cause I'm gonna sue you for false arrest. I got two attorneys sitting right here, right next to me, and I've got their cards and they've already said that I haven't done anything wrong and they're gonna be witnesses. You'd better write down your own witnesses 'cause you're gonna need 'em." I found out later that I was right. That I wasn't guilty of disorderly conduct.

But an ironic thing was that the guy who arrested me had a twelve-year-old son with multiple sclerosis who was in an electric wheelchair! When I was in his office taking care of the paperwork we were talking about his son and I said, "I'll tell you something. I feel better about taking a stand and doing this than I *ever* felt about my role in the war in Vietnam. I know that what I'm doing right here is right. I know right from wrong and I know that this policy humiliates people and irregardless of its intention to evacuate people in the event of a survivable crash, and that was even suspect if that was the real intention, it's categoric discrimination," I said. "Because when they see me as a nonambulatory person they categorically discriminated against me because they have me stereotyped as being helpless. I have no problem about how they get me out of the plane, *if* they get me out. I've got a problem about how they treat me *before* the crash. They could put the blanket above the seat in the compartment, they could put it under the seat. Do they think I'm gonna sit there and twiddle my thumbs in the seat waitin' for the stewardess to come back and get me on the blanket? I weigh two hundred pounds! Give me a break! I'm gonna be out of that seat just like I got in it, 'cause I know that when people start headin' for the exits, they're not comin' back for their purse, right? I mean, they're gonna be in the aisle, right down back, and there's gonna be this big cluster of people around the doors jumpin' out and I'll be right behind 'em. There are like eighty-, ninety-year-old people who get on that plane with the help of a walker and their grandson and they help 'em sit down and they kiss 'em good-bye. I'm telling you, if there was a survivable crash, those people, because of arthritis and age, couldn't get out. They'd be more helpless in a situation than I would, but they're ambulatory, you see, so they don't have to sit on a blanket. I mean, I had 'em cold, it was just unbelievable. I could have brought paraplegics in there who can lift five hundred pounds. I mean, I can prove that paraplegics are not helpless people.

If I had been in that pilot's place, of course I wouldn't have done what he did. 'Course not, because I think I have more common sense than he had. I mean, I think I'd realize that if there was really a survivable crash, you're just gonna grab somebody and try to drag 'em out, no one's going to think about which one. I'll tell you something that I've always suspected. In their minds, they didn't just see me as a helpless person, they saw me as an incontinent person. They had probably had experiences of people who were paralyzed and incontinent and they're trying to protect the upholstery of their seats. That's not unusual, that paternalism. You know, I lobby all the time. I'll talk to people a half hour in their office—senators, congressmen—and on the way out I'll get patted on the back like I'm a little kid. I mean, even very high officials. They're so far out of tune with what's goin' on in the disabled movement and the women's movement, the black movement, I mean, they're just so engrossed, I guess, in doing their job, that they lose contact.

I've got a blind friend who we see every once in a while. One day I'm walking down the street with this guy—and he's got dark glasses and a white cane—and a guy pulls over and says to me, "Hey! Could you tell me how to get to the Prudential Building?" Well, I had been here only a year and a half and I know the major roads, but I don't know the names of the streets so my friend starts talkin' and tells the guy how to get there and the guy pulls off and like five feet later pulls over and asks somebody else, 'cause he says to himself, "Blind guys don't know where anything is." But my friend can get around that town as well as anybody else. If anybody's gonna memorize how to get around, he is. But yeah, that's not untypical of the nondisabled population.

One of the things that happens when you stigmatize people is, you see, if I can call people "niggers" in my mind, I don't think of these people as human beings. There's not equality, you know. They're not my peers. If I call a Vietnamese a gook, it's easier to kill him than Mr. Hung Yung or whatever his name would be, right? So we do it. Americans do it, everyone, man. We call people krauts, limeys, gooks, niggers, and handicapped. People are refusing to recognize people as people, as having human traits. It's easier to just stereotype a large group of people than it is to deal with the problems and the need.

We always deal with problems in this country either technologically or monetarily, and that's how this country has decided to deal with disabled people. Hey, I get my butt shot up in Vietnam, I come back here, they're not interested in what I'm gonna do, you know. They're not interested in my head problems about Vietnam or getting over all that trauma. It's later for that. We'll dump some money on you, just like, stay home. But if I say, "Look, later with your money. Stop subsidizing my life, just allow me equal opportunity to make my way in this life to the best that I can and all I want you to do is provide me accessible transportation so that I can get to and from my job, or make that post office that's two blocks away from here accessible so I can mail a letter and maintain my dignity while I'm doing it, rather than have somebody go up and do it for me," they refuse to do that. They'll dump money on you though, so you can stay home.

I don't even know if I could really give an answer as to why I didn't sit on the blanket. I know good people, good friends of mine, who have sat on that blanket, and I consider them to be real advocates. They did it because, I guess, it was like the easiest course to take. Most people's lives, I think, probably are like water. Water runs to the easiest course and most people would prefer to go around a confrontation than actually confront somebody. Oh for sure I would have preferred that. I mean, nobody enjoys confrontation, really. I think you'd have to be sick to really enjoy confrontation. There's a lot that's gone on in my life that goes way back. There's building blocks, I guess, and you see things and it takes time. You are what you are today because of what you were yesterday and the day before. We are an accumulation.

I think by the time I got out of the army, I said to myself, "I'm gonna start making the decisions in my life." Because I was always saying, "I should have listened to myself." Well, I started really making decisions for myself for the first time when I was layin' in a bloody mess in Vietnam. It was the first time, okay? Up until then I'd always been doing these crazy things on the advice of other people. I grew up in a time where we saw too many John Wayne movies, okay? I was a World War II baby, I was born in July of forty-five and I grew up with all this Audie Murphy, John Wayne type of thing. The good guy goes to war, gets a bullet in the shoulder, meets and marries the pretty nurse, and they live happily ever after. That was war to me—and besides, we always won. We were always the good guys and we were always moral and ethical and all that. That was the propaganda that I was fed all my life, through movies, television. When I was young, "Combat" was the big show. Vic Morrow, who just died, was the buck sergeant. I grew up in South Texas, my dad was a marine in World War II. I fell for it. I don't think that the movie industry really thought that they were propagandizing, but that's what it is. 'Cause you were subjected to only one side. I mean, the Nazis were always bad, every Nazi was bad, every bad guy had a foreign accent. The Japanese were the people who were always torturing people. My God, we'd never do a thing like that! Oh no! But I believed it. I mean, I was twenty years old and I believed it. I had *never learned* to question.

Actually I started questioning before I got shot but that changed my life completely. When I got shot I took a different road, I guess, from the one I might have taken. I probably would have come back from 'Nam and gone back to school and been workin' in a bank with a couple kids, probably divorced, I'm sure, that type of thing. But it's strange, you know. Being shot has made my life probably a lot more exciting. I would have probably lived a normal, average mundane kind of life. But it's like I entered a whole new field. I started learning real fast that disabled people were not considered the general population and I started wondering why.

I learned what things meant and the language and semantics got important to me. I was six foot two, a hundred seventy-five pounds, I'd never been disabled or in a hospital in my life. I had never seen anybody die before, then all of a sudden in a short period of time I'm killing people, people are trying to kill me, then I do get shot and almost killed. I get back and *then* I'm subjected to the worst bunch of crap I've ever seen in my life. I started being treated like dirt. It was ironic. Up until the time I got shot I was like Number One citizen. My country was spendin' *billions* of dollars for me. Thousands of dollars just to train me how to kill, thousands more dollars to send me halfway around the world to save us from "Communism." And they let it thrive ninety miles away! When I got in the army, that's when I started thinkin', wait a minute. Like I'm on this airplane and all of a sudden I realized, this is a one-way ticket! I'd been enslaved to keep this country "free." I'd been drafted for two years and if you don't think it's slavery, you just try to walk away from it! And so I said, okay, number one, I'm a slave, then I say, where am I? I'm goin' halfway around the world 'cause we had to pick a fight with some little, Southeast Asian country to save the world from Communism! I had never even met a Vietnamese. I didn't even know what one *looked* like. I couldn't tell one from a Japanese and I'm going to go over there and kill these people? I thought, "This is ridiculous."

I was like twenty-one when I got there and the average age of everybody in 'Nam was nineteen. Which meant that the average age of the infantry, the guy on the line, was about seventeen and a half. And I just couldn't believe it. I just couldn't believe what was goin' on there. And we were goin' around in circles, you know, killin' people, and they were killin' us and it was like no war that we ever had. You never took ground, you never went north—you know, *that's* where the enemy is, Goddamn!

I think that we are a nation of dissenters. Our nation was created by dissenters. Anybody that's ever made a major change in this world has been someone who was a dissenter. It's been done by somebody, you know, who you would call an unreasonable person. It was George Bernard Shaw who said the reasonable man looks at the world as it is and tries to adapt himself to suit the world. And the unreasonable man sees the world as it is and tries to change the world to suit himself. Therefore, said Shaw, all progress depends on the unreasonable man. I think that's absolutely true! And it's those dissenters that I think really are like a drumbeat ahead, you know, from the rest of the band. They are the people that are leading. Hey! If there were no dissenters, if there were no "unreasonable" people there'd just simply be the status quo. We'd still be goin' around as cave men. But somebody had to have a better idea. And it seems like every time somebody's got a better idea, the status quo is there to start callin' him names.

Like what I did. People would say, "Man, that was an unnatural thing to do." And it *is* unnatural, because thousands of people have sat on the damn blanket before me. I guess they didn't consider it unnatural. But I'm telling ya, people are going to *have* to start becoming more unnatural, if that's what you want to call it, more unreasonable; less tolerant with those greedy people.

I don't know what makes people principled dissenters. I'll tell ya, you're searching for somethin' and it's kinda like searching for something smaller than the atom. You *know* something's there, but it's those building blocks or the makeup or whatever that substance is that makes people good people or bad people. You know something's there, you're tryin' to search for it but I just don't think that we're there yet. I don't think we know what it is. I don't know. Everybody's different in their intellect, their ability. I'm no genius. I'm not really great with the books. I have to study real hard. I'm not super smart or anything, but I just think I was born with the right genes or something that just gave me good *common sense.* Good common sense to know right from wrong, good from bad and make good decisions in my life. And every once in a while we blow it.

I remember the first time I ever recognized discrimination in my life. I was on a bus and this great big, huge black lady gets on the bus and sits down and faces me and the bus driver stopped the bus and said, "I'm sorry, lady, you're gonna have to move to the back of the bus." And she says somethin' like, "Look I have a right to sit here. I don't have to sit back there. My feet are hurtin' me. I've been working all day. I don't want to walk back down there." Just like Rosa Parks.[1] And he says, "Look, that's the law! Either you sit in the back of the bus or this bus don't go anywhere." So she was at that tired, worn-out stage and says okay, I'm ready for a rest. So *she* was a principled dissenter as far as I'm concerned. First one I ever heard of. And she says, "Then you do what you have to do. I'm gonna sit here, I'm tired." So he got off the bus, went to the corner, and got this cop who was directin' traffic, and this cop come on and like put a handcuff on her and took her off the bus. Boy! I thought, what's goin' on here? I never realized, see, up until that time that black people had to sit in the back of the bus. I just thought, they wanted to sit there, that they liked it there. I guess I was about nine. I thought, well, I guess I'm always sittin' near white people 'cause I want to, but I never thought about goin' back there. I just never thought of it. And then, all of a sudden, boom! I started thinkin' about it. All the way when I was goin' home I was thinkin', what'd she do? I didn't see her do anything. I thought maybe she had pickpocketed or robbed a purse. I didn't know. Why did they take her off the bus? I didn't know anything about it. And

---

[1] *Rosa Parks:* When she was arrested for sitting in the front of a bus instead of in back where blacks were supposed to sit, black people in Montgomery, Alabama boycotted the bus lines in 1955.

so I went home and I said to my mother, "What happened? This lady was arrested. I don't understand. Why couldn't she sit there?" And my mother said, "That's just the way things are. They've always been like that and that's the way they're always gonna be. Don't worry about it. Go outside and play." So I went outside and I remember sittin' on the porch for a long time and thinkin' about it, and *knowin'* that, now, I'm not getting the right answer here. Somethin's goin' on here, you know, like, even if it's always been that way and it's always goin' to be that way, well, why? Why is it that way? That's what I asked. I didn't get any answer to my question and back then that's probably the first time I started questioning like an adult would do. You know, I never thought of that again from that time on until after I got shot and I was in the VA hospital. The nurses were leavin' at four-thirty to go out and stand on the bus stop and take the bus and somebody said, "Why don't we go and take a bus and go down and have a drink with the nurses?" And everybody laughed. Ha. Ha. And there it went—boy! When that guy said that, I went back, back, seeing that person on the bus. And all of a sudden I went, "I don't believe this!" That's the first time that I had ever been discriminated against in my life!

I had been fortunate to live until that time as a white person in this racist society, and I'd never experienced any kind of discrimination, none. All of a sudden I realized—you know my life was so screwed up, it was like a big jigsaw puzzle and I had found one piece to start putting my life back together and I wanted to talk about it. Like, hey! There's a big puzzle out here and I know that if we can fit all the pieces together I'll understand everything that's happening to me. And that was the first significant piece of the puzzle I found out.

Listen, I'll tell you a story. This happened to me in New York. I came back from Los Angeles on TWA and I got to the terminal at Kennedy International and I was getting a transfer to Delta, okay? It had nothin' to do with the blanket, but another problem. Delta's terminal is in a separate terminal. It's about a half a mile around. And there's no curb cuts or anything. So I get there, it's midnight, and I get my bags on my lap and I'm goin' out and I figure I'll catch a cab around. So I ask a guy about cabs and he says, "Well, you're gonna have a hard time. Those cabbies have been sittin' in line two hours and they want a big fare to go downtown." I says, "Well, I'll get one." So I went out and I told this lady who was the dispatcher. "I want a cab." She says, "Where ya goin'?" I said, "Delta Airlines." She says, "Nope! Nobody'll take ya!" So I say, "Look, then if I can't get over there, I want to go downtown, stay in a hotel overnight." She says, "Okay." Cab comes up, I get in, the guy puts my chair in the trunk and he says, "Where ya goin'?" "Delta Airlines." "Nope. I'm waiting here for a fare to go downtown." And I says, "Well, I ain't goin' downtown, I want to go to Delta Airlines." The dispatcher says, "You said you were goin' downtown." I said, "I changed my mind." He says, "Get out of the cab, I'm not goin' to take you over there. I've been sittin' here two hours." "No, I'm not going to get out." So *he* gets out and he takes my chair out of the trunk. I locked his doors. And he says, "Look, I'll call the police," And I said, "Call 'em. You call 'em and then I'll sue *you.*" I says, "If you call 'em you're gonna be involved the whole damn night, you won't get another fare the whole night. Either you want to do that or take me to Delta. I don't know specifically what the law is here but I guarantee you you can't refuse to take me where I want to go. That's discrimination. Besides, if you don't take me to Delta, I'm not gonna letcha back in the cab!" And he says, "Look, man, don't make me break into my own cab!" I says, "I'm gonna tell ya, take me to Delta or I'm gonna crawl over this seat and drive this goddamned cab myself over there!" We went to Delta Airlines. That has happened to me, like, three times! I've locked the door. I'm just not gonna do that you know. And I know damn well ninety-nine percent of disabled people would *never* do anything like that because the movement is in its infancy stage. But we're getting there.

It *bugs* me that people in this country are always talkin' about civil rights, you know. When I think of rights, I think of something more—a civil right is something that is written in law and that's all bullshit anyway. We don't need any laws, we don't need any constitution, we don't need the Declaration of Independence. All we need to do is treat people with respect.

I grew up about twenty miles from this town called Alvin, Texas, and there used to be a sign out there—I was in junior high school the last time I saw it. I think since then they've had to take the thing down. It was a sign out in front of the town that said, "Nigger, don't let the sun set on your head." Not until I was twenty years old did I get out of South Texas. I'm not a racist. I might have been. I remember one time I pushed the button on the water fountain marked "white" and no water would come out of it, so I pushed the button marked "colored" and water came out, but I would not drink it. At that time we would think nothing about tellin' a racist joke—and laughing. Maybe that's a way of finding out who's a real racist. Something's happened to me. I don't think I've lost my sense of humor, I'm pretty funny, I laugh—we've been laughing here—but I just don't appreciate those kinds of jokes. The important thing was, I think, not just one incident, but I kept seeing incidents like that.

When I went into the army I was in Germany and I had never associated a whole lot with black people before, and suddenly I'm sleeping next to black people and showering with black people, drinkin' with black people and *fightin'* with black people. And I remember we were sittin' down on a cot and it was Christmastime and this one guy who was black got this big long bar of candy with these nuts all around it and he took this big bite out of it and handed it to me for me to get a bite of. Man! It was like somebody had handed me a piece of *shit* to take a bite of. Boy! Did that candy look good! But I hesitated you know, and he says, "Oh, forgit it!" And I said, "Hey, no, give it here." I still think of it and that was 1967 and Jesus! It makes you realize that, you know, they got me. They got a piece of me. There we were, havin' a good time, drinkin' beer and everything's great until I did somethin' like that, and I realized, well here I am, I'm a prejudiced ass. We grow though, we grow, hopefully.

What made me not like what was happening, those jokes, the water fountain, what made me dislike that or understand that it's not right, I don't know. I think that's what you're really looking for. Why would somebody young and immature know in his soul and his heart and his mind that this is not right? Actually I did think about it a lot then. When I would see things like that happening, I would dwell on them. And I could look in the eyes of people when they were being done a number on and I could see it. I could see the hate, frustration, anger and I could see that what was happening here, this policy that would create that kind of reaction by somebody, is a policy that should be eliminated. We should have no policies that create that kind of tension in somebody, that kind of anxiety, that sense of disaster. I think I probably always felt that way. Not just for the racist-type things I saw, but as I grew up if I saw some kid being punished by his father or something, you know, when the punishment far surpassed what was just, if I saw somebody getting beat up on the playground, I was just the kind of person that would kind of go help the person.

I remember one time. It got me in really bad trouble. I was in eighth grade and I was a big kid. I was six feet tall and we had this one guy who was the only disabled person I'd ever met in my life. He had CP and he couldn't talk very good and we were friends. Well, it had been rainin' on the playground and some kid threw him in this hole. Just for fun! Boy, I'll tell ya, when they threw this guy into the mud, it just made me sick and I ran over there to help him and these people were gonna throw *me* in the mud! And then we were both so muddy—it was raining like cats and dogs. And then when we were almost out of the hole, these kids kicked mud in our faces. So I told the kid, "I want to see you after school. I'll get you." And before I realized what I was sayin', I was talkin' to like one of the toughest guys in the school! And later I was sittin' in my class and my knees were almost shakin'. I'm thinkin', "I'm gonna get killed. What do I do now? If I back down now I'll be *dirt* for four years, all through high school." So I said, "Jeez, I gotta go get beat up." So I went over and met him at the drugstore. And I thought, "If I let this guy hit me, I'm gonna die, so I'm gonna get the first punch in anyway." So I walked out of this drugstore door, it was like eight steps down to the sidewalk and the glass door was framed in wood and it was closing behind this guy and he walked out and took that first step and I caught him in midair. I turned around and *smacked* this guy right in the face. I connected so good in his face that I could just feel the guy's nose crack. Blood went all over and he flew back and went right through the glass door. Just flew! And then all of a sudden I changed from being wimpo, like "I'm gonna get killed," to "Come on, man! Let's get going!" Yeah, I was *bad* you know. Next thing I knew, I was worried 'cause the guy wasn't wakin' up. And I'm goin', "Wheow! What power!" Next thing I know, they call the police and I ran. No one squealed on me. I got away with the whole thing. I mean, the guy was so bad, if it had ever been a fair fight, I would have been dead. But the guy had some kind of respect for that kind of power and I just didn't. I had no respect for myself, see, 'cause I had sucker punched the guy, right? I hadn't really used any kind of power and after that he's thinkin' I'm this bad dude, don't mess with Sabatier, man. I had this great big reputation for nothin'. I said, "Thank God, nobody else'd pick a fight with me!" So I never really had much respect, I think, for strength as far as authority over other people. Maybe those kinds of things that happen throughout your life kinda teach that just because somebody has authority over you, has the power to do a number on you, doesn't make them the kind of person you have to respect. I don't think, when you fight, there's anything fair about it. When you fight, it's kinda like war—you win. The *only* thing that counts is to win. You defend yourself by destroying another person, that's all there is to it. I don't care what anybody says.

I enjoyed the fighting and I enjoyed being able to defend myself. That's a nice thing—to know that you can defend yourself. That you don't take much guff. That's good and every kid needs that, at least men in our society need that. It was just demanded when we were kids. If you grow up wimpy, brother! People are going to start stepping on you so you have to be able to take care of yourself. No one ever really got hurt. That's the thing women miss most, I think, the fact that there's nothin' like winnin' a fight. If you get in a fight and you win, boy! The feeling of success and victory and power—there's somethin' about it that is a *good* feeling. And that's why when we get to be adults we get into violence. We like the violence.

It's kinda strange what happened to me. Just killing somebody, you know, is something that you never get over, and when I left Vietnam I think I was more committed to learning as much as I could and trying to understand and be empathetic about people and I gained more respect for human life than I ever had before. I was put in a situation that had little respect for human life—either on our side or theirs. We had free fire zones and in the free-fire zone, anybody walking, you kill. You know, no respect. You don't ask any questions, in the free-fire zone you just kill 'em. And I think killin' somebody close up is more of an experience than doing a number on somebody in a bush that you don't see. You just fire at the bush or something and you walk by and you don't know what happened.

I had some really close experiences where I have actually killed somebody *very* close. And I killed a woman who was unarmed and *that* was somethin' I will *never* shake. We had set up this perimeter and we were there eleven days and every day we'd run out, search and destroy, and come back. Well, it just so happened that there were about thirty Vietcong who were digging these tunnels, and we had caught them out in the open and didn't know it and when we set up our perimeter it was right on top of them. They hadn't dug the other entrance and so they were all closed in. They were like, after eleven days, tryin' to sneak out of the perimeter. They didn't have any food, they'd run out of water and they were on their way out. And it was about four o'clock in the morning. I'd just got off guard duty and I was going to sleep and I heard this guy on this tank next to my armored personnel carrier. He started yelling, "Infantry, there's somebody in the perimeter. There's gooks in the perimeter!" And I said, "Okay, we'll go check it out." So I jumped up, I took a couple of guys from my squad and I went to the other side of this tank and he says, "There's somebody in the bomb crater. I killed two on the side of the bomb crater." We saw their bodies, they weren't moving and we could hear someone in the bomb crater. I had this tunnel light, this big flashlight that we used when we'd go through tunnels, and I shined it in the bomb crater and this guy's got these two big old bullet holes right on each side of his neck and he's breathing, erh, arh, erh, arh, like that, and blood's burbling right out of the holes in his neck and he's *buck* naked and he's got a grenade in each hand and he's layin' on his back and the tanker yells, "Go get a medic." And I says, "There's no medic going to go down there. The guy's dyin', man," I says. "Besides, he's got grenades in his hands. What fool's goin' to go down there?" So the guy calls the medic and the medic wouldn't go down there and the guy ended up, like five minutes later he died. But I wouldn't have gone down there either. And so I said, "Look, let's fan out around this bomb crater." I'm right next to the bomb crater and there's a guy like two feet to my left and two feet to his left there's another and we're gonna walk around this bomb crater and then I realize, hey! I'm the guy that has the light! So I thought, I can use my power here, you know, I'm a sergeant. I could say, "Hey, psst, take this light." But they'd say, "Take *this*." So I didn't say that. I said to myself, "Wow! What am I gonna do?" So I held this light wa-a-ay out to my left and I could feel this guy's hand pushing it back over toward me, so I went way over to my right, where nobody was and I take one step and it was so dark I couldn't see anything and I took one step and this gal jumped up in front of me on her knees and screamed out something, two or three words, and I just *instinctively* pulled the trigger on my M-16 and I just used up a whole ammo pack, twenty rounds, just destroyed her. Blood flew on me and she like flew forward and then backward and she hit me as I jumped down. I thought any second, after that, everybody's gonna open up and this guy's gonna start shootin' back or his friends will or something, but no one did. I jumped down and when I jumped down I jumped on her and I rolled off and I reached over. I was ready to fight this person, right? And of course she was dead and I grabbed her and when I grabbed her I thought, "Boy this is a little person," you know, "this is like grabbing my little niece or something." So, it was real quiet. We just lay there for a second or two and then I took the light and I said, "Let's take a look." And I put the light on her and she had her hair all up on top of her head and I cut this string that she had tied it with and boy! She had beautiful hair. It went all the way down, like past her knees.

Beautiful long black hair. And I searched her and she had this wallet, the only thing in it was a picture of her and a guy that was probably her husband and two little kids and a razor blade, an old rusty razor blade. I don't know why she had that, but that's all that was in her wallet. So I took the picture. We went around and ended up killing three or four more people and capturing about eight others and the next morning, the sun came up and the CO called me over and said, "What's the statistics here?" And I told him how many dead and how many captured and he says, "Was there a woman there?" And I said, "Yeah, there was a woman." And he said, "Was she armed?" And I says, "No, we didn't find any weapons." But hell, I didn't have time to say, "Hey, do you have a weapon?" There were bullet holes in her ankles, in her arms, in her face, it was terrible. So he says, "Well, who killed her?" And I says, "I did." And this fool, he's got one of these guys that we captured and he happened to be her husband. He's in his tent and he's having this conversation with this guy with the interpreter and the interpreter tells the guy that I'm the one that killed his wife. So right away, man, the guy comes *runnin'* at me, you know, his hands are tied behind his back, and I just threw him down on the ground. And the guy just went berserk, you know, crazy. I mean, he was like a chicken with its head cut off. He wasn't comin' at anybody, he just went runnin' into everything, throwing dirt up into the air and kicking and hollerin' and screamin' and like he'd lost his mind, which he did. So there I was, you know, and that night everybody's callin' me the woman killer. Like it's a big joke. You know, the woman killer, it's a joke. That was the heaviest thing that's ever happened to me. And so I think, Jesus, I don't know whatever happened to that guy. Whether he ever got his mind together. I don't know what happened to her kids. I don't know if they're dead or alive. Unbelievable! The next day we ended up gettin' in a big firefight and burning down by accident, by all the fire and ammo and everything, all these hooches and stuff and the captain told me that that was the village that this lady lived in. So in a day I had killed an unarmed lady, seen her husband go crazy, and then burned down her village—and I'm the *good* guy! I'm the good guy? And I'm thinkin', "I've gotta get out of here." God, she wasn't even armed. She was diggin' a tunnel, you know, carrying water back and forth for these people and what are they doin'? They're trying to get these foreigners out of their country, you know. That was us.

You know, I called them gooks. I used this term and everything. I played that game but I never, never really thought that I was going to be in a position—that's how stupid and naïve I was—I never thought that *I* would really have to shoot somebody and that I would get shot. It was just stupid, just so stupid. I am convinced, I've talked to all those guys, you know, *none* of those people ever thought that they were actually gonna pull a trigger on somebody or that they would ever get killed. You know, what happens is that the country confused the war with the warriors. We lost the war, therefore the warriors are losers. We can make jokes about them. They're psychos, they're nuts, they're baby killers, they're losers! We are discriminated against as much as if we had been the ones over there being killed.

I thought a *lot* about that when I didn't have nothin' to do except think. I was always in the field and sneakin' all the time and walkin' down trails and thinking, what am I doing? If I get killed today, will I go to hell or heaven? Am I guilty or innocent? Am I a war criminal? Am I violating people's human rights? Would I appreciate them in my country doing this? I'd walk in people's hooches and I mean, we'd go through a village at four-thirty in the morning. We don't knock on the door, we walk through and they're sleeping with their wives and babies and they're scared, you know, and you see these people, their faces. I felt like I was the Gestapo in World War II, walking in somebody's house without knocking on the door. 'Course that bothers me. I don't like doin' that. I'm not that kind of a person. But what am I gonna do? Refuse to go on a search-and-destroy mission? Jesus, so all I was hopin' to do was stay alive and get home and never find myself in that position again.

And so I *really* started thinking about all this right and wrong, good and bad and human rights, and what I would die for, what I wouldn't die for. And I came to the conclusion that there's just human rights. Human rights, not civil rights. And human rights are not conditional. Any commitment to a *conditional* human right is no commitment at all. And that's exactly what we got, we disabled people. Here's a President who says he's committed to social justice and all this business and at the same time it's being conditioned on your ability to get on the bus, or on your ability to see something. Things that really shouldn't matter. And so a commitment for conditional human rights to me is no commitment at all. Exactly none. And I'll do everything in my power to make sure that people understand that if you're gonna be committed toward something you can't talk commitment and in your actions do something else. You can't say you're in favor of affirmative action and then go out and discriminate.

I mean all the people of the different populations should recognize things like that. Not many people look inward. They look outward to see where the problem is. They don't look in and say, "Yeah, I've wasted twenty people off the face of the earth and for what? You know, I'm guilty, okay, from there I'll make sure this never happens again and I'll try to stop it whenever I see it." You know, whenever I see that current of hate or that current of discrimination, or see that president or that mayor or the governor or somebody making bad decisions, whenever I see it, I got to stand up and stop it. At least I owe those people, or their souls that! I have to. I figure, if *I* don't, who will? I owe it.

---

**Review Questions**

1. Why did the airlines say they asked Charlie to sit on the blanket? Why did he believe he was asked to sit on it?
2. Do you agree or disagree with his reasons? Why?
3. What did Charlie believe a person could do to stop thinking of other people as human beings?
4. Why did Charlie feel that being shot probably made his life a lot more exciting?
5. Why did Charlie come to the conclusion that "all progress depends on the unreasonable man [sic]"?
6. What did Charlie feel could go in place of all the civil rights laws?

7. What did Charlie enjoy about the fighting?
8. In what way do you think it affected Charlie to kill the unarmed woman?

## Letter from Birmingham Jail

### Martin Luther King, Jr.

The modern civil rights movement began in traditionally black colleges during the 1950s. It soon expanded and involved many Americans, black and white. One of the most memorable episodes of the movement was the campaign to racially integrate Birmingham, Alabama. Reverend Dr. Martin Luther King, Jr., was arrested there, along with many others. While he was incarcerated in Birmingham, King wrote a response to a letter by other clergy that had recently been published.

*April 16, 1963*

My Dear Fellow Clergymen:

While confined here in the Birmingham city jail, I came across your recent statement calling my present activities "unwise and untimely." Seldom do I pause to answer criticism of my work and ideas. If I sought to answer all the criticisms that cross my desk, my secretaries would have little time for anything other than such correspondence in the course of the day, and I would have no time for constructive work. But since I feel that you are men of genuine good will and that your criticisms are sincerely set forth, I want to try to answer your statement in what I hope will be patient and reasonable terms.

I think I should indicate why I am here in Birmingham, since you have been influenced by the view which argues against "outsiders coming in." I have the honor of serving as president of the Southern Christian Leadership Conference, an organization operating in every southern state, with headquarters in Atlanta, Georgia. We have some eighty-five affiliated organizations across the South, and one of them is the Alabama Christian Movement for Human Rights. Frequently we share staff, educational and financial resources with our affiliates. Several months ago the affiliate here in Birmingham asked us to be on call to engage in a nonviolent direct-action program if such were deemed necessary. We readily consented, and when the hour came we lived up to our promise. So I, along with several members of my staff, am here because I was invited here. I am here because I have organizational ties here.

But more basically, I am in Birmingham because injustice is here. Just as the prophets of the eighth century B.C. left their villages and carried their "thus saith the Lord" far beyond the boundaries of their home towns, and just as the Apostle Paul left his village of Tarsus and carried the gospel of Jesus Christ to the far corners of the Greco-Roman world, so am I compelled to carry the gospel of freedom beyond my own home town. Like Paul, I must constantly respond to the Macedonian call for aid.

Moreover, I am cognizant of the interrelatedness of all communities and states. I cannot sit idly by in Atlanta and not be concerned about what happens in Birmingham. Injustice anywhere is a threat to justice everywhere. We are caught in an inescapable network of mutuality, tied in a single garment of destiny. Whatever affects one directly, affects all indirectly. Never again can we afford to live with the narrow, provincial "outside agitator" idea. Anyone who lives inside the United States can never be considered an outsider anywhere within its bounds.

You deplore the demonstrations taking place in Birmingham. But your statement, I am sorry to say, fails to express a similar concern for the conditions that brought about the demonstrations. I am sure that none of you would want to rest content with the superficial kind of social analysis that deals merely with effects and does not grapple with underlying causes. It is unfortunate that demonstrations are taking place in Birmingham, but it is even more unfortunate that the city's white power structure left the Negro community with no alternative.

In any nonviolent campaign there are four basic steps: collection of the facts to determine whether injustices exist; negotiation; self-purification; and direct action. We have gone through all these steps in Birmingham. There can be no gainsaying the fact that racial injustice engulfs this community. Birmingham is probably the most thoroughly segregated city in the United States. Its ugly record of brutality is widely known. Negroes have experienced grossly unjust treatment in the courts. There have been more unsolved bombings of Negro homes and churches in Birmingham than in any other city in the nation. These are the hard, brutal facts of the case. On the basis of these conditions, Negro leaders sought to negotiate with the city fathers. But the latter consistently refused to engage in good-faith negotiation.

Then, last September, came the opportunity to talk with leaders of Birmingham's economic community. In the course of the negotiations, certain promises were made by the merchants—for example, to remove the stores' humiliating racial signs. On the basis of these promises, the Reverend Fred Shuttlesworth and the leaders of the Alabama Christian Movement for Human Rights agreed to a moratorium on all demonstrations. As the weeks and months went by, we realized that we were the victims of a broken promise. A few signs, briefly removed, returned; the others remained.

As in so many past experiences, our hopes had been blasted, and the shadow of deep disappointment settled upon us. We had no alternative except to prepare for direct action, whereby we would present our very bodies as a means of laying our case before the conscience of the local and the national community. Mindful of the difficulties involved, we decided to undertake a process of self-purification. We began a series of workshops on nonviolence, and we repeatedly asked ourselves: "Are you able to accept blows without retaliating?" "Are you able to endure the ordeal of jail?" We decided to schedule our direct-action program for the Easter season, realizing that except for Christmas, this is the main shopping period of the year. Knowing that a strong economic-withdrawal program would be the by-product of direct action, we felt that this would be the best time to bring pressure to bear on the merchants for the needed change.

Then it occurred to us that Birmingham's mayoral election was coming up in March, and we speedily decided to postpone action until after election day. When we discovered that the Commissioner of Public Safety, Eugene "Bull" Connor, had piled up enough votes to be in the run-off, we decided again to postpone action until the day after the run-off so that the demonstrations could not be used to cloud the issues. Like many others, we waited to see Mr. Connor defeated, and to this end we endured postponement after postponement. Having aided in this community need, we felt that our direct-action program could be delayed no longer.

You may well ask: "Why direct action? Why sit-ins, marches and so forth? Isn't negotiation a better path?" You are quite right in calling for negotiation. Indeed, this is the very purpose of direct action. Nonviolent direct action seeks to create such a crisis and foster such a tension that a community which has constantly refused to negotiate is forced to confront the issue. It seeks so to dramatize the issue that it can no longer be ignored. My citing the creation of tension as part of the work of the nonviolent-resister may sound rather shocking. But I must confess that I am not afraid of the word "tension." I have earnestly opposed violent tension, but there is a type of constructive, nonviolent tension which is necessary for growth. Just as Socrates felt that it was necessary to create a tension in the mind so that individuals could rise from the bondage of myths and half-truths to the unfettered realm of creative analysis and objective appraisal, so must we see the need for nonviolent gadflies to create the kind of tension in society that will help men rise from the dark depths of prejudice and racism to the majestic heights of understanding and brotherhood.

The purpose of our direct-action program is to create a situation so crisis-packed that it will inevitably open the door to negotiation. I therefore concur with you in your call for negotiation. Too long has our beloved Southland been bogged down in a tragic effort to live in monologue rather than dialogue.

One of the basic points in your statement is that the action that I and my associates have taken in Birmingham is untimely. Some have asked: "Why didn't you give the new city administration time to act?" The only answer that I can give to this query is that the new Birmingham administration must be prodded about as much as the outgoing one, before it will act. We are sadly mistaken if we feel that the election of Albert Boutwell as mayor will bring the millennium to Birmingham. While Mr. Boutwell is a much more gentle person than Mr. Connor, they are both segregationists, dedicated to maintenance of the status quo. I have hope that Mr. Boutwell will be reasonable enough to see the futility of massive resistance to desegregation. But he will not see this without pressure from devotees of civil rights. My friends, I must say to you that we have not made a single gain in civil rights without determined legal and non-violent pressure. Lamentably, it is an historical fact that privileged groups seldom give up their privileges voluntarily. Individuals may see the moral light and voluntarily give up their unjust posture; but, as Reinhold Niebuhr[1] has reminded us, groups tend to be more immoral than individuals.

We know through painful experience that freedom is never voluntarily given by the oppressor; it must be demanded by the oppressed. Frankly, I have yet to engage in a direct-action campaign that was "well timed" in the view of those who have not suffered unduly from the disease of segregation. For years now I have heard the word "Wait!" It rings in the ear of every Negro with piercing familiarity. This "Wait" has almost always meant "Never." We must come to see, with one of our distinguished jurists, that "justice too long delayed is justice denied."

We have waited for more than 340 years for our constitutional and God-given rights. The nations of Asia and Africa are moving with jetlike speed toward gaining political independence, but we still creep at horse-and-buggy pace toward gaining a cup of coffee at a lunch counter. Perhaps it is easy for those who have never felt the stinging darts of segregation to say, "Wait." But when you havé seen vicious mobs lynch your mothers and fathers at will and drown your sisters and brothers at whim; when you have seen hate-filled policemen curse, kick and even kill your black brothers and sisters; when you see the vast majority of your twenty million Negro brothers smothering in an airtight cage of poverty in the midst of an affluent society; when you suddenly find your

---

[1]*Moral Man and Immoral Society,* written by Reinhold Niebuhr, an American clergyman and theologian (1892–1971).

tongue twisted and your speech stammering as you seek to explain to your six-year-old daughter why she can't go to the public amusement park that has just been advertised on television, and see tears welling up in her eyes when she is told that Funtown is closed to colored children, and see ominous clouds of inferiority beginning to form in her little mental sky, and see her beginning to distort her personality by developing an unconscious bitterness toward white people; when you have to concoct an answer for a five-year-old son who is asking: "Daddy, why do white people treat colored people so mean?"; when you take a cross-country drive and find it necessary to sleep night after night in the uncomfortable corners of your automobile because no motel will accept you; when you are humiliated day in and day out by nagging signs reading "white" and "colored"; when your first name becomes "nigger," your middle name becomes "boy" (however old you are) and your last name becomes "John," and your wife and mother are never given the respected title "Mrs."; when you are harried by day and haunted by night by the fact that you are a Negro, living constantly at tiptoe stance, never quite knowing what to expect next, and are plagued with inner fears and outer resentments; when you are forever fighting a degenerating sense of "nobodiness"—then you will understand why we find it difficult to wait. There comes a time when the cup of endurance runs over, and men are no longer willing to be plunged into the abyss of despair. I hope, sirs, you can understand our legitimate and unavoidable impatience.

You express a great deal of anxiety over our willingness to break laws. This is certainly a legitimate concern. Since we so diligently urge people to obey the Supreme Court's decision of 1954 outlawing segregation in the public schools, at first glance it may seem rather paradoxical for us consciously to break laws. One may well ask: "How can you advocate breaking some laws and obeying others?" The answer lies in the fact that there are two types of laws: just and unjust. I would be the first to advocate obeying just laws. One has not only a legal but a moral responsibility to obey just laws. Conversely, one has a moral responsibility to disobey unjust laws. I would agree with St. Augustine that "an unjust law is no law at all."

Now, what is the difference between the two? How does one determine whether a law is just or unjust? A just law is a man-made code that squares with the moral law or the law of God. An unjust law is a code that is out of harmony with the moral law. To put it in the terms of St. Thomas Aquinas: An unjust law is a human law that is not rooted in eternal law and natural law. Any law that uplifts human personality is just. Any law that degrades human personality is unjust. All segregation statutes are unjust because segregation distorts the soul and damages the personality. It gives the segregator a false sense of superiority and the segregated a false sense of inferiority. Segregation, to use the terminology of the Jewish philosopher Martin Buber, substitutes an "I–it" relationship for an "I–thou" relationship and ends up relegating persons to the status of things. Hence segregation is not only politically, economically and sociologically unsound, it is morally wrong and sinful. Paul Tillich has said that sin is separation. Is not segregation an existential expression of man's tragic separation, his awful estrangement, his terrible sinfulness? Thus it is that I can urge men to obey the 1954 decision of the Supreme Court, for it is morally right; and I can urge them to disobey segregation ordinances, for they are morally wrong.

Let us consider a more concrete example of just and unjust laws. An unjust law is a code that a numerical or power majority group compels a minority group to obey but does not make binding on itself. This is *difference* made legal. By the same token, a just law is a code that a majority compels a minority to follow and that it is willing to follow itself. This is *sameness* made legal.

Let me give another explanation. A law is unjust if it is inflicted on a minority that, as a result of being denied the right to vote, had no part in enacting or devising the law. Who can say that the legislature of Alabama which set up that state's segregation laws was democratically elected? Throughout Alabama all sorts of devious methods are used to prevent Negroes from becoming registered voters, and there are some counties in which, even though Negroes constitute a majority of the population, not a single Negro is registered. Can any law enacted under such circumstances be considered democratically structured?

Sometimes a law is just on its face and unjust in its application. For instance, I have been arrested on a charge of parading without a permit. Now, there is nothing wrong in having an ordinance which requires a permit for a parade. But such an ordinance becomes unjust when it is used to maintain segregation and to deny citizens the First-Amendment privilege of peaceful assembly and protest.

I hope you are able to see the distinction I am trying to point out. In no sense do I advocate evading or defying the law, as would the rabid segregationist. That would lead to anarchy. One who breaks an unjust law must do so openly, lovingly, and with a willingness to accept the penalty. I submit that an individual who breaks a law that conscience tells him is unjust, and who willingly accepts the penalty of imprisonment in order to arouse the conscience of the community over its injustice, is in reality expressing the highest respect for law.

Of course, there is nothing new about this kind of civil disobedience. It was evidenced sublimely in the refusal of Shadrach, Meshach and Abednego to obey the laws of Nebuchadnezzar, on the ground that a higher moral law was at stake. It was practiced superbly by the early Christians, who were willing to face hungry lions and the excruciating pain of chopping blocks rather than submit to certain unjust laws of the Roman Empire. To a degree, academic freedom is a reality today because Socrates practiced civil disobedience. In our own nation, the Boston Tea Party represented a massive act of civil disobedience.

We should never forget that everything Adolf Hitler did in Germany was "legal" and everything the Hungarian freedom fighters did in Hungary was "illegal." It was "illegal" to aid and comfort a Jew in Hitler's Germany. Even so, I am sure that, had I lived in Germany at the time, I would have aided and comforted my Jewish brothers. If today I lived in a Communist country where certain principles dear to the Christian faith are suppressed, I would openly advocate disobeying that country's anti-religious laws.

I must make two honest confessions to you, my Christian and Jewish brothers. First, I must confess that over the past few years I have been gravely disappointed with the white moderate. I have almost reached the regrettable conclusion that the Negro's great stumbling block in his stride toward freedom is not the White Citizen's Counciler or the Ku Klux Klanner, but the white moderate, who is more devoted to "order" than to justice; who prefers a negative peace which is the absence of tension to a positive peace which is the presence of justice; who constantly says: "I agree with you in the goal you seek, but I cannot agree with your methods of direct action"; who paternalistically believes he can set the timetable for another man's freedom; who lives by a mythical concept of time and who constantly advises the Negro to wait for a "more convenient season." Shallow understanding from people of good will is more frustrating than absolute misunderstanding from people of ill will. Lukewarm acceptance is much more bewildering than outright rejection.

I had hoped that the white moderate would understand that law and order exist for the purpose of establishing justice and that when they fail in this purpose they become the dangerously structured dams that block the flow of social progress. I had hoped that the white moderate would understand that the present tension in the South is a necessary phase of the transition from an obnoxious negative peace, in which the Negro passively accepted his unjust plight, to a substantive and positive peace, in which all men will respect the dignity and worth of human personality. Actually, we who engage in nonviolent direct action are not the creators of tension. We merely bring to the surface the hidden tension that is already alive. We bring it out in the open, where it can be seen and dealt with. Like a boil that can never be cured so long as it is covered up but must be opened with all its ugliness to the natural medicines of air and light, injustice must be exposed, with all the tension its exposure creates, to the light of human conscience and the air of national opinion before it can be cured.

In your statement you assert that our actions, even though peaceful, must be condemned because they precipitate violence. But is this a logical assertion? Isn't this like condemning a robbed man because his possession of money precipitated the evil act of robbery? Isn't this like condemning Socrates because his unswerving commitment to truth and his philosophical inquiries precipitated the act by the misguided populace in which they made him drink hemlock? Isn't this like condemning Jesus because his unique God-consciousness and never-ceasing devotion to God's will precipitated the evil act of crucifixion? We must come to see that, as the federal courts have consistently affirmed, it is wrong to urge an individual to cease his efforts to gain his basic constitutional rights because the quest may precipitate violence. Society must protect the robbed and punish the robber.

I had also hoped that the white moderate would reject the myth concerning time in relation to the struggle for freedom. I have just received a letter from a white brother in Texas. He writes: "All Christians know that the colored people will receive equal rights eventually, but it is possible that you are in too great a religious hurry. It has taken Christianity almost two thousand years to accomplish what it has. The teachings of Christ take time to come to earth." Such an attitude stems from a tragic misconception of time, from the strangely irrational notion that there is something in the very flow of time that will inevitably cure all ills. Actually, time itself is neutral; it can be used either destructively or constructively. More and more I feel that the people of ill will have used time much more effectively than have the people of good will. We will have to repent in this generation not merely for the hateful words and actions of the bad people but for the appalling silence of the good people. Human progress never rolls in on wheels of inevitability; it comes through the tireless efforts of men willing to be co-workers with God, and without this hard work, time itself becomes an ally of the forces of social stagnation. We must use time creatively, in the knowledge that the time is always ripe to do right. Now is the time to make real the promise of democracy and transform our pending national elegy into a creative psalm of brotherhood. Now is the time to lift our national policy from the quicksand of racial injustice to the solid rock of human dignity.

You speak of our activity in Birmingham as extreme. At first I was rather disappointed that fellow clergymen would see my nonviolent efforts as those of an extremist. I began thinking about the fact that I stand in the middle of two opposing forces in the Negro community. One is a force of complacency, made up in part of Negroes who, as a result of long years of oppression, are so drained of self-respect and a sense of "somebodiness" that they have adjusted to segregation; and in part of a few middle-class Negroes who, because of a degree of academic and economic security and because in some ways they profit by segregation, have become insensitive to the problems of the masses. The other force is one of bitterness and hatred, and it comes perilously close to advocating violence. It is expressed in the various black nationalist groups that are springing up across the nation, the largest and best-known being Elijah Muhammad's Muslim movement. Nourished by the Negro's frustration over the continued existence of racial discrimination, this movement is made up of people who have lost faith in America, who have absolutely repudiated Christianity, and who have concluded that the white man is an incorrigible "devil."

I have tried to stand between these two forces, saying that we need emulate neither the "do-nothingism" of the complacent nor the hatred and despair of the black nationalist. For there is the more excellent way of love and nonviolent protest. I am grateful to God that, through the influence of the Negro church, the way of nonviolence became an integral part of our struggle.

If this philosophy had not emerged, by now many streets of the South would, I am convinced, be flowing with blood. And I am further convinced that if our white brothers dismiss as "rabble-rousers" and "outside agitators" those of us who employ nonviolent direct action, and if they refuse to support our nonviolent efforts, millions of Negroes will, out of frustration and despair, seek solace and security in black-nationalist ideologies—a development that would inevitably lead to a frightening racial nightmare.

Oppressed people cannot remain oppressed forever. The yearning for freedom eventually manifests itself, and that is what has happened to the American Negro. Something within has reminded him of his birthright of freedom, and something without has reminded him that it can be gained. Consciously or unconsciously, he has been caught up by the *Zeitgeist,* and with his black brothers of Africa and his brown and yellow brothers of Asia, South America and the Caribbean, the United States Negro is moving with a sense of great urgency toward the promised land of racial justice. If one recognizes this vital urge that has engulfed the Negro community, one should readily understand why public demonstrations are taking place. The Negro has many pent-up resentments and latent frustrations, and he must release them. So let him march; let him make prayer pilgrimages to the city hall; let him go on freedom rides—and try to understand why he must do so. If his repressed emotions are not released in nonviolent ways, they will seek expression through violence; this is not a threat but a fact of history. So I have not said to my people: "Get rid of your discontent." Rather, I have tried to say that this normal and healthy discontent can be channeled into the creative outlet of nonviolent direct action. And now this approach is being termed extremist.

But though I was initially disappointed at being categorized as an extremist, as I continued to think about the matter I gradually gained a measure of satisfaction from the label. Was not Jesus an extremist for love: "Love your enemies, bless them that curse you, do good to them that hate you, and pray for them which despitefully use you, and persecute you." Was not Amos an extremist for justice: "Let justice roll down like waters and righteousness like an ever-flowing stream." Was not Paul an extremist for the Christian gospel: "I bear in my body the marks of the Lord Jesus." Was not Martin Luther an extremist: "Here I stand; I cannot do otherwise, so help me God." And John Bunyan: "I will stay in jail to the end of my days before I make a butchery of my conscience." And Abraham Lincoln: "This nation cannot survive half slave and half free." And Thomas Jefferson: "We hold these truths to be self-evident, that all men are created equal . . . " So the question is not whether we will be extremists, but what kind of extremists we will be. Will we be extremists for hate or for love? Will we be extremists for the preservation of injustice or for the extension of justice? In that dramatic scene on Calvary's hill three men were crucified. We must never forget that all three were crucified for the same crime—the crime of extremism. Two were extremists for immorality, and thus fell below their environment. The other, Jesus Christ, was an extremist for love, truth and goodness, and thereby rose above his environment. Perhaps the South, the nation and the world are in dire need of creative extremists.

I had hoped that the white moderate would see this need. Perhaps I was too optimistic; perhaps I expected too much. I suppose I should have realized that few members of the oppressor race can understand the deep groans and passionate yearnings of the oppressed race, and still fewer have the vision to see that injustice must be rooted out by strong, persistent and determined action. I am thankful, however, that some of our white brothers in the South have grasped the meaning of this social revolution and committed themselves to it. They are still all too few in quantity, but they are big in quality. Some—such as Ralph McGill, Lillian Smith, Harry Golden, James McBride Dabbs, Ann Braden and Sarah Patton Boyle—have written about our struggle in eloquent and prophetic terms. Others have marched with us down nameless streets of the South.

They have languished in filthy, roach-infested jails, suffering the abuse and brutality of policemen who view them as "dirty nigger-lovers." Unlike so many of their moderate brothers and sisters, they have recognized the urgency of the moment and sensed the need for powerful "action" antidotes to combat the disease of segregation.

Let me take note of my other major disappointment. I have been so greatly disappointed with the white church and its leadership. Of course, there are some notable exceptions. I am not unmindful of the fact that each of you has taken some significant stands on this issue. I commend you, Reverend Stallings, for your Christian stand on this past Sunday, in welcoming Negroes to your worship service on a nonsegregated basis. I commend the Catholic leaders of this state for integrating Spring Hill College several years ago.

But despite these notable exceptions, I must honestly reiterate that I have been disappointed with the church. I do not say this as one of those negative critics who can always find something wrong with the church. I say this as a minister of the gospel, who loves the church; who was nurtured in its bosom; who has been sustained by its spiritual blessings and who will remain true to it as long as the cord of life shall lengthen.

When I was suddenly catapulted into the leadership of the bus protest in Montgomery, Alabama, a few years ago, I felt we would be supported by the white church. I felt that the white ministers, priests and rabbis of the South would be among our strongest allies. Instead, some have been outright opponents, refusing to understand the freedom movement and misrepresenting its leaders; all too many others have been more cautious than courageous and have remained silent behind the anesthetizing security of stained-glass windows.

In spite of my shattered dreams, I came to Birmingham with the hope that the white religious leadership of this community would see the justice of our cause and, with deep moral concern, would serve as the channel through which our just grievances could reach the power structure. I had hoped that each of you would understand. But again I have been disappointed.

I have heard numerous southern religious leaders admonish their worshipers to comply with a desegregation decision because it is the law, but I have longed to hear white ministers declare: "Follow this decree because integration is morally right and because the Negro is your brother." In the midst of blatant injustices inflicted upon the Negro, I have watched white churchmen stand on the sideline and mouth pious irrelevancies and sanctimonious trivialities. In the midst of a mighty struggle to rid our nation of racial and economic injustice, I have heard many ministers say: "Those are social issues, with which the gospel has no real concern." And I have watched many churches commit themselves to a completely otherworldly religion which makes a strange, un-Biblical distinction between body and soul, between the sacred and the secular.

I have traveled the length and breadth of Alabama, Mississippi and all the other southern states. On sweltering summer days and crisp autumn mornings I have looked at the South's beautiful churches with their lofty spires pointing heavenward. I have beheld the impressive outlines of her massive religious-education buildings. Over and over I have found myself asking: "What kind of people worship here? Who is their God? Where were their voices when the lips of Governor Barnett dripped with words of interposition and nullification? Where were they when Governor Wallace gave a clarion call for defiance and hatred? Where were their voices of support when bruised and weary Negro men and women decided to rise from the dark dungeons of complacency to the bright hills of creative protest?"

Yes, these questions are still in my mind. In deep disappointment I have wept over the laxity of the church. But be assured that my tears have been tears of love. There can be no deep disappointment where there is not deep love. Yes, I love the church. How could I do otherwise? I am in the rather unique position of being the son, the grandson and the great-grandson of preachers. Yes, I see the church as the body of Christ. But, oh! How we have blemished and scarred that body through social neglect and through fear of being nonconformists.

There was a time when the church was very powerful—in the time when the early Christians rejoiced at being deemed worthy to suffer for what they believed. In those days the church was not merely a thermometer that recorded the ideas and principles of popular opinion; it was a thermostat that transformed the mores of society. Whenever the early Christians entered a town, the people in power became disturbed and immediately sought to convict the Christians for being "disturbers of the peace" and "outside agitators." But the Christians pressed on, in the conviction that they were "a colony of heaven," called to obey God rather than man. Small in number, they were big in commitment. They were too God-intoxicated to be "astronomically intimidated." By their effort and example they brought an end to such ancient evils as infanticide and gladiatorial contests.

Things are different now. So often the contemporary church is a weak, ineffectual voice with an uncertain sound. So often it is an archdefender of the status quo. Far from being disturbed by the presence of the church, the power structure of the average community is consoled by the church's silent—and often even vocal—sanction of things as they are.

But the judgment of God is upon the church as never before. If today's church does not recapture the sacrificial spirit of the early church, it will lose its authenticity, forfeit the loyalty of millions, and be dismissed as an irrelevant social club with no meaning for the twentieth century. Every day I meet young people whose disappointment with the church has turned into outright disgust.

Perhaps I have once again been too optimistic. Is organized religion too inextricably bound to the status quo to save our nation and the world? Perhaps I must turn my faith to the inner spiritual church, the church within the church, as the true *ekklesia* and the hope of the world. But again I am thankful to God that some noble souls from the ranks of organized religion have broken loose from the paralyzing chains of conformity and joined us as active partners in the struggle for freedom. They have left their secure congregations and walked the streets of Albany, Georgia, with us. They have gone down the highways of the South on tortuous rides for freedom. Yes, they have gone to jail with us. Some have been dismissed from their churches, have lost the support of their bishops and fellow ministers. But they have acted in the faith that right defeated is stronger than evil triumphant. Their witness has been the spiritual salt that has preserved the true meaning of the gospel in these troubled times. They have carved a tunnel of hope through the dark mountain of disappointment.

I hope the church as a whole will meet the challenge of this decisive hour. But even if the church does not come to the aid of justice, I have no despair about the future. I have no fear about the outcome of our struggle in Birmingham, even if our motives are at present misunderstood. We will reach the goal of freedom in Birmingham and all over the nation, because the goal of America is freedom. Abused and scorned though we may be, our destiny is tied up with America's destiny. Before the pilgrims landed at Plymouth, we were here. Before the pen of Jefferson etched the majestic words of the Declaration of Independence across the pages of history, we were here. For more than two centuries our forebears labored in this country without wages; they made cotton king; they built the homes of their masters while suffering gross injustice and shameful humiliation—and yet out of a bottomless vitality they continued to thrive and develop. If the inexpressible cruelties of slavery could not stop us, the opposition we now face will surely fail. We will win our freedom because the sacred heritage of our nation and the eternal will of God are embodied in our echoing demands.

Before closing I feel impelled to mention one other point in your statement that has troubled me profoundly. You warmly commended the Birmingham police force for keeping "order" and "preventing violence." I doubt that you would have so warmly commended the police force if you had seen its dogs sinking their teeth into unarmed, nonviolent

Negroes. I doubt that you would so quickly commend the policemen if you were to observe their ugly and inhumane treatment of Negroes here in the city jail; if you were to watch them push and curse old Negro women and young Negro girls; if you were to see them slap and kick old Negro men and young boys; if you were to observe them, as they did on two occasions, refuse to give us food because we wanted to sing our grace together. I cannot join you in your praise of the Birmingham police department.

It is true that the police have exercised a degree of discipline in handling the demonstrators. In this sense they have conducted themselves rather "nonviolently" in public. But for what purpose? To preserve the evil system of segregation. Over the past few years I have consistently preached that nonviolence demands that the means we use must be as pure as the ends we seek. I have tried to make clear that it is wrong to use immoral means to attain moral ends. But now I must affirm that it is just as wrong, or perhaps even more so, to use moral means to preserve immoral ends. Perhaps Mr. Connor and his policemen have been rather nonviolent in public, as was Chief Pritchett in Albany, Georgia, but they have used the moral means of nonviolence to maintain the immoral end of racial injustice. As T. S. Eliot has said: "The last temptation is the greatest treason: To do the right deed for the wrong reason."

I wish you had commended the Negro sit-inners and demonstrators of Birmingham for their sublime courage, their willingness to suffer and their amazing discipline in the midst of great provocation. One day the South will recognize its real heroes. They will be the James Merediths, with the noble sense of purpose that enables them to face jeering and hostile mobs, and with the agonizing loneliness that characterizes the life of the pioneer. They will be old, oppressed, battered Negro women, symbolized in a seventy-two-year-old woman in Montgomery, Alabama, who rose up with a sense of dignity and with her people decided not to ride segregated buses, and who responded with ungrammatical profundity to one who inquired about her weariness: "My feets is tired, but my soul is at rest." They will be the young high school and college students, the young ministers of the gospel and a host of their elders, courageously and nonviolently sitting in at lunch counters and willingly going to jail for conscience' sake. One day the South will know that when these disinherited children of God sat down at lunch counters, they were in reality standing up for what is best in the American dream and for the most sacred values in our Judaeo-Christian heritage, thereby bringing our nation back to those great wells of democracy which were dug deep by the founding fathers in their formulation of the Constitution and the Declaration of Independence.

Never before have I written so long a letter. I'm afraid it is much too long to take your precious time. I can assure you that it would have been much shorter if I had been writing from a comfortable desk, but what else can one do when he is alone in a narrow jail cell, other than write long letters, think long thoughts and pray long prayers?

If I have said anything in this letter that overstates the truth and indicates an unreasonable impatience, I beg you to forgive me. If I have said anything that understates the truth and indicates my having a patience that allows me to settle for anything less than brotherhood, I beg God to forgive me.

I hope this letter finds you strong in the faith. I also hope that circumstances will soon make it possible for me to meet each of you, not as an integrationist or a civil-rights leader but as a fellow clergyman and a Christian brother. Let us all hope that the dark clouds of racial prejudice will soon pass away and the deep fog of misunderstanding will be lifted from our fear-drenched communities, and in some not too distant tomorrow the radiant stars of love and brotherhood will shine over our great nation with all their scintillating beauty.

Yours for the cause of Peace and Brotherhood,
*Martin Luther King, Jr.*

---

**Review Questions**

1.  How does King deal with those that oppose his movement?
2.  What is civil disobedience?
3.  When, in your opinion, is it right to break the law?
4.  Are there any phrases from this letter that you have seen printed before?
5.  Who did King feel was the greatest stumbling block for Negroes? Why did he feel that way?
6.  Who was the audience for this letter?
7.  Why was King in jail?

# *The Equality of Innocence:*
# *Washington, D.C.*

### *Jonathan Kozol*

Jonathan Kozol has written several books critical of the public school system in the United States. *Death at an Early Age, The Night Is Dark and I Am Far from Home,* and *Rachel and Her Children* each address this theme. His most recent book, *Savage Inequalities,* takes a close look at inner-city schools. This chapter focuses on school financing.

Most academic studies of school finance, sooner or later, ask us to consider the same question: "How can we achieve more equity in education in America?" A variation of the question is a bit more circumspect: "How can we achieve both equity and excellence in education?" Both questions, however, seem to value equity as a desired goal. But, when the recommendations of such studies are examined, and when we look as well at the solutions that innumerable commissions have proposed, we realize that they do not quite mean "equity" and that they have seldom asked for "equity." What they mean, what they prescribe, is *something that resembles equity but never reaches it:* something close enough to equity to silence criticism by approximating justice, but far enough from equity to guarantee the benefits enjoyed by privilege. The differences are justified by telling us that equity must always be "approximate" and cannot possibly be perfect. But the imperfection falls in almost every case to the advantage of the privileged.

In Maryland, for instance, one of several states in which the courts have looked at fiscal inequalities between school districts, an equity suit filed in 1978, although unsuccessful, led the state to reexamine the school funding system. When a task force set up by the governor offered its suggestions five years later, it argued that 100 percent equality was too expensive. The goal, it said, was *75 percent equality*—meaning that the poorest districts should be granted no less than three quarters of the funds at the disposal of the average district. But, as the missing 25 percent translates into differences of input (teacher pay, provision of books, class size, etc.), we discover it is just enough to demarcate the difference between services appropriate to different social classes, and to formalize that difference in their destinies.

"The equalized 75 percent," says an educator in one of the state's low-income districts, "buys just enough to keep all ships afloat. The unequal 25 percent assures that they will sail in opposite directions."

It is a matter of national pride that every child's ship be kept afloat. Otherwise our nation would be subject to the charge that we deny poor children public school. But what is now encompassed by the one word ("school") are two very different kinds of institutions that, in function, finance and intention, serve entirely different roles. Both are needed for our nation's governance. But children in one set of schools are educated to be governors; children in the other set of schools are trained for being governed. The former are given the imaginative range to mobilize ideas for economic growth; the latter are provided with the discipline to do the narrow tasks the first group will prescribe.

Societies cannot be all generals, no soldiers. But, by our schooling patterns, we assure that soldiers' children are more likely to be soldiers and that the offspring of the generals will have at least the option to be generals. If this is not so, if it is just a matter of the difficulty of assuring perfect fairness, why does the unfairness never benefit the children of the poor?

"Children in a true sense," writes John Coons of Berkeley University, "are all poor" because they are dependent on adults. There is also, he says, "a sameness among children in the sense of [a] substantial uncertainty about their potential role as adults." It could be expressed, he says, "as an equality of innocence." The equality of adults, by comparison, "is always problematical; even social and economic differences among them are plausibly ascribed to their own deserts . . . In any event, adults as a class enjoy no presumption of homogeneous virtue and their ethical demand for equality of treatment is accordingly attenuated. The differences among children, on the other hand, cannot be ascribed even vaguely to fault without indulging in an attaint of blood uncongenial to our time."

Terms such as "attaint of blood" are rarely used today, and, if they were, they would occasion public indignation; but the rigging of the game and the acceptance, which is nearly universal, of uneven playing fields reflect a dark unspoken sense that other people's children are of less inherent value than our own. Now and then, in private, affluent suburbanites concede that certain aspects of the game may be a trifle rigged to their advantage. "Sure, it's a bit unjust," they may concede, "but that's reality and that's the way the game is played. . . .

"In any case," they sometimes add in a refrain that we have heard now many times, "there's no real evidence that spending money makes much difference in the outcome of a child's education. We have it. So we spend it. But it's probably a secondary matter. Other factors—family and background—seem to be a great deal more important."

In these ways they fend off dangers of disturbing introspection; and this, in turn, enables them to give their children something far more precious than the simple gift of pedagogic privilege. They give them uncontaminated satisfaction in their victories. Their children learn to shut from mind the possibility that they are winners in an unfair race, and they seldom let themselves lose sleep about the losers. There are, of course, unusual young people who, no matter what their parents tell them, do become aware of the inequities at stake. We have heard the voices of a few such students in this book. But the larger numbers of these favored children live with a remarkable experience of ethical exemption. Cruelty is seldom present in the thinking of such students, but it is contained within insouciance.

Sometimes the residents of affluent school districts point to certain failings in their own suburban schools, as if to say that "all our schools" are "rather unsuccessful" and that "minor differentials" between urban and suburban schools may not therefore be of much significance. "You know," said the father of two children who had gone to school in Great Neck, "it isn't just New York. We have our problems on Long Island too. My daughter had some high school teachers who were utterly inept and uninspired. She has had a devil of a time at Sarah Lawrence. . . . " He added that she had friends who went to private school and who were given a much better preparation. "It just seems terribly unfair," he said.

Defining unfairness as the difficulty that a Great Neck graduate encounters at a top-flight private college, to which any child in the South Bronx would have given her right arm to be admitted, strikes one as a way of rendering the term so large that it means almost nothing. "What is unfair," he is saying in effect, "is what I *determine* to be unfair. What I find unfair is what affects my child, not somebody else's child in New York." Competition at the local high school, said another Great Neck parent, was "unhealthy." He described the toll it took on certain students. "Children in New York may suffer from too little. Many of our children suffer from too much." The loss of distinctions in these statements serves to blur the differences between the inescapable unhappiness of being human and the needless misery created by injustice. It also frees the wealthy from the obligation to concede the difference between inconvenience and destruction.

Poor people do not need to be reminded that the contest is unfair. "My children," says Elizabeth, a friend of mine who lives in a black neighborhood of Boston, "know very well the system is unfair. They also know that they are living in a rich society. They see it on TV, and in advertisements, and in the movies. They see the president at his place in Maine, riding around the harbor in his motor boat and playing golf with other wealthy men. They know that men like these did not come out of schools in Roxbury or Harlem. They know that they were given something extra. They don't know exactly what it is, but they have seen enough, and heard enough, to know that men don't speak like that and look like that unless they have been fed with silver spoons—and went to schools that had a lot of silver spoons and other things that cost a lot. . . .

"So they know this other world exists, and, when you tell them that the government can't find the money to provide them with a decent place to go to school, they don't believe it and they know that it's a *choice* that has been made—a choice about how much they matter to society. They see it as a message: 'This is to tell you that you don't much matter. You are ugly to us so we crowd you into ugly places. You are dirty so it will not hurt to pack you into dirty places.' My son says this: 'By doing this to you, we teach you how much you are hated.' I like to listen to the things my children say. They're not sophisticated so they speak out of their hearts."

One of the ideas, heard often in the press, that stirs the greatest sense of anger in a number of black parents that I know is that the obstacles black children face, to the extent that "obstacles" are still conceded, are attributable, at most, to "past injustice"—something dating maybe back to slavery or maybe to the era of official segregation that came to its close during the years from 1954 to 1968—but not, in any case, to something recent or contemporary or ongoing. The nostrum of a "past injustice"— an expression often spoken with sarcasm—is particularly cherished by conservatives because it serves to undercut the claim that young black people living now may have some right to preferential opportunities. Contemporary claims based on a "past injustice," after all, begin to seem implausible if the alleged injustice is believed to be a generation, or six generations, in the past. "We were not alive when these injustices took place," white students say. "Some of us were born to parents who came here as immigrants. None of these things are our responsibility, and we should not be asked to suffer for them."

But the hundreds of classrooms without teachers in Chicago's public schools, the thousands of children without classrooms in the schools of Irvington and Paterson and East Orange, the calculated racial segregation of the children in the skating rink in District 10 in New York City, and the lifelong poisoning of children in the streets and schools of East St. Louis are not matters of anterior injustice. They are injustices of 1991.

Over 30 years ago, the city of Chicago purposely constructed the high-speed Dan Ryan Expressway in such a way as to cut off the section of the city in which housing projects for black people had been built. The Robert Taylor Homes, served by Du Sable High, were subsequently constructed in that isolated area as well; realtors thereafter set aside adjoining neighborhoods for rental only to black people. The expressway is still there. The projects are still there. Black children still grow up in the same neighborhoods. There is nothing "past" about most "past discrimination" in Chicago or in any other northern city.

In seeking to find a metaphor for the unequal contest that takes place in public school, advocates for equal education sometimes use the image of a tainted sports event. We have seen, for instance, the familiar image of the playing field that isn't level. Unlike a tainted sports event, however, a childhood cannot be played again. We are children only once; and, after those few years are gone, there is no second chance to make amends. In this respect, the consequences of unequal education have a terrible finality. Those who are denied cannot be "made whole" by a later act of government. Those who get the unfair edge cannot be later stripped of what they've won. Skills, once attained—no matter how unfairly—take on a compelling aura. Effectiveness seems irrefutable, no matter how acquired. The winners in this race *feel* meritorious. Since they also are, in large part, those who govern the discussion of this issue, they are not disposed to cast a cloud upon the means of their ascent. People like Elizabeth are left disarmed. Their only argument is justice. But justice, poorly argued, is no match for the acquired ingenuity of the successful. The fruits of inequality, in this respect, are self-confirming.

There are "two worlds of Washington," the *Wall Street Journal* writes. One is the Washington of "cherry blossoms, the sparkling white monuments, the magisterial buildings of government. . . , of politics and power." In the Rayburn House Office Building, the *Journal* writes, "a harpist is playing Schumann's 'Traumerei,' the bartenders are tipping the top brands of Scotch, and two huge salmons sit on mirrored platters." Just over a mile away, the other world is known as Anacostia.

In an elementary school in Anacostia, a little girl in the fifth grade tells me that the first thing she would do if somebody gave money to her school would be to plant a row of flowers by the street. "Blue flowers," she says. "And I'd buy some curtains for my teacher." And she specifies again: "Blue curtains."

I ask her, "Why blue curtains?"

"It's like this," she says. "The school is dirty. There isn't any playground. There's a hole in the wall behind the principal's desk. What we need to do is first rebuild the school. Another color. Build a playground. Plant a lot of flowers. Paint the classrooms. Blue and white. Fix the hole in the principal's office. Buy doors for the toilet stalls in the girls' bathroom. Fix the ceiling in this room. It looks like somebody went up and peed over our heads. Make it a beautiful clean building. Make it *pretty*. Way it is, I feel ashamed."

Her name is Tunisia. She is tall and thin and has big glasses with red frames. "When people come and see our school," she says, "they don't say nothing, but I know what they are thinking."

"Our teachers," says Octavia, who is tiny with red sneakers and two beaded cornrows in her hair, "shouldn't have to eat here in the basement. I would like for them to have a dining room. A nice room with a salad bar. Serve our teachers big thick steaks to give them energy."

A boy named Gregory tells me that he was visiting in Fairfax County on the weekend. "Those neighborhoods are different," Gregory reports. "They got a golf course there. Big houses. Better schools."

I ask him why he thinks they're better schools.

"We don't know why," Tunisia says. "We are too young to have the information."

"You live in certain areas and things are different," Gregory explains.

Not too long ago, the basement cafeteria was flooded. Rain poured into the school and rats appeared. Someone telephoned the mayor: "You've got dead rats here in the cafeteria."

The principal is an aging, slender man. He speaks of generations of black children lost to bitterness and failure. He seems worn down by sorrow and by anger at defeat. He has been the principal since 1959.

"How frustrating it is," he says, "to see so many children going hungry. On Fridays in the cafeteria I see small children putting chicken nuggets in their pockets. They're afraid of being hungry on the weekend."

A teacher looks out at her class: "These children don't smile. Why should they learn when their lives are so hard and so unhappy?"

Seven children meet me in the basement cafeteria. The flood that brought the rats is gone, but other floods have streaked the tiles in the ceiling.

The school is on a road that runs past several boarded buildings. Gregory tells me they are called "pipe" houses. "Go by there one day—it be vacant. Next day, they bring sofas, chairs. Day after that, you see the junkies going in."

I ask the children what they'd do to get rid of the drugs.

"Get the New Yorkers off our streets," Octavia says. "They come here from New York, perturbed, and sell our children drugs."

"Children working for the dealers," Gregory explains.

A teacher sitting with us says, "At eight years old, some of the boys are running drugs and holding money for the dealers. By 28, they're going to be dead."

Tunisia: "It makes me sad to see black people kill black people."

"Four years from now," the principal says when we sit down to talk after the close of school, "one third of the little girls in this fifth grade are going to be pregnant."

I look into the faces of these children. At this moment they seem full of hope and innocence and expectation. The little girls have tiny voices and they squirm about on little chairs and lean way forward with their elbows on the table and their noses just above the table's surface and make faces at each other and seem mischievous and wise and beautiful. Two years from now, in junior high, there may be more toughness in their eyes, a look of lessened expectations and increasing cynicism. By the time they are 14, a certain rawness and vulgarity may have set in. Many will be hostile and embittered by that time. Others will coarsen, partly the result of diet, partly self-neglect and self-dislike. Visitors who meet such girls in elementary school feel tenderness; by junior high, they feel more pity or alarm.

But today, in Anacostia, the children are young and whimsical and playful. If you hadn't worked with kids like these for 20 years, you would have no reason to feel sad. You'd think, "They have the world before them."

"The little ones come into school on Monday," says the teacher, "and they're hungry. A five-year-old. Her laces are undone. She says, 'I had to dress myself this morning.' I ask her why. She says, 'They took my mother off to jail.' Their stomachs hurt. They don't know why. We feed them something hot because they're hungry."

I ask the children if they go to church. Most of them say they do. I ask them how they think of God.

"He has a face like ours," Octavia says.

A white face or a black face?

"Mexican," she says.

Tunisia: "I don't know the answer to that question."

"When you go to God," says Gregory, "He'll remind you of everything you did. He adds it up. If you were good, you go to Heaven. If you were selfish, then He makes you stand and wait awhile—over there. Sometimes you get a second chance. You need to wait and see."

We talk about teenagers who get pregnant. Octavia explains: "They want to be like rock stars. Grow up fast." She mentions a well-known singer. "She left school in junior high, had a baby. Now she got a swimming pool and car."

Tunisia says, "That isn't it. Their lives are sad."

A child named Monique goes back to something we discussed before: "If I had a lot of money, I would give it to poor children."

The statement surprises me. I ask her if the children in this neighborhood are poor. Several children answer, "No."

Tunisia (after a long pause): "We are all poor people in this school."

The bell rings, although it isn't three o'clock. The children get up and say good-bye and start to head off to the stairs that lead up from the basement to the first floor. The principal later tells me he released the children early. He had been advised that there would be a shooting in the street this afternoon.

I tell him how much I liked the children and he's obviously pleased. Tunisia, he tells me, lives in the Capital City Inn—the city's largest homeless shelter. She has been homeless for a year, he says; he thinks that this may be one reason she is so reflective and mature.

Delabian Rice-Thurston, an urban planner who has children in the D.C. schools, says this: "We did a comparison of schools in Washington and schools out in the suburbs. A group of business leaders went with us. They found it sobering. One of them said, 'If anybody thinks that money's not an issue, let the people in Montgomery County put their children in the D.C. schools. Parents in Montgomery would riot.' "

She runs through a number of the schools they visited in Washington: "There was a hole in the ceiling of a classroom on the third floor of the Coolidge School. They'd put a 20-gallon drum under the hole to catch the rain. The toilets at the Stevens School were downright unpleasant. But, if you really want to see some filth, you go to the Langston School. You go down into the basement—to the women's toilet. I would not go to the bathroom in that building if my life depended on it.

"Go to Spingarn. It's a high school in the District. The time we visited, it was a hot, humid day in June. It was steaming up there on the third floor. Every window on one side had been nailed shut. A teacher told me that a child said to her, 'This school ain't shit.' She answered him, 'I have to teach you here. We both know what it is.'

"If you're rich in Washington, you try to send your kids to private school. Middle-class people sometimes put their kids in certain public schools. Parents in those neighborhoods raise outside money so their kids get certain extras. There are boundaries for school districts, but some parents know the way to cross the borders. The poorer and less educated parents can't. They don't know how.

"The D.C. schools are 92 percent black, 4 percent white, 4 percent Hispanic and some other ethnics. There is no discussion of cross-busing with the suburbs. People in Montgomery and Fairfax wouldn't hear of it. It would mean their children had to cross state borders. There is regional cooperation on a lot of other things. We have a regional airport, a regional public-transit system, and a regional sewage-disposal system. Not when it comes to education.

"Black people did not understand that whites would go to such extremes to keep our children at a distance. We never believed that it would come to this: that they would flee our children. Mind you, many of these folks are government officials. They are setting policy for the entire nation. So their actions, their behavior, speak to something more than just one system.

"If you're black you have to understand—white people would destroy their schools before they'd let our children sit beside their children. They would leave their homes and sell them for a song in order not to live with us and see our children socializing with their children. And if white people want the central city back someday, they'll get it. If they want to build nice homes along the Anacostia River, they'll get Anacostia too. We'll be sent off to another neighborhood, another city."

Poor people in the District, she explains, want very much to keep the middle-class children, white and black, from fleeing from the city's schools. In order to keep them, they are willing to accept a dual system in the District, even while recognizing that the better schools, the so-called "magnet schools," for instance, will attract the wealthier children and will leave more concentrated numbers of the poorest children in the poorest schools. In other words, she says, in order not to have an all-poor system with still less political and fiscal backing than they have today, they will accept the lesser injustice of two kinds of schools within one system. Even within a single school, they will accept a dual track—essentially, two separate schools within one building.

This compromise would not be needed if the city were not isolated from the suburbs in the first place. A similar dynamic is at stake in New York City and Chicago, where, as we have seen, at least two separate systems coexist disguised as one. If the urban schools were not so poor, if there were no ghetto and therefore no ghetto system, people wouldn't be obliged to make this bleak accommodation. But once a city of primarily poor people has been isolated and cut off, the poorest of the poor will often acquiesce in this duality out of the fear of losing some of the side-benefits of having less-poor people in the system.

So it is a loser's strategy: "Favor the most fortunate among us or they'll leave us too. Then we will have even fewer neighbors who can win political attention for our children." There is always the example of a place like Paterson or East St. Louis, where almost all residents are poor. These pitiful trade-offs would not be required if we did not have a dual system in the first place. But one dual system (city versus suburbs) almost inevitably creates a second dual system (city-poor versus city-less-than-poor). So it is that inequality, once it is accepted, grows contagious. . . .

"Despite a lot of pious rhetoric about equality of opportunity . . . ," writes Christopher Jencks, "most parents want their children to have a more than equal chance of success"—which means, inevitably, that they want others, not all others but some others, to have less than equal chances. This is the case in health care, for example—where most wealthy people surely want to give their children something better than an equal choice of being born alive and healthy, and have so apportioned health resources to assure this—and it is the case in education too.

Test scores in math and reading in America are graded not against an absolute standard but against a "norm" or "average." For some to be above the norm, others *have* to be below it. Preeminence, by definition, is a zero-sum matter. There is not an ever-expanding pie of "better-than-average" academic excellence. There can't be. Two thirds of American children can never score above average. Half the population has to score below the average, and the average is determined not by local or state samples but by test results for all Americans. We are 16,000 districts when it comes to opportunity but one nation when it comes to the determination of rewards.

When affluent school districts proudly tell their parents that the children in the district score, for instance, "in the eightieth percentile," they are measuring local children against children everywhere. Although there is nothing invidious about this kind of claim—it is a natural thing to advertise if it is true—what goes unspoken is that this preeminence is rendered possible (or, certainly, *more* possible) by the abysmal scores of others.

There is good reason, then, as economist Charles Benson has observed, that "discussion about educational inequalities is muted." People in the suburbs who deplore *de facto* segregation in the cities, he observes, "are the ones who have a major stake in preserving the lifetime advantages that their privileged, though tax-supported, schools offer their children." The vocal elements of the community, he says, "find it hard to raise their voices on the one issue over which, in the present scheme of things, they can lose most of all." . . .

Two years ago [1989], George Bush felt prompted to address this issue. More spending on public education, said the president, isn't "the best answer." Mr. Bush went on to caution parents of poor children who see money "as a cure" for education problems. "A society that worships money . . . ," said the president, "is a society in peril."

The president himself attended Phillips Academy in Andover, Massachusetts—a school that spends $11,000 yearly on each pupil, not including costs of room and board. If money is a wise investment for the education of a future president at Andover, it is no less so for the child of poor people in Detroit. But the climate of the times does not encourage this belief, and the president's words will surely reinforce that climate.

**Review Questions**

1.   What is the big question in school financing?
2.   Why does Kozol call affluent children winners in an unfair race?
3.   Why was Tunisia ashamed of her school? Who should be ashamed?
4.   What do the "two worlds" of Washington, DC teach the children who go to Anacostia schools?
5.   What makes the high test scores in the affluent schools possible?

## English and Good English

### Geoffrey Nunberg

> In this essay, which introduced an edition of the *American Heritage Dictionary*, Nunberg talks about the concerns voiced by people who feel good English is disappearing. He maintains that the fate of the language does not rest with copywriters or bureaucrats, but with poets, novelists, and other artists.

It is natural enough that the parties in the debate over what makes for "good English" should be preoccupied with their differences, but what tends to get overlooked in the process is that all sides share a great many common assumptions and that these assumptions are in fact every bit as particular and curious as the more notorious idiosyncracies of English spelling. It is not so much the linguistic virtues we recognize that are unusual. All of us admire language that is vivid, euphonious, rhythmic, and eloquent as well as clear, logical, and concise. But it is only these last that we elevate to the status of civic and moral responsibilities. We may pity the speaker with a tin ear, but so long as he expresses himself clearly and logically, we are not likely to hold him up as a horrible example of the failure of the educational system.

What is even more curious, we apply the canons of good usage only when we are considering the relatively restricted writing that we classify as expository prose. Essays on the sad state of the language seem invariably to begin with a ritual invocation to "the tongue of Shakespeare and Dickens," but the evidence of degeneration that they cite is never drawn from recent poetry or fiction. Instead examples of errors culled from advertisements, newspaper stories, and government reports are given, as if the fate of English lay entirely in the hands of its copywriters and bureaucrats rather than its artists.

All of this would have been puzzling to Dante or Cyrano—or to Shakespeare, for that matter. And others would find it odd, as well, that English grammarians made no effort to establish a single correct accent but rather allowed each nation—or, in America, each locality—to establish its own local standards of pronunciation. And finally, they would surely wonder why in centuries of bickering about usage the English-speaking world has never seriously tried to establish an academy to set things right once and for all. In short, asking a foreigner to understand our concept of usage would be rather like asking a present-day banker to understand why Dante cast the usurers down to the seventh circle.

Our ideas of good usage were for the most part shaped in the eighteenth century. They owed something to the growth of literacy and the rise of the middle class, something to the replacement of the Stuart court by the German-speaking Hanovers, and something to a new perception of English as the language not just of England but also of the larger community of Great Britain and the colonies. The new attitudes were most closely associated with the rise of a new class of writers and intellectuals, freed for the first time from direct dependence on aristocratic patronage, who assumed cultural authority during the period. To a striking extent these men were outsiders: the Scotsmen Hume, Adam Smith, and Smollett, the Irishmen Burke, Steele, Swift, and Goldsmith, the Catholic Alexander Pope, and the middle-class provincials Gay, Sterne, and Dr. Johnson. Their object was to replace the social values of the declining aristocratic tradition with new values determined by a "natural" elite based on wit and learning, and they moved immediately to assume authority over the language, the only coin they had it in their power to mint. Never before or since have so many great minds occupied themselves with the problem of defining and rationalizing the English language—not just Johnson but Swift, Addison, Chesterfield, Priestley, Webster, and many more whose names are no longer familiar. If they did not succeed in "ascertaining" the language, as many had hoped, they did at least manage to fix the criteria by which language use would be judged for the next two hundred years.

The eighteenth-century grammarians never seriously questioned the doctrine that usage should be the "supreme arbiter" of linguistic correctness. As the great grammarian George Campbell observed in his 1776 *Philosophy of Rhetoric*, "Every tongue whatever is founded in use or custom." At stake was whose usage should rule and why. In earlier days English standards had been set in the relatively changeable speech of the aristocracy and its captive clergy, and a usage was justified largely according to the prestige of its users. The prescriptive grammarians, as they have come to be called, insisted instead that standards must be fixed and rational. To this end they argued the supremacy of literary precedents, in particular those of critical prose, as recorded and systematized in the comprehensive dictionaries and grammars that had begun to appear for

the first time. Such models were more permanent and more democratic—for the great writers were selected, not by accidents of birth, but
by natural talent and public approbation. More radical than their conti-
nental contemporaries, the grammarians argued that linguistic authority
should be sharply separated from any national institutions. In 1712 Swift
had been one of many to suggest the formation of an academy, to be
composed partly of writers and partly of aristocrats, and one might actually have been constituted if the Tories had remained in power. But by
mid-century the idea was universally rejected as inimical to what
Johnson called the spirit of English liberty.

   But the chief virtue of literary models of good usage, from the grammarians' point of view, was not in their fixity or their popular acceptance
but in the fact that their merits could be explicitly justified by appeals to
analogy, etymology, and logic; for the Age of Reason good usage had to be
rationalized. Thus there began to appear such now-familiar dictates as
the injunctions against usages like *It is me, more perfect, the tallest of
the two*, and *as old, or older than*, among many others, all justified by
reference to what logic should require. And a sharp distinction was
drawn between those aspects of usage that allowed of rational justification and others, like pronunciation, that remained tied to social prestige.

   In their zeal many of the grammarians—like their modern succes-
sors—seemed sometimes to want to make all usage subject to their idi-
osyncratic ideas of logic, without due respect for the idiomaticity of
language. As modern linguists have been at pains to show, language has
a logic of its own, which does not always reveal itself to casual reflection.
To take just one example, linguists have noted that the rule requiring
words like *everyone* and *each* to be followed by singular pronouns becomes a cropper when the pronoun occurs outside of the clause that contains its antecedent. We simply cannot say, for example, *Everyone took
his coat, and he left without saying good-bye.* But linguists err when
they conclude that the "logical" justifications that the grammarians offered for good usage were really intended as excuses to justify the usage
of the ruling classes. The specific rules that the grammarians insisted on
may sometimes have been ill-considered, but that is less important than
the general principle that the rules were intended to illustrate: good usage is determined in rational reflection on language.

   What is more, while the literate middle class to which the prescriptive grammarians were speaking may have been by modern standards a small elite, it was much larger than the aristocracy whose
linguistic standards it usurped, and in advancing the notion that linguistic values required an independent, rational justification the prescriptive

grammarians set themselves squarely on the side of merit against hereditary privilege. Until recently, at least, English prescriptive grammar has been a doctrine closely associated with liberal ideals, as can be seen from the roster of its defenders, from Johnson to Matthew Arnold to George Orwell, W. H. Auden, and Lionel Trilling.

By the middle of the twentieth century, however, the social battle lines had been substantially redrawn. Earlier grammarians had given little time to inveighing against the speech of the provinces or the lower classes. It was simply understood that such models were unacceptable. But the twentieth century brought with it a new pluralistic idea of how cultural values should be determined, and prescriptive grammarians sometimes found themselves having to defend the very sorts of class values that had been attacked two hundred years before as they tried to show that middle-class language was superior in logic or clarity to the language of the lower classes or of ethnic minorities. At this point, moreover, the battle was joined by proponents of the new linguistics, who quite correctly pointed out that every language variety has its own internal logic and who questioned the authority of mere writers and critics to speak to matters that required considerable technical expertise. In the name of science the linguists insisted that there were no hard grounds for preferring the usage of one group over another and went on to argue that the entire notion of correctness rested on an ill-justified elitism.

By the time the controversy had reached its pitch, in the furor over the publication of more "permissive" dictionaries and grammar textbooks, there had been a curious ideological shift. Now the grammarians were attacked as apologists for the entrenched order, while the opponents of traditional doctrines of usage were branded mobocrats. As in other areas, the old liberals found themselves in alliance with the new right as writers like William F. Buckley, Jr. began to sound the same themes that George Orwell had insisted on a generation earlier.

At present we are at an impasse. Both sides fulgurate, while in the middle the lexicographers and educators often counsel an enlightened hypocrisy: even if the canons of good usage have no real justification, it is best that people be taught to conform to them so as not to give offense to traditionalists. And to be sure, there are no easy solutions, since each side has a part of the right in the matter. On the one hand, it is clear that there is no going back to the days of a homogeneous, literate elite whose linguistic authority is accepted unquestioningly. Nor can the technical authority of modern linguistics be repealed, any more than that of psychiatry, sociology, or the other sciences that have taken over a large part of the intellectual territory that used to belong to the critical public. The day is past when the dictates of any single lexicographer or grammarian could hope to command the attention, much less the deference, of the literate public.

At the same time, the linguists have not the fondest hope of convincing the public that all widely practiced forms of usage are equally acceptable; if anything, there is more support now for traditional standards than there was twenty years ago. And this is surely good, for if the idea that good usage has a rational justification is abandoned, people will return to the doctrine that the correctness of a usage is based entirely on the social prestige of the speaker—the very notion that both the eighteenth-century grammarians and the modern radicals have found intolerable. This has always been the English speaker's attitude toward pronunciation, which has been considered to lie outside the scope of rational justification; if the laissez-faire party had its way, all other aspects of usage would be reduced equally to matters of pure snobbery.

---

### Review Questions

1. Why doesn't America have an academy to correct English usage as France does for French?
2. When were most of our ideas about good usage developed?
3. Why do words like "everyone" present usage problems?
4. Are usage rules elitist? Support your answer.
5. What's a language traditionalist?

## The Definition and Determination of "Correct" English

### Robert C. Pooley

This essay evaluates English usage according to the social classes of people who use it. Pooley wrote this essay in 1946, and, while almost no one says these things today, see how many of his assumptions about how the language you use mark your social status are still true. The idea that Americans do not have a class system has persisted in spite of continuing evidence that it does exist. Pooley gave examples of differences in speech patterns that continue despite compulsory education. Have these differences changed much over the years?

In the year 1712 Dean Swift wrote a letter to the Earl of Oxford outlining a plan for the foundation of an English academy similar to the French Academy for the purpose of regularizing and establishing correct

English. Although his plan was received with interest, it was never acted upon, and many later attempts to found an academy have failed. The purists of the later eighteenth century did much of what Swift desired, but fortunately for the life and vigor of our tongue it has never been submitted to the restraint of a board of authorities. Several theories of "correctness" in English have therefore been formulated and have influenced writers and teachers of the past and present. One of the most important of these theories was that enunciated by George Campbell in 1776, that "correctness" rests in good custom, defined as "national," "reputable," and "present." This definition was accepted by practically all the nineteenth-century grammarians (although they frequently did it violence in specific instances), and may be found in a number of the high-school composition books of the present day. Another theory, really a modification of Campbell's, proposed by Fitzedward Hall and other nineteenth-century students of language, is that "good usage is the usage of the best writers and speakers." This definition is also very widely used in the textbooks of today, and is probably the expressed or implied standard of good English in almost every American school room. Both of these definitions, useful as they have been and are, present many difficulties in application to the teaching of current usage.

The chief difficulty lies in the interpretation of the terms "reputable" and "the best writers and speakers." For example, nearly all grammar books list as undesirable English the use of the split infinitive, the dangling participle or gerund, the possessive case of the noun with inanimate objects, the objective case of the noun with the gerund, the use of *whose* as a neuter relative pronoun, and many others; yet all of these uses may be found in the authors who form the very backbone of English literature and who are "reputable" and the "best writers" in every sense of the words. If the standard-makers defy the standards, to whom shall we turn for authority? Moreover, the use of literary models tends to ignore the canon of *present* usage, for by the time an author has come to be generally recognized as *standard* his usage is no longer *present*. And among present speakers, who are best? The writer has heard a large number of the most prominent platform speakers of the day, yet he has still to hear one who did not in some manner violate the rules of the books. Are all great writers and speakers at fault, or is it possible that the rules are inaccurate?

The way out of this perplexity is to shift the search for standards away from "authorities" and traditional rules to the language itself as it is spoken and written today. Just as the chemist draws his deductions from the results of laboratory experiments, the biologist from his observation of forms of life, and the astronomer from his telescope, so must students of language draw their deductions from an observation of the facts of language. In establishing the laws of language, our personal desires, preferences, and prejudices must give way to the scientific determination and interpretation of the facts of language. What language we use ourselves may take any form we desire, but the making of rules and the teaching of rules must rest upon objective facts. We must take the attitude of a distinguished scholar who said recently of *due to,* "I don't like it, but there is no doubt about its establishment in English."

If we discard the authority of rules and of "reputable" writers, to what can we turn for a definition of "correct" English? At the outset it must be acknowledged that there can be no absolute, positive definition. "Correct English" is an approximate term used to describe a series of evaluations of usage dependent upon appropriateness, locality, social level, purpose, and other variables. It is a relative term, in decided contrast with the positive nature of (1) *reputability,* the determination of good usage by reference to standard authors; (2) *preservation,* the obligation to defend and maintain language uses because they are traditional, or are felt to be more elegant; (3) *literary,* the identification of good usage with formal literary usage. By discarding these traditional conceptions, and turning to the language itself as its own standard of good usage, we may find the following definition adequate for our present needs. *Good English is that form of speech which is appropriate to the purpose of the speaker, true to the language as it is, and comfortable to speaker and listener. It is the product of custom, neither cramped by rule nor freed from all restraint; it is never fixed, but changes with the organic life of the language.*

Such a definition is linguistically sound because it recognizes the living, organic nature of language; it is historically sound, for the language of the present is seen to be the product of established custom; it is socially sound in recognizing the purpose of language and its social acceptability in *comfort* to speaker and writer.

Teachers of English will recognize that the acceptance of this or a similar definition of good English necessitates great changes in the presentation of usage in textbooks and in the classroom. Those who are accustomed to rule and authority, to an absolute right and wrong in language, will find great difficulty in making the mental readjustment imperative for a relative rather than an absolute standard of usage. Much of the conventional teaching of grammar and correctness will have to be vastly modified or discarded. There will be much confusion and some distress. But eventually there will grow up in the schools a new theory of good English so closely knit with the language itself that the perplexity now arising from the discrepancies between rule and usage will no longer have cause for existence. But in discarding an absolute right and wrong for a relative standard of appropriateness and social acceptability, we shall have to determine the areas or levels of language usage, to define and illustrate them, and to apply them as standards for the written and spoken English in the schools. . . .

It is obvious that when such terms as *appropriate, customary, comfortable,* or *socially desirable* are used in defining the nature of good English usage, the conception of a single standard or level of correctness can no longer prevail. Speech is a form of human behavior, and like all forms of human behavior, is subject to almost infinite variety. But in even the most primitive societies human behavior is made subject to certain restraints, determined and maintained by the social group. Some of these are fundamental, essential to the life of the group, like the prohibition of murder; others are ceremonial in character, applying to all members of the group at certain times, or to some members of the group at all times. In somewhat similar fashion language usages are subjected to the restraints of society. At all times those who speak a language are required to keep within the limits of intelligibility in order to be understood; language which departs from custom so far as to be incomprehensible defeats its own purpose. But in addition to fundamental understanding there are ceremonial distinctions in language to be found in the most primitive societies; the language of the council fire or religious observance differs in vocabulary and tone from that of the hunt or the harvest. In civilized societies the same principle prevails, except that greater complexity of life calls forth a wider range of differentiations in usage. It will cause no surprise upon reflection to realize that we all more or less unconsciously distinguish three or more gradations or levels in our language usage; there is the informal intimate speech of the home and of our hours of recreation; the slightly restrained speech of semi-public occasions, like conversation with strangers; and the carefully chosen, deliberate language of public address on formal occasions. Each of these has its analogue in writing. Moreover, business and professional people are very apt to employ a technical vocabulary among their colleagues, sometimes almost incomprehensible to the uninitiated. It seems beyond doubt reasonable, therefore, that this differentiation of language usage, a fundamental law of language, should be our first consideration in the study of "correct" English and in the presentation of English usage in the classroom. The purpose of this chapter is to define and illustrate the levels of English usage and to point out their relative values in the social group.

### The Illiterate Level

The words and phrases typical of this level of English usage mark the user as belonging definitely outside the pale of cultivated, educated society. They have no standing whatever in literature, except in the dialect conversation of characters deliberately portrayed as illiterate or uncultivated. Although comparatively few in number, they are widespread and extremely common in the speech of the uneducated. They cannot be tolerated in the classroom except in deliberate attempts to reproduce the conversation of illiterate characters.

**Examples**

If I had *of* come, he wouldn't *of* done it.

I got the measles *off* Jimmie.

He *give* me the book. (past tense)

They *was*, we *was*, you *was*

I *is*, you *is*, they *is*, them *is*

He *come, done, seen, run*, etc.

*Have went, have came, have did, have saw, have ran, have drank,* etc.

The double negative, as in: *didn't have no, won't never, can't never, couldn't get no*, etc.

*Them* books

*Youse*

I *ain't*, you *ain't*, etc.

*Growed, knowed, blowed, seed*, etc.

*That there, this here*

He looked at me and *says*

*Leave* me do it.

He did *noble, good, swell*, etc.

### The Homely Level

The words and phrases typical of this level are outside the limits of standard, cultivated usage, yet are not completely illiterate. They characterize the speech of many worthy men and women with some claim to literacy, who by the accident of birth, occupation, or geographical location are denied the society of more cultivated persons. The children in many of our rural schools come from homes in which the parents speak the English of this level. It behooves the teacher, therefore, to have an understanding sympathy for this type of speech, and while zealously seeking to build up in the children a dialect more closely approaching standard English, to refrain from ridiculing the speech of the home or from characterizing it unreservedly as "bad English." Tactful understanding will do far more than rigid purism in creating among these children a respect for the more standard forms of speech and a desire to attain a higher standard of usage.

### Examples

He *don't* come here any more.

I *expect* you're hungry.

Stop the bus; I *want out.*

Mary's mother, *she* isn't very smart.

I *got* an apple right here in my hand.

I *haven't hardly* time.

We *can't scarcely* do it.

Just where are we *at?*

He *begun, sung, drunk, eat,* etc.

The various forms of confusion in *lie* and *lay, sit* and *set, rise* and *raise*

I *want for* you to do it.

The dessert was made with *whip cream.*

He comes *of a Sunday.*

John *was raised* in Kentucky.

This is *all the farther* we can go.

*Calculate* (or cal'late, reckon) for *guess, suppose*

A light-*complected* girl

*Hadn't he ought* to do it?

To this homely level of English speech belong also the local dialect uses not generally recognized over the United States, like the *to home,* for *at home,* of New England; the *admire* for *like* of the South; the *loco* for *crazy* of the West; and the characteristic idioms of the mountaineers in the Blue Ridge and Ozark ranges.

### *Standard English, Informal Level*

The range of Standard English is necessarily very wide. It must include all the words, phrases, forms, and idioms employed by the great mass of English-speaking people in the United States whose dialect lies between the homely level and the decidedly literary level. It must be wide enough to include the variations of language usage common among people of education; the speech of the home, of the hours of business and recreation, as well as that of the party and formal reception. In written form it must include the most informal of personal correspondence to the formal phrasing of the business and social note. Standard English is, in fact, *the language;* it is present, ordinary, comfortable usage, with sufficient breadth in limits to permit of the shades of difference appropriate to specific occasions.

The informal level of Standard English includes words and phrases commonly used by people of culture and education in their more informal moments, but which are generally excluded from formal public address, social conversation with strangers, and formal social correspondence. Informal Standard English should be the normal usage of the teacher in the classroom and the goal which is set for the pupils to attain. A large part of the confusion arising from the teaching of usage in schools has been the result of trying to maintain the formal standard dialect, appropriate to careful writing, for the conversational needs of the schoolroom. There is no more need for children to be bookish in their schoolroom speech than for the teacher herself to be bookish in her intimate conversation.

The examples listed here for the informal standard level include only those items which may be employed informally but which are generally excluded from formal Standard English.

### Examples

He *blamed* the accident on me.
The *picnic* was a failure, *due to* a heavy shower.
No one knows what *transpires* in Washington.
Does anyone know *if* he *was* there?
I have never seen anyone act *like* he does.
His attack on my paper was most *aggravating.*
*Most everyone* is familiar with this picture.
Where can you get *these kind* of gloves?
We had just two dollars *between* the four of us.
I *can't help but* go to the store.
*Who* did you send for?
John is the *quickest* of the two.
They were *very pleased* with the new house.
It was *good and cold (nice and warm)* in the room.
I *will try and do* it.
They invited John and *myself.*
Did you *get through with* your work?
*As long as you have come,* we can start.

### Standard English, Formal Level

It is quite in accord with the customs of language usage that "correct" English have considerable variety in range of appropriateness, two levels of which are distinguished in this study by the terms *informal* and *formal* Standard English. In general the leading characteristics of the more formal level of Standard English are (1) greater restraint in vocabulary, with the avoidance of words distinctly informal in tone; (2) greater attention to formal agreement in number, both in subject-verb and pronoun-antecedent relationships, in tense sequence, and in case-agreement of pronouns; (3) greater attention to word order, particularly with respect to the position of modifying words, phrases, and clauses, and the use of a more complex sentence structure.

In the schoolroom this formal level of Standard English should be the goal set for careful theme-writing, especially in what is commonly called the "thought theme," whether expository or argumentative. Narration and the various kinds of informal essays, as well as friendly letters, need not be held to the more exacting requirements of the formal standard level. It is, however, of great importance that children recognize the characteristics of both levels, and are able to use either appropriately.

To this level of English usage belong not only the public speech and formal writing of educated people, but also much of the printed material generally classed as "literature." Writing designed primarily for communication, as for example news articles, editorials, textbooks, and other expository compositions, unless distinctly technical or artistic in aim, employ the usages of the formal standard level.

It is rather difficult to offer many distinctive examples of formal standard usage, inasmuch as it is characterized by a general tone of restraint and care more than by the use of certain expressions. A few examples, however, may be found which are quite typical of the formal standard level.

#### Examples

I *shall* be glad to help you.

Neither of the parties *was* injured.

Here are three *whom* we have omitted from the list.

I *had rather* stay at home.

We *had* better complete this investigation.

*Under the circumstances,* he did as well as might be expected.

The use of connectives like *furthermore, notwithstanding, despite, inasmuch as, on the contrary*

### The Literary Level

It must be granted at the outset that the definition of the literary level of English usage employed in this study is somewhat arbitrary, and is more narrow in scope than the definitions of many textbooks. But since much of the difficulty in the teaching of English usage centers about the confusion of the terms *literary, Standard,* and *correct* English, a most earnest attempt has been made in this book to differentiate the terms and to clarify their meanings and applications. It is therefore assumed that what is commonly called "correct" English includes the usages of at least three levels: the informal standard, the formal standard, and the literary levels, the correctness of any specific item in any given instance being dependent upon its appropriateness. The first two levels have been defined; it remains to describe the third.

Literary English is taken to mean that form of speech or writing which in aim goes beyond mere utility to achieve beauty. It differs from formal Standard English not so much in kind as in purpose and effect. In diction it seeks not only accuracy in meaning but also a subjective quality of suggestion aroused by the sound of the word or the associated ideas and feelings. In form it goes beyond mere orderliness to achieve rhythm, symmetry, and balance. In every respect it surpasses the ordinary prose of communication in the attainment of aesthetic values transcending the needs of everyday expression.

An illustration of the difference between standard formal English and literary English may be seen in the opening sentence of Lincoln's "Gettysburg Address." Had Lincoln said, "Eighty-seven years ago our ancestors established on this continent a new nation, inspired by the spirit of liberty, and actuated by the theory that all men are created equal," he would have met adequately the demands of clear, formal communication. But in his phrasing, "Four score and seven years ago, our fathers brought forth on this continent a new nation, conceived in liberty, and dedicated to the proposition that all men are created equal," there are to be found those characteristics of the literary style which transcend communication. The literary tone of *four score and seven, fathers, dedicated to the proposition* is at once apparent; the associations awakened by the words *brought forth, conceived,* and *dedicated* give them emotional depths unsounded by *established, inspired,* or *actuated;* moreover, the sentence as a whole moves with an effect of solemnity achieved only by the happy arrangement of accents and the sonorous quality of the vowels employed. These qualities combine to make this sentence artistic, literary prose of the highest order.

It is obvious that the literary level cannot be made a requirement for all students in schoolroom composition. It is too much the product of mental maturity and highly developed skill to be attainable by the average student, or indeed, by the average teacher. Therefore, while examples of beautiful prose should be given to pupils to study, and the few who are gifted should be encouraged to strive toward the development of a literary tone and style, the great body of school children should be expected to do no more than to cultivate the clear, direct English of communication, together with a feeling for the appropriateness of word and idiom to the purpose intended. Students in whom these perceptions have been engendered will always use "correct," adequate English.

---

### Review Questions

1.  Since almost everyone owns televisions and radios, why don't all Americans speak pretty much alike?
2.  What is the difference between Standard and present usage?
3.  Is good English a fixed form?
4.  When Pooley says illiterate-level language is widespread but must not be tolerated in the classroom, is there an assumption about the people who use it?
5.  Would you ever use literate-level English in regular speech? Do writers use this form today?

## *Local News: Reality as Soap Opera*

### *Elayne Rapping*

In this selection from her book, *The Looking Glass World of Nonfiction* (1987), Rapping analyzes the local television news for what it says about those who watch it. She comes to the conclusion that those who watch the news get what they want and that does not include clear, factual, significant information about local, national, and world events.

Local news was not always the jazzy package we have come to think of as "Happy News," "Eyewitless News" and "Newzak." In fact, local news, until recently, wasn't much of anything. Even national news was, until the early 1960s, a mere fifteen minute segment which affiliates were reluctant to carry because it was not a moneymaker. National news has always been a difficult thing to sell. An FCC ruling requires that it be a regular programming feature, but it doesn't draw viewers well and has never warranted primetime scheduling. Even the special events and reports, which networks carry largely for prestige and to fulfill the "public interest" requirements of the FCC, lose money.[1] Apparently, most people, most of the time, don't like to be educated or informed; after a hard day's work they prefer lighter fare, escapism, something that either numbs or stimulates intense emotions.

The expansion of national news to thirty minutes came about because of technical innovations at a time when public life was particularly dramatic. The 1960s were heady days for American newswatchers. The Vietnam War, violent police reactions to massive protests, ghetto riots, public figure assassinations, "all converged to attract nightly viewers in unprecedented numbers."[2] The sophistication of the new TV technologies, especially the portable minicam which allowed live, on-the-spot coverage of breaking news, added to the appeal. So did the highly televisible space flights with their accompanying development of global satellite communications technology. Now major news stories from distant places, as well as the most mundane local fire or car accident, could be brought to audiences as they happened, in full, bold color.

Local news was the primary beneficiary of this technology because it enabled stations to turn trivial local events into sensational, colorful dramas. But there was another reason for local news' rise to prominence. By the 1960s, local news had become almost the only original programming produced by affiliates. The networks had become so powerful that they had been able to produce and sell their own shows to affiliates very successfully. They offered an arrangement the locals could not refuse. In exchange for running nationally produced programs, rather than their own, affiliates received "compensation" from the networks. Since the local affiliates could sell their own spots in the network shows, the arrangement was both profitable and efficient. Affiliates no longer had to hire large production staffs and produce elaborate programs. They merely used nationally relayed material, which was slick and popular. Thus, local happenings became the only area which required local production.[3]

Another factor in the rise of local news was its growing role in the evening's primetime schedule. Local news is, by default, the program which establishes the personality and tone, the "signature," for each local affiliate. Whatever the quality of the news team and its coverage, that is what viewers come to identify as the quality of the entire station. And whatever local news show develops the biggest audience is also the show

---

[1] Ron Powers, *The Newscasters* (New York, 1977), p. 53.

[2] *ibid.,* p. 6.

[3] *ibid.,* p. 29.

which is most likely to carry its viewers with it through the rest of the evening's shows. Network news as well as the entire schedule of primetime programming for each network thus depend on the ratings of their affiliates' local newscasts. So do the affiliates own revenues for local commercials.

As a result of this importance, as early as the 1960s audience research specialists were hired to help in attracting audiences. Paul Klein, a brilliant analyst hired by NBC, came up with the concept of "Least Objectionable Programming." It was based on the insightful idea that audiences did not really "watch a program" so much as they "watched television." The handwriting was on the wall. The move from information to broadly appealing entertainment was a foregone conclusion.[4]

The affiliates, sensing the rising appeal of news in general, as well as its pivotal importance in primetime ratings, began to think about the news more carefully. With their eyes fixed on greater profits, commercialization of local news was inevitable. As Ron Powers has said, "the TV newscast was a victim of its own success."[5] Advertisers were quick to zero in on the growing audiences and were willing to pay higher rates for even bigger ones. How to deliver them? The answer came through the services of market research consultants. And when their services paid off more handsomely than anyone had anticipated, the future of TV news was a *fait accompli*. It was to be—in ways more profound and disturbing than anyone imagined—a commodity, a combination of various show business staples packaged and promoted like perfume or pet food.

In 1974, local use of media consultants hit the jackpot. NBC's New York affiliate was running a poor third in ratings. Compared to its 333,000 adult viewers, ABC had 697,000 and CBS a whopping 937,000.[6] NBC hired some experts who, using standard marketing techniques, found they could gauge audiences' tastes and their attitudes toward various news features and styles more effectively than the networks had dreamed possible. Seventeen months later, NBC's *News Center 4* was number one with 708,000 viewers to CBS' 696,000 and ABC's 610,000.

At that point "television news had become too important to be left to the newspeople." Marketing whiz kids and TV production experts began determining the content, look, and delivery of what was supposed to be important political information and analysis. No expense was spared in what was quickly recognized as a near foolproof investment. Suddenly budgets went sky high. NBC built a $300,000 set, raised anchor Tom

---

[4]*ibid.*, p. 30.

[5]*ibid.*, p. 6.

[6]*ibid.*, p. 17.

Snyder's salary to $500,000 a year and put a staff of 200—"the largest group anywhere putting out a news program, local or national"[7]—to work. Local news had become big business, big show business to be exact.

Marketing research is a system developed to determine "what people want," but always within the limits of what the market is prepared to offer. Viewers participating in the research had their past experience to use as a guideline—not some ideal informational universe in which relevant, significant events were offered in a meaningful context. The choices presented by researchers necessarily reflected some variation of selections from within that range. Similarly, once the results of the research are put into practice, and ratings rise accordingly, viewers are not necessarily confirming that their needs have been met. They are merely confirming that as network news goes, they prefer the new arrangement to the old.

The researchers discovered that what viewers "chose" to see on local news—and increasingly, over time, on all news—wasn't more in depth reporting on politics or social issues. Far from it. They were dying for something which was not technically news or information at all. They wanted more human interest stories, more personable anchors who would communicate a sense of intimacy and warmth, more sports, more weather, more jazzy graphics, and more on-the-spot coverage of community events—no matter what they were. In a word, audiences wanted local newscasters to create for them a sense of "community."

If the results of these findings, in terms of news production, have at times seemed appalling, that is by no means because of "what people wanted," at least not in some absolute sense. The direction of local news reflects two facts about contemporary life and network TV. In the first place, it reconfirms [that] the social role of television, in its broadest sense, is to provide that lost sense of community integrity in a fragmented world. That is a legitimate need and, to the extent that local news alone provides it, its popularity is justified. That this society needs to manufacture a synthetic version of community in this way is a reflection of its structural values, not its citizens. It is the economic drive of capitalism, after all, that subverted the homogeneous communities of the past. And it is capitalist economics, more than any human "want," that led to the particularly plastic version of "community" local news came to offer.

To provide "what people wanted," local news producers began to revamp their entire newscasts. Everyone needed a "media consultant"—it

---

[7]Edwin Diamond, *The Tin Kazoo* (Cambridge, Mass., 1975), p. 76.

was not enough to have a general sense of what was wanted. Competition demanded specialists in creating sets, weather maps, and other graphic aids. National trends began to emerge, as each station adopted a tried and true format established elsewhere. *Eyewitness News, News Center 4,* and so on, came to represent standardized sets and program formats seen all over the nation. Even some packaged, generic-style news items began to appear. Human interest and other light features are highly transportable in a society which has increasingly given up local color for the modern uniformity of mass-produced shopping malls, fast food chains, and eight-screen movie complexes showing the same eight movies from Anchorage to Atlanta.

All of this is considered nonfiction. It pretends to present "reality" in the raw. But in truth it could hardly be further from reality. The superficially unique but essentially clonelike communities portrayed on local newscasts everywhere are utopian fantasies. They are Emerald Cities conjured up by the hidden Wizards of marketing research. They construct a false version of reality, a false sense of community and intimacy which, in many lives, must substitute for the real thing. That these Tinker Toy towns are taken at face value by most viewers, are embraced and smiled upon as their own, is a sadder commentary on American life than the much scapegoated media "sex and violence." For the "have schmaltz will travel" anchors that smile out at us from news desks and other cozy local spots are not journalists, strictly speaking, but rather paid performers, impersonating the friends and neighbors we all wish we had.

It is all too easy to condemn the audiences whose apparent attitudes and desires brought all this about. That, in fact, is the standard line we get from most educated people and indeed many media workers themselves. It is worth looking at the implications of this position. On the one hand, there is no question that the networks are in the business of manipulation and profiteering. They need to attract and hold audiences and they have found that the best way to do this is with this pseudo-news. But if people enjoy and look forward to watching this stuff, it is not because they are stupid; it is because their immediate human needs are not being met elsewhere. What people in this country crave, and increasingly feel the absence of, is human intimacy and a sense of meaning in their lives. They are lonely, confused, and increasingly terrified of what the world "out there" might have in store for them.

The lack of interest in hard news and analysis is in part attributable to this greater felt need for security and well being. But it is also a function of the educational institutions—of which the media is by now perhaps the most influential—through which we develop our ideas about the world. Functional illiteracy in America is a well known scandal. Even those who are "educated" are not taught to see events in an historic context or to question the information they receive. When you put together the commercial, show biz style of TV generally, the lack of critical skills in the population at large, and the very real—almost heartbreaking—need for emotional and social gratification, you have a world readymade for the gift of Newzak.

### A Day in the Life of Hometown, USA

Local news is now quite standardized. It is made up of a series of formulaic features organized in a way which prioritizes things for us. To scan the agenda and time allotments of the items featured on a typical local newscast is to see at a glance what a typical American day is supposed to have been like in Anytown, USA. I have selected, at random, an 11 P.M. Action Newscast from the ABC affiliate in Pittsburgh, on the night of September 26, 1984. First there was a report of a fatal car crash. Then a three-year-old "was found beaten to death." Then came the death of an eleven month old baby, possibly a result of neglect. A man, we heard next, was sentenced to twenty-five years for arson, followed by a report about a local county's budget problems. All this took four minutes. It was followed by a "teaser" for upcoming stories and a commercial break.

At 11:06:50 the national and international news began—with a noticeable local slant. First, and supposedly most important, a local speech by Anwar Sadat's widow was cancelled because of a bomb scare. Then came a quick report on the activities of the President, Secretary of State, and Vice President—all of whom had spent their important days delivering speeches. After a quick report on a study of the dangers of tobacco, and another commercial, we were ready, at 11:13, for the sports segment, which ran over six minutes—as compared to the seconds-long reports on political and social matters.

After the sports came a report on the beginning of the Jewish New Year, a report on the lottery winners, and a commercial break preceded by a teaser for the weather report. The weather itself, second in time-measured importance only to sports, ran for over five minutes. It included footage of the weather reporter's visit to a local grade school that day, complete with pictures of the signs made by the kids—"The Weatherman Cares"—and the refreshment table, Jell-O molds and all. Finally the anchor told a cute story about tourists stealing sherry glasses from an English Earl and said good night.

    With a variety of other similarly earthshaking options, this is what
local news does. It sends us off to bed with certain images, ideas, and
attitudes dancing in our heads. First there is local catastrophe, the more
heartrending the better. Kids in need of organ transplants are often featured in the early minutes, along with pleas for money and/or donors.
Lately, reports on missing children have also become big news. Any story
in which warm feelings combine with dramatic visuals is a shoe-in. Pets
stuck in trees, or kids falling into wells are always hot. They allow for
sympathy and for a chance to show our local fire fighters and law enforcers on the job, being heroic, making our neighborhoods safe and happy.
Whatever national news is shown is usually locally oriented and, if possible, sensational too. Big names are featured doing ceremonial things.
If there is a bomb scare, all the better. The local heroes are on the job
again.

    This series of disasters and tragedies may not seem particularly
cheering at first glance, but given the realities of modern life, it presents
a picture that is in many ways reassuring. In fact, the world it presents to
us is remarkably like the fictional world of daytime soap opera. There is
a preponderance of trouble and disaster, to be sure; but the trouble and
disaster take timebound, physical forms. The tragedy is always personal,
not political, even in the major national news items. It takes the form of
illness, natural catastrophe, and human failure of a very personal, immediate kind. The father who beats his child is, by the very fact of his deeds
having been reported, already taken into custody. And if the missing
child, the child in need of an organ transplant, the victim of fire, are in
very bad—even terminally bad—shape, it is not the fault of society or the
political system. On the contrary, to the extent that local or national
officials enter the picture, they are seen as heroes, good guys—not by dint
of any political virtues, but because of their official status. The implication is that given disaster and tragedy in our community, more often than
not, there are good professional father figures around inventing new sur-
gical procedures, putting criminals and child abusers where they belong,
saving family homes from fire.

    The very ways in which social leaders are portrayed is reassuringly
apolitical and noncontroversial. Speeches, acts of derring do, and so on,
have no political, social or historic context or implication. Local news,
again like soap opera, makes no judgments about issues, except an occa-
sional emotional endorsement of "Democracy" and repudiation of
"Communism." It omits any historic or social background information
to tie personal events—and even national speeches by individual leaders
are personalized—together or make them part of a larger social world. It

moves from visually sensational or heart stirring image to image quickly, with each report separated from the other by breaks. Overall, it provides a sense that the average citizen, as victim, patient, frightened worker, or homeowner, is important, is cared about and cared for.[8]

Local news stations do deal with larger, more ongoing social issues in their own way. But it is not a way which leads to deeper understanding or raises any kind of question about differing policies or strategies for solving such problems. Rather, the ways of solving social problems on local news are wholly in keeping with the ways of solving private problems. From time to time, special reports are run on recurring problems. If there has been a rash of rapes, teen suicides, or the like, locals will often run a series of brief reports on the topic. Incest, teen sexuality, and other sexually titillating topics are particularly popular. Mostly, they are nothing but interviews with victims and local experts in the field. A director of a shelter for battered women may say a few sentences about the number of cases and the gory details of the typical situations. Footage of crying children, bandaged women, and—if all else fails—the exteriors of family homes is *de rigueur.*

These special reports are usually run during the sweeps seasons to boost ratings at the time when advertising rates are set. When media consultants are brought in, the topics covered can be pretty flimsy. "Bikini fashions" was a hit in one city. A series on "Super Rats" sighted around town actually boosted a Chicago station's audience by 30,000 homes. "We thought it was a joke," said one of the reporters involved. While media experts tend to believe that the popularity of this kind of thing "brings out the worst in human nature," there is more to it than that. This, after all, is just the kind of thing people in a small, close knit community would talk about quite naturally. It is only because of the atomization and impersonality of most cities that we do not normally have these discussions, even when the situation at hand is one that affects an entire community. People often do not know their neighbors anymore, and may even be hostile or fearful of them. Local TV, by acting as neighbor substitute and telling us this kind of story, may not be giving us the news, but it is giving us something we don't get anywhere else and would naturally find interesting or at least useful for small talk.

Another feature of local news which is both disheartening and understandable is the increasing use of prepackaged items distributed by

---

[8]Herbert Schiller's *The Mind Managers* (Boston, 1973) deals with many of these features in detail, and discusses their ideological effects. His seminal work is done in the tradition of strict manipulation theory, however.

independent producers or the networks. While the independent items are generally used as fillers on slow nights, the network packages are different. They are produced and distributed so the affiliates can publicize, through popular local newscasts, the network's other programming. As competition from cable and video cassettes impinges on network entertainment audiences, it has become common for the networks to send affiliates whole series of pseudo-promotional clips to be run as news. Most typically, a "report" on a sitcom or soap opera will air, accompanied by guest appearances by stars, or even appearances by newscasters in the shows themselves.

This serves two purposes. First it helps boost the shows. But more interestingly, it adds to the personalization of the newscasters, to their transformation from journalists to show business personalities. There they are, acting out a fantasy viewers can only dream of—mingling with popular stars and appearing as actors on television. Never mind that they are already more actors than information gatherers. This ploy intensifies and glamorizes a process which is not consciously understood by most viewers, but which is perhaps the most important ingredient in the success of local news.

On another level, of course, there is a great deal of public awareness of much of what I have just described, although not in any coherent, systematic context. And the media itself, in its other forms, often satirizes and criticizes the excesses of news trivialization. Recently, one of the networks aired a very good TV movie about the dangers of sensationalizing the news, and the moral and social issues the practice raises. This is where television acts in its most healthy capacity. The tendency of TV movies to individualize and limit issues is always present, but the process of consciousness raising is nonetheless begun.

Late night TV comedy has always been the domain in which social satire flourishes best, and TV news has often been its target. As early as the 1960s, *That Was the Week That Was* began mocking TV news as a genre. HBO's current *Not Necessarily the News* updates the effort. In fact, the best TV comedy today—*Second City TV* and *David Letterman* for instance—takes its humor from its knowing "defrocking" of the hallowed traditions of its own medium. The demise of *Saturday Night Live* was probably in part attributable to its failure to focus on a salient aspect of the social world and mock it. Its best features, in its early days, were its parodies of classic TV genres. That it is now the media itself that most demands satiric comment is a reflection of the "looking glass" hypothesis: that social reality, as we experience it, comes largely through the mediated glass of network convention.

### Howdy, Neighbors!

If satiric take-offs on TV news have focused mostly on newscasters themselves, it is because the personalities of these people, "the news teams," as they are euphemistically called, are the dominant elements of the genre and the biggest factors in the ratings wars. Most local newscasters have had no experience in print journalism. They were trained and hired to do what local news does: create a sense of "family." So important is this role that local newspeople have become marketable commodities. No longer do they hail from the cities they report on, and pretend to be a part of. They move from town to town in search of the bigger buck, the bigger market, the bigger chance to hit the TV bigtime. "They circulate through the ranks of the farm-league stations on their way to the majors with maximum fanfare."[9] You only need to check the trade paper, *Variety*, to see what has happened. Each week, space is devoted to the moves and salaries of local newscasters. Anyone with appeal will move from Omaha to Denver to Washington so fast they will have no time to learn the local landscape, slang or dialect. Newscasters even have agents to negotiate their salaries and career moves.

In order to capitalize on, and increase, the sense of family closeness and community solidarity which the news team is supposed to reflect, stations now regularly hire ad agencies to create very elaborate, almost sitcom-like ads for their crews. They are seen doing their shopping, visiting their grandmothers, tending their babies, and so on. They are tracked to the bank, the local diner, and the Little League in order to promote their local roots and "just folks" personalities. An anchor who has just barely unpacked will say "I love my neighborhood" to attract viewers. And during the sweeps season, when the ratings are monitored, the stations go all out to do more and more of what works best—colorful, emotion-charged stories full of sensational visuals and community spirit.

There are anchors who cannot pronounce the English language, much less names and cities of other cultures. There are anchors who cannot read a sentence and make it seem as though they understand their own words. And these people may be the most popular. Grooming, dress, and the all-important ability to interact in a chummy way with the other reporters and exude cheeriness and charm are what producers look for. After all, with a script full of half-minute hard news stories stuck between mountains of shocks and tearjerkers, the only reactions really needed are horror, pity, and sentimentality.

---

[9]Ann Salisbury, "News That Isn't Really," *TV Guide* (February 11, 1984), pp. 5–10.

The advancement of women into anchor spots has been heralded as a victory for feminists. Certainly there is truth in this. The change in newscaster image, from the fatherly authority of Walter Cronkite to the informal sister-brother camaraderie of today's local and national teams is one of the many salutary effects of feminism on the mass media. It is also one of the most dramatic illustrations of the often kinky workings of hegemony. On the one hand, even that bastion of male privilege, *60 Minutes*, has introduced a woman, Jessica Savitch, to the team. And Barbara Walters' position of prominence in the news world would have been unthinkable a decade ago. On the other hand, the image projected by these women is not exactly a model of feminist dignity. And the worst of the negative features foisted upon women newscasters is seen in local news.

It is difficult to sort out the convoluted minglings of the demands of feminism and the marketplace in discussing women on the news. For if, on the other hand, women newscasters—like women in every field—must be faster, brighter, and more aggressive than their male counterparts, they must also conform to an image of femininity which is saturated with negative stereotypes. Women anchors are invariably young, pretty, and ever-smiling. Since they are meant to perform as good neighbors and family members, they mimic the most traditional female versions of those roles. They coo at babies, cluck at naughtiness, sigh emotionally at stories of human tragedy.

The case of Christine Craft, the thirty-eight year old local anchor who brought suit against her ex-employer on grounds of sex discrimination, explains it all. Craft was let go because, among other things, she did not take enough care of her appearance and failed to show "deference" to males. The attractive, personable woman won her case, although it was appealed and is still unresolved. But the contradictions in local news shows brought out in the case were enlightening. For it is not only women, but men too, who have been "feminized" by Newszak. Good journalism is in fact a matter of aggressiveness and integrity, not deference or grooming. But since ratings and human interest, not truth, are most valued in local news, show business standards overtake those of journalism. And show business is built on charm and affability. For women, this translates into an image too close to "sweet young thing" for comfort. For men, it comes across as "good old boy." In both cases, it reflects a move from the "watchdog" role of professional, independent journalists to a more entertainment-oriented image of the untroubled Yuppie enjoying his or her lifestyle.

In the process of creating the "team," local news has followed another trend set by dramatic series—presenting an image of the family in which authority figures are downplayed, while youth and equality are stressed. Sitcoms have long projected this view of family life. Father has not known best in TV families for a long time now. More often, as in *Family Ties* and *All in the Family*, it is the youngsters, more in tune with social reality and often more sophisticated and intelligent, who shine. Bumbling old Dad, with his outdated ideas about life, is the butt of many jokes on TV. (The popularity of *The Bill Cosby Show* may reflect popular discomfort with this trend and a return to patriarchal dignity.)

As a trend, the elimination of the strong father figure, and his replacement with a group of palsy-walsy kids who get along fine without him, is at the heart of the news team concept. Expertise and authority are less and less centered in the home, after all. And a family living the good life presented on TV is in fact caught up equally in the concern with youthfulness, fun and being "with it." And so, while Dan Rather and Ted Koppel still affect a patriarchal kind of authoritativeness, the local teams, reflecting personal life and private values, share in the playful, egalitarian image of family life projected by commercials. Sometimes—often, actually—a team will burst into theatrical giggles when a line is flubbed. This collective cracking up emphasizes the childishness of what's going on, the playfulness and the element of leisure activity. Needless to say, such behavior would be unseemly in a serious analysis of the arms race. But such material is not found on local news.

In place of old fashioned journalism, local news inserts interpersonal relations, jokes and teasing. "Where did you get that jacket?" says a woman anchor to the weatherman—who has developed a reputation for slightly out of the ordinary attire. Or perhaps we hear about someone's failure to change her snow tires or stick to his diet. Just like you and me, we think, as we smile warmly to ourselves.

The actual coverage of events, and choice of stories, reflects these human, neighborly criteria for news. In fact, the media—especially local news—have become a kind of substitute for all the things a good society is supposed to provide, but which our society dramatically lacks. We live in a world in which social service agencies are underfunded, inefficient and often cruel and insensitive. The police and the courts are filled with corruption and bias in their enforcement of "justice." The sense of community has been replaced by a plastic, nationally uniform series of commercial enterprises. Do you need child care? You won't find much in the way of public assistance and what is available is expensive and corporately owned and managed. Do you worry about the dangers of drugs and violence for your kids? The streets and schools are full of both and there is little being done about it. Government agencies are often as not in on the take or responsible for the violence.

But when you turn on the local news, it's a different world entirely. There you see any number of encouraging and reassuring things. The pretty reporter who jokes with the weatherman every day is right there in front of City Hall, or the local prison, keeping us informed of the latest developments in a scary situation. The robber is just now being apprehended, she'll assure us. The city council is carefully considering bills to stop drug traffic, to tighten up regulations for child care licenses, to bring more jobs to our city. We ourselves might be frightened to go out and observe these things—especially with the media so eager to scare us to death about street violence—but we know if "our Mary" is on-the-spot, it cannot be too bad for too long.

### News Teams as Public Servants

Serious city council debates on troublesome issues do not in fact bring results very often. So, besides reassuring us that things are being "considered," local newscasters have another, even more important job. As the world and its problems worsen, and the proposed plans to make things better fall by the wayside and are forgotten, the media has become the primary source of its own "good news." It is no exaggeration to say that most of what passes for good news—as opposed to reports that our officials are on the job, working on solutions to social problems—is manufactured by local news stations themselves. More and more, local news stations have been taking their responsibilities as agents of the public interest seriously. News stations and crews are responsible for any number of campaigns and programs to solve community problems.

The sign in the grade school lunchroom announcing "The Weatherman Cares" is a symbol of the main role of local TV. It presents an image of an institution—the media itself—that is wholly concerned with us and our needs. Newspeople now traditionally visit schools, lead parades, head charity drives, and open malls—all in the name of public interest. In any city you visit you will find that each network affiliate has its own little do-gooder bailiwick. One may focus on collecting food for the unemployed and homeless. One may provide information for returning veterans. One may provide health information.

This trend began with the now standard "Action Line" segments in cities everywhere. People, desperate for help in solving everyday problems, took to calling their local TV stations for advice and information. From there it was a quick move to the institutionalization of a special feature in which anyone with a problem calls a certain number and talks to the person in charge of that beat. Say the garbage on your street has been sitting there for weeks, attracting rats and looking generally grotesque. Call "Action Line" and the newscaster will put in a special call on your behalf to the appropriate agency. In a flash your problem is solved. Then you will find yourself on the evening news telling your story to other sufferers of governmental neglect.

This is a technique which President Reagan has used with great success. Single out one person, solve her or his problem, and then announce to the world that the system works. Never mind that it took clout to do the job for which every citizen pays taxes. Never mind that one case means nothing in the scheme of things. The point is that help is available, caring, and effective. No need to organize, protest, or—perish the thought—change any institutional structures or power relations. In fact, one result of this technique is to individualize the whole concept of social problem solving. While giving us a sense of belonging to a cohesive, caring community, it also reinforces the sense that each problem is unique and personal and must be solved on a case by case basis.

When this technique took off, stations recognized a real gold mine of viewer loyalty and commercial revenues. And since the world is getting harder and harder to deal with anyway, it was inevitable that bigger problems and bigger media extravaganzas would soon arrive. Following in the tradition of the TV marathon for charity, the stations began running lengthy broadcasts devoted to one particularly serious community issue. Typical issues treated in several-hour long, or even whole day, marathons are those which first speak to local concerns and crises, and second, have great emotional appeal. The plight of Vietnam vets, for example, might be treated as a day long "workshop" in which local news teams and public officials participate.

This "group effort" image is one of the most important aspects of this kind of program. It adds to the image of the station as a caring, effective community institution. The hitch is that the TV crews can do nothing beyond publicizing, and exaggerating, the existing programs and agencies and their effectiveness in "solving problems." In fact, these problems have deep social, historic, and political causes. They arise because we live in a society which does not provide needed services and benefits for those on the bottom, those who have the least opportunity and are therefore most often exploited—a perfect description of the Vietnam vets. But the day long attention to their "problems" gives the false impression that this society is functioning in a healthy, just way.

One of the most common issues to be treated in this way recently is unemployment. No fewer than sixty cities have in the last few years run lengthy primetime extravaganzas called "Job-a-thons."[10] These shows, sponsored by local stations in areas hard hit by unemployment, are paradigms—almost parodies, really—of what local news is all about. Following the charity marathon format, they pretend to be offering a vital service: a "job exchange." The entire news team is on hand to facilitate the event. Publicity begins early and is relentless, leading anyone with a problem finding work to anticipate the day with great hope. First, every possible employer in need of workers lists openings, complete with job description, requirements, and pay. Then everyone seeking work is invited to come on the show and give her or his story and work qualifications. Viewers—both employers and jobseekers—can also call in to offer jobs and request interviews for those listed.

This format—part *Queen for a Day,* part cattle auction—is both dishonest and exploitative. First of all, the jobs listed are almost invariably minimum wage dead ends that no one else wants. Some are downright Dickensian in their demands. A position as the sole live-in "counselor" at a halfway house for delinquent and addicted teenagers is typical. Most of the opportunities are of the custodial nature, and many are very short term. The "applicants" for these positions are often positively tragic. Most are highly qualified for much more meaningful work. They are people laid off from good jobs, with families to support, and are forced, through sheer desperation, to parade themselves before the TV audience, dressed in their best and nervously trying to make a good impression as they tell their stories. What should elicit outrage brings pity. The always smiling newscasters look dutifully sympathetic and concerned—as they do about everything else they report on. The experience is humiliating and, worse yet, largely useless. In Pittsburgh, one of the hardest hit cities economically, 4,600 people, many with advanced degrees and special skills, applied for about 1,500 jobs. Only 300 fulltime jobs were filled. Almost all were far beneath the talents of their applicants. In Milwaukee, 860 jobs were offered. Of 2,800 applicants, 460 found jobs. Most were with food chains.[11]

The sheer number of offerings and ringing phones, seen and heard on the TV screen, give the impression that there is a lot happening, that people are being helped out of seemingly hopeless situations, that a huge social problem is being solved. This impression comes almost entirely from the visual and dramatic format of the programs. The hosts seem to be sweating away, aching hearts in throats, in the interest of the poor

---

[10] Tim Patterson, "Eyewitless News: An Amusing Aid to Digestion," in *Alternative Papers: Selection from the Alternative Press* (Philadelphia, 1982), p. 458.

[11] "Cross Currents," *Channels of Communication* (May–June, 1983), p. 11.

souls they exploit as they comfort. Soup kitchens are shown feeding smiling children. Volunteer health care workers describe free health care. Never mind that in reality these institutions are few, understaffed, and very limited in the services they are able to provide. It looks impressive on TV. Periodically, local politicians come on or call in to applaud the effort and pledge their support (whatever that means). President Reagan himself called in to the "Virginia Job Day" program. And why not? That is just the sort of "safety net" he loves—one which gets lots of media coverage and almost no meaningful results.

The society at large is clearly not dealing with the problem of unemployment, or health care, or illiteracy, or any other widescale social crisis affecting the poor, the disabled, the minorities of the country. Nothing vaguely related to the real causes of structural unemployment, or any other social crisis, ever comes up in these shows. There is no analysis of historic causes, no economic analysis, no attempt to look for broad solutions to endemic problems of capitalism. Instead, out of a few bad jokes, crocodile tears, and completely misleading images of activity and progress, the viewer is led to believe that no matter what might befall you in these United States, help is just around the corner.

So successful have these features become that many stations take on long term commitments to their pet social crises. The station that ran the Job-a-thon in Pittsburgh has continued to collect food for the unemployed on weekends. Each week you see your local favorites—out of their tailored suits and dressed in jeans and parkas—going out to various town centers to personally collect canned goods from viewers and load them onto trucks. Such is the job of a TV reporter. Not only do these people fail to report news, they often collude in increasingly important ways with the corporations and government agencies responsible for the policies that create these problems. This is because they tend to create a false sense that society is in fact working more effectively than is the case to solve problems. Where collective agitation to demand government action might be a more useful response to a crisis, those who might protest are led to believe the issue is being resolved, that no further action is necessary. In this sense, the media have become an indispensable part of the established power structure, ameliorating anxiety and defusing mass anger.

### *The Real News: Game Cancelled Because of Rain*

As dramatic as these special marathons are, they are obviously not what keeps people watching local news every day. What makes up the bulk of the nightly newscasts are sports and weather—issues of no social import at all. Each of these segments runs far longer than any hard news story, no matter how earthshaking. The allocation of time for these segments is based on the findings of market analysts. It was sports and weather, in particular, that viewers were interested in having expanded. Over the years, this has been happening almost on a daily basis. Anyone returning from a trip of any length at all will notice at least minor embellishments to the weather and sports reports. Maps of various aspects of the weather proliferate endlessly. And sports reports are continuously being changed, and changed again, in efforts to make even more attractive what is already the highlight of the broadcast.

Sports and weather may be the most vacuous things on the air. They provide very little in the way of real information, and what is presented is nearly drowned in glitz. Sports news is the most repetitious and non-analytical thing on TV. There is no sense that economic or social factors come into play in the sports world. On the contrary, the typical sportscast is predictable to the point of self-parody. Athletes are interviewed about a game coming up or just played. The questions and answers are always the same. "How do you think you'll do this season, Bud?" "Well, gee, we're just gonna get out there and give it our best and all," is recognizably typical. (Actually, it is the prototype of most TV interviewing. "How do you feel about your daughter's murder?" "Well, it's hard to put into words. We're just broken up about it." Pointless questions and obvious answers are the stuff of TV "reporting.")

The appeal of these reports cannot be understood in terms of news criteria. It is the very desire to escape from "news," from the pressures of social reality and personal woes, that draws viewers to sports and weather. In that sense, the blurring of entertainment and information creates a situation in which critics, puzzling over entertainment presented as news, may be missing the point. It is because sports is so universal a form of "fun" and relaxation for Americans that it is so talked about and watched. It provides needed "play" after a busy day.

That sports seems to be news is related to the role of sports teams in community identity. If football is fun to watch, rooting for a home team is a more significant pastime. It provides one of the strongest forms of community "glue" left to us. There are few activities—none in collective daily life—that provide that sense of belonging and sharing that sports do. In workplaces, where competition and tension rule, the time spent talking about local teams is a welcome respite from the anxiety and hostility of other activities.

The weather report plays a similar role. Even those who don't like sports must discuss and concern themselves with the weather. It too binds us together as a community; it too is a common element of our collective daily life. When personal problems—money fears, sexual anxieties—plague us, we often hide them from others. With the weather, we really do share them. That is an important social fact. An interview with Phil McHugh, of the media consultant firm McHugh and Hoffman, explained some of the reasons for emphasizing weather on local news. The interview took place in 1974, at a time when weather was only, on average, about three and one-half minutes of the newscasts. In ten years it has just about doubled. According to McHugh, "People are very much interested in weather. They plan their life around it . . . the mass audience, the people who have to go to work for a living . . . all the mothers want to know how to dress their kids for school."[12]

The elaborate, sometimes downright gorgeous graphics used to show us everything we could conceivably want to know about the weather are interesting examples of the way in which television's visual sophistication has improved its ability to provide this kind of shared intimacy and personal advice. Because there are so many different maps and radarscopes available, the weatherperson can stay on screen, saying nothing much, for a very long time. Weather people are usually the homiest, wittiest (actually silliest in most cases), and most informal members of the news team. They are often loved by community members, who will choose a particular news station as much for the weatherperson as anything else. If there is no one at home to commiserate with about the eight days of rain we've just had; no one to complain to about having to cut the grass, miss the softball game; or whatever may happen, we still have good old Bill What's-His-Name to share it with. He understands just how we feel. He too forgot his umbrella, or had to shovel his walk four times in one week.

That these weather reporters are in some sense informing us of a phenomenon which has all the trappings of science produces interesting side effects. For one thing, the sexy blondes who reported weather in the 1950s have gone the way of all such blatantly sexist stereotyping on local news. Men do most weather reports, and the women who do it are all business. In that sense, weather and women have made progress toward respectability. But on another level, the pseudoscientific mystification produced by the sets and charts is excessive. It reflects another trend in media toward taking authority away from us and putting our fates in the hands of scientific experts who are knowledgeable about things beyond our comprehension. Science and pseudoscience are the delights

---

[12]*ibid.*

of television, for they justify so much that is done to us and for us. The folklore and finger knowledge that Grandma used often worked after all. She didn't need TV to tell her what nature was up to. While there are positive elements to this trend, it also creates one more area of daily life over which we have lost control and forgotten how to use our common sense.

In essence, all these aspects of local news combine to create a feeling of family for those who have none, and for those who have little in common with the one they do have. In so doing they reinforce the corporate definition of family relations too. As one TV station promo promised: "It's not like watching news, it's like watching family!" And it is a family more to your liking than the one you may be stuck with at that. There is a phrase that has gained currency among TV folk lately: "Reality Programming." It is the industry term for the phenomenon signalled by the success of local news—the fact that more and more people seem to prefer nonfiction to fiction on TV. They watch local news in the same spirit that they watch soap operas—in an effort to feel some intense, ongoing human drama in which no matter how bad things may get or seem, there is always a silver lining, an upbeat ending, a hero to solve the problem or at least explain it. They get that from local news. But it is in many ways a more dangerous addiction than the soaps. Soaps after all are—for all but the borderline psychotic—clearly unreal. Local news, on the other hand, is presented and accepted as all too real. What it tells, what it leaves out, how it explains and solves problems, have a lot to do with the way people have come to understand and respond to their daily experience. And yet local news is every bit as much a creation, a fiction, a story as a soap opera. Its characters are playing roles, its stories are distorted and falsified versions of life, and its values are those of the people who make the decisions governing our lives, not our own.

---

**Review Questions**
1.  Why did news broadcasting change in the 1960s?
2.  What do people most want to see on the news?
3.  What is the primary goal of the TV news program?
4.  How is the news like a soap opera?
5.  What are the big newscasters hired to do?
6.  How do "Action Lines" create a false image of efficient social functioning?

# C. P. Ellis

## Studs Terkel

One of the hardest things for a person who is not racist to understand is a person who *is* racist. C. P. Ellis offers insights on how racism became a part of his life and how it left it. Studs Terkel (b. 1912) is widely respected as a gatherer of oral histories from ordinary people in a way that makes their lives real and sympathetic to the reader.

*We're in his office in Durham, North Carolina. He is the business manager of the International Union of Operating Engineers. On the wall is a plaque: "Certificate of Service, in recognition to C. P. Ellis, for your faithful service to the city in having served as a member of the Durham Human Relations Council. February 1977."*

*At one time, he had been president (exalted cyclops) of the Durham chapter of the Ku Klux Klan. . . .*

*He is fifty-three years old.*

My father worked in a textile mill in Durham. He died at forty-eight years old. It was probably from cotton dust. Back then, we never heard of brown lung. I was about seventeen years old and had a mother and sister depending on somebody to make a livin'. It was just barely enough insurance to cover his burial. I had to quit school and go to work. I was about eighth grade when I quit.

My father worked hard but never had enough money to buy decent clothes. When I went to school, I never seemed to have adequate clothes to wear. I always left school late afternoon with a sense of inferiority. The other kids had nice clothes, and I just had what Daddy could buy. I still got some of those inferiority feelin's now that I have to overcome once in a while.

I loved my father. He would go with me to ball games. We'd go fishin' together. I was really ashamed of the way he'd dress. He would take this money and give it to me instead of putting it on himself. I always had the feeling about somebody looking at him and makin' fun of him and makin' fun of me. I think it had to do somethin' with my life.

My father and I were very close, but we didn't talk about too many intimate things. He did have a drinking problem. During the week, he would work every day, but weekends he was ready to get plastered. I can understand when a guy looks at his paycheck and looks at his bills, and he's worked hard all the week, and his bills are larger than his paycheck. He'd done the best he could the entire week, and there seemed to be no hope. It's an illness thing. Finally you just say: "The heck with it. I'll just get drunk and forget it."

My father was out of work during the depression, and I remember going with him to the finance company uptown, and he was turned down. That's something that's always stuck.

My father never seemed to be happy. It was a constant struggle with him just like it was for me. It's very seldom I'd see him laugh. He was just tryin' to figure out what he could do from one day to the next.

After several years pumping gas at a service station, I got married. We had to have children. Four. One child was born blind and retarded, which was a real additional expense to us. He's never spoken a word. He doesn't know me when I go to see him. But I see him, I hug his neck. I talk to him, tell him I love him. I don't know whether he knows me or not, but I know he's well taken care of. All my life, I had work, never a day without work, worked all the overtime I could get and still could not survive financially. I began to say there's somethin' wrong with this country. I worked my butt off and just never seemed to break even.

I had some real great ideas about this great nation. (Laughs.) They say to abide by the law, go to church, do right and live for the Lord, and everything'll work out. But it didn't work out. It just kept gettin' worse and worse.

I was workin' a bread route. The highest I made one week was seventy-five dollars. The rent on our house was about twelve dollars a week. I will never forget: outside of this house was a 265-gallon oil drum, and I never did get enough money to fill up that oil drum. What I would do every night, I would run up to the store and buy five gallons of oil and climb up the ladder and pour it in that 265-gallon drum. I could hear that five gallons when it hits the bottom of that oil drum, splatters, and it sounds like it's nothin' in there. But it would keep the house warm for the night. Next day you'd have to do the same thing.

I left the bread route with fifty dollars in my pocket. I went to the bank and I borrowed four thousand dollars to buy the service station. I worked seven days a week, open and close, and finally had a heart attack. Just about two months before the last payments of that loan. My wife had done the best she could to keep it runnin'. Tryin' to come out of that hole, I just couldn't do it.

I really began to get bitter. I didn't know who to blame. I tried to find somebody. I began to blame it on black people. I had to hate somebody. Hatin' America is hard to do because you can't see it to hate it. You gotta have somethin' to look at to hate. (Laughs.) The natural person for me to hate would be black people, because my father before me was a member of the Klan. As far as he was concerned, it was the savior of the white people. It was the only organization in the world that would take care of the white people. So I began to admire the Klan.

I got active in the Klan while I was at the service station. Every Monday night, a group of men would come by and buy a Coca-Cola, go back to the car, take a few drinks, and come back and stand around talkin'. I couldn't help but wonder: Why are these dudes comin' out every Monday? They said they were with the Klan and have meetings close-by. Would I be interested? Boy, that was an opportunity I really looked forward to! To be part of somethin'. I joined the Klan, went from member to chaplain, from chaplain to vice-president, from vice-president to president. The title is exalted cyclops.

The first night I went with the fellas, they knocked on the door and gave the signal. They sent some robed Klansmen to talk to me and give me some instructions. I was led into a large meeting room, and this was the time of my life! It was thrilling. Here's a guy who's worked all his life and struggled all his life to be something, and here's the moment to be something. I will never forget it. Four robed Klansmen led me into the hall. The lights were dim, and the only thing you could see was an illuminated cross. I knelt before the cross. I had to make certain vows and promises. We promised to uphold the purity of the white race, fight communism, and protect white womanhood.

After I had taken my oath, there was loud applause goin' throughout the buildin', musta been at least four hundred people. For this one little ol' person. It was a thrilling moment for C. P. Ellis.

It disturbs me when people who do not really know what it's all about are so very critical of individual Klansmen. The majority of 'em are low-income whites, people who really don't have a part in something. They have been shut out as well as the blacks. Some are not very well educated either. Just like myself. We had a lot of support from doctors and lawyers and police officers.

Maybe they've had bitter experiences in this life and they had to hate somebody. So the natural person to hate would be the black person. He's beginnin' to come up, he's beginnin' to learn to read and start votin' and run for political office. Here are white people who are supposed to be superior to them, and we're shut out.

I can understand why people join extreme right-wing or left-wing groups. They're in the same boat I was. Shut out. Deep down inside, we want to be part of this great society. Nobody listens, so we join these groups.

At one time, I was state organizer of the National Rights party. I organized a youth group for the Klan. I felt we were getting old and our generation's gonna die. So I contacted certain kids in schools. They were havin' racial problems. On the first night, we had a hundred high school students. When they came in the door, we had "Dixie" playin'. These kids were just thrilled to death. I begin to hold weekly meetin's with 'em, teachin' the principles of the Klan. At that time, I believed Martin Luther King had Communist connections. I began to teach that Andy Young was affiliated with the Communist party.

I had a call one night from one of our kids. He was about twelve. He said: "I just been robbed downtown by two niggers." I'd had a couple of drinks and that really teed me off. I go downtown and couldn't find the kid. I got worried. I saw two young black people. I had the .32 revolver with me. I said: "Nigger, you seen a little young white boy up here? I just got a call from him and was told that some niggers robbed him of fifteen cents." I pulled my pistol out and put it right at his head. I said: "I've always wanted to kill a nigger and I think I'll make you the first one." I nearly scared the kid to death, and he struck off.

This was the time when the civil rights movement was really beginnin' to peak. The blacks were beginnin' to demonstrate and picket downtown stores. I never will forget some black lady I hated with a purple passion. Ann Atwater. Every time I'd go downtown, she'd be leadin' a boycott. How I hated—pardon the expression, I don't use it much now— how I just hated that black nigger. (Laughs.) Big, fat, heavy woman. She'd pull about eight demonstrations, and first thing you know they had two, three blacks at the checkout counter. Her and I have had some pretty close confrontations.

I felt very big, yeah. (Laughs.) We're more or less a secret organization. We didn't want anybody to know who we were, and I began to do some thinkin'. What am I hidin' for? I've never been convicted of anything in my life. I don't have any court record. What am I, C. P. Ellis, as a citizen and a member of the United Klansmen of America? Why can't I go to the city council meeting and say: "This is the way we feel about the matter? We don't want you to purchase mobile units to set in our schoolyards. We don't want niggers in our schools."

We began to come out in the open. We would go to the meetings, and the blacks would be there and we'd be there. It was a confrontation every time. I didn't hold back anything. We began to make some inroads with the city councilmen and county commissioners. They began to call us friend. Call us at night on the telephone: "C. P., glad you came to that meeting last night." They didn't want integration either, but they did it secretively, in order to get elected. They couldn't stand up openly and say it, but they were glad somebody was sayin' it. We visited some of the city leaders in their home and talk to 'em privately. It wasn't long before councilmen would call me up: "The blacks are comin' up tonight and makin' outrageous demands. How about some of you people showin' up and have a little balance?" I'd get on the telephone: "The niggers is comin' to the council meeting tonight. Persons in the city's called me and asked us to be there."

We'd load up our cars and we'd fill up half the council chambers, and the blacks the other half. During these times, I carried weapons to the meetings, outside my belt. We'd go there armed. We would wind up just hollerin' and fussin' at each other. What happened? As a result of our fightin' one another, the city council still had their way. They didn't want to give up control to the blacks nor the Klan. They were usin' us.

I began to realize this later down the road. One day I was walkin' downtown and a certain city council member saw me comin'. I expected him to shake my hand because he was talkin' to me at night on the telephone. I had been in his home and visited with him. He crossed the street. Oh shit, I began to think, somethin's wrong here. Most of 'em are merchants or maybe an attorney, an insurance agent, people like that. As long as they kept low-income whites and low-income blacks fightin', they're gonna maintain control.

I began to get that feeling after I was ignored in public. I thought: Bullshit, you're not gonna use me any more. That's when I began to do some real serious thinkin'.

The same thing is happening in this country today. People are being used by those in control, those who have all the wealth. I'm not espousing communism. We got the greatest system of government in the world. But those who have it simply don't want those who don't have it to have any part of it. Black and white. When it comes to money, the green, the other colors make no difference. (Laughs.)

I spent a lot of sleepless nights. I still didn't like blacks. I didn't want to associate with 'em. Blacks, Jews, or Catholics. My father said: "Don't have anything to do with 'em." I didn't until I met a black person and talked with him, eyeball to eyeball, and met a Jewish person and talked to him, eyeball to eyeball. I found out they're people just like me. They cried, they cussed, they prayed, they had desires. Just like myself. Thank God, I got to the point where I can look past labels. But at that time, my mind was closed.

I remember one Monday night Klan meeting. I said something was wrong. Our city fathers were using us. And I didn't like to be used. The reactions of the others was not too pleasant: "Let's just keep fightin' them niggers."

I'd go home at night and I'd have to wrestle with myself. I'd look at a black person walkin' down the street, and the guy'd have ragged shoes or his clothes would be worn. That began to do somethin' to me inside. I went through this for about six months. I felt I just had to get out of the Klan. But I wouldn't get out.

Then something happened. The state AFL-CIO received a grant from the Department of HEW, a $78,000 grant: how to solve racial problems in the school system. I got a telephone call from the president of the state AFL-CIO. "We'd like to get some people together from all walks of life." I said: "All walks of life? Who you talkin' about?" He said: "Blacks, whites, liberals, conservatives, Klansmen, NAACP people."

I said: "No way am I comin' with all those niggers. I'm not gonna be associated with those type of people." A White Citizens Council guy said: "Let's go up there and see what's goin' on. It's tax money bein' spent." I walk in the door, and there was a large number of blacks and white liberals. I knew most of 'em by face 'cause I seen 'em demonstratin' around town. Ann Atwater was there. (Laughs.) I just forced myself to go in and sit down.

The meeting was moderated by a great big black guy who was bushyheaded. (Laughs.) That turned me off. He acted very nice. He said: "I want you all to feel free to say anything you want to say." Some of the blacks stand up and say it's white racism. I took all I could take. I asked for the floor and I cut loose. I said: "No, sir, it's black racism. If we didn't have niggers in the schools, we wouldn't have the problems we got today."

I will never forget. Howard Clements, a black guy, stood up. He said: "I'm certainly glad C. P. Ellis come because he's the most honest man here tonight." I said: "What's that nigger tryin' to do?" (Laughs.) At the end of that meeting, some blacks tried to come up shake my hand, but I wouldn't do it. I walked off.

Second night, same group was there. I felt a little more easy because I got some things off my chest. The third night, after they elected all the committees, they want to elect a chairman. Howard Clements stood up and said: "I suggest we elect two co-chairpersons." Joe Beckton, executive director of the Human Relations Commission, just as black as he can be, he nominated me. There was a reaction from some blacks. Nooo. And, of all things, they nominated Ann Atwater, that big old fat black gal that I had just hated with a purple passion, as co-chairman. I thought to myself: Hey, ain't no way I can work with that gal. Finally, I agreed to accept it, 'cause at this point, I was tired of fightin', either for survival or against black people or against Jews or against Catholics.

A Klansman and a militant black woman, co-chairmen of the school committee. It was impossible. How could I work with her? But after about two or three days, it was in our hands. We had to make it a success. This give me another sense of belongin', a sense of pride. This helped this inferiority feelin' I had. A man who has stood up publicly and said he despised black people, all of a sudden he was willin' to work with 'em. Here's a chance for a low-income white man to be somethin'. In spite of all my hatred for blacks and Jews and liberals, I accepted the job. Her and I began to reluctantly work together. (Laughs.) She had as many problems workin' with me as I had workin' with her.

One night, I called her: "Ann, you and I should have a lot of differences and we got 'em now. But there's somethin' laid out here before us, and if it's gonna be a success, you and I are gonna have to make it one. Can we lay aside some of these feelin's?" She said: "I'm willing if you are." I said: "Let's do it."

My old friends would call me at night: "C. P., what the hell is wrong with you? You're sellin' out the white race." This begin to make me have guilt feelin's. Am I doin' right? Am I doin' wrong? Here I am all of a sudden makin' an about-face and tryin' to deal with my feelin's, my heart. My mind was beginnin' to open up. I was beginnin' to see what was right and what was wrong. I don't want the kids to fight forever.

We were gonna go ten nights. By this time, I had went to work at Duke University, in maintenance. Makin' very little money. Terry Sanford give me this ten days off with pay. He was president of Duke at the time. He knew I was a Klansman and realized the importance of blacks and whites getting along.

I said: "If we're gonna make this thing a success, I've got to get to my kind of people." The low-income whites. We walked the streets of Durham, and we knocked on doors and invited people. Ann was goin' into the black community. They just wasn't respondin' to us when we made these house calls. Some of 'em were cussin' us out. "You're sellin' us out, Ellis, get out of my door. I don't want to talk to you." Ann was gettin' the same response from blacks: "What are you doin' messin' with that Klansman?" One day, Ann and I went back to the school and we sat down. We began to talk and just reflect. Ann said: "My daughter came home cryin' every day. She said her teacher was makin' fun of me in front of the other kids." I said: "Boy, the same thing happened to my kid. White liberal teacher was makin' fun of Tim Ellis's father, the Klansman. In front of other peoples. He came home cryin'." At this point—(he pauses, swallows hard, stifles a sob)—I begin to see, here we are, two people from the far ends of the fence, havin' identical problems, except hers bein' black and me bein' white. From that moment on, I tell ya, that gal and I worked together good. I begin to love the girl, really. (He weeps.)

The amazing thing about it, her and I, up to that point, had cussed each other, bawled each other, we hated each other. Up to that point, we didn't know each other. We didn't know we had things in common.

We worked at it, with the people who came to these meetings. They talked about racism, sex education, about teachers not bein' qualified. After seven, eight nights of real intense discussion, these people, who'd never talked to each other before, all of a sudden came up with resolutions. It was really somethin', you had to be there to get the tone and feelin' of it.

At that point, I didn't like integration, but the law says you do this and I've got to do what the law says, okay? We said: "Let's take these resolutions to the school board." The most disheartening thing I've ever faced was the school system refused to implement any one of these resolutions. These were recommendations from the people who pay taxes and pay their salaries. (Laughs.) I thought they were good answers. Some of 'em I didn't agree with, but I been in this thing from the beginning, and whatever comes of it, I'm gonna support it. Okay, since the school board refused, I decided I'd just run for the school board.

I spent eighty-five dollars on the campaign. The guy runnin' against me spent several thousand. I really had nobody on my side. The Klan turned against me. The low-income whites turned against me. The liberals didn't particularly like me. The blacks were suspicious of me. The blacks wanted to support me, but they couldn't muster up enough to support a Klansman on the school board. (Laughs.) But I made up my mind that what I was doin' was right, and I was gonna do it regardless what anybody said.

It bothered me when people would call and worry my wife. She's always supported me in anything I wanted to do. She was changing, and my boys were too. I got some of my youth corps kids involved. They still followed me.

I was invited to the Democratic women's social hour as a candidate. Didn't have but one suit to my name. Had it six, seven, eight years. I had it cleaned, put on the best shirt I had and a tie. Here were all this high-class wealthy candidates shakin' hands. I walked up to the mayor and stuck out my hand. He give me that handshake with that rag type of hand. He said: "C. P., I'm glad to see you." But I could tell by his handshake he was lyin' to me. This was botherin' me. I know I'm a low-income person. I know I'm not wealthy. I know they were sayin': "What's this little ol' dude runnin' for school board?" Yet they had to smile and make like they're glad to see me. I begin to spot some black people in that room. I automatically went to 'em and that was a firm handshake. They said: "I'm glad to see you, C. P." I knew they meant it—you can tell about a handshake.

Every place I appeared, I said I will listen to the voice of the people. I will not make a major decision until I first contacted all the organizations in the city. I got 4,640 votes. The guy beat me by two thousand. Not bad for eighty-five bucks and no constituency.

The whole world was openin' up, and I was learnin' new truths that I had never learned before. I was beginnin' to look at a black person, shake hands with him, and see him as a human bein'. I hadn't got rid of all this stuff. I've still got a little bit of it. But somethin' was happenin' to me.

It was almost like bein' born again. It was a new life. I didn't have these sleepless nights I used to have when I was active in the Klan and slippin' around at night. I could sleep at night and feel good about it. I'd rather live now than at any other time in history. It's a challenge.

Back at Duke, doin' maintenance, I'd pick up my tools, fix the commode, unstop the drains. But this got in my blood. Things weren't right in this country, and what we done in Durham needs.to be told. I was so miserable at Duke, I could hardly stand it. I'd go to work every morning just hatin' to go.

My whole life had changed. I got an eighth-grade education, and I wanted to complete high school. Went to high school in the afternoons on a program called PEP—Past Employment Progress. I was about the only white in class, and the oldest. I begin to read about biology. I'd take my books home at night, 'cause I was determined to get through. Sure enough, I graduated. I got the diploma at home.

I come to work one mornin' and some guy says: "We need a union." At this time I wasn't pro-union. My daddy was anti-labor too. We're not gettin' paid much, we're havin ' to work seven days in a row. We're all starvin' to death. The next day, I meet the international representative of the Operating Engineers. He give me authorization cards. "Get these cards out and we'll have an election." There was eighty-eight for the union and seventeen no's. I was elected chief steward for the union.

Shortly after, a union man come down from Charlotte and says we need a full-time rep. We've got only two hundred people at the two plants here. It's just barely enough money comin' in to pay your salary. You'll have to get out and organize more people. I didn't know nothin' about organizin' unions, but I knew how to organize people, stir people up. (Laughs.) That's how I got to be business agent for the union.

When I began to organize, I began to see far deeper. I began to see people again bein' used. Blacks against whites. I say this without any hesitancy: Management is vicious. There's two things they want to keep: all the money and all the say-so. They don't want these poor workin' folks to have none of that. I begin to see management fightin' me with everything they had. Hire anti-union law firms, badmouth unions. The people were makin' a dollar ninety-five an hour, barely able to get through weekends. I worked as a business rep for five years and was seein' all this.

Last year, I ran for business manager of the union. He's elected by the workers. The guy that ran against me was black, and our membership is seventy-five percent black. I thought: Claiborne, there's no way you can beat that black guy. People know your background. Even though you've made tremendous strides, those black people are not gonna vote for you. You know how much I beat him? Four to one. (Laughs.)

The company used my past against me. They put out letters with a picture of a robe and a cap: Would you vote for a Klansman? They wouldn't deal with the issues. I immediately called for a mass meeting. I met with the ladies at an electric component plant. I said: "Okay, this is Claiborne Ellis. This is where I come from. I want you to know right now, you black ladies here, I was at one time a member of the Klan. I want you to know, because they'll tell you about it."

I invited some of my old black friends. I said: "Brother Joe, Brother Howard, be honest now and tell these people how you feel about me." They done it. (Laughs.) Howard Clements kidded me a little bit. He said: "I don't know what I'm doin' here, supportin' an ex-Klansman." (Laughs.) He said: "I know what C. P. Ellis come from. I knew him when he was. I knew him as he grew, and growed with him. I'm tellin' you now: follow, follow this Klansman." (He pauses, swallows hard.) "Any questions?" "No," the black ladies said. "Let's get on with the meeting, we need Ellis." (He laughs and weeps.) Boy, black people sayin' that about me. I won one thirty-four to forty-one. Four to one.

It makes you feel good to go into a plant and butt heads with professional union busters. You see black people and white people join hands to defeat the racist issues they use against people. They're tryin' the same things with the Klan. It's still happenin' today. Can you imagine a guy who's got an adult high school diploma runnin' into professional college graduates who are union busters? I gotta compete with 'em. I work seven days a week, nights and on Saturday and Sunday. The salary's not that great, and if I didn't care, I'd quit. But I care and I can't quit. I got a taste of it. (Laughs.)

I tell people there's a tremendous possibility in this country to stop wars, the battles, the struggles, the fights between people. People say: "That's an impossible dream. You sound like Martin Luther King." An ex-Klansman who sounds like Martin Luther King. (Laughs.) I don't think it's an impossible dream. It's happened in my life. It's happened in other people's lives in America.

I don't know what's ahead of me. I have no desire to be a big union official. I want to be right out here in the field with the workers. I want to walk through their factory and shake hands with that man whose hands are dirty. I'm gonna do all that one little ol' man can do. I'm fifty-two years old, and I ain't got many years left, but I want to make the best of 'em.

When the news came over the radio that Martin Luther King was assassinated, I got on the telephone and begin to call other Klansmen. We just had a real party at the service station. Really rejoicin' 'cause that son of a bitch was dead. Our troubles are over with. They say the older you get, the harder it is for you to change. That's not necessarily true. Since I changed, I've set down and listened to tapes of Martin Luther King. I listen to it and tears come to my eyes 'cause I know what he's sayin' now. I know what's happenin'.

POSTSCRIPT: *The phone rings. A conversation.*

*"This was a black guy who's director of Operation Breakthrough in Durham. I had called his office. I'm interested in employin' some young black person who's interested in learnin' the labor movement. I want somebody who's never had an opportunity, just like myself. Just so he can read and write, that's all."*

---

## Review Questions

1. What was C. P. Ellis's childhood like?
2. Why was the 265-gallon oil drum a problem for Ellis?
3. Why couldn't Ellis hate America?
4. Who are the majority of people belonging to the KKK, according to Ellis?
5. How did Ellis think the important people in his town were using him and the Klan?
6. Why did the blacks in the school committee trust Ellis?
7. What happened to Ann Atwater's daughter and C. P. Ellis's son that changed Ellis's racist attitudes?
8. How did Ellis's life change when he gave up the Klan?

## *The Beauty Myth*

### *Naomi Wolf*

Wolf argues that the way women are focused on their appearance has much more to do with social control than it does with vanity. In the aftermath of a feminist movement that was supposed to liberate women, many feel less free, rather than more. She does not see this problem as a conspiracy by any individual, sex, or industry. Societies lie to themselves the same way people do, she says.

At last, after a long silence, women took to the streets. In the two decades of radical action that followed the rebirth of feminism in the early 1970s, Western women gained legal and reproductive rights, pursued higher education, entered the trades and the professions, and overturned ancient and revered beliefs about their social role. A generation on, do women feel free?

The affluent, educated, liberated women of the First World, who can enjoy freedoms unavailable to any women ever before, do not feel as free as they want to. And they can no longer restrict to the subconscious their sense that this lack of freedom has something to do with—with apparently frivolous issues, things that really should not matter. Many are ashamed to admit that such trivial concerns—to do with physical appearance, bodies, faces, hair, clothes—matter so much. But in spite of shame, guilt, and denial, more and more women are wondering if it isn't that they are entirely neurotic and alone but rather that something important is indeed at stake that has to do with the relationship between female liberation and female beauty.

The more legal and material hindrances women have broken through, the more strictly and heavily and cruelly images of female beauty have come to weigh upon us. Many women sense that women's collective progress has stalled; compared with the heady momentum of earlier days, there is a dispiriting climate of confusion, division, cynicism, and above all, exhaustion. After years of much struggle and little recognition, many older women feel burned out; after years of taking its light for granted, many younger women show little interest in touching new fire to the torch.

During the past decade, women breached the power structure; meanwhile, eating disorders rose exponentially and cosmetic surgery became the fastest-growing medical specialty. During the past five years, consumer spending doubled, pornography became the main media category, ahead of legitimate films and records combined, and thirty-three thousand American women told researchers that they would rather lose ten to fifteen pounds than achieve any other goal. More women have more money and power and scope and legal recognition than we have ever had before; but in terms of how we feel about ourselves *physically*, we may actually be worse off than our unliberated grandmothers. Recent research consistently shows that inside the majority of the West's controlled, attractive, successful working women, there is a secret "underlife" poisoning our freedom; infused with notions of beauty, it is a dark vein of self-hatred, physical obsessions, terror of aging, and dread of lost control.

It is no accident that so many potentially powerful women feel this way. We are in the midst of a violent backlash against feminism that uses images of female beauty as a political weapon against women's advancement: the beauty myth. It is the modern version of a social reflex that has been in force since the Industrial Revolution. As women released themselves from the feminine mystique of domesticity, the beauty myth took over its lost ground, expanding as it waned to carry on its work of social control.

The contemporary backlash is so violent because the ideology of beauty is the last one remaining of the old feminine ideologies that still has the power to control those women whom second wave feminism would have otherwise made relatively uncontrollable: It has grown stronger to take over the work of social coercion that myths about motherhood, domesticity, chastity, and passivity, no longer can manage. It is seeking right now to undo psychologically and covertly all the good things that feminism did for women materially and overtly.

This counterforce is operating to checkmate the inheritance of feminism on every level in the lives of Western women. Feminism gave us laws against job discrimination based on gender; immediately case law evolved in Britain and the United States that institutionalized job discrimination based on women's appearances. Patriarchal religion declined; new religious dogma, using some of the mind-altering techniques of older cults and sects, arose around age and weight to functionally supplant traditional ritual. Feminists, inspired by Friedan, broke the stranglehold on the women's popular press of advertisers for household products, who were promoting the feminine mystique; at once, the diet and skin care industries became the new cultural censors of women's intellectual space, and because of their pressure, the gaunt, youthful model supplanted the happy housewife as the arbiter of successful womanhood. The sexual revolution promoted the discovery of female sexuality; "beauty pornography"—which for the first time in women's history artificially links a commodified "beauty" directly and explicitly to sexuality—invaded the mainstream to undermine women's new and vulnerable sense of sexual self-worth. Reproductive rights gave Western women control over our own bodies; the weight of fashion models plummeted to 23 percent below that of ordinary women, eating disorders rose exponentially, and a mass neurosis was promoted that used food and weight to strip women of that sense of control. Women insisted on politicizing health; new technologies of invasive, potentially deadly "cosmetic" surgeries developed apace to re-exert old forms of medical control of women.

Every generation since about 1830 has had to fight its version of the beauty myth. "It is very little to me," said the suffragist Lucy Stone in 1855, "to have the right to vote, to own property, etcetera, if I may not keep my body, and its uses, in my absolute right." Eighty years later, after women had won the vote, and the first wave of the organized women's movement had subsided, Virginia Woolf wrote that it would still be decades before women could tell the truth about their bodies. In 1962, Betty Friedan quoted a young woman trapped in the Feminine Mystique: "Lately, I look in the mirror, and I'm so afraid I'm going to look like my mother." Eight years after that, heralding the cataclysmic second wave of feminism, Germaine Greer described "the Stereotype": "To her belongs all that is beautiful, even the very word beauty itself . . . she is a doll . . . I'm sick of the masquerade." In spite of the great revolution of the second wave, we are not exempt. Now we can look out over ruined barricades: A revolution has come upon us and changed everything in its path, enough time has passed since then for babies to have grown into women, but there still remains a final right not fully claimed.

The beauty myth tells a story: The quality called "beauty" objectively and universally exists. Women must want to embody it and men must want to possess women who embody it. This embodiment is an imperative for women and not for men, which situation is necessary and natural because it is biological, sexual, and evolutionary: Strong men battle for beautiful women, and beautiful women are more reproductively successful. Women's beauty must correlate to their fertility, and since this system is based on sexual selection, it is inevitable and changeless.

None of this is true. "Beauty" is a currency system like the gold standard. Like any economy, it is determined by politics, and in the modern age in the West it is the last, best belief system that keeps male dominance intact. In assigning value to women in a vertical hierarchy according to a culturally imposed physical standard, it is an expression of power relations in which women must unnaturally compete for resources that men have appropriated for themselves.

"Beauty" is not universal or changeless, though the West pretends that all ideals of female beauty stem from one Platonic Ideal Woman; the Maori admire a fat vulva, and the Padung, droopy breasts. Nor is "beauty" a function of evolution: Its ideals change at a pace far more rapid than that of the evolution of species, and Charles Darwin was himself unconvinced by his own explanation that "beauty" resulted from a "sexual selection" that deviated from the rule of natural selection; for women to compete with women through "beauty" is a reversal of the way in which natural selection affects all other mammals. Anthropology has overturned the notion that females must be "beautiful" to be selected to mate: Evelyn Reed, Elaine Morgan, and others have dismissed sociobiological assertions of innate male polygamy and female monogamy. Female higher primates are the sexual initiators; not only do they seek out and enjoy sex with many partners, but "every nonpregnant female takes her turn at being the most desirable of all her troop. And that cycle keeps turning as long as she lives." The inflamed pink sexual organs of primates are often cited by male sociobiologists as analogous to human arrangements relating to female "beauty," when in fact that is a universal, nonhierarchical female primate characteristic.

Nor has the beauty myth always been this way. Though the pairing of the older rich men with young, "beautiful" women is taken to be somehow inevitable, in the matriarchal Goddess religions that dominated the Mediterranean from about 25,000 B.C.E. to about 700 B.C.E., the situation was reversed: "In every culture, the Goddess has many lovers. . . . The clear pattern is of an older woman with a beautiful but expendable youth—Ishtar and Tammuz, Venus and Adonis, Cybele and Attis, Isis and Osiris . . . their only function the service of the divine 'womb.' " Nor is it something only women do and only men watch: Among the Nigerian Wodaabes, the women hold economic power and the tribe is obsessed with male beauty; Wodaabe men spend hours together in elaborate makeup sessions, and compete—provocatively painted and dressed, with swaying hips and seductive expressions—in beauty contests judged by women. There is no legitimate historical or biological justification for the beauty myth; what it is doing to women today is a result of nothing more exalted than the need of today's power structure, economy, and culture to mount a counteroffensive against women.

If the beauty myth is not based on evolution, sex, gender, aesthetics, or God, on what is it based? It claims to be about intimacy and sex and life, a celebration of women. It is actually composed of emotional distance, politics, finance, and sexual repression. The beauty myth is not about women at all. It is about men's institutions and institutional power.

The qualities that a given period calls beautiful in women are merely symbols of the female behavior that that period considers desirable: *The beauty myth is always actually prescribing behavior and not appearance.* Competition between women has been made part of the myth so that women will be divided from one another. Youth and (until recently) virginity have been "beautiful" in women since they stand for experiential and sexual ignorance. Aging in women is "unbeautiful" since women grow more powerful with time, and since the links between generations of women must always be newly broken: Older women fear young ones, young women fear old, and the beauty myth truncates for all the female life span. Most urgently, women's identity must be premised upon our "beauty" so that we will remain vulnerable to outside approval, carrying the vital sensitive organ of self-esteem exposed to the air.

Though there has, of course, been a beauty myth in some form for as long as there has been patriarchy, the beauty myth in its modern form is a fairly recent invention. The myth flourishes when material constraints on women are dangerously loosened. Before the Industrial Revolution, the average woman could not have had the same feelings about "beauty" that modern women do who experience the myth as continual comparison to a mass-disseminated physical ideal. Before the development of technologies of mass production—daguerreotypes, photographs, etc.—an ordinary woman was exposed to few such images outside the Church. Since the family was a productive unit and women's work complemented men's, the value of women who were not aristocrats or prostitutes lay in their work skills, economic shrewdness, physical strength, and fertility. Physical attraction, obviously, played its part; but "beauty" as we understand it was not, for ordinary women, a serious issue in the marriage marketplace. The beauty myth in its modern form gained ground after the upheavals of industrialization, as the work unit of the family was destroyed, and urbanization and the emerging factory system demanded what social engineers of the time termed the "separate sphere" of domesticity, which supported the new labor category of the "breadwinner" who left home for the workplace during the day. The middle class expanded, the standards of living and of literacy rose, the size of families shrank; a new class of literate, idle women developed, on whose submission to enforced domesticity the evolving system of industrial capitalism depended. Most of our assumptions about the way women have always thought about "beauty" date from no earlier than the 1830s, when the cult of domesticity was first consolidated and the beauty index invented.

For the first time new technologies could reproduce—in fashion plates, daguerreotypes, tintypes, and rotogravures—images of how women should look. In the 1840s the first nude photographs of prostitutes were taken; advertisements using images of "beautiful" women first appeared in mid-century. Copies of classical artworks, postcards of society beauties and royal mistresses, Currier and Ives prints, and porcelain figurines flooded the separate sphere to which middle-class women were confined.

Since the Industrial Revolution, middle-class Western women have been controlled by ideals and stereotypes as much as by material constraints. This situation, unique to this group, means that analyses that trace "cultural conspiracies" are uniquely plausible in relation to them. The rise of the beauty myth was just one of several emerging social fictions that masqueraded as natural components of the feminine sphere, the better to enclose those women inside it. Other such fictions arose contemporaneously: a version of childhood that required continual maternal supervision; a concept of female biology that required middle-class women to act out the roles of hysterics and hypochondriacs; a conviction that respectable women were sexually anesthetic; and a definition of women's work that occupied them with repetitive, time-consuming, and painstaking tasks such as needlepoint and lacemaking. All such Victorian inventions as these served a double function—that is, though they were encouraged as a means to expend female energy and intelligence in harmless ways, women often used them to express genuine creativity and passion.

But in spite of middle-class women's creativity with fashion and embroidery and child rearing, and, a century later, with the role of the suburban housewife that devolved from these social fictions, the fictions' main purpose was served: During a century and a half of unprecedented feminist agitation, they effectively counteracted middle-class women's dangerous new leisure, literacy, and relative freedom from material constraints.

Though these time- and mind-consuming fictions about women's natural role adapted themselves to resurface in the post-war Feminine Mystique, when the second wave of the women's movement took apart what women's magazines had portrayed as the "romance," "science," and "adventure" of homemaking and suburban family life, they temporarily failed. The cloying domestic fiction of "togetherness" lost its meaning and middle-class women walked out of their front doors in masses.

So the fictions simply transformed themselves once more: Since the women's movement had successfully taken apart most other necessary fictions of femininity, all the work of social control once spread out over the whole network of these fictions had to be reassigned to the only strand left intact, which action consequently strengthened it a hundredfold. This reimposed onto liberated women's faces and bodies all the limitations, taboos, and punishments of the repressive laws, religious injunctions and reproductive enslavement that no longer carried sufficient force. Inexhaustible but ephemeral beauty work took over from inexhaustible but ephemeral housework. As the economy, law, religion, sexual mores, education, and culture were forcibly opened up to include women more fairly, a private reality colonized female consciousness. By using ideas about "beauty," it reconstructed an alternative female world with its own laws, economy, religion, sexuality, education, and culture, each element as repressive as any that had gone before.

Since middle-class Western women can best be weakened psychologically now that we are stronger materially, the beauty myth, as it has resurfaced in the last generation, has had to draw on more technological sophistication and reactionary fervor than ever before. The modern arsenal of the myth is a dissemination of millions of images of the current ideal; although this barrage is generally seen as a collective sexual fantasy, there is in fact little that is sexual about it. It is summoned out of political fear on the part of male-dominated institutions threatened by women's freedom, and it exploits female guilt and apprehension about our own liberation—latent fears that we might be going too far. This frantic aggregation of imagery is a collective reactionary hallucination willed into being by both men and women stunned and disoriented by the rapidity with which gender relations have been transformed: a bulwark of reassurance against the flood of change. The mass depiction of the modern woman as a "beauty" is a contradiction: Where modern women are growing, moving, and expressing their individuality, as the myth has it, "beauty" is by definition inert, timeless, and generic. That this hallucination is necessary and deliberate is evident in the way "beauty" so directly contradicts women's real situation.

And the unconscious hallucination grows ever more influential and pervasive because of what is now conscious market manipulation: powerful industries—the $33-billion-a-year diet industry, the $20-billion cosmetics industry, the $300-million cosmetic surgery industry, and the $7-billion pornography industry—have arisen from the capital made out of unconscious anxieties, and are in turn able, through their influence on mass culture, to use, stimulate, and reinforce the hallucination in a rising economic spiral.

This is not a conspiracy theory; it doesn't have to be. Societies tell themselves necessary fictions in the same way that individuals and families do. Henrik Ibsen called them "vital lies," and psychologist Daniel Goleman describes them working the same way on the social level that they do within families: "The collusion is maintained by directing attention away from the fearsome fact, or by repackaging its meaning in an acceptable format." The costs of these social blind spots, he writes, are destructive communal illusions. Possibilities for women have become so open-ended that they threaten to destabilize the institutions on which a male-dominated culture has depended, and a collective panic reaction on the part of both sexes has forced a demand for counterimages.

The resulting hallucination materializes, for women, as something all too real. No longer just an idea, it becomes three-dimensional, incorporating within itself how women live and how they do not live: It becomes the Iron Maiden. The original Iron Maiden was a medieval German instrument of torture, a body-shaped casket painted with the limbs and features of a lovely, smiling young woman. The unlucky victim was slowly enclosed inside her; the lid fell shut to immobilize the victim, who died either of starvation or, less cruelly, of the metal spikes embedded in her interior. The modern hallucination in which women are trapped or trap themselves is similarly rigid, cruel, and euphemistically painted. Contemporary culture directs attention to imagery of the Iron Maiden, while censoring real women's faces and bodies.

Why does the social order feel the need to defend itself by evading the fact of real women, our faces and voices and bodies, and reducing the meaning of women to these formulaic and endlessly reproduced "beautiful" images? Though unconscious personal anxieties can be a powerful force in the creation of a vital lie, economic necessity practically guarantees it. An economy that depends on slavery needs to promote images of slaves that "justify" the institution of slavery. Western economies are absolutely dependent now on the continued underpayment of women. An ideology that makes women feel "worth less" was urgently needed to counteract the way feminism had begun to make us feel worth more. This does not require a conspiracy; merely an atmosphere. The contemporary economy depends right now on the representation of women within the beauty myth. Economist John Kenneth Galbraith offers an economic explanation for "the persistence of the view of homemaking as a 'higher calling' ": the concept of women as naturally trapped within the Feminine Mystique, he feels, "has been forced on us by popular sociology, by magazines, and by fiction to disguise the fact that woman in her role of consumer has been essential to the development of our industrial society. . . . Behavior that is essential for economic reasons is transformed into a social virtue." As soon as a woman's primary social value could no longer be defined as the attainment of virtuous domesticity, the beauty myth redefined it as the attainment of virtuous beauty. It did so to substitute both a new consumer imperative and a new justification for economic unfairness in the workplace where the old ones had lost their hold over newly liberated women.

Another hallucination arose to accompany that of the Iron Maiden: The caricature of the Ugly Feminist was resurrected to dog the steps of the women's movement. The caricature is unoriginal; it was coined to ridicule the feminists of the nineteenth century. Lucy Stone herself, whom supporters saw as "a prototype of womanly grace . . . fresh and fair as the morning," was derided by detractors with "the usual report" about Victorian feminists: "a big masculine woman, wearing boots, smoking a cigar, swearing like a trooper." As Betty Friedan put it presciently in 1960, even before the savage revamping of that old caricature: "The unpleasant image of feminists today resembles less the feminists themselves than the image fostered by the interests who so bitterly opposed the vote for women in state after state." Thirty years on, her conclusion is more true than ever: That resurrected caricature, which sought to punish women for their public acts by going after their private sense of self, became the paradigm for new limits placed on aspiring women everywhere. After the success of the women's movement's second wave, the beauty myth was perfected to checkmate power at every level in individual women's lives. The modern neuroses of life in the female body spread to woman after woman at epidemic rates. The myth is undermining—slowly, imperceptibly, without our being aware of the real forces of erosion—the ground women have gained through long, hard, honorable struggle.

The beauty myth of the present is more insidious than any mystique of femininity yet: A century ago, Nora slammed the door of the doll's house; a generation ago, women turned their backs on the consumer heaven of the isolated multiapplianced home; but where women are trapped today, there is no door to slam. The contemporary ravages of the beauty backlash are destroying women physically and depleting us psychologically. If we are to free ourselves from the dead weight that has once again been made out of femaleness, it is not ballots or lobbyists or placards that women will need first; it is a new way to see.

---

### Review Questions

1. Wolf talks about second-wave feminism. What was the first wave?
2. Who is the woman Friedan Wolf refers to?
3. Why does Wolf call age and weight the "new religious dogma"?
4. Wolf calls the beauty myth a "collective reactionary hallucination." What are some other similar hallucinations societies have experienced? Did the Nazis have such a hallucination?
5. Why do feminists often get labeled as ugly?

# Appendix

# *Using Reference Material*

Brief Discussion of Format
- 1.1 Using Quotations in Your Essay
- 1.2 Using References
- 1.3 Citation Form
- 1.4 Titles: Underline or Quotation Marks?

Books
- 2.1 One Author
- 2.2 Two or Three Authors
- 2.3 One Editor of an Anthology
- 2.4 Multiple Editors of an Anthology
- 2.5 Encyclopedias or Dictionaries
- 2.6 Pamphlets
- 2.7 Government Publications

Other Printed Material
- 3.1 Magazines
- 3.2 Journals
- 3.3 Newspapers

Nonprint Sources
    4.1  Television and Radio Programs
    4.2  Films or Videotapes
    4.3  Compact Discs, Audiotapes, or Records
    4.4  Lectures
    4.5  Interviews

## BRIEF DISCUSSION OF FORMAT

### *1.1  Using Quotations in Your Essay*

If you give it some consideration, you can often think of sources of information that will strengthen your position in an argument. Each of us tends to notice information that agrees with the way we think on an issue, and that may assist you in using outside support for your essays. As you read the daily paper, listen to lectures in other classes, or even enjoy your favorite music, you will often notice things that support an idea that you have previously thought about. Do not hesitate to use this information in your essays. It can often form an example that assists your audience in seeing the reasonable elements in your argument because they can see why you came to your conclusion. This appendix is designed to assist you in properly citing or referencing your sources. Use the appendix contents to find the material that you wish to use. Look up the example under the listed numbers and follow the pattern for citing your references.

The way you present the material you are using in your essay will have a large impact on how effective it is in supporting the point you selected it to support. You can do a great deal of research for an essay but still not make good use of the material. You may quote large portions of text but have your argument get lost because you did not make the reason for the material clear to your audience. When you want to quote material to support a point or provide an example, make sure your audience sees that material as an addition to your essay. Composition essays are designed for you to develop your own arguments and polish your writing. When you quote large chunks of material, you appear to be evading writing your own argument. Most referenced material for a composition class should be brief: three or four sentences at most.

All material that is copied word-for-word must have quotation marks around it and be referenced. Changing just a few words (or paraphrasing) is a form of plagiarism if you do not reference the material, even though you do not have to use quotation marks. If you do not quote the reference directly, but you use information you've read or heard, you still need to acknowledge the source. If you are not sure how to use quotation marks in material you are using, look at the examples that follow. You can find a variety of ways to integrate material in an essay and select patterns that work for your material. Quoting entire sentences is often not the most effective way to use the material, and, frequently, the clearest method is to just quote the part that applies directly to your argument. Be careful that you do not change the ideas in your source by shortening the quotation, though.

If, for example, you wish to quote just a part of the opening lines of the Gettysburg Address, you would put three periods (called "ellipsis points") with a space before, between, and after them to indicate that some of the text has been left out. This is the whole sentence:

> "Four score and seven years ago our fathers brought forth, upon this continent, a new nation, conceived in Liberty, and dedicated to the proposition that all men are created equal."

If you just wanted to use a portion of the sentence, you could abridge it in this fashion.

> "Four score and seven years ago our fathers brought forth, upon this continent, a new nation . . . dedicated to the proposition that all men are created equal."

The three periods indicate that material is missing from the text you have quoted. Use four periods with spaces between each period to indicate you have eliminated a sentence or sentences in the material you have quoted.

> "Four score and seven years ago our fathers brought forth, upon this continent, a new nation, conceived in Liberty, and dedicated to the proposition that all men are created equal. . . . we here highly resolve that these dead shall not have died in vain. . . ."

Whenever you quote from your source, reduce the quoted material to the briefest form you can manage and still make the point you selected the quotation to make. If you have to put in words of your own to make the quotation fit smoothly, that is fine. Just make sure the quotation marks indicate what is yours and what belongs to the source material. Look at how the quotation marks indicate which words are part of the original Gettysburg Address and which are not.

>   Eighty-seven years ago, "our fathers brought forth, upon this con-
>   tinent, a new nation . . . dedicated to the proposition that all men are
>   created equal."

If you wish to put information *into* a quotation, place your words
between brackets to indicate that they are yours and not part of the quotation.

>   Eighty-seven years ago, "our fathers [and mothers] brought forth,
>   upon this continent, a new nation conceived in Liberty, dedicated to
>   the proposition that all men are created equal."

If you want to include a large block of material, such as the entire
Gettysburg Address, you do not have to use quotation marks. You simply word process the material exactly as it is written in your source
and then indent both right and left margins ten spaces. A colon usually introduces a quote such as this. You put the last name of the
author at the end of the material, and then a full citation in your bib-
liography.

When you do not want to quote the material directly but you do want
to use the ideas, you do not have to use quotation marks. If you do not
reference the source of those ideas, however, you will have plagiarized
the material.

## 1.2   Using References

**Plagiarism.**   Both the reader's journal and the reaction papers discussed in Chapter 2 are intended for readings that are assigned out of this
book. If you do other reading for the essays you write, you must use a
different way of recording them, because not everyone will have read the
same material. You can use a wide variety of materials from outside your
writing class to support your thesis position. A similar topic may have
been discussed in another class or covered in a related reading. You might
have seen an article in a newspaper or magazine, heard a news report, or
listened to a lecture that offered support for your argument. None of
these sources required library research on your part, but they are still
excellent ones to use.

Any time you read something that you intend to refer to in your
essay, you must cite a reference for that source. You must also cite a
reference if you heard someone speak to a group on the subject. If you do
not do that, you will be plagiarizing that material and, whether or not
you intended to cheat, you will be guilty of cheating.

---

**Plagiarism**  To use ideas, words, and/or information provided by an identifiable source without acknowledging that source.

---

**Recording your sources.**  In order to avoid this problem, you must properly record all outside material you use in your writing. Proper citation is not difficult to do once you have taken a minute or two to make the pattern clear in your mind, and it is a seriously regarded responsibility of every educated person. Check with your instructor for the method of citation you will be expected to use and become familiar with it. The Modern Language Association (MLA) form is given here. It will give you the proper form for acknowledging material you have read and also the form for citing informal sources, such as information you heard on the news some time in the past.

When you first find material that you think will help you, you need to write down all the information you will need to cite the reference. Usually, that is: author, title of book or article, publisher, date of publication, and page numbers. (More exact instructions are given below.) Finding the exact article you saw while in the library is often very difficult unless you have written down the information in your reader's journal, in your notes, or on the reaction paper you wrote for that reading assignment. Once your notes are complete, the material will be easy to cite when you are writing the essay.

The second step is writing a few notes to remind yourself of exactly what the material said. If you wish to include a brief quotation, write down the part you want to use word-for-word, including the exact punctuation. You do not have to summarize the whole article or a large piece of material. The instructor is going to be interested in *your* thinking and *your* writing, not the thinking and writing of the person who wrote the material you have found. While it is sometimes useful to use outside material in supporting your position, you must not try to let outside readings take the place of your own thinking.

### 1.3  Citation Form

The Modern Language Association (MLA) form of referencing provides a pattern for giving credit to the source of the material a writer wants to cite in order to gain support for an argumentative position. Doing this citation carefully is very important in order to avoid the appearance of plagiarism.

This appendix is not intended to cover every type of referencing situation. It is intended as a guide to help you with the most common situations that composition students may encounter as they prepare their papers. If you have a problem with referencing that is not covered in the examples included here, ask your instructor or a librarian for assistance. The complete text of *MLA Handbook for Writers of Research Papers* is available in your library.

The form for referencing material can seem very complicated and difficult to follow if you attempt to memorize all the rules. Reference material is not difficult to cite correctly, however, if you simply note your reference in your first draft and then look up the citation form for the material you are using before presenting the draft to an audience. When you use the citation format as a reference, it becomes a step-by-step procedure that requires you only to follow the directions. While you must pay close attention to the details of those directions, you do not have to memorize them for the next time you reference. All that is necessary is for you to record the information on your notes when you are in the library.

### 1.4   Titles: Underline or Quotation Marks?

The pattern of when to underline a title and when to put it in quotation marks can best be remembered by thinking about the difference between a boat and a ship.

1. A boat is a little vessel, and it can be compared to the titles that are put in quotation marks. An article from a journal or magazine, a short poem, or an essay are all smaller works, and their titles are put between quotation marks.

2. A ship is very big, and it can be compared to the titles that are underlined. A book, an entire play, or an epic poem are much larger than a short poem or an article, so the titles of books, plays, and long poems are underlined as well. See the examples that follow:

| | |
|---|---|
| BOOK | Of Mice and Men |
| CHAPTER IN A BOOK | "Riddles in the Dark," from The Hobbit |
| PLAY | Romeo and Juliet |
| SPEECH | "The Gettysburg Address" |
| ESSAY | "This Country Was a Lot Better Off When the Indians Were Running It" |
| POEM | "Dover Beach" |
| LONG POEM | Paradise Lost |

| MAGAZINE | "Coast Trash Increasing." <u>Gulf Coast</u> |
| NEWSPAPER | "Recycling Proving Successful." St. Louis <u>Post-Dispatch</u> |
| TELEVISION | <u>Shocking America</u> |

**Exceptions.**   Sacred books are not underlined, even though they are very large works. The books or chapters within those works are not underlined or put in quotation marks.

| | | |
|---|---|---|
| Bible | Genesis | King James Version |
| Talmud | Koran | Upanishads |

# BOOKS

## *2.1   One Author*

The following quotation was taken from the sort of book you might find after looking up *Recycling* in the subject heading of your card catalog or library computer system. Both the author and the name of the book are identified in the essay, so only the page number is required in the body of the text.

> Deep Ecology is the name given to a very radical segment of the environmental movement. Gary Snyder, Charlene Spretnek, and Wendall Berry are some of the writers who best exemplify the ideals of the deep ecology movement. One of the better known advocates of this movement is the sociologist Tim Ingalsmith. In his book <u>Technology from Compost</u>, Ingalsmith advocates making paper products from lawn clippings: "A household blender can easily be converted to use to make paper products for all occasions" (95). Following the lead of thinkers such as Ingalsmith, people can end their dependence on international trade networks that waste countless amounts of energy in transportation and exploit workers in less developed countries.

**Work cited**

Ingalsmith, Timothy.  <u>Technology from Compost</u>.  Portland, OR: Save the Planet, 1989.

Put the information for book works cited in this order:

Author's (or authors') name(s), period (.), and two spaces. The author is listed with the last name first.

Title of the book, underlined, period (.), and two spaces

Edition of the book (2nd ed. or rev. ed.), period (.), and two spaces

Place of the publication, colon (:), name of the publisher, comma (,),
date of publication, and period (.)

Page numbers (if not cited in the text of the essay), period (.)

## 2.2   *Two or Three Authors*

The following book is another example you might find in the library
if you were assigned to write an essay on ecology. It might be listed under
the subjects *Southwest Ecology, Desert Agriculture,* and *World Food Crisis.* Books are often listed under several subject headings that might apply to them. In this quotation all the authors and the name of the book
are identified in the essay so only the page number is required in the body
of the text.

> Marcos Contreras, Dolores Garcia, and Martin Montoya, the
> authors of <u>Saving the Southwest</u>, which studies the ecology as well
> as the social health of the American Southwest, have invented sev-
> eral new uses for a cactus plant called Nopal. They argue that nopal
> is the answer to world hunger (188): "Both the leaves and the fruit
> are edible. It doesn't need to be watered and its spines protect it from
> destruction by marauding animals" (189).

**Work cited**

Contreras, Marcos J., Dolores M. Garcia, and Martin D. Montoya.
   <u>Saving the Southwest</u>.  Fresno: Atzlan, 1991.

The information for a book by multiple authors is listed in this order.

When there are multiple authors, list the last name of the first
   author, put in a comma, and then list the first name and middle
   initial of the first author. Put a comma after the first author's
   name; commas separate the names of each of the remaining
   authors, which are written in natural order: first name, middle
   initial, and last name.

Title of the book, underlined, period (.), and two spaces

Edition of the book, period (.), and two spaces

Place of the publication, colon (:), name of the publisher, comma (,),
   date of publication, and period (.)

Page numbers (if not cited in the text of the essay), period (.)

## 2.3   *One Editor of an Anthology*

If you like to fish and you are assigned an essay on ecology, you might
want to write about ecology and fishing. You think that the two have a

lot in common but you are not sure how to express that. You might look up fishing in the subject catalog and find a subcategory on fishing and ecology. There you might find an anthology such as this one. (An anthology is collection of stories or essays.) You could read quickly through the essays to find the ones you want to read more carefully.

In this quotation the author and the title of his essay are identified, so only the page number is needed to allow readers to find it if they wish to do so.

> Fly fishermen and other outdoor enthusiasts often serve as advocates of the streams and similar environments to which their sport takes them. According to Jon Page's essay, "Fly Fishing as a Modern Religion," part of the love of nature is the desire to protect and nurture it, as in any emotional relationship (227).

**Work cited**

Page, Jon. "Fly Fishing as a Modern Religion." <u>Aspects of Fishing</u>. Ed. Greeley Thompson. Eugene: Northwest, 1992. 226–37.

The editors of this anthology must be identified after the title of the book. The abbreviation *Ed.* indicates Greeley Thompson was the editor of this anthology, and it is under his name that the book will be found in the library. In the case of multiple editors, the book is listed under the name of the first editor listed.

The information from an anthology is arranged in this order:

Author's (or authors') name(s), period (.), and two spaces

Title of the article or story written by the author enclosed in quotation marks, period (.), and two spaces

Title of the book, underlined, period (.), and two spaces

Name of the editor with (Ed.) in front of the name and a period (.) and two spaces afterward

Edition of the book, period (.), and two spaces

Place of the publication, colon (:), name of the publisher, comma (,), date of publication, and period (.)

Page numbers (if not cited in the text of the essay), period (.)

## 2.4  Multiple Editors of an Anthology

In this reference, the name of the work being quoted and the author of that work are not mentioned in the text, so the last name of the author must be included with the page number. No punctuation is required within the parentheses.

This reference is the sort you might find if you were doing research on the hole in the ozone layer.

> A scientist on the faculty of the University of British Columbia who is too well-known to be considered an alarmist stated, "Our current estimates of ozone deterioration are probably much too conservative" (Chang 127).

**Work cited**

Chang, Lucinda H.  "The Rate of Ozone Deterioration."  <u>Our Environment: Essays for the Twenty-First Century</u>.  Eds. P. Lyn Synclair and Timothy A. Nebergall.  Vancouver, BC: British Columbia UP, 1991.  239–48.

This is the order of information for an anthology with multiple editors.

Author's (or authors') name(s), period (.), and two spaces

Title of the article or story written by the author, period (.), quotation marks, and two spaces

Title of the book, underlined, period (.), and two spaces

The abbreviation *Ed.* indicates P. Lyn Synclair was the first listed editor of this anthology, and it is under her name that the book will be found in the library. Three or more editors are listed with commas separating their names.

Edition of the book, period (.), and two spaces

Place of the publication, colon (:), name of the publisher, comma (,), date of publication, and period (.)

Page numbers (if not cited in the text of the essay), period (.)

## 2.5  *Encyclopedias or Dictionaries*

The specific encyclopedia was not mentioned in the text example that follows, so it had to be referenced within the parentheses.

Some people argue that even pedigreed dog kennels should be regulated because of the overpopulation of animals. If that were to happen, some breeds of animals that have remained consistent over the centuries might be lost. According to the encyclopedia, the Norwegian Elkhound is one of the oldest recognized breeds of dog, originating in Norway in 5000 to 4000 BC (Norwegian Elkhound 426). The Norwegian Elkhound has never been a common dog because its heavy coat requires regular grooming, and it would be at risk for extinction if breeder regulations were put into effect. It would be difficult to favor this breed over another so that the diversity of dog breeds was maintained. Given that some animals are a link with history, pedigreed kennels should remain unrestricted except for the present laws requiring humane treatment of the animals.

**Work cited**

"Norwegian Elkhound." <u>World Book Encyclopedia</u>. 1978 ed.

The editor does not have to be cited in an encyclopedia, but if the author of the referenced information is given, that name should be included after the article title. The volume or page number may be omitted if the material is arranged alphabetically and the article reference gives clear indication of where the material was found. The same pattern applies to both encyclopedias and dictionaries.

## 2.6  *Pamphlets*

Not every source you may want to cite is in the library. There may be an extension office of the U.S. Department of Agriculture in your community. There you might find a pamphlet such as the following one. Some stores in your community might also have information centers with similar pamphlets.

A pamphlet should be treated as if it were a book, even though it is not book-sized. The title should be underlined. Because the author is often not mentioned in a pamphlet, the full citation will begin with the title of the pamphlet or the company that published it, and the citation in the text will be the first word of the title.

> Often farmers turn to chemicals when other methods of pest control are equally effective. However, "[b]iological agents can be used in place of the chemicals to destroy many of the pests that prey upon the cotton plant" (<u>Biological</u> 5). Using this information, a farmer in areas considered until recently too pest-infested to grow cotton could return to the production of that crop profitably.

**Work cited**

<u>Biological Agents of Cotton Pests</u>. Baton Rouge: Louisiana State Agricultural and Mechanical University, 1991.

If the city that this publication was printed in were not in the United States (or not well known), you would put an abbreviation of the country after the city and state or province.

## 2.7   Government Publications

Many large libraries have a section devoted to government publications. It is also possible to write to state and federal government offices, and they will send you publications on many subjects. Government publications come from many sources, and they present special problems in citation. When the writer of the document is not known, cite the government agency as the author. A sample citation is listed below for a reference from the congressional record. "United States" with a page number would be used exactly as an author's name is used in the textual citation.

### Work cited

United States.  Cong.  Joint Committee on the Investigation of the
Pearl Harbor Attack.  Hearings.  79th Cong., 1st and 2nd Sess.
32 vols.  Washington: GPO, 1946.

# OTHER PRINTED MATERIAL

The pattern for material taken from periodicals like magazines, journals, and newspapers that are issued daily, weekly, monthly, or quarterly is similar to that used for material taken from anthologies. The additional pieces of information will assist the reader in finding the date (and the city for newspapers) in which the material was issued. Information will be given in the following order:

Author's name (if given), followed by a period (.) and two spaces
Title of the article and a period enclosed in quotation marks, followed by two spaces
Name of the periodical, underlined (do not include a beginning article such as *The* or *A*)
Series number or name (if applicable)
Volume number (for a scholarly journal)
Issue number (if applicable)
Date of publication
Page numbers for the entire article

## 3.1   Magazines

Libraries have sections for periodicals (magazines and journals). You might also want to use a magazine you found outside the educational setting as support for an argument. In magazine and journal citations, the name of the periodical should be underlined, and the name of the article should be in quotation marks.

> According to <u>Gulf Coast</u> magazine, over 30,000 pounds of trash was gathered on the Texas Gulf Coast between Galveston and South Padre Island on June 1990 Arbor Day. The clean up, which was sponsored by the Audubon Society in connection with local organizations, increased its collection by twenty percent over the previous year (Collins 27).

**Work cited**

Collins, Gary. "Coast Trash Increasing." <u>Gulf Coast</u> Sep. 1990: 24–27.

When the author's name is given, it is placed at the beginning with the last name first. The title of the article is given inside quotation marks and then the name of the periodical after two spaces.

### 3.2 *Journals*

Scholarly journals do not require much extra citation in the text of an essay if the author's name is mentioned. The following example shows the citation form for a journal.

> The seriousness of America's soil erosion crisis gets very little media attention. Eric Rasmussen of the Soil Study Institute of St. Paul, Minnesota, writes, "Every decade the so-called bread basket of America, the Midwest, loses .25 of an inch of topsoil. This may not seem like much but it is not being replaced" (60).

**Work cited**

Rasmussen, Eric R. "Results of a Twenty Year Study of Soil Erosion." <u>The Journal of Agronomy</u> 30 (1988): 59–60.

Some journals number pages continuously through the year. If that is the case, instead of the month or quarter, you only need to cite the page number, because it will automatically guide the reader to the correct issue.

### 3.3 *Newspapers*

You can often find not only your own community newspaper, but other major national and sometimes international newspapers in your library. There are reference guides to help you look up articles by subject. Newspaper references must have the page number and the section letter; otherwise, the reader would not know which section to look in when looking up the article.

> Local elementary school children have had an effect on the government of the city of St. Louis. They were the ones who first began asking for a recycling program. The St. Louis Post-Dispatch reports that the city began receiving letters from school children asking for the introduction of curbside recycling last year (D12). "At first we thought it was too expensive, but further research proved it was cost effective," said the superintendent of the city Solid Waste Department (Bishoff).

**Work cited**

Bishoff, John. "Recycling Proving Successful." St. Louis
  Post-Dispatch 15 Sep. 1992: D2.

Newspapers differ from magazines and journals only in that the specific date and the section of the paper must be cited in addition to the other information. The day of the month is noted before the month in order to avoid confusion with the year. Sometimes the city name is not part of the newspaper name, as in the citation above, and sometimes it is, as in the New York Times. Only underline the actual title of the newspaper. If the city's name does not make the state apparent (there are cities named Springfield in many states, for example), indicate the state after the city name.

# NONPRINT SOURCES

The reason why you hold the opinions that you do is often related to ideas that came from sources in the media. You see something on the television news, a documentary program, or in a movie, and you remember it. This source of information can also be cited in an essay and will help you to explain the source of your ideas.

## 4.1  *Television and Radio Programs*

This example demonstrates the form for a television reference.

> The scandal in the American poultry industry is so serious it should be called "Chickengate." On June 8, 1992, I saw a segment on

<u>Shocking America</u> about the poultry industry that revealed appalling facts about how chickens are treated. The film showed chickens living in overcrowded, unsanitary conditions at farms in several states.

**Work cited**

<u>Shocking America</u>.  Narr. Phil Nebergall.  NBC News Special.
   WBDQ, Denver.  8 June 1992.

Much of this information can be found in the television program guide in the newspaper, and the rest will be in the credits that are run at the end of the show.

## 4.2   *Films or Videotapes*

Underline the title of films and videotapes.

A film called <u>Urban Gardening</u> can help people planning their first garden. It shows in great detail how soil should be prepared before anything is planted. According to this film, leaves from deciduous trees can be put on the garden plot in the fall, rather than just being bagged and sent to the landfill.

**Work cited**

<u>Urban Gardening</u> videotape.  United States Extension Service.
   1986.

When possible, the director should follow the title with the main actors in a dramatic presentation following the director. Periods follow the director and the list of primary actors.

## 4.3   *Compact Discs, Audiotapes, or Records*

Underline record titles and put song titles in quotation marks. Indicate the medium: compact disc, audiotape, or record, immediately after the title. If the group name is more important than the name of one individual, put the group name first. Place the library catalog number, if available, after the manufacturer's name.

Everyone has the right to a decent environment! It is not right that humans think they are the only ones with feelings and that we can ignore the suffering we impose on other species. As Cedar Oldgrowth says in her latest CD, "We are the animals; the animals are us!" (Oldgrowth)

**Work cited**

Oldgrowth, Cedar. "Forest Anthem." <u>Meet You in Montana</u>.
    CD. Rec. 20 March 1992. Columbia, 1993.


## 4.4 *Lectures*

You learn things in all your classes, and your learning will become more meaningful to you when you can see how the things you are learning in your various classes fit together. For this reason, it is always a good idea to use the information you learn in one class to enhance an essay you write for another. Many colleges and universities also hold public lectures, where experts on many subjects speak, and those lectures are good sources of information for your essays as well. When you use information you have acquired in this fashion, cite it as demonstrated by the following example.

> Being in the presence of animals can have a calming influence on human beings, according to Professor Joseph McTavish who teaches my psychology class. Even urban dwellers can have a bird or other small pet in their apartments, and the animal's presence can lower blood pressure.

**Work cited**

McTavish, Joseph. Psychology 206 Lecture. University of Oregon.
    Eugene, 10 Oct. 1994.


## 4.5 *Interviews*

Interviews can be excellent support for an argument. However, interviews must also be properly cited in order to give credit to those who helped you to develop your ideas. If the interview was one you saw on television or heard on radio, then give credit to the program and the person doing the interviewing.

> When I talked to my mother about her memories of early union activity and the Industrial Workers of the World (IWW), I found out my grandfather and his brothers played an active role in some interesting historical events (Walker). I called my sister to see what she knew about the story and she gave me the name of a book, <u>Wobbly War</u>, that includes references to my grandfather and great-uncles (Smith).

**Work cited**

Walker, Ethel L. Personal interview. 15 November 1993.
Smith, Paula R. Telephone interview. 7 November 1993.

# Index

Active voice, 134
Agreement
   subject/pronoun, 109
   subject/verb, 108
Apostrophe, 190
Argument, 26–37, 62, 74, 144–148
Article use, 105
Audience, 31, 49–70, 75

Brainstorming, 73

Capitalization, 191
Citing sources, 86, 93
Clustering, 73
Comma errors, 196
   and compound sentences, 198
   interrupting material, 197
Commas, 201–204
Common ground, 50–70
Common knowledge, 81
Complex subject, 130
Contractions, 191
Connie, 193
Correctness, 61
Craig, 68
Critical reading, 16

Darla, 39, 45
Deduction, 145
Dependent clause, 128
Dialect, 59
Dialectic, 129
Dictionary, 88
Diversity, 50–70

Earned conclusion, 92, 115
Economic status, 54
English as a second
   language, 105
Eric, 63
Ethics, 148
Ethnic, 62
Experience, 35, 37
Expert, 34
Extended subject, 130

First person, 37
Floppy disk, 177
Freewriting, 72

Gender, 51
Gender neutral, 192
Generative sentences, 73

Grammar, 100
Grammar checker, 63, 184

Homonyms, 126
Homophones, 181

Independent clause, 128
Induction, 145
Invention, 71–74

*Kevin*, 79, 84, 89

Library use, 44, 92
Logic, 147
Logical fallacies, 149
    appeal to popularity, 150
    appeal to tradition, 153
    authority, 154
    doubtful clause, 151
    either/or dilemma, 152
    generalization, 150
    personal attack, 152
    slippery slope, 151
    straw man, 153
    two wrongs make a right, 154

*Marie*, 10, 13
Mechanics, 100
Modern Language Association
    (MLA), 87
Modifiers, 130

*Natalie*, 123, 135
Noun, 126

Object, 130–134
Opposition, 12, 74, 97
    opposing, 4

Paragraph, 98, 137–143
    evaluating, 141
Passive voice, 134
Peer reviewing, 94–112
Persuasion, 147
Plagiarism, 87
Plato, 129

Politics, 55
Possessive apostrophe, 190
Possessive pronouns, 191
Preposition, 131–134
Prepositional phrase, 131–134
Pronoun, 125
Pronoun reference, 110
Proofing, 188
Proverbial, 147
Punctuation, 170
    end punctuation, 172

Question at issue, 18, 32

Reaction paper, 21
    sample, 25
Reader's journal, 21
Region, 56
Religion, 53
Rhetorical question, 116, 173

Saving text, 177
Second person, 37
Semicolon, 199
Sentence structure, 125–135
Slang, 61
Spell checker, 83, 181
Standard English, 58–62, 106, 195
Subject, 129
Subordinate, 128
Syllogism, 146

Thesaurus, 88
Thesis, 96, 113–122
Thesis statement, 113–114
Third person, 37
Transitions, 45, 142

Verb, 126, 130
Verb tense, 106–109
Viruses, 179

Warrant, 50–70
Wordiness, 87
Word processing, 9, 175